Cairo

Andrew Humphreys

LONELY PLANET PUBLICATIONS
Melbourne • Oakland • London • Paris

Cairo
2nd edition – February 2002
First published – April 1998

Published by
Lonely Planet Publications Pty Ltd ABN 36 005 607 983
90 Maribyrnong St, Footscray, Victoria 3011, Australia

Lonely Planet offices
Australia Locked Bag 1, Footscray, Victoria 3011
USA 150 Linden St, Oakland, CA 94607
UK 10a Spring Place, London NW5 3BH
France 1 rue du Dahomey, 75011 Paris

Photographs
Many of the images in this guide are available for licensing from
Lonely Planet Images.
email: lpi@lonelyplanet.com.au
Web site: www.lonelyplanetimages.com

Front cover photograph
Billboards galore on the streets of Cairo (Eddie Gerald)

Map section title-page photograph
Sunset over Cairo tower (Dan Herrick)

ISBN 1 86450 115 4

text & maps © Lonely Planet Publications Pty Ltd 2002
photos © photographers as indicated 2002

Printed by Craft Print International Ltd, Singapore

Contents – Text

THE PYRAMIDS & MEMPHIS NECROPOLIS   149

PLACES TO STAY   168

PLACES TO EAT   178

ENTERTAINMENT   194

SHOPPING   205

EXCURSIONS   216

LANGUAGE   223

GLOSSARY   229

THANKS   231

INDEX   233

Contents – Maps

The Author

Andrew Humphreys

Andrew has been living, travelling and working in the Middle East on and off since 1988 when he arrived in Cairo on holiday and took three years to leave. Originally trained in London as an architect, he slid into writing through a growing fascination with Islamic buildings. Following a spell in mainstream journalism based for several years in the Baltic States, Andrew hooked up with Lonely Planet for a return to the Middle East and has since authored or co-authored Lonely Planet guides to Central Asia, the Middle East, Israel & the Palestinian Territories, Jerusalem, Egypt and Syria.

Andrew is one of the co-founders of the *Cairo Times*, an Egypt-based, English-language newspaper. He currently lives in London but wonders for how long.

FROM THE AUTHOR

Big thanks to Joann Fletcher for her authoritative voice on all things Egyptological, to Louisa Young, Fiona Sibald, Paul Geday and the *Egypt Almanac*, and most of all to Gadi Farfour who assisted with much of the research.

This Book

Andrew Humphreys researched and wrote the 1st and 2nd editions of *Cairo*. Some of the text for the 1st edition was adapted from the 4th edition of *Egypt*, which was written by Damien Simonis, Leanne Logan and Geert Cole.

From the Publisher

The 2nd edition of Cairo was edited by Isabelle Young, with assistance from Cherry Prior, Tom Smallman and Lynne Preston. Sarah Sloane was responsible for mapping and design. Emma Koch organised the Language chapter; Jenny Jones and Daniel New designed the cover; Matt King supervised the illustrative content; Annie Horner from LPI coordinated the photographic images; Melissa Kirkby designed the chapter ends; Shahara Ahmed put together the map legend; and Mark Germanchis provided Quark support. Brigitte Ellemor and Brett Moore oversaw the whole project.

Finally, a special thanks to Andrew for his continuing enthusiasm for Cairo, the book and the city.

THANKS
Many thanks to the travellers who used the last edition and wrote to us with helpful hints, advice and interesting anecdotes. Your names appear in the back of this book.

Foreword

ABOUT LONELY PLANET GUIDEBOOKS

The story begins with a classic travel adventure: Tony and Maureen Wheeler's 1972 journey across Europe and Asia to Australia. Useful information about the overland trail did not exist at that time, so Tony and Maureen published the first Lonely Planet guidebook to meet a growing need.

From a kitchen table, then from a tiny office in Melbourne (Australia), Lonely Planet has become the largest independent travel publisher in the world, an international company with offices in Melbourne, Oakland (USA), London (UK) and Paris (France).

Today Lonely Planet guidebooks cover the globe. There is an ever-growing list of books and there's information in a variety of forms and media. Some things haven't changed. The main aim is still to help make it possible for adventurous travellers to get out there – to explore and better understand the world.

At Lonely Planet we believe travellers can make a positive contribution to the countries they visit – if they respect their host communities and spend their money wisely. Since 1986 a percentage of the income from each book has been donated to aid projects and human rights campaigns.

Updates Lonely Planet thoroughly updates each guidebook as often as possible. This usually means there are around two years between editions, although for more unusual or more stable destinations the gap can be longer. Check the imprint page (following the colour map at the beginning of the book) for publication dates.

Between editions up-to-date information is available in two free newsletters – the paper *Planet Talk* and email *Comet* (to subscribe, contact any Lonely Planet office) – and on our Web site at www.lonelyplanet.com. The *Upgrades* section of the Web site covers a number of important and volatile destinations and is regularly updated by Lonely Planet authors. *Scoop* covers news and current affairs relevant to travellers. And, lastly, the *Thorn Tree* bulletin board and *Postcards* section of the site carry unverified, but fascinating, reports from travellers.

Correspondence The process of creating new editions begins with the letters, postcards and emails received from travellers. This correspondence often includes suggestions, criticisms and comments about the current editions. Interesting excerpts are immediately passed on via newsletters and the Web site, and everything goes to our authors to be verified when they're researching on the road. We're keen to get more feedback from organisations or individuals who represent communities visited by travellers.

Lonely Planet gathers information for everyone who's curious about the planet – and especially for those who explore it first-hand. Through guidebooks, phrasebooks, activity guides, maps, literature, newsletters, image library, TV series and Web site we act as an information exchange for a worldwide community of travellers.

Research Authors aim to gather sufficient practical information to enable travellers to make informed choices and to make the mechanics of a journey run smoothly. They also research historical and cultural background to help enrich the travel experience and allow travellers to understand and respond appropriately to cultural and environmental issues.

Authors don't stay in every hotel because that would mean spending a couple of months in each medium-sized city and, no, they don't eat at every restaurant because that would mean stretching belts beyond capacity. They do visit hotels and restaurants to check standards and prices, but feedback based on readers' direct experiences can be very helpful.

Many of our authors work undercover, others aren't so secretive. None of them accept freebies in exchange for positive write-ups. And none of our guidebooks contain any advertising.

Production Authors submit their manuscripts and maps to offices in Australia, USA, UK or France. Editors and cartographers – all experienced travellers themselves – then begin the process of assembling the pieces. When the book finally hits the shops, some things are already out of date, we start getting feedback from readers and the process begins again …

WARNING & REQUEST

Things change – prices go up, schedules change, good places go bad and bad places go bankrupt – nothing stays the same. So, if you find things better or worse, recently opened or long since closed, please tell us and help make the next edition even more accurate and useful. We genuinely value all the feedback we receive. A well-travelled team reads and acknowledges every letter, postcard and email and ensures that every morsel of information finds its way to the appropriate authors, editors and cartographers for verification.

Everyone who writes to us will find their name listed in the next edition of the appropriate guidebook. They will also receive the latest issue of *Planet Talk*, our quarterly printed newsletter, or *Comet*, our monthly email newsletter. Subscriptions to both newsletters are free. The very best contributions will be rewarded with a free guidebook.

We may edit, reproduce and incorporate your comments in all Lonely Planet products, such as guidebooks, Web sites and digital products, so let us know if you don't want your comments reproduced or your name acknowledged.

Send all correspondence to the Lonely Planet office closest to you:

Australia: Locked Bag 1, Footscray, Victoria 3011
USA: 150 Linden St, Oakland, CA 94607
UK: 10a Spring Place, London NW5 3BH

Or email us at: talk2us@lonelyplanet.com.au

For news, views and updates see our Web site: www.lonelyplanet.com

HOW TO USE A LONELY PLANET GUIDEBOOK

The best way to use a Lonely Planet guidebook is any way you choose. At Lonely Planet we believe the most memorable travel experiences are often those that are unexpected, and the finest discoveries are those you make yourself. Guidebooks are not intended to be used as if they provide a detailed set of infallible instructions!

Contents All Lonely Planet guidebooks follow roughly the same format. The Facts about the Destination chapters or sections give background information ranging from history to weather. Facts for the Visitor gives practical information on issues like visas and health. Getting There & Away gives a brief starting point for researching travel to and from the destination. Getting Around gives an overview of the transport options when you arrive.

The peculiar demands of each destination determine how subsequent chapters are broken up, but some things remain constant. We always start with background, then proceed to sights, places to stay, places to eat, entertainment, getting there and away, and getting around information – in that order.

Heading Hierarchy Lonely Planet headings are used in a strict hierarchical structure that can be visualised as a set of Russian dolls. Each heading (and its following text) is encompassed by any preceding heading that is higher on the hierarchical ladder.

Entry Points We do not assume guidebooks will be read from beginning to end, but that people will dip into them. The traditional entry points are the list of contents and the index. In addition, however, some books have a complete list of maps and an index map illustrating map coverage.

There may also be a colour map that shows highlights. These highlights are dealt with in greater detail in the Facts for the Visitor chapter, along with planning questions and suggested itineraries. Each chapter covering a geographical region usually begins with a locator map and another list of highlights. Once you find something of interest in a list of highlights, turn to the index.

Maps Maps play a crucial role in Lonely Planet guidebooks and include a huge amount of information. A legend is printed on the back page. We seek to have complete consistency between maps and text, and to have every important place in the text captured on a map. Map key numbers usually start in the top left corner.

Although inclusion in a guidebook usually implies a recommendation we cannot list every good place. Exclusion does not necessarily imply criticism. In fact there are a number of reasons why we might exclude a place – sometimes it is simply inappropriate to encourage an influx of travellers.

Introduction

Encountering Cairo for the first time can turn out to be one of those life defining experiences. It's a city that people tend to react to, and react in fairly extreme ways. For some visitors the result of their encounter is a Dorothy in Oz sort of realisation that there's just 'no place like home' – given a pair of red shoes, they would click their heels three times and be gone from Cairo forever. At the other extreme, there are just as many, if not more, visitors who revel in the fact that not only is Cairo unlike home, but it's unlike any other place on earth.

For my part, I'm a reveller. I first came to Cairo on holiday, filling in a month between jobs in London; in the end, it was three years before I returned home. What ensnared and entranced me – and still does – was the sheer intensity of the city. As home to more than 16 million Egyptians, sundry other Arabs, Africans and international hangers-on, and with one of the world's greatest densities of people, being in Cairo means submitting to an all-out assault on the senses. Some days the most unambitious stroll around town can leave you with the same sort of feeling you might get after a sadistically vigorous massage: tender, unsteady on your feet and stinkingly sweaty, but also strangely satisfied.

Cairo's like that, it is not a gentle city. It doesn't have graceful boulevards and cobbled squares and the kind of dolled-up, prettified buildings that cry out to be photographed and stuck in an album. It doesn't have the resources to spare to be picturesque. Buildings that in almost any other city would take pride of place, Cairo has in abundance, from 10th-century mosques to pseudo-Hindu temples. But they're not fussed over and primped, appended with coach parks and souvenir kiosks. Instead, they're buried in age-old quarters of the city that have yet to be tamed and made tourist-friendly in the way that they have in places such as Istanbul or Jerusalem. They probably never will be, for the simple reason that Cairo's medieval quarters still support a huge population that has nowhere else to go.

This lack of room to develop or expand constantly throws up startling juxtapositions. In one central Nile-side district, less than 500m from a new computer superstore there are mud-brick houses where goats wander through living rooms and where water is available from spigots in the street. Across town, a nightclub/restaurant complex has gone up on the fringes of a 1000-year-old cemetery, which is still in use with the dead vying for space with the living.

Cairenes see nothing strange in this. Possibly as a result of living in such close proximity to 4½ millennia of history (the Pyramids are visible from the upper storeys of buildings all over the city), they aren't driven by the Western obsession to update and upgrade. The latest model Toyota is obliged to share lane space with a donkey and cart; you go to buy paper for your fax machine and the sales assistant tallies the bill on an abacus. Of course, a lack of money and opportunity may also have something to do with it, but Cairo has such an overwhelming sense of its own history that it can take or leave the 21st century.

If I had to attempt to identify just one quality, it's this pervasive sense of timelessness that really has me hooked. It's possible to move from the medieval backstreets of Islamic Cairo to the Pharaonic monumentalism of the Pyramids, take time out in a coffeehouse identical to those portrayed in 19th-century prints and then drink in a bar time-locked in the pre-Revolutionary days. And what really matters here is that none of these places feels 'historical', they all just feel like Cairo. That's to say, they're chaotic, noisy, totally unpredictable and seething with humanity.

Life is what this city is about and, to paraphrase a cliche, only a person who's tired of life itself could fail to see the charm of Cairo.

Facts about Cairo

HISTORY

Cairo is not a Pharaonic city, though the presence of the Pyramids leads many to believe otherwise. At the time of the Pyramids' construction the capital of ancient Egypt was Memphis, about 24km south of the Giza plateau. The site of present-day Cairo was probably a royal estate at this time, a temporary encampment housing the hundreds of thousands of workers required to hack, smooth and haul the massive stone blocks that were piled up into the awesome forms they survive in today, the Pyramids of Giza.

Babylon-in-Egypt

As the glory days of ancient Egypt were drawing to an end around the end of the 2nd millennium BC, the dwindling empire was subject to attack from outsiders; by Libyans in the north, Kushites in the south, then the Assyrians, Persians and eventually the Greeks under the command of Alexander the Great. The Macedonian warrior king entered Memphis where his right to rule Egypt was legitimised by the old priests but he otherwise ignored the ancient capital to found his own city on the Mediterranean, Alexandria.

It was left to the Romans, who won Egypt from the last of the Greek-Egyptian rulers, Cleopatra, to establish a presence on the site now known as Cairo. Take the metro a few stops south from the city centre to the station at Mar Girgis and there, just a few steps from the platform, are the earliest archaeological remains so far discovered in the city. In a pretty poor state of preservation are walls and towers belonging to a Roman fortress constructed around the 1st century AD and referred to in texts of the time as 'Babylon-in-Egypt'. The fortress stood on the site of an established Pharaonic river crossing, beside the rocky island of Rhoda, into which the ancient Egyptians had cut a Nilometer, used to measure the annual rise and fall of the river waters. The Romans' fortress controlled access to the upper Nile and as such was a major frontier stronghold and busy port.

Despite the adoption of Pharaonic iconography, styles of dress and architecture, all meant to legitimise their presence in Egypt, Roman rule was rarely popular. When Christianity was embraced by growing numbers of the local populace after being introduced some time around AD 40 by the preachings of St Mark, the Romans regarded the new religion as a potential threat and persecuted its followers. Even after Christianity was adopted as the official religion of the Roman Empire in AD 323, the Egyptians still ran foul of Rome since their Monophysitic doctrine believed Christ was divine, rather than both human and divine. The Egyptians were therefore declared heretical and expelled from the rest of the Christian world, while within Egypt the Roman overlords continued their persecutions of the local populace. This oppressive state of affairs came to an end in AD 640 with the arrival of an army of mounted warriors riding out of the deserts of the Arabian peninsula bearing the flag of another new religion, Islam.

Fustat: the First Islamic Capital

The besieged Romans surrendered to the conquering Muslim Arabs, who were welcomed by the Egyptian populace as liberators. Under the command of their general Amr ibn al-As, the Islamic army chose not to occupy Babylon and instead set up their own tent city, Fustat, immediately adjacent on wasteland to the north of the Roman walls. In a pleasing echo of ancient events, Babylon, known now as Coptic Cairo, remains a predominantly Christian enclave surrounded by the modern, almost wholly Muslim city.

At the centre of Fustat was a mosque (its direct descendant, the Mosque of Amr ibn al-As, still stands) around which the original tent city was rapidly replaced by mud-brick and wood constructions. The population was increased by the arrival of more tribes from Arabia, and the new city prospered.

City Builders – Amr ibn al-As

Amr ibn al-As (r. 640–44) was a warrior not a builder, but in defeating the Romans in Egypt and establishing a Muslim camp (Fustat) beside the Nile he laid the foundations for the city that was to evolve into Cairo. In 644, when he was recalled from Egypt, he left an organised capital behind him garrisoned by 10,000 soldiers. He founded the first mosque in North Africa, which, enlarged and rebuilt many times, survives to this day on its original site.

Like Christianity before it, Islam, though still in its infancy, was already subject to splinter factions and dynasties. In AD 658 the Umayyads, an Arab dynasty based in Damascus, became rulers, or caliphs, of the whole Muslim world, including Egypt. Less than a century passed before Umayyad rule was supplanted by the Abbasid dynasty of Baghdad, whose influence also extended to the lands of the Nile from AD 750. Abbasid control of Egypt was maintained through a governor appointed in Baghdad and lodged in Al-Askar, a new administrative quarter appended to the north-east corner of Fustat. But a mere hundred years later a new governor, Ahmed ibn Tulun (835–84), found Al-Askar too crowded for his liking. He built a new compound further north, Al-Qatai (The Districts), complete with quarters for 10,000 soldiers, palaces and, so legend relates, a pleasure garden – complete with a pool filled with quicksilver on which the governor floated on silk cushions towed by slave girls. Ibn Tulun grew powerful enough to cut loose from Baghdad, controlling Egypt as his personal kingdom and passing succession to his son. But the dynasty was short-lived and in AD 905 an Abbasid army reconquered Egypt and levelled Al-Qatai, all apart from Ibn Tulun's grand central mosque, which still stands to this day, more than a millennium later.

Fustat continued to thrive as one of the richest components of the new Muslim world order. Its wealth was based on Egypt's excessively rich soil and the taxes imposed on the heavy Nile traffic. Descriptions left by 10th-century travellers portray Fustat as a cosmopolitan metropolis with public gardens, street lighting and buildings up to 14 storeys high. It was a glittering treasury and in August AD 969 the army of the Fatimids, an Islamic dynasty from North Africa, marched in from the west to claim it.

Al-Qahira: the City Victorious

As Amr ibn al-As, the Abbasids and Ibn Tulun had done before them, the Fatimids chose to escape the crush of the existing quarters and break new ground to the north. The area for the new city, so the story goes, was pegged out and labourers were waiting for a signal from the astrologers to begin digging. The signal was to be the ringing of bells attached to the ropes marking off the construction area but a raven landed on the rope and set off the bells prematurely. As the planet Mars (Al-Qahir) was in the ascendant, the Fatimid caliph decided to call the city Al-Qahira, also meaning 'The Victorious'. European tongues would later garble this name into something more easily pronounceable to non-Arabs – Cairo.

A square kilometre or so, walled around and entered only via massive fortified gates, the Fatimid city began life as a royal precinct of palaces, parade grounds and gardens – a precursor of the Forbidden City of Beijing. It was off limits to the citizens of Fustat. The

City Builders – Al-Muizz

Al-Muizz (r. 969–75) was the cultivated and energetic fourth caliph of the Fatimids, a dynasty based in Tunisia, who sent out an army to 'conquer Egypt and build a city that would rule the world'.

On a sandy plain north of the existing Fustat his victorious general Gawhar marked out a walled royal precinct for Egypt's new rulers. This new city Al-Qahira remained the core of Cairo well into the 19th century and several of its great gates (including Bab al-Futuh, Bab an-Nasr and Bab Zuweila) and mosques (including Al-Azhar and Al-Hakim) survive.

division between those within the walls and those without was made even greater by the fact that the Fatimids were Shiite, a brand of Islam at odds with the orthodox Sunnism of the indigenous populace.

The unhappy relationship between rulers and their subjects was not helped by the fact that the Fatimids produced a succession of caliphs all with varying degrees of insanity, the most infamous of whom, Al-Hakim, ordered his troops to lay waste to Fustat, a move that came close to sparking all-out civil war. The former tent city was eventually destroyed by the Fatimids, but not until some 150 years after the death of Al-Hakim.

In 1168 the European Crusaders, having bloodily rampaged through Palestine, were advancing into Egypt. Fearing that Fustat was indefensible and would be quickly occupied by the Crusaders, from where they could comfortably lay siege to Al-Qahira, the Fatimids ordered the lower city evacuated and put to the torch. It burnt for 54 days until virtually nothing remained (vast areas of what was Fustat have never been built over and remain barren to this day). However, the Crusaders never attacked. They were driven off by the Seljuk Turks of Damascus to whom the Fatimids had appealed for help. The Seljuks were Sunni Muslims and once in Al-Qahira they went on to depose the Shiite dynasty they had come to the aid of.

The restorer of Sunni rule and the new overlord of Cairo was Salah ad-Din Ayyub, known to his Crusader enemies as Saladin. He established a new ruling dynasty, the Ayyubids. A soldier foremost, Salah ad-Din erected a defensive wall enclosing Cairo and Fustat together, and established the fortified Citadel that still dominates the city skyline to this day.

The Ayyubid line ran to only four rulers before a bizarre and bloody episode that saw Egypt being briefly ruled by its only female Islamic potentate (for more details, see under Mausoleum of Shagaret ad-Durr in the Things to See & Do chapter) and resulted in the rise to power of a new dynasty.

City Builders – Salah ad-Din

Salah ad-Din (r. 1171–93) is better known as the chivalrous Islamic general Saladin who sparred with the Crusader king Richard the Lionheart. But he was also, from 1171 to his death, ruler of Egypt. No matter that he only spent eight years in his capital – which he left in 1182 and never revisited before dying; in that short time he built a great fortified citadel on a projecting spur of the Muqattam Hills, and encompassed the whole of Al-Qahira and Fustat within a wall. The Citadel remains, and sections of Salah ad-Din's city walls still fringe the eastern edge of Islamic Cairo.

The Mamluks: City of the 1001 Nights

The Mamluks were originally slave boys, brought from the Caucasus by Cairo's Ayyubid rulers, heeding the old Baghdad adage that 'One obedient slave is better than 300 sons'. Trained in martial arts they became an elite fighting force, organised in a quasi-feudal manner, with the numerous 'households' of Mamluks each attached to their own lord or emir. With no family ties, loyalty to household and master was absolute. Their military service was rewarded with gifts of land and when As-Salih Ayyub (great nephew of Salah ad-Din) died, the Mamluks, as the most powerful force in the country, were well positioned to assume control.

Mamluk ranks were maintained not by recruitment or breeding, but by the purchase of new slaves. There was no system of hereditary lineage; it was rule by the strongest, with rival emirs manoeuvring, scheming and warring for the sultancy. During the 267 years that this slave-soldier caste held power, rare was the sultan who died of old age.

On the battlefields of the Near East the Mamluk armies were unstoppable. Superb horsemen who utilised the latest in weapons technology from the East (the lightest of swords, the recurved composite bow), they checked the Mongol hordes that had ravished Persia and Syria and succeeded in driving the Western Crusaders out of the

Holy Land. Cairo became the capital of the strongest military power of its age, lording over an empire that included Jerusalem, Damascus and lands all the way north to what's now south-eastern Turkey, as well as the Arabian peninsula and the holy cities of Mecca and Medina.

As a result of territorial gains, the Mamluks also effectively controlled all trade between the East (Arabia, India and China) and the West (Europe). A Pharaonic-era canal connecting the Red Sea with the Nile had been reopened by Amr ibn al-As and by the time of the Mamluks this waterway (which flowed right by the city walls along the route of the present-day Sharia Port Said) was a vital commercial route. Cairo's Bab al-Hadid port (now the site of Midan Ramses) was one of the world's busiest and the city flourished like no other since perhaps the glory of ancient Rome. In 1481 an Italian rabbi arrived in Egypt recording in his journal that he'd 'come to see the Cairenes and their deeds'. He went on to write 'I swear that if it were possible to put Rome, Venice, Milan, Padua, Florence and four more cities together, they would not equal in wealth and population half that of Cairo'.

The wealth that flowed into the city triggered a building boom. Bursting its walls, Al-Qahira spilled over, filling the empty lands between Bab Zuweila and the Citadel (present-day Darb al-Ahmar) and spreading into the desert, where successive sultans spent lavishly on a series of great funerary monuments (now the Northern Cemetery).

The splendid architecture – mosques, palaces and mausoleums all embellished with marble, stucco, exquisite stone carving and gold leaf – remains, and constitutes one of modern Cairo's most precious legacies. Crowded with architectural finery, filled with merchants from distant lands, laden with bazaars of exotic wares, ruled by cruel and fickle sultans – this was the city that inspired many of the tales that make up *The Thousand and One Nights* (for more information see the boxed text 'City of the Thousand and One Nights' in the Things to See & Do chapter).

City Builders – Qaitbey

Qaitbey (r. 1468–96) typifies the combination of brutality and artistic excellence that characterises the Mamluk era. Bought as a slave for 50 dinars, he witnessed the brief reigns of nine sultans before he clawed his way to the throne. Once in power he rapaciously taxed his subjects and dealt out vicious punishments with his own hands, on one occasion tearing out the eyes and tongue of a court chemist who had failed to transform lead into gold. Yet he bequeathed the city some of its most beautiful monuments, notably his exquisite mosque in the Northern Cemetery.

The end of these fabled days came in the closing years of the 15th century when Vasco da Gama discovered the sea route around the Cape of Good Hope, so freeing European merchants from the heavy taxes imposed by Cairo. At around the same time, on the northern fringes of the Mamluk-controlled territories, a mighty new power, the Ottoman Turks of Constantinople, was looking to extend its influence throughout the rest of the Islamic world. The Mamluks were obliged to meet the threat and in 1516, led by the then-venerable sultan Al-Ghouri, a Mamluk army rode forth from Cairo. They met the Ottoman Turks in battle in Syria and suffered a crushing defeat. Al-Ghouri was unhorsed and trampled to death. In January of the following year the Ottoman sultan Selim entered Cairo.

The Ottomans: the Provincialisation of Cairo

Cairo's days as a great imperial centre were at an end. Under the Ottomans it was reduced to the level of a provincial city. All trading revenues went back to Constantinople, as did the taxes that were squeezed from the Egyptian population. But that's not to say the development of the city halted. Under the Ottomans Cairo experienced sustained growth. The Al-Qahira area, already densely settled, underwent little change, but surrounding areas became urbanised, notably west of the Khalij, or Canal (present-day Sharia Port Said), and particularly around a large pond known as the Ezbekiyya, named after one of its earliest settlers, the emir Ezbek.

Although the Mamluk sultanate had been abolished, the Mamluks lived on in the form of lords known as beys and maintained considerable power. Over time the Ottoman hold on Egypt became weaker as its own empire went into decline. In 1796 one of the Mamluk beys was confident enough to take on the Ottoman garrison in Cairo, defeat them and dispatch the governor back to Constantinople. But the Mamluk re-emergence was short-lived. Within two years they were unseated again, not by the Ottomans but by a new force in Egypt – Europeans, in the form of Napoleon and the French army.

The French in Cairo

France was at war with Britain. One of the prizes of the fight was India, then very much a British colony. In order to sever communication between the two and establish a base from where he might march East, Napoleon landed at Alexandria in 1798 and then marched on to Cairo where his modern musket-bearing army decimated the old-fashioned sword-wielding Mamluk forces. The diminutive general set up headquarters in a Mamluk palace on the edge of the Ezbekiyya pond with the expressed intention of exerting a benevolent rule. However, benevolent or not, this was an occupation by a non-Muslim foreign army. The citizens of Cairo resisted with open revolt, which was only quelled by the French bombarding the city from the terraces of the Citadel.

Sitting on a powder keg in Cairo, with the British and dispossessed Ottomans allying in Syria, Napoleon decided to cut his losses and get out. The general he left behind was murdered by the Egyptians and in 1801, with the British, the Turks and the Mamluks all gathered on the edges of Cairo, the remaining French forces readily agreed to an armistice and departed the way they had come.

Ottoman rule was tenuously reinstated in Cairo but the reality was something of a power vacuum. This was soon to be filled by an Albanian mercenary named Mohammed Ali who, within five years of the French army's departure, had successfully established himself as viceroy of Egypt – nominally the vassal of Constantinople but in practice enjoying absolute independence.

Mohammed Ali: Cairo, City of the Orient

As long as the Mamluks were still around they posed a potential threat to Mohammed Ali's security. This was settled by the infamous slaughter that took place at the Citadel in 1811 – see the boxed text 'The Massacre of the Mamluks' in the Things to See & Do chapter. In the weeks that followed, a further 3500 Mamluks were murdered in Cairo, bringing a 560-year chapter of the city's history to a bloody close.

Although Mohammed Ali's means of achieving his ends could be barbarous, his reign is pivotal in the history of Cairo as it was under his uncompromising rule that the city began its transition from medieval-style feudalism to something approaching industrialisation. He encouraged foreigners with talent to come to Cairo, including teachers

City Builders – Mohammed Ali

Mohammed Ali (r. 1805–48) inherited a Cairo where 900 years of continuity had been brought to an end by the invasion of Napoleon. His reign marks the beginning of the city's entry into the modern world. Wide, straight roads meant for wheeled carriages (such as Sharia Mohammed Ali) were ploughed through the old labyrinthine street patterns. Buildings were constructed in styles foreign to local traditions; for example, there was a prohibition (nominally for safety reasons) on *mashrabiyya*, the traditional wooden lattice window screens, and a switch to the use of glass windows. In 1847, under the supervision of four artillery officers, houses on Cairo's streets received numbers.

and experts in all fields, to help modernise his capital and country. His reign also saw the city open up to a stream of intrepid early travellers, including Mark Twain, Gustave Flaubert and Florence Nightingale, as well as artists such as the Scot David Roberts, whose painstakingly detailed lithographs of Cairo continue to adorn countless calendars and postcards and are reproduced in just about every book on Cairo and Egypt. Their journals and lithographs were eagerly devoured by romantically inclined readers enraptured by accounts of temples in the sand, veiled harems and the bare-breasted women of the slave markets.

Ironically, it was the interests and influence of the Europeans that were very soon to completely change Cairo from a city of the East to one that looked almost exclusively to the West.

Ismailia: the New European Cairo

Although Mohammed Ali was in many respects a moderniser, in appearance Cairo remained firmly medieval. Look at the drawings of David Roberts, made in 1838 but portraying street scenes and views that might easily date from the heyday of the Mamluks. It was left to his grandson to change that. Ismail didn't immediately succeed Mohammed Ali but had to wait out the rule of a brother (Abbas) and father (Said) before assuming power. However, once in power the French-educated ruler (now with the title khedive, an Ottoman recognition of the right of the heirs of Mohammed Ali to hereditary sovereignty of Egypt) did more to alter the appearance of Cairo than anybody since the Fatimids founded Al-Qahira.

It was Ismail who expanded the city west of its medieval borders right up to the banks of the Nile, in effect establishing a new European-style Cairo, known initially as Ismailia, beside the old Islamic one. It was also during Ismail's reign that workers completed the Suez Canal. The inaugural celebrations accompanying the canal's opening in 1869 were attended by royalty, presidents and prime ministers from all over the world, making Ismail's new Cairo the focus of international attention.

City Builders – Khedive Ismail

Khedive Ismail (r. 1863–79) was the founder of modern Cairo, the first ruler in nine centuries to conceive an overall plan for the city's development. Basically the city west of Ezbekiyya (a lake transformed into a garden, now a lawn beside the twin midans of Ataba and Opera) is Ismail's creation. His plan echoed Western models, specifically the Paris of Haussman, and introduced to Cairo European-style apartment blocks complete with gas lighting and water. He also added a railway connection to Alexandria, trams, new bridges and a general grandiose air that had the ambitious khedive declare of his new city, 'Now…we are civilised'.

By this time Cairo was attracting ever-increasing numbers of foreign tourists, particularly with the advent of the railway connecting it to the Mediterranean port of Alexandria. By 1860 Thomas Cook had already begun leading organised tours to Cairo and Egypt, and new hotels ringed the Ezbekiyya area. Pride of these was Shepheard's hotel, which in its day was the city's most famous landmark after the Pyramids. Established in 1841 by Samuel Shepheard, a farmer's son from northern England, the hotel occupied the site of Napoleon's former headquarters on the Ezbekiyya. It was the base camp for all travellers in the Middle East and Africa. Early guests included General Gordon before he set forth on his ill-fated mission to Khartoum, Stanley bound for Africa and his historic meeting with Livingstone, Sir Richard Burton after his pilgrimage to Mecca, and Rudyard Kipling en route between England and India.

In addition to visitors, the city had rapidly acquired a large resident foreign population. By 1872 there were some 25,000 Europeans and Americans living in Cairo involved in running businesses and conducting trade. The city almost had the character of a gold-rush town. Pickings were particularly rich for the European bankers who, with the connivance of their governments, bestowed lavish loans upon Ismail for his grandiose schemes. They advanced the kind of money Egypt could never conceivably repay, at insatiable rates of interest. In 1882, the British stepped in and announced that until Egypt could repay its debts, they were taking control.

The British in Cairo

The British allowed the heirs of Mohammed Ali to remain on the throne but all power was concentrated in the hands of the British agent, the governor by another name. What Britain was interested in was reaping the profits from Egyptian cotton and ensuring the security of the Suez Canal, the passageway to British India.

The British often saw their role in Cairo as a stern sort of paternalism, acting for a country that couldn't look after itself. They introduced a form of Egyptian legislative assembly and improved public transport, and many local landowners benefited from the cotton trade and built fantastic villas in the new, planned suburbs such as Garden City, Zamalek and Heliopolis, but again the bottom line was that it was occupation by military might.

Egypt's desire for self-determination was strengthened by the Allies' use of Cairo as a glorified barracks during WWI, even though Egypt was never itself a theatre of the war. Saad Zaghloul, the most brilliant of a newly emerging breed of young Egyptian politicians, spoke for his nation when he said, 'I have no quarrel with the British personally…but I want to see an independent Egypt'.

As a sop to nationalist sentiments the British granted Egypt its 'sovereignty' but this was very much an empty gesture – King Fuad enjoyed little popularity among his people and the British kept tight hold of the reins.

More than that, they came in ever greater numbers with the outbreak of WWII. To the thousands of Allied troops posted in Cairo following Germany's invasion of North Africa, the city seemed like bliss. It was hot and luxurious, food and beer were in plentiful supply and there were many other welcome diversions from the war being fought out in the desert. Officers were billeted in apartments beside the Gezira Club or overlooking the Nile in Garden City and frequented Shepheard's terrace, Groppi's, the Turf Club and Madame Badia's Cabaret, with its famed belly dancers.

While many Egyptians, particularly shopkeepers and businessmen, were also enjoying the benefits of this, the most glamorous of wars, there was a vocal element among the locals who saw the Germans as potential liberators. Students held rallies in support of German field marshal Rommel and in the Egyptian army a small cabal of officers, which included future presidents Nasser and Sadat, plotted to aid the German advance on their city. Sadat was, in fact, jailed for a time by the British for his involvement in an infamous episode involving a German spy named John Eppler. Eppler was arrested on a Nile houseboat after being smuggled into the city across the Western Desert guided by a Hungarian adventurer Ladislaus 'Laszlo' Almásy – a character immortalised half a century later in the novel and film *The English Patient*.

There was a brief scare as Rommel pushed the Allied forces back almost to Alexandria, which had the British embassy and GHQ hurriedly burning documents in such quantity that the skies over Cairo turned dark with the ash, but the Germans never broke through. Instead, the British were to remain for almost 10 more years before a day of greater and fiercer flames was to drive them out for good.

Masr: Capital of the Arab World

On Saturday 26 January 1952 – Black Saturday – Cairo was set on fire. After years of demonstrations, strikes and riots against the continued presence of the British in Egypt, the British storming of a rebellious Egyptian police station in the Suez Canal zone provided the necessary spark to ignite the capital. Foreign-owned and foreigner-frequented shops and businesses all over town were targeted by mobs and set ablaze. Shepheard's hotel went up in flames as did many other landmarks of 80 years of British rule, all reduced to charred ruins within the space of one day.

The British must have realised that, as far as they were concerned, Egypt was ungovernable, so when just a few weeks later a group of young army officers seized power in a coup it was accepted as a *fait accompli*. On 26 July 1952, the Egyptian puppet-king Farouk, descendant of the Albanian Mohammed Ali, departed Alexandria harbour aboard the royal yacht, leaving Egypt to be ruled by Egyptians for the first time since the pharaohs.

As the leader of the revolutionary Free Officers, Colonel Gamal Abdel Nasser ascended to power and was confirmed as president by elections in 1956. His priority was domestic transformation to create a situation whereby the Egyptians would be masters in their own land. To this end all the old feudal estates were broken up and the land was distributed among the fellaheen, Egypt's large and long put-upon agrarian workforce. While members of Cairo's huge foreign community were not forced to go, they nevertheless hurriedly began to sell up and stream out of the country.

Meanwhile, Cairo grew spectacularly in population and the urban planners struggled

to keep pace. The west bank of the Nile was concreted over with new suburbs, including Medinat Mohandiseen (Engineers' City) and Medinat Sahafayeen (Journalists' City).

Nasser's skills as a tough negotiator and his ability to stand up to the Western powers (spectacularly so in the case of the 1956 Suez Crisis) earned him plaudits all over the developing world, and Cairo became the beacon for a nascent Arab nationalism.

Cairo: City of Islam?

Local opinion regarding Anwar Sadat, Nasser's successor, is more divided. Egypt's second president initiated a complete about turn, ditching the socialist idealisms of Nasser and instead wholeheartedly embracing capitalism. After a decade and a half of keeping a low profile the wealthy resurfaced and were joined by a large, new, moneyed middle class grown rich on the back of a much-touted *intifah* or 'open-door policy'. The likes of Mohandiseen and Medinat Nasr (Nasr City), originally conceived as Soviet-style workers' dormitories, became the addresses of choice for the new money and favoured locations for rashes of boutiques and car showrooms.

More contentious was Sadat's willingness to talk peace with the state of Israel. This cost him his life when he was assassinated during a 1981 military parade by members of what are usually described for convenience as 'Muslim fundamentalists', a loose term for a collection of Islamic groups with a different vision for the state. Mass roundups of Islamists and suspected Islamists were immediately carried out on the orders of Sadat's successor Hosni Mubarak, a former air-force general and vice-president.

Less flamboyant than Sadat and less charismatic than Nasser, Mubarak has often been criticised as being both unimaginative and indecisive. Nevertheless, in the early years of his rule he managed to carry out a dicey balancing act on several fronts, abroad and at home. He rehabilitated Egypt in the eyes of an Arab world who had previously shown disgust at the peace with Israel, while keeping a lid on the Islamic extremists.

City Builders – Nasser

Gamal Abdel Nasser (r. 1956–71), the first president of the fledgling Arab Republic of Egypt, initiated a wholesale state-sponsored reshaping of Cairo. Public spending was used to counter overcrowding, with the creation of vast new concrete mid-rise suburbs on the city fringes; ring roads (such as the Salah Salem highway) were designed to route traffic around the city; communications were improved with new bridges. All of this was very practical and very necessary, but none of it was pretty to look at. The most fitting monument to the Nasser era is Midan Tahrir's hideous Mogamma building, a Stalinist-styled monolithic monument to well-intentioned but bungling socialist bureaucracy.

But in the early 1990s the lid blew off. Despite the Islamists' use of religious symbolism, theirs is essentially a political movement that has grown out of harsh socioeconomic conditions. In the 1980s discontent had been brewing among the poorer sections of society. Government promises had failed to keep up with the population explosion and a generation of youths were finding themselves without jobs and living in squalid, overcrowded housing with little or no hope for the future. With a repressive political system that allowed little chance to legitimately voice opposition, the only hope lay with the Islamic parties and their calls for change.

Denied recognition by the state as a legal political entity, the Islamists turned to force. There were frequent attempts on the life of the president and his ministers and frequent clashes with the security forces. Perhaps even more alarmingly, the matter escalated from a domestic issue to a matter of international concern when the Islamists began to target one of the state's most vulnerable sources of income: tourists.

Several groups of foreign tourists were shot at or bombed in the last months of 1992 and into 1993, resulting in a handful of deaths. The government responded with a heavy-handed lightning crackdown, arresting thousands and introducing the death penalty for terrorism. Egypt, after all, is a police state, if a less repressive one than others in the region. Justice here is not for the squeamish. Human rights groups were up in arms at the mass arrests and reports of confessions extracted by torture and other police brutalities, but by the mid-1990s, the violence had receded from the capital, retreating to the religious heartland of Middle Egypt. The Egyptian government proclaimed the Islamic extremists 'utterly crushed'.

Cairo Today

Cairo has seen significant, if agonisingly slow, improvements during Mubarak's 20 years in power. The city has gained arterial roads and an underground metro system, new residential projects are springing up in the desert and old inner-city quarters are being regenerated. The changes, however, fall well short of keeping pace with the litany of woes (including overcrowding, collapsing infrastructure, the widening poverty gap, unemployment and health-endangering pollution) afflicting the overstretched and greatly abused metropolis. The city's major source of revenue, its history in the shape of the Pyramids at Giza, the antiquities of the Egyptian Museum and the Islamic monuments, is also under threat from pollutant-accelerated decay, neglect and downright bad management.

While Cairo has five millennia's worth of a glorious and rich history, as we begin the new millennium the future for the city looks far less grand.

GEOGRAPHY

Cairo sits on the Nile at the point at which the river fans out to become the fertile green Delta. The city covers some 214 sq km, most of which is on the east bank. As with Egypt itself (where the country's population is strung out along the narrow stem of the Nile valley), Cairo clings to the river, stretching 40km from north to south. Its lateral spread east used to be constrained by the bare-rock Muqattam Hills, which give way to the Eastern Desert, but in recent

City Builders – Osman

Osman Ahmed Osman, now deceased, was the founder of the Osman Ahmed Osman Contracting Company, aka Arab Contractors, the country's biggest pourers of concrete. He rose to prominence during the Nasser years and since then almost every major construction project has had his name on it. The company is so big and so much a part of the political establishment that it's almost a ministry of construction. All those flyovers casting their dank shadow over central Cairo – they're his. Same with many of the most ghastly tower blocks. In fact, pick any eyesore and odds are that it's got that OAO stamp on it. No environmental awards then, but who cares when the company's worth this much?

years, population pressure has meant that the Muqattam have been leapfrogged, and the once-barren desert is now a vast and messy construction site for a series of overspill-soaking satellite cities.

Cairo's expansion on the west bank is much smaller. Here, if you stray more than a half-dozen kilometres from the Nile, the loamy valley soil gives way to the fine sand of the Western Desert. From the Pyramids, on the westernmost edge of Cairo, there is little but sand between the city and the Libyan border some 600km distant.

CLIMATE

Most of the year, except for the winter months of December, January and February, Cairo is hot and dry. In summer a punishing sun keeps temperatures up around 35° to 38°C (95° to 100°F), though a relatively low humidity generally makes the heat bearable. During the winter, daytime temperatures drop to a very comfortable 15° to 20°C (59° to 68°F). Jumpers or a light jacket are useful but a coat is not necessary. However, the evenings can be quite chilly in winter, with temperatures plummeting to as low as 8°C (47°F). This is made worse by the fact that there is no such thing as central heating in Cairo apartments.

Rainfall is modest, about 25mm per year, occurring during January and February in an infrequent spattering of downpours.

Between March and April, Cairo is occasionally subject to the *khamseen*, a dry, hot and very dusty wind that blows in from the parched Western Desert at up to 150km per hour. The name comes from the Arabic word for 'fifty' and refers to the 50 days for

which the winds are supposed to blow. In fact, during the khamseen period the storms rarely occur more than once a week and last for just a few hours at a time.

ECOLOGY & ENVIRONMENT

There are no two ways about it, Cairo is bad for your health. Chief among the city's afflictions is air pollution, but water pollution, noise pollution, unsafe buildings and overcrowding are also seriously problematic issues. Caring about the environment is a luxury that, traditionally, few Egyptians have had time to indulge in, but this is starting to change. In 1997 the post of Minister of State for the Environment was created. While the post is sometimes criticised as being little more than a sop to critics, some action has been taken on industrial polluters in Cairo and plans are being drawn to deal with the waste that cruise boats dump into the Nile.

Air Pollution

In the words of Tony Horwitz, author of *Baghdad Without a Map*, Cairo is the great upturned ashtray. Its air is so full of filth and ill health that breathing it is said to be equivalent to smoking a packet of cigarettes a day. During summer, a few minutes on the streets of central Cairo is enough to acquire a gritty coating that turns tissues black when you wipe them across your perspiring forehead. The month of November in both 1999 and 2000 saw the city overshadowed by a dense black cloud that, if nothing else, at least brought home the seriousness of the situation. More than one million vehicles, most old and badly maintained, jam the city's roads, belching out clouds of noxious fumes. There is next to no control on vehicle emissions, and unleaded fuel has yet to catch on. Add to that the factories on the edge of town that spew pollution into the air and the net result is that Cairo may well be the world's second-most-polluted urban centre after Mexico City. USAID reports that Cairo has the world's highest levels of lead and suspended solid particles (the main cause of respiratory problems), accounting for somewhere between 10,000 and 25,000 deaths per year.

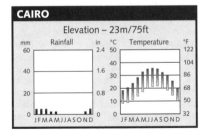

CAIRO

Elevation – 23m/75ft

The government is finally sufficiently alarmed to do something about all this: factories are now required to install filters (reportedly, few have so far done so); there are now several thousand taxis running on liquid natural gas; and a US$200 million USAID-sponsored air-improvement project has been launched. But for the time being residents of Cairo are forced to resign themselves to the nasty habit of passive smoking.

Overcrowding

If the latest census results are accurate then Egypt's long-running family planning campaigns may be on the way to tackling the country's problem of uncontrolled population growth, particularly regarding Cairo. According to the statistics, Egypt's population growth rate has fallen from 2.8% a decade ago to the current 2.1%. On top of that, the census showed that the trend of urbanisation has been reversed, with fewer people migrating to the capital.

That said, around 16.5 million people still inhabit Cairo. By the government's own admission, parts of the city have the densest number of people per kilometre anywhere in the world (the south Cairo suburb of Dar as-Salaam is known locally as 'Little China'). The strain placed on the city's decaying infrastructure is enormous. The result is one of the world's most lethal public transport systems, with a regular roll-call of train wrecks and bus smashes, and cities of hastily thrown-up buildings which all too frequently crash to the ground again, with horrific consequences. Problems are particularly acute in what are termed the 'unplanned housing districts' or, in less wilfully obscure words, slums. Some 20% of Cairenes live in slums with makeshift sewers that leak into the streets, no fresh water supply, no garbage collection and the most rudimentary types of dwellings.

GOVERNMENT & POLITICS

In terms of the state, Egypt and Cairo are virtually synonymous; in Arabic the traditional name for both is the same, Masr. In the minds of many academics, business-people, media people and politicians, little

beyond the capital matters. While the Ministry of Tourism might ponder upon Upper Egypt and the resort areas of Sinai, and the Ministry of Foreign Affairs may look to Paris or Washington, the gaze of government is fixed almost exclusively on the capital. While Cairo does have a governor (in fact it has three: one for Cairo, one for Giza and one for Qalyubiyya, a grouping of the city's northern districts) all major initiatives and decisions concerning the city are dealt with at ministerial level.

The public interface with these unreachable, and very much unaccountable, holders of office is through the multilayered complexity of Cairo's bureaucracy. If there is one unquestionable achievement of the Egyptian administration since 1952, when President Nasser guaranteed a job to each and every university graduate, it has been to raise the inanity of bureaucracy to the point of surrealism. No application or request may be accepted before it has been stamped four times, signed and countersigned at least the same number of times, passed by the desks of a half-dozen individuals, and a certain amount of small bills have changed hands. For the average Cairene, whose interest in politics has been blunted by fraudulent elections and the marginalisation of opposition parties, bureaucracy *is* government.

ECONOMY

The most widely quoted statistic about Cairo's economy was that the average government employee did just 27 minutes of work per day. That changed in the mid-1990s when the talk switched to Egypt being one of the world's most attractive emerging markets, with great potential for fast growth. After decades of subsidising unproductive and overstaffed state-owned industries, the government began dismantling the Nasserist system of central planning, selling off businesses and introducing packages of liberalising reforms to encourage foreign investment. The new policies paid early dividends with millions flowing into a newly rejuvenated Cairo stock exchange and a surge in foreign investment. In spring 1997 Rolls Royce set up a showroom in Cairo, hot on the heels of Jaguar; Nile-side apartment blocks went on the market at starting prices of US$1.3 million; and US-style shopping malls sprung up around town filled with designer clothes stores, Belgian confectioners and sushi bars.

However, all this comes with its own problems. As part of the reform program the government is also committed to cutting subsidies on housing, food, electricity and transport, and the greater part of society is soon going to be wondering why the cost of their daily bread is rising while they're seeing more and more luxury cars on the roads. This isn't yet Brazil, but with the present absence of any real wealth redistribution Cairo is looking at a startling widening of the rich-poor divide.

POPULATION & PEOPLE

Cairo is reckoned to be home to about 27% of the country's population; if the latest census statistics are accurate, this means that the city is heaving with some 16.5 million. There are more Cairenes than there are Austrians, Belgians or Greeks. Each day this number is swollen by thousands of commuters from the Delta villages and towns arriving at Ramses train station and the city's various bus stations.

ARTS

For information on the visual arts, see the boxed text 'Art & Artists' in the Things to See & Do chapter.

Architecture

Cairo is not a place to visit if you are looking for cutting-edge modern buildings. As the 21st century begins, architecture in the city is in a sad state – in fact, according to one published survey, the highest rate of depression in Egypt in 2000 was among architects. Apart from the new Opera House, the city doesn't possess a single building of architectural worth that dates from after the 1950s. The current vogue is for pastiche Pharaonic, best illustrated by the most high profile of all the city's current developments, the new Supreme Constitutional Court, designed by young, up-and-coming architect Ahmed Mito, which is presently under construction on a Nile-side site down in Ma'adi. It's bold and displays some invention; however, it's also bombastic and vaguely ridiculous, more suited to an operatic production of *Aïda* than the sombre requirements of law and justice.

The current sad state of affairs wasn't always so. The city possesses a splendid legacy of late-19th- and early-20th-century apartment blocks, villas and public buildings, some of which are mentioned in the boxed text 'Paris on the Nile' in the Things to See & Do chapter. Even more splendid is the city's fantastic legacy of medieval architecture. Starting with the Mosque of Amr ibn al-As (AD 642), the earliest existing Islamic structure in Cairo, it's possible to trace the development of Muslim architecture through more than 1000 years of history.

For the first 300 years or so (a period known as Early Islamic) there was no uniform style and the few buildings in Cairo

Ottoman minarets are slender and pencil-like; Mamluk minarets have three characteristic tiers.

that remain from this period vary in inspiration; the Mosque of Ibn Tulun, for example, has its stylistic precedents in Iraq. A common architectural vocabulary only began to develop with the Fatimids, who were the first to introduce the use of the dome and the keel arch, the pointed arch that has come to typify Islamic architecture. The Fatimids also introduced the use of heavy stone masonry, where previously mud-brick and stucco had been the main building materials. The Ayyubids did little to advance these building techniques, though Salah ad-Din made good use of stone in constructing the walls of Cairo's Citadel.

However, under the influence of the Mamluks, Islamic architecture quickly became very sophisticated and expressive. During their time in power, the Mamluks extended the existing repertoire of buildings to include not only mosques, walls and gates but also *madrassas* (Islamic colleges), *khanqahs* (Sufi monasteries) and mausoleum complexes. These buildings, especially in the later part of the Mamluk era, are often characterised by the banding of red and white stonework (a technique known as *ablaq*) and by the elaborate stalactite carvings *(muqarnas)* and patterns around the windows and in the recessed portals. The Mamluks were also responsible for the transformation of the minaret from a squat, stubby, often square tower into the slender cylindrical structure typical of Cairo. Decorative stone carving also reached its zenith, best seen on the myriad domes swelling on the city skyline. As the masons' skills developed, patterns progressed from simple zigzags to geometric star patterns and then floral designs. In the Northern Cemetery you can witness this development in the space of 400m and 60 years, from the Khanqah-Mausoleum of Ibn Barquq (AD 1411; zigzags) to the complex of Sultan Ashraf Barsbey (1432; stars) and the final glory of the Mosque of Qaitbey (1474; floral).

The Mamluks were eventually defeated by the Ottoman Turks, who ruled out of Istanbul, and Cairo became a provincial capital. Most of the city's Ottoman buildings are therefore small, practical structures, including houses, *wikalas* (caravanserais) and *sabil-kuttabs* (Quranic school and fountain complexes). However, there's also a handful of mosques, instantly recognisable by their slim pencil-shaped minarets.

Anyone interested in knowing more about Cairo's Islamic architecture should pick up the excellent *Islamic Monuments in Cairo: A Practical Guide* or *An Introduction to the Islamic Architecture of Cairo*, both readily available in the city's bookshops.

Literature

Awarded the Nobel Prize for Literature in 1988, native Cairene Naguib Mahfouz can claim to have single-handedly shaped the nature of Arabic literature in the 20th century. Born in 1911 in the Islamic Cairo quarter of Gamaliyya, Mahfouz began writing when he was 17. His first efforts were very much influenced by European models, but over the course of his long writing career he developed a voice that was uniquely of the Arab world and that drew its inspiration from the talk in the coffeehouses and the dialect and slang of Cairo's streets. His ability to write was savagely ended in 1994 by a knife attack that left the author partially paralysed.

His masterpiece is usually considered to be *The Cairo Trilogy*, a generational saga of family life set in the districts of Mahfouz's youth, but perhaps more interesting are the later works such as *The Harafish*, *Children of the Alley* and *Arabian Nights and Days*, all written in an episodic, almost folkloric style that owes much to the tradition of *The Thousand and One Nights*.

On the strength of what's available in English it's all too easy to view Egyptian literature as beginning and ending with Mahfouz, but he's only the best known of a group of respected writers who include Taha Hussein (1889–1973), a blind author and intellectual who spent much of his life in trouble with whichever establishment happened to be in power; Tewfiq al-Hakim (1899–1987), a prodigious playwright, novelist and short-story writer; and Yousef Idris (1927–92), a writer of powerful short stories largely based on his own life experiences.

Unfortunately, none of these authors has gained anything like the international attention they deserve and they're only published in English-language editions by the AUC Press, a small Cairo-based academic publishing house.

Curiously, though under-represented at home, Egypt's women writers are arguably enjoying more international success than the men. Nawal al-Saadawi's fictional work *Woman at Point Zero* has been published, at last count, in 28 languages. An outspoken critic on behalf of women, she is very much marginalised at home – her nonfiction book *The Hidden Face of Eve*, which considers the role of women in the Arab world, is banned in Egypt. For many years Al-Saadawi was also forced to stay out of the country after Islamists issued death threats against her.

Equally as forthright and uncompromising is Salwa Bakr, another writer who tackles taboo subjects such as sexual prejudice and social inequality.

All of which is a world away from Egypt's current best-known cultural export, Ahdaf Soueif. Though Egyptian, born and brought up in Cairo, she's something of an anomaly in that she writes in English. She lives and is published in London, where she's very much part of the UK literary scene. So far, most of her work has yet to appear in Arabic. Her 790-page coming-of-age (and highly autobiographical) novel about a middle-class Cairene girl *In the Eye of the Sun* and her two short-story collections *Aisha* and *Sandpiper* flit between grey, drizzly Britain and the close, muggy city of her birth. The predominant theme of much of her work is, not surprisingly, the notion of foreignness. Her latest novel *The Map of Love* was short-listed for the UK's most prestigious literary prize, the Booker. Although she didn't win, her profile is sky high and the book remains on the bestseller lists.

Recommended Reading If you're new to Egyptian writers, the following is a short list of must-read Cairo books, all of which are (or have been) available in English-language translations.

Beer at the Snooker Club by Waguih Ghali. A fantastic novel that deserves to be far better known; the Egyptian *Catcher in the Rye*.

City of Love and Ashes by Yousef Idris. Although Idris is best known for his short stories, this is a novel, set in January 1952 as Cairo struggles free of 70 years of British occupation.

A Daughter of Isis by Nawal al-Saadawi. Autobiographical work that has completely divided critics over the author's sour take on the world.

The Golden Chariot by Salwa Bakr. Inmates in a women's prison exchange life stories; surprisingly upbeat, funny and bawdy even.

The Harafish by Naguib Mahfouz. The desert-island choice if we were allowed only one work by Mahfouz, but everything he's done is worth reading.

The Map of Love by Ahdaf Soueif. Bestselling (in the UK) historical novel about love and clashing cultures.

Proud Beggars by Albert Cossery. Egyptian but resident in Paris since 1945, Cossery's novels are widely available in French, less so in English, not at all in Arabic.

Zaat by Sonallah Ibrahim. The 'Zaat' of the title is a particularly helpless heroine, ignored, abused and put upon in this scathing piece of satire on contemporary Egyptian life. *Bridget Jones's Diary* as written by Kafka.

Zayni Barakat by Gamal al-Ghitani. Intrigue, backstabbing and general Machiavellian goings-on in the twilight of Mamluk-era Cairo.

Music
Unlike literature and painting, there's no getting away from music in Cairo. Taking a taxi, shopping or just walking the streets, the routines of daily life are played out to a constant musical accompaniment blasted from wheezing and tinny cassette players. The music you hear can be broadly divided into two categories: classical and pop.

Classical In the 1940s and '50s, classical Arabic music peaked. It fitted the age. These were the golden days of a rushing tide of nationalism and then, later, of Nasser's rule when Cairo was the virile heart of the Arab-speaking world. Its singers were icons and through the radio their impassioned words captured and inflamed the spirits of listeners from Algiers to Baghdad. Chief icon of all was Umm Kolthum, the most famous Arab singer of the 20th century. Her protracted love songs and *qasa'id* (long poems) were the very expression of the Arab world's collective identity. Egypt's love affair with Umm Kolthum was such that on the afternoon of the first Thursday of each month, streets would become deserted as the whole country sat beside a radio to listen to her regular live-broadcast performance.

She had her male counterparts in Abdel Halim Hafez and Farid al-Attrache, but they never attracted anything like the devotion accorded to 'Al-Sitt' (the Lady). She sang well into the mid-1970s, and when she died in 1975 her death caused havoc, with millions of grieving Egyptians pouring out onto the streets of Cairo.

Her cassettes still sell as well now as any platinum pop and her presence is strongly felt in the media, including a radio station that broadcasts four hours of her music daily. Her appeal hasn't been confined to the Arab world either. In an article in *Vanity Fair* magazine in 2000, Elvis Costello nominated an Umm Kolthum anthology as one of his '500 albums you need', while former Led Zeppelin vocalist Robert Plant has said that one of his life's ambitions is to re-form the Middle Eastern Orchestra, Umm Kolthum's group of backing musicians (he and Jimmy Page have toured backed by an Egyptian orchestra).

The kind of orchestra in question is a curious cross-fertilisation of East and West, with the instruments familiar to Western ears augmented by the oud (a type of lute), *nay* (reed pipe), *qanun* (zither) and tabla (a small hand-held drum).

Pop Although to this day the likes of Umm Kolthum and Abdel Halim Hafez are still eulogised and revered, as Cairo experienced a population boom and the mean age decreased, a gap in popular culture developed that the memory of the greats couldn't fill. Enter Ahmed Adawiyya, who did for Arabic music what punk did in the West. Throwing out traditional melodies and melodramas, his backstreet, streetwise and, to some, politically subversive songs captured the spirit of the times and dominated popular culture throughout the entire 1970s.

London-Cairo Remix

An Anglo-Arab with her roots in Egypt and Morocco, Natacha Atlas is an ethno-techno diva whose work fuses traditional Egyptian songwriting, orchestrations and vocals with a London dance-club sensibility. Although she can be guilty of overplaying the Oriental card and indulging in unnecessary warbling (many Cairenes find her phoney), she nonetheless has a cult following and has worked with a number of cutting-edge artists including TransGlobal Underground, David Arnold and flavour-of-the-moment Nitin Sawhney. She's released four albums to date, recorded jointly in Cairo and London with a mix of British and Egyptian musicians: *Diaspora* (1995), *Halim* (1997), *Gedida* (1998) and *Ayeshteni* (2000).

Adawiyya set the blueprint for a new kind of music known as *al-jeel* (the generation), characterised by a clattering, hand-clapping rhythm overlaid with synthesised twirling and a catchy, repetitive vocal. Highly formularised, poorly recorded and mass-produced on cheap cassettes, this form of Egyptian pop was nothing if not tacky and highly disposable. So it remained right up until the late 1980s until producers began to catch up with the times. Since then the Cairo sound has become ever more chic and slickly produced as the big-name artists (the whole music scene is dominated by solo vocalists, there are no such things as 'bands') look towards the international market. Head of the pack is Amr Diab, the chubby foremost purveyor of Western-style pop.

Adawiyya's legacy also spawned something called *shaabi* (from the word for 'popular'), which is currently the real music of the working class. It's much cruder than al-jeel and its lyrics are often satirical or politically provocative. The acceptable face of shaabi is TV-friendly Hakim, whose albums regularly sell around the million mark. However, most other shaabi artists are considered too close to the bone and are kept well away from state media – Shaaban Abdel Rahim, for example, whose wryly funny song 'I Hate Israel' was huge in 2000/2001 but couldn't be played on radio or TV because of its taboo sentiments. Shaaban, however, was hired by McDonald's Egypt to sing the praises of its new product, the McFelafel, until, that is, the US headquarters learnt of his provocative hit and had him sacked for fear of Israeli McBoycotts.

But while the greatest names in 20th-century Arabic music were nearly all Egyptian, that is most definitely not the case in the 21st. The majority of current big sellers in Cairo cassette shops hail from Lebanon, Syria, Tunisia and even Iraq. It's something of a sore point. The consolation is that Egypt still provides the best backing musicians, songwriters and production facilities in the Arab world, not to mention the biggest audiences.

Recommended Listening The following selection will give you a pretty good taste of what Egyptian music is about. You never know, you might even get to like it. Some of these albums are available internationally on CD.

Aho by Hakim. 'Hey People' – a loud, anthemic shout rooted in a traditional shaabi (working class) sound.
Awadouny by Amr Diab. Slick, slick, slick – Spanish guitars and huge sing-along choruses from Egypt's answer to Ricky Martin.
Fi'Ishq al-Banat by Mohammed Mounir. Latest album by the thinking person's pop star, a Nubian who fuses traditional Arabic music with jazz.
Inta Omri by Umm Kolthum. Sixty minutes long and an absolute classic. You could also try *Fakharuni* and *Al-Atlal*.
Khosara by Abdel Halim Hafez. The riff from this song was apparently ripped off by US rapper Jay-Z for his track 'Big Pimpin'.
Layali by Nawal al-Zoghby. She may be Lebanese but she's huge in Egypt, helped no end by fronting a local TV campaign for Pepsi.
Lo Laki by Ali Hameida. Pivotal 1988 track that set the formula for much of the Egyptian pop to follow. Listen at your peril.
Maatadarsh by Shaaban Abdel Rahim. A man who used to make his living from ironing clothes, Rahim is the shaabiest of shaabi singers, hugely popular for singing the words that few others in the public spotlight would dare say.

Nagham al-Hawa by Warda. Algerian by birth but an honorary Cairene by residency. This double CD includes one of her best songs, 'Batwanes Beek'.
Zahma by Ahmed Adawiyya. Social comment (the title means 'Crowded') from the 1970s when Adawiyya's irreverent backstreet sound was at the peak of its popularity.

Also look out for *Yalla* (1990), a compilation of Egyptian street music released by Mango Records, which is a division of Island. Also worth looking out for are *Songs from the City Victorious*, a collaboration between Jaz Coleman (from Killing Joke), Anne Dudley (from Art of Noise) and a bunch of Egyptian musicians. The Egyptians like it so much that it's all over state TV. It's available on cheap cassette in Egypt under the name *Masryat*.

Belly Dance

Tomb paintings in Egypt prove that the tradition of formalised dancing goes back as far as the pharaohs. During medieval times, dancing became institutionalised in the form of the *ghawazee*, a cast of dancers who travelled with storytellers and poets and performed publicly or for hire. Performances were often segregated, with women dancers either performing for other women or appearing before men veiled.

The arrival of 19th-century European travellers irrevocably changed this tradition. Religious authorities, outraged that Muslim women were performing for 'infidel' men, pressured the government to impose heavy taxes on the dancers. When the high prices failed to stop the Western thrill seekers, the dancers were banished from Cairo. Cut off from most of their clientele, many turned to prostitution to survive. For intrepid male travellers, this only increased their lure and they went out of their way to fulfil their erotic fantasies. Visitors such as French author Gustave Flaubert, who travelled through Egypt in 1849, supplied lurid accounts of their experiences (for example, in *Flaubert in Egypt*), titillating Victorian Europeans and helping to cement the less-than-respectable reputation of Egyptian dance:

Sisters Are Dancin' it for Themselves

'Why did you make the heroine of your novels a belly dancer?' I get asked with some regularity. 'Because she gets to hang out in low dives and swanky hotels, wear fabulous outfits and consider the historical background to a woman's power over her own body, from Salome to contemporary prostitution, via Flaubert and sexual tourism in the developing world,' I reply.

It's easy to forget, when you're being dragged up on to a tiny nightclub stage by a strapping Ukrainian lass in a sequined bikini, that belly dancing is older than the hills, deeply private and an icon of post-feminism. Men and foreigners tend to see it as a sexual show but for many Arab women – and an increasing number of Western women – it is a personal activity incorporating identity, history and community alongside fun, exercise and girl-bonding.

The Babylonian goddess Ishtar, when she went down to the underworld to get her dead husband Tammuz back, danced with her seven veils at each of the seven entrances. Ancient Egyptian wall paintings, the Bible, Greek legend and *The Thousand and One Nights* are full of women dancing by and for themselves and each other. Salome's dance for Herod – the seven veils again – was so powerful because she was bringing into public what normally only happened in the women's quarters.

Arab domestic dancing nowadays tends to involve tea, cakes, female friends and relations, little girls and old ladies, a scarf around the hips and a lot of laughter and gossip. Western versions – particularly in the US and Germany – are the bastard children of aerobics classes, women's groups, New Age Goddess awareness, and the perennial female weakness for fancy underwear and being able to show off in it. Belly dancing is extremely good exercise – for the back, the figure, stamina and sex life. It's also good for the soul – it's an art, and requires the distilled concentration, self-respect and 'heart' necessary to art.

None of this is wasted on the great female public (especially in the US), who have taken the ideas, practices and above all the sequins of belly dancing to their hearts. A spin on the Web brings up a plethora of local groups, videos, magazines, performances and costume suppliers. Links lead on to sites covering yoga, costumiers, unicorns, goddess worship and pornography, so you can see where belly dancing sits in the Western consciousness. The real reason for its popularity? In belly dancing, not only do you not *have* to be thin to be gorgeous, you *mustn't* be. Plus there's no age cut-off – in fact it's better to be experienced. Fun for women who are more than eight stone and 18? No wonder we don't see it on TV.

Louisa Young, author of *Baby Love*, *Desiring Cairo* and *Tree of Pearls*

They both wore the same costume – baggy trousers and embroidered jacket, their eyes painted with kohl. The jacket goes down to the abdomen, whereas the trousers, held by an enormous cashmere belt folded over several times, begin approximately at the pubis, so that the stomach, the small of the back and the beginning of the buttocks are naked, seen through a bit of black gauze held in place by the upper and lower garments. The gauze ripples on the hips like a transparent wave with every movement they make.

And that was just the men.

Belly dancing as we see it today began to gain credibility and popularity in Egypt with the advent of cinema, when dancers were lifted out of nightclubs and put on the screen before mass audiences. The cinema imbued belly dancing with glamour and made household names of a handful of dancers. It also borrowed liberally from Hollywood, adopting Tinseltown's fanciful costumes of hip-hugging bikini bottoms, sequined bras and swathes of diaphanous veils.

Also imported from the Western movie industry was the modern phenomenon of the belly dancer as a superstar capable of commanding Hollywood-style fees for an appearance. Dancers such as Samia Gamal and Tahia Carioca, who became the stars of B&W films of the 1930s and '40s, can still be seen today as the old films are endlessly rerun on Egyptian TV. Such is the present-day earning power of the top dancers that in 1997 a series of court cases was able to haul in E£900 million in back taxes from 12 of the country's top artists.

Despite its long history and the wealth of some of its practitioners, belly dancing is still not considered completely respectable and, according to many aficionados, is slowly dying out. In the early 1990s, Islamic conservatives patrolled weddings in poor areas of Cairo and forcibly prevented women from dancing or singing, cutting off a vital source of income for lower-echelon performers. In an attempt to placate the religious right, the government joined in and declared that bare midriffs, cleavage and thighs were out. At the same time, a number of high-profile entertainers donned the veil and retired, denouncing their former profession as sinful. Since then, bellies have once more been bared, but the industry has not recovered.

For more details on who's who on the current belly-dance scene and where to watch them, see under Nightlife in the Entertainment chapter. For information on belly-dance lessons in Cairo, see under Courses in the Things to See & Do chapter.

In the UK, Jacqueline Chapman (☎ 020-8777 6662, W www.bellydancer.org.uk) is one of the leading names in belly-dance classes and each year she takes her students on tour to see the real thing in Cairo.

Cinema

In the halcyon years of the 1940s and '50s Cairo's film studios turned out over 100 movies annually, filling cinemas throughout the Arab world. These days, the average number of films made is around 20 a year. The chief reason for the decline, according to the producers, is excessive government taxation and restrictive censorship. Asked what sort of things they censor, one film-industry figure replied, 'Sex, politics, religion – that's all'. However, at least one Cairo film critic has suggested that another reason

for the demise of local film is that so much of what is made is trash. The ingredients of the typical Egyptian film are shallow plot lines, farcical slapstick humour, over-the-top acting and perhaps a little belly dancing.

There are exceptions. Every year one or two films come out that do display artistic skill and quite often handle social themes of a controversial nature. The one director who consistently stands apart from the mainstream detritus is Yousef Chahine. Born in 1926, he has directed 37 films to date in a career that defies classification. Accorded messiah-like status by critics in Egypt (though he's far from being a huge hit with the general public), he's been called Egypt's Fellini and he was honoured at Cannes in 1997 with a lifetime achievement award. Chahine's films are also some of the very few Egyptian productions that are ever subtitled into English or French, and they regularly do the rounds of international film festivals. His most recent works are 1999's *Al-Akhar* (The Other), 1997's *Al-Masir* (Destiny) and from three years earlier *Al-Muhagir* (The Emigrant), effectively banned in Egypt because of Islamist claims that it portrays scenes from the life of the Prophet. Others to look out for are *Al-Widaa Bonaparte* (Adieu Bonaparte), a historical drama about the French occupation, and *Iskandariyya Ley?* (Alexandria Why?), an autobiographical meditation on the Mediterranean city of Chahine's birth.

For anyone wondering what happened to Omar Sherif, star of *Dr Zhivago* and *Lawrence of Arabia*, he's living in Cairo making very poor films for the local market and appearing in TV ads pushing ceramic tiles.

SOCIETY & CONDUCT

There's no simple definition of Cairo society. On the one hand there's traditional conservatism, reinforced by poverty, in which the diet is one of *fuul* and *ta'amiyya*, traditional dietary staples; women wear the long black, all-concealing *abeyyas* and men *galabeyyas*; cousins marry; going to Alexandria constitutes the trip of a lifetime; and all is 'God's will'. On the other hand, there are sections of society who order out from McDonald's;

whose daughters wear little black slinky numbers and flirt outrageously; who think nothing of regular trips to the US; and who never set foot in a mosque until the day they're laid out in one.

Most Cairenes fall somewhere between these two poles. The average family lives in the hemmed-in side streets of a suburb like Shubra or Dar as-Salaam, in a six-floor concrete tenement with cracking walls. If they're lucky, they may own a small Fiat or Lada, which will be 10 or more years old; otherwise father will take the metro to work or, more likely, fight for a handhold on one of the city's sardine-can buses. He may well be a university graduate (about 40,000 people graduate each year), although that is no longer any guarantee of a job. Chances are he'll be one of the million-plus paper-pushing civil servants, earning a pittance to while away each day in an undemanding job. This at least allows him to slip away early each afternoon to borrow his cousin's taxi for a few hours and bring in some much needed supplementary income. His wife remains at home each day cooking, looking after the three or more children, and swapping visits with his mother, her mother and various family members.

The aspirations of this typical family are to move up the social scale. With no class system as such or aristocracy, movement upwards is completely dependent on money. In the 1970s Sadat's free-market policies resulted in a lot of people becoming very rich. These people now form Cairo's middle classes. They largely inhabit the newer concrete districts of Mohandiseen, Doqqi and Medinat Nasr, where they cruise the wide tree-lined avenues in Mercedes, Audis and BMWs, dropping off the kids at the club.

While this latter group is definitely in the minority, due to their money and status they exert an influence on society vastly disproportionate to their numbers. Occasionally there is a backlash, as in 1997 when around 80 sons and daughters of the Westernised elite were rounded up on charges of Satan worshipping. They were accused of drinking the blood of rats, digging up corpses and

burning the Quran when in reality all they had done was listen to Western music (CDs confiscated ranged from Guns 'n' Roses to Beethoven), dress like kids of the MTV generation, and enjoy access to satellite TV and the Internet. Within two weeks they were all released without charges. The round-up of 'gay' men (see Gay & Lesbian Travellers in the Facts for the Visitor chapter) that took place in 2001 is part of a similar confusion on the part of the authorities. Cairo is undeniably becoming ever more Western in outlook but certain sections of society are running a little bit too far ahead of the rest.

Dos & Don'ts

Dress See under Women Travellers in the Facts for the Visitor chapter for advice on appropriate dress for women. Dressing prudently is also an issue for male travellers. In places less used to tourists the sight of a man in shorts is considered offensive, while in Cairo you'll be looked at like someone who's forgotten to put his trousers on. Count the number of Egyptian men in shorts.

Drink While alcohol is *haram* (forbidden) in the eyes of many Muslims, it is tolerated by most, drunk by a fair few and quite freely available. That said, getting blasted is not a widespread national pastime. It's advisable not to go reeling around Cairo's streets otherwise you may end up cooling your heels in a police cell. We speak from experience.

RELIGION

About 90% of Egypt's population are Muslims; most of the rest are Coptic Christians. Generally speaking the two communities enjoy a more or less easy coexistence. Though Western newspapers from time to time run stories claiming that Copts are a persecuted minority, virtually all prominent Christians in Egypt insist they are neither persecuted nor a minority. Intermarrying between Christians and Muslims is uncommon.

Islam

Islam is the predominant religion of Egypt. It shares its roots with two of the world's other major religions: Judaism and Christianity.

The Mosque & How it Functions

Embodying the Islamic faith, and representing its most predominant architectural feature, is the mosque, or *masgid* or *gamaa*. The house belonging to the Prophet Mohammed is said to have provided the prototype. The original setting was an enclosed rectangular courtyard with huts (housing Mohammed's wives) along one wall and a rough portico providing shade. This plan developed, with the courtyard becoming the *sahn*, the portico the arcaded *riwaqs* and the houses the *haram* or prayer hall.

Typically divided into a series of aisles, the centre aisle in the prayer hall is wider than the rest and leads to a vaulted niche in the wall called the mihrab, which indicates the direction of Mecca, the direction Muslims must face when they pray.

Islam does not have priests as such. The closest equivalent is the mosque's imam, a man schooled in Islam and Islamic law. He often doubles as the muezzin, who calls the faithful to prayer from the tower of the minaret – except these days recorded cassettes and loudspeakers do away with the need for him to climb up there. At the main Friday noon prayers, the imam gives a *khutba* (sermon) from the *minbar*, a wooden pulpit that stands beside the mihrab. In older, grander mosques these minbars are often beautifully decorated.

Before entering the prayer hall and participating in the communal worship, Muslims must perform a ritual washing of hands, forearms and face. For this purpose mosques have traditionally had a large ablutions fountain at the centre of the courtyard, often carved from marble and worn by centuries of use. Modern mosques just have rows of taps.

The mosque also serves as a kind of community centre, and often you'll find groups of children or adults receiving lessons (usually in the Quran), people in quiet prayer and others simply dozing – mosques provide wonderfully tranquil havens from the chaos of the street.

Visiting Mosques

With just a couple of exceptions, non-Muslims are quite welcome to visit any Cairo mosque at any time other than during Friday prayers. (Two of the mosques that cannot be entered by non-Muslims are the mosques of Sayyida Zeinab and Sayyidna al-Hussein.) You must dress modestly. For men that means no shorts; for women no shorts, tight pants, shirts that aren't done up, or anything else that might be considered immodest. You must also either take off your shoes or use the shoe coverings that are available at most mosques for just a few piastres.

KELLI HAMBLET

Mosque of Qaitbey in the Northern Cemetery

Adam, Abraham (Ibrahim), Noah, Moses and Jesus are all accepted as Muslim prophets, although Jesus is not recognised as the son of God. Muslim teachings correspond closely to the Torah (the foundation book of Judaism) and the Christian Gospels. The essence of Islam is the Quran (or Koran) and the Prophet Mohammed, who was the last and truest prophet to deliver messages from Allah to the people.

Islam was founded by Mohammed, who was born around AD 570 in Mecca (now in Saudi Arabia). Mohammed received his first divine message at about the age of 40. The revelations continued for the rest of his life and they were transcribed to become the holy Quran. To this day not one dot of the Quran has been changed, making it, Muslims claim, the direct word of Allah.

Mohammed's teachings were not an immediate success. He started preaching in 613, three years after the first revelation, but could only attract a few dozen followers. Having attacked the ways of Meccan life, especially the worship of a wealth of idols, he made many enemies. In 622 he and his followers retreated to Medina, an oasis town some 360km from Mecca. This *hejira*, or migration, marks the start of the Muslim calendar. Mohammed died in 632 but the new religion continued its rapid spread, reaching all of Arabia by 634 and Egypt by 640.

Islam means 'submission' and this principle is visible in the daily life of Muslims. The faith is expressed by observance of the five pillars of Islam. Muslims must:

- Publicly declare that 'there is no God but Allah and Mohammed is his Prophet'.
- Pray five times a day: at sunrise, noon, mid-afternoon, sunset, and night.
- Give *zakat*, alms, for the propagation of Islam and to help the needy.
- Fast during daylight hours during the month of Ramadan.
- Complete the haj, the pilgrimage to Mecca.

The first pillar is accomplished through prayer, which is the second pillar. Prayer is an essential part of the daily life of a believer. Five times a day the muezzin bellows out the call to prayer through speakers on top of the minarets. It is perfectly permissible to pray at home or elsewhere; only the noon prayer on Friday should be conducted in the mosque. It is preferred that women pray at home. (For information about Islamic holidays and festivals, see Public Holidays & Special Events in the Facts for the Visitor chapter.)

The fourth pillar, Ramadan, is the ninth month of the Muslim calendar, when all believers fast during the day. Pious Muslims do not allow *anything* to pass their lips in daylight hours. Although many Muslims do not follow the injunctions to the letter, most conform to some extent. Although non-Muslims are not expected to fast it is considered impolite to eat or drink in public during fasting hours. The evening meal during Ramadan, called *iftar* (breaking the fast), is always a celebration. In some parts of town tables are laid out in the street as charitable acts by the wealthy to provide food for the less fortunate.

Coptic Christianity

Egyptian Christians are known as Copts. The term is laden with history. It's the Western form of the Arabic *qibt*, which is derived from the Greek *aegyptios* (Egyptian). In turn this is a corruption of the ancient Egyptian *hi-kuptah* (meaning 'the castle of the ka of Ptah'); Ptah is an ancient name for the Pharaonic capital Memphis. Hence the claims by some Egyptian Christians to be the true direct descendants of the pharaohs.

Before the arrival of Islam, Christianity was the predominant religion in Egypt. St Mark, companion of the apostles Paul and Peter, began preaching Christianity in Egypt around AD 40 and, although it didn't become the official religion of the country until the 4th century, Egypt was one of the first countries to embrace the new faith. Egyptian Christians split from the Orthodox church of the Eastern (or Byzantine) Empire, of which Egypt was then a part, after the main body of the church described Christ as both human and divine. Dioscurus, the patriarch of Alexandria, refused to accept this description. He embraced the theory that Christ is totally absorbed by his divinity and that it is blasphemous to consider him human.

The Coptic Church is ruled by a patriarch (presently Pope Shenouda), other members of the religious hierarchy, and an ecclesiastical council of laypeople. It has a long history of monasticism and can justly claim that the first Christian monks, St Anthony and St Pachomius, were Copts. The Coptic language is still used in religious ceremonies, sometimes in conjunction with Arabic for the benefit of the congregation. It has its origins in Egyptian hieroglyphs and ancient Greek. Today, Coptic language is based on the Greek alphabet with an additional seven characters taken from hieroglyphs.

The Copts have long provided something of an educated elite in Egypt, filling many important government and bureaucratic posts, and they've always been an economically powerful minority. Internationally, the most famous Copt today is the former United Nations secretary-general, Boutros Boutros Ghali.

LANGUAGE

Arabic is the official language of Egypt. However, the Arabic spoken on the streets differs greatly from the Modern Standard Arabic written in newspapers, spoken on the radio or recited in prayers at mosques throughout the Arab world. Egyptian Colloquial Arabic (ECA) is a dialect of Arabic, but so different in many respects to Modern Standard Arabic as to be virtually another language. As with most dialects, it is the everyday language that differs the most from that of Egypt's other Arabic-speaking neighbours. More specialised or educated language tends to be pretty much the same across the Arab world, although pronunciation may vary considerably. An Arab from, say, Jordan or Iraq, will have no problem having a chat about politics or literature with an Egyptian, but might have trouble making himself understood in the bakery.

For further notes on Egyptian Colloquial Arabic, plus a vocabulary and pronunciation guide, see the Language chapter at the back of the book.

Facts for the Visitor

WHEN TO GO

Climatically, Cairo has only two seasons: summer and 'not-summer' (for more details, see Climate in the Facts about Cairo chapter). Given the choice, you would be far better advised to visit during 'not-summer', a period that stretches roughly from September to April or May. While January and February can be a little overcast with the occasional downpour, the months immediately either side are comfortably warm, with daytime temperatures leavened by breezes.

During summer the city is insufferably hot and grimy. There are very few places in which to take respite from the heat (shops and public buildings are not usually air-conditioned) and you'll find yourself wanting to shower and change your clothes at least twice daily. Cairenes who can afford to tend to sit out the summer in Alexandria.

It's also worth considering the timing of the various Muslim festivals, in particular Ramadan (see Public Holidays & Special Events later in this chapter), when for a whole month many businesses only work half-days, museums and tourist sites shut early, and many restaurants stay closed until sundown.

MAPS

Lonely Planet has a handy, pocket-sized *Cairo City Map*, produced on laminated card and combining maps of the city centre, Islamic Cairo, the Pyramids and the metro, along with an index of streets and sights. Otherwise, Falk produces a detailed map of Cairo (1:13,000), but you have to appreciate the map's style of unravelling – you either like it or you hate it. The map you'll see around most (it has a very dated photo of the Cairo Tower on the cover) is the *Cairo Tourist Map* (1:12,500) produced by Lehnert & Landrock. It's a terrible map and is hard to read. Better is the *City Map of Cairo* (1:25,000), which, despite the small scale, is clear; it also has larger scale inserts of Downtown, Heliopolis and Ma'adi.

If you're spending a long time in Cairo you may find the *Cairo A-Z* helpful, although its 150 pages make it very bulky and quite heavy. There's a slimmer, handier booklet, *Cairo Maps*, produced by the AUC Press but, as tends to be the problem with atlases and A-Zs, it fails to give any sense of how the place fits together as a whole.

RESPONSIBLE TOURISM

Tourism is vital to the Egyptian economy and the country would be in a mess without it but, at the same time, millions of visitors a year can't help but add to Cairo's ecological and environmental overload. The problem is particularly acute at sites such as the Pyramids and Saqqara. As long as visitors have been stumbling upon or searching for such ancient wonders, they have also been crawling all over them, chipping off bits or leaving their own contributions engraved in the stones. This is no longer sustainable. The organised menace of mass tourism threatens to destroy the very monuments that people flock to see. At sites such as Saqqara, south of Giza, thousands of visitors a day mill about in cramped tombs designed for one occupant. The deterioration of the painted wall reliefs alarms archaeologists, whose calls for limits on the numbers of visitors to sites such as these have largely fallen on deaf ears. Even the Pyramids, which have so far survived 4500 years, are suffering. Cracks have begun to appear in inner chambers and authorities have been forced to limit visitors and to close the great structures periodically to give them a bit of rest and recuperation. It can only be a matter of time before similar measures are enforced elsewhere.

In the meantime, it's up to you to behave responsibly. Don't be tempted to *baksheesh* (tip) guards so you can use your flash in tombs. Don't clamber over toppled masonry. Don't touch painted reliefs. It's all just common sense.

TOURIST OFFICES
Local Tourist Offices

Cairo's main tourist office (Map 2, #31; ☎ 391 3454) is at 5 Sharia Adly, near Midan Opera. The staff can be helpful if they've nothing better to do, but they're not very clued-up. The office is open from 8.30am to 8pm daily (9am to 5pm during Ramadan).

There are tourist offices at both Terminal I (☎ 667 475) and Terminal II (☎ 291 4255) at Cairo international airport. The office at Terminal II should be open 24 hours, but don't bank on it. There's also a tourist office (☎ 385 0259) at the Pyramids, opposite the entrance to the Oberoi Mena House, open from 9am to 5pm daily. There are other small offices at the Manial Palace (Map 5) and Ramses train station (Map 8).

The tourist police (Map 2, #31; ☎ 390 6028) are on the 1st floor in the alley to the left of the main tourist office on Sharia Adly.

Tourist Offices Abroad

Following is a selected list of tourist offices outside Egypt:

Australia
(☎ 02-6273 4260, fax 6273 4629) Press & Information Bureau, Embassy of the Arab Republic of Egypt, 1 Darwin Ave, Yarralumla, Canberra, ACT 2600

Canada
(☎ 514-861 4420, fax 861 8071) Egyptian Tourist Authority, Suite 250, 1253 McGill College Ave, Montreal, Quebec H3B 2Y5

France
(☎ 01 45 62 94 42, fax 01 42 89 34 81) Bureau de Tourisme, Ambassade de la RAE, 90 Ave des Champs Élysées, Paris

Germany
(☎ 69-25 23 19, fax 23 98 76) Aegyptisches Fremdenverkehrsamt, 64A Kaiserstrasse, 60329 Frankfurt-am-Main

Italy
(☎ 396-482 79 85) Egyptian Tourist Authority, Via Bissolati 19, Rome

Spain
(☎ 341-559 2121) Oficina de Turismo Egipto, Torre de Madrid Planta 5, Oficina 3, Madrid

UK
(☎ 020-7493 5283, fax 7408 0295, ⓔ egypt@freenetname.co.uk) Egyptian Tourist Authority, 3rd floor West, Egyptian House, 170 Piccadilly, London W1V 9DD

USA
Chicago: (☎ 312-280 4666, fax 280 4788) Egyptian Tourist Authority, Suite 829, 645 North Michigan Ave, Chicago, IL 60611
Los Angeles: (☎ 323-653 8815, fax 653 8961) Egyptian Tourist Authority, San Vincente Plaza, Suite 215, 8383 Wilshire Boulevard, Wilshire, Beverly Hills, CA 90211
New York: (☎ 212-332 2570, fax 956 6439) Egyptian Tourist Authority, Suite 1706, 630 Fifth Ave, New York, NY 10111

TRAVEL AGENCIES

The area around Midan Tahrir is teeming with travel agencies but don't expect any amazing deals. In fact there are a lot of dodgy operators here and we would strongly advise taking your business elsewhere. For tours of Cairo and surrounds and for trips down to Luxor or Aswan, try Hamis Travel (☎ 575 2757, fax 574 9276, ⓔ hamis@hamis.com.eg, Ⓦ www.hamis.com.eg), with offices on the 1st floor in the annexe just south of the main booking hall at Ramses train station. The company is managed by Anny, a friendly Dutch lady who speaks excellent English. It's open from 9am to 9pm daily.

One of the best and most reputable agencies in town, though it's way down in the dormitory suburb of Ma'adi, is Egypt Panorama Tours (☎ 359 0200, fax 359 1199, ⓔ ept@link.net, Ⓦ www.eptours.com) at 4 Road 79 just outside Al-Ma'adi metro station. They're good on cheap air fares and tours within Egypt and around the Mediterranean region. If you don't want to make the trip down to Ma'adi, Panorama takes bookings over the phone (the staff speak excellent English) and will courier the tickets to you.

The official Egyptian government travel agency, Masr Travel (Map 2, #71; ☎ 393 0168, fax 392 4440), is at 7 Talaat Harb, Downtown.

DOCUMENTS
Visas

All foreigners entering Egypt, except nationals of Malta, South Africa and Zimbabwe, must obtain visas from Egyptian consulates overseas or at the airport or port on arrival. As a general rule, it is cheaper to get a visa at Cairo airport, where the whole process takes only a few minutes; the required stamps are bought from one of the 24-hour bank exchange booths just before passport control and no photo is required. The cost is US$15/UK£12.

Elsewhere, the length of time for processing of visa applications varies. In the USA and the UK, processing takes about 24 to 48 hours if you drop your application off in person, or anything from 10 days to six weeks if you mail it.

A single-entry visa is valid for three months and entitles the holder to stay in Egypt for one month. Multiple-entry visas (for three visits) are also available, but although good for presentation for six months, they still only entitle the bearer to a total of one month in the country.

Costs at embassies and consulates vary depending on your nationality and the country in which you apply. As an example, a single-entry tourist visa costs most Western applicants UK£15 (about US$22) in the UK.

Visa Extensions & Re-entry Visas All visa business, including extensions, is carried out at the Mogamma (Map 2), the 14-storey monolithic white building on Midan Tahrir, which is open from 8am to 2pm Saturday to Thursday. Travellers from overseas need to go up to the 1st floor, pass through the door on the right, then circle around to the left and go straight down the corridor ahead (marked with a No 4). Go to window No 50 and ask for a form (extension or re-entry). In the case of the former, hand in the completed form at window No 27, 28 or 29. You can ask for an extension of up to 12 months and it costs E£8.50 (for the form) plus E£3.10 for stamps. You need photocopies of the photograph and visa pages in your passport, one photograph and a modicum of patience.

Re-entry forms are handed in at window No 16 or 17; you'll need one photograph. Single/multiple re-entry visas cost E£10/14.

There is a two-week grace period beyond the expiry date of your visa, ie, a one-month stay is to all intents and purposes six weeks.

If you stay beyond that, a fine of E£60 is imposed on exit, plus before you can leave you have to sort out an extension. Apparently this can be done at the airport, but it takes time.

Travel Insurance

A travel insurance policy to cover theft, loss and medical problems is a good idea. Some policies offer lower and higher medical-expense options; the higher ones are chiefly for countries such as the USA, which have extremely high medical costs. There is a wide variety of policies available, so check the small print. Some policies specifically exclude 'dangerous activities', which can include scuba diving, motorcycling, even trekking. A locally acquired motorcycle licence is not valid under some policies.

You may prefer a policy that pays doctors or hospitals directly rather than you having to pay on the spot and claim later. If you have to make a claim later, make sure you keep all documentation. Some policies ask you to call back (reverse charges) to a centre in your home country where an immediate assessment of your problem is made.

Check that the policy covers an emergency flight home.

Driving Licence

If you plan to drive in Cairo you should obtain an international driving permit from your local automobile association before you leave home. You'll need a passport photo and a valid licence.

Student Cards

For years it has been notoriously easy to get a legitimate International Student Identification Card (ISIC) in Cairo. That situation has now changed. Proof of student status is now required before an ISIC card will be issued. That proof must be an ID card or letter from your own college or university. ISIC now works exclusively in Egypt with Egyptian Student Travel Services (ESTS) in Cairo. ESTS issues the ISIC, the International Teacher Identity Card (ITIC) and the International Youth Travel Card (IYTC). It also provides a full range of student travel services. For more information, contact

ESTS (Map 5, #20; ☎ 531 0330, fax 363 7251, e ests@rusys.eg.net) at 23 Al-Manial in the medical faculty of Cairo University.

Most of Cairo's backpacker hotels and budget travel agencies can also get the cards but you still require proof of student status.

It is well worth having a student card as it entitles you to a 50% discount on admission to almost all the antiquities sites and museums, as well as significant reductions on train travel.

Vaccination Certificates

You'll need proof that you have been vaccinated against yellow fever only if you are coming from an infected area (such as most of sub-Saharan Africa and South America). Yellow fever is not endemic in Egypt.

Copies

All important documents (passport data page and visa page, credit cards, travel insurance policy, air/bus/train tickets, driving licence etc) should be photocopied before you leave home. Leave one copy with someone at home and keep another with you, separate from the originals.

EMBASSIES & CONSULATES
Egyptian Embassies & Consulates

Following are the addresses and telephone numbers of Egyptian embassies and consulates in major cities around the world:

Australia (☎ 02-6273 4437/8) 1 Darwin Ave, Yarralumla, Canberra, ACT 2600
Consulate in Melbourne: (☎ 03-9654 8869/8634) 9th floor, 124 Exhibition St, Melbourne, Vic 3000
Consulate in Sydney: (☎ 02-9332 3388) 112 Glenmore Rd, Paddington, NSW 2021
Canada (☎ 613-234 4931/35/58) 454 Laurier Ave East, Ottawa, Ontario K1N 6R3
Consulate: (☎ 514-866 8455) 1 Place Ville Marie, 2617 Montreal, Quebec H3B 4S3
France (☎ 01 47 23 06 43, 01 53 67 88 30) 56 Ave d'Iena, 75116 Paris
Consulate in Marseille: (☎ 04 91 25 04 04) 166 Ave d'Hambourg, 13008 Marseille
Consulate in Paris: (☎ 01 45 00 49 52, 01 45 00 77 10) 58 Ave Foch, 75116 Paris

Germany (☎ 228-956 83 11/2/3) Kronprinzen-strasse 2, Bad Godesberg, 53173 Bonn
Embassy branch: (☎ 30-477 10 48) Waldstrasse 15, 13156 Berlin
Consulate: (☎ 69-59 05 57/8) Eysseneck-strasse 34, 60322 Frankfurt-am-Main
Ireland (☎ 01-660 6566, 660 6718) 12 Clyde Rd, Dublin 4
Israel (☎ 03-546 4151/2) 54 Rehov Basel, Tel Aviv
Consulate: (☎ 07-597 6115) 68 Afraty St, Bna Betkha, Eilat
Italy (☎ 06-844 0191, e amb.egi@pronet.it) Villa Savoia, Via Salaria 267, Rome
Consulate: (☎ 02-951 6360) Via Gustavo Modena 3/5, Milan
Jordan (☎ 06-605202, fax 604082) Karbata Ben ad-Dawar St, 4th floor, Amman, PO Box 35178
Consulate: (☎ 03-316171/81) Al-Wahdat al-Jarbiyya, Al-Istiqlal St, Aqaba
Libya (☎ 61-92488, fax 96291) Omar Khayyam Hotel, 5th floor, Benghazi
Netherlands (☎ 070-354 2000) Badhuisweg 92, 2587 CL, The Hague
Spain (☎ 91-577 6308, e gyptemb@teleline.es) Velazquez 69, 28006 Madrid
Sudan (☎/fax 11-778741) Sharia al-Gama'a, al-Mogran, Khartoum
Consulate: (☎ 11-772191) Sharia al-Gomhurriya, Khartoum
UK (☎ 020-7499 2401) 26 South St, Mayfair, London W1
Consulate: (☎ 020-7235 9777/19) 2 Lowndes St, London SW1
USA (☎ 202-895 5400) 3521 International Court NW, Washington, DC 20008
Consulate in Chicago: (☎ 312-828 9162/64/67) Suite 1900, 500 N Michigan Ave, Chicago, IL 60611
Consulate in Houston: (☎ 713-961 4915/6) Suite 2180, 1990 Post Oak Blvd, Houston, TX 77056
Consulate in New York: (☎ 212-759 7120/1/2) 1110 2nd Ave, New York, NY 10022
Consulate in San Francisco: (☎ 415-346 9700/2) 3001 Pacific Ave, San Francisco, CA 94115

Embassies & Consulates in Cairo

Most embassies and consulates in Cairo are open from around 8am to 3pm Sunday to Thursday.

The addresses of some of the foreign embassies and consulates in Cairo are listed in this section.

Your Own Embassy

It's important to realise what your own embassy – the embassy of the country of which you are a citizen – can and can't do to help you if you get into trouble. Generally speaking, it won't be much help in emergencies if the trouble you're in is remotely your own fault. Remember that you are bound by the laws of the country you are in. Your embassy will not be sympathetic if you end up in jail after committing a crime locally, even if such actions are legal in your own country.

In genuine emergencies you might get some assistance, but only if other channels have been exhausted. For example, if you need to get home urgently, a free ticket home is exceedingly unlikely – the embassy would expect you to have insurance. If you have all your money and documents stolen, it might assist with getting a new passport, but a loan for onward travel is out of the question.

Some embassies used to keep letters for travellers or have a small reading room with home newspapers, but these days the mail-holding service has usually been stopped and even newspapers tend to be out of date.

If you need to ask directions to find an embassy say 'Feyn sifarat [country name]'.

Australia (Map 3, #33; ☎ 575 0444, fax 578 1638) World Trade Centre, 11th floor, 1191 Corniche el-Nil, Bulaq
Canada (Map 2, #127; ☎ 794 3110, fax 796 3548) 5 Al-Saraya al-Kubra, Garden City
Denmark (Map 3, #68; ☎ 735 2503, fax 736 1780) 12 Hassan Sabry, Zamalek
Ethiopia (Map 3, #9; ☎ 335 3696, fax 335 3699) 6 Abdel Rahman Hussein, Doqqi
France (Map 4, #29; ☎ 570 3916, fax 571 0276) 29 Sharia Giza, Giza
  Consulate: (Map 2, #51; ☎ 393 4645) 5 Sharia Fadl, off Talaat Harb, Downtown
Germany (Map 3, #82; ☎ 736 0015, fax 736 0530) 8 Hassan Sabry, Zamalek, Cairo
Ireland (Map 3, #42; ☎ 735 8264, fax 736 2863) 7th floor, 3 Abu al-Feda, Zamalek
Israel (Map 4, #25; ☎ 361 0528, fax 361 0414) 18th floor, 6 Ibn al-Malek, Giza
Italy (Map 5, #3; ☎ 794 0658, fax 794 0657) 15 Abd al-Rahman Fahmy, Garden City

Jordan (Map 4, #15; ☎ 348 5566, fax 360 1027) 6 Al-Shaheed Bassem al-Katab, Doqqi
Kenya (Map 4, #11; ☎ 345 3907, fax 344 3400) 7 Sharia al-Mohandis Galal, Doqqi
Lebanon (Map 3, #41; ☎ 738 2823) 22 Mansour Mohammed, Zamalek
Libya (Map 3, #67; ☎ 735 1864, fax 735 0072) 7 Sharia Salah ad-Din, Zamalek
Netherlands (Map 3, #70; ☎ 735 1936, fax 736 5249) 18 Hassan Sabry, Zamalek
New Zealand (Map 2, #70; ☎ 575 5326) 4th floor, 2 Talaat Harb, Downtown
Saudi Arabia (Map 4, #24; ☎ 349 0757, fax 349 3495) 2 Ahmed Nessim, Giza
Spain (Map 3, #52; ☎ 735 6437, fax 735 2132) 41 Ismail Mohammed, Zamalek
Sudan (Map 2, #126; ☎ 794 5043, fax 794 2693) 4 Sharia Ibrahimy, Garden City
  Consulate: (Map 2, #126; ☎ 354 9661) 1 Mohammed Fahmy as-Said, Garden City
Syria (Map 4, #12; ☎ 337 7020, fax 335 8232) 18 Abdel Rahim Sabry, Doqqi
UK (Map 2, #125; ☎ 794 0850, fax 794 0959) 7 Ahmed Ragheb, Garden City
USA (Map 2, #124; ☎ 795 7371, fax 797 3200, Ⓦ www.usembassy.egnet.net) 5 Sharia Latin America, Garden City

CUSTOMS

The duty-free limit on arrival is 1L of alcohol, 1L of perfume, 200 cigarettes and 25 cigars. On top of that, you can buy another 3L of alcohol plus a wide range of other duty-free articles once you are in the country but this must be done within 24 hours of arrival at one of the special Egypt Free duty-free shops.

A grand total of E£1000 can be imported into or exported out of the country. There are no restrictions on the import of foreign currencies, although you are supposed to declare all you have when you enter the country, and you aren't supposed to take out more than you have brought in and declared. This is all highly theoretical and we've never heard of anyone being asked to declare any currency.

Sometimes the Customs Declaration Form D is given to arriving tourists to list all cameras, jewellery, cash, travellers cheques and electronics (personal stereos, computers, radios, VCRs etc). No-one seems to be asked for this form on departure, and few tourists are given it on arrival.

Travellers are, however, regularly asked to declare their video cameras and some have reported being slapped with a hefty 'import tax'.

Prohibited and restricted articles include books, printed matter, motion pictures and materials which the government considers 'subversive or constituting a national risk or incompatible with the public interest'. Articles for espionage or 'intelligence activities' and explosives are banned.

Duty-Free Shops

You can make duty-free purchases at branches of the Egypt Free Shops Company. These shops carry imported spirits, wine, beer and cigarettes, plus a range of electrical goods and other items. Wine costs from US$8 to US$20, whisky, gin and vodka from US$12 upwards, and a crate of 24 cans of Heineken beer is US$16. Take your passport.

Major branches in Cairo include the following:

Doqqi (Map 4, #18; ☎ 348 9059) Cairo Sheraton
Downtown (Map 2, #88; ☎ 393 1985) 19 Sharia Talaat Harb, no alcohol or cigarettes are sold at this branch; (Map 2, #94; ☎ 391 5134) 17 Sharia al-Gomhuriyya
Mohandiseen (Map 4, #1; ☎ 349 7094) 106 Sharia Gamiat ad-Dowal al-Arabiyya

MONEY
Currency

The official currency is the Egyptian pound (E£), or *guinay* in Arabic. One pound consists of 100 piastres (pt). There are notes in denominations of 25pt, 50pt, E£1, E£5, E£10, E£20, E£50, E£100 and E£200. Coins in circulation are for denominations of 10pt, 20pt and 25pt.

Prices may be written in pounds or piastres. For example, E£3.35 can also be written as 335pt.

There is a severe shortage of small change in Cairo. The 25pt, 50pt and E£1 notes, which are useful for tipping, local transport (taxis especially) and avoiding the painfully repetitious scenario of not being given the correct change, are not always easy to come by. Hoard them.

Exchange Rates

Bad news for Egypt but a boon for travellers – in 2000 the long-time stable Egyptian pound wobbled and devalued, dropping against all major currencies. From a traditional E£3.40 or so to the US dollar it fell to as low as E£4. It recovered slightly, but at the time of writing has yet to return to strength. Economists reckon it is unlikely to make a full recovery any time soon.

Exchange rates for a range of foreign currencies were as follows when this book went to print:

country	unit		Egyptian pound
Australia	A$1	=	E£2.16
Canada	C$1	=	E£2.73
Euro zone	€1	=	E£3.75
Israel	NIS1	=	E£0.99
Japan	¥100	=	E£3.43
Jordan	JD1	=	E£5.95
New Zealand	NZ$1	=	E£1.78
UK	UK£1	=	E£5.98
USA	US$1	=	E£4.20

Exchanging Money

Most branches of the big banks – Banque al-Ahli (National Bank of Egypt), Banque du Caire, Banque Masr, Misr International Bank (MIBank), Commercial International Bank (CIB), National Société Générale Bank (NSGB) and the Egyptian American Bank (EAB) – have exchange desks, but for the most efficient service head for those branches in the five-star hotels such as the Hiltons, Sheratons, Marriott and Semiramis Inter-Continental. For slightly better rates you could try the city's foreign exchange (forex) bureaus, of which there are several along Sharia Adly (Map 2), Downtown. Banking hours are from 8am or 8.30am to 2pm Sunday to Thursday. Many banks open again from 5pm or 6pm for two or three hours, largely for foreign exchange transactions. During Ramadan, banks are open between 10am and 1.30pm only. Banque Masr branches at the Nile Hilton (Map 2, #65) and Helnan Shepheard's (Map 2, #113) hotels are open 24 hours. Forex bureaus tend to be open until 8pm or 9pm.

Look at the money you're given when exchanging and don't accept any badly defaced, shabby or torn notes (there are plenty of them around) because you'll have great difficulty off-loading them later. The same goes for transactions in shops and taxis etc.

Travellers Cheques While there is no problem cashing well-known brands of travellers cheques at major banks, many forex bureaus don't take them. Cheques issued on post office accounts (common in Europe) or cards linked to such accounts cannot be used in Egypt.

Banks sometimes have a small handling charge on travellers cheques, usually about 50pt per cheque, plus E£2 to E£3 for stamps. Always ask about commission as it can vary. Forex bureaus that do take cheques tend not to charge any commission.

American Express (AmEx) and Thomas Cook travellers cheques can also be cashed at one of their offices in Cairo. There's a small handling charge. Some souvenir shops and hotels will also accept payment with travellers cheques, but check with them beforehand.

ATMs These are becoming ever more widespread and it's possible to get by in Cairo relying solely on plastic. However, of the numerous types of ATMs in Egypt, not all are compatible with cards issued outside Egypt. Those belonging to Banque Masr, CIB, the EAB and HSBC are good. If you have your PIN number, these machines will dispense cash on Visa and MasterCard and any Cirrus or Plus compatible cards. In central Cairo (Map 2), ATMs are conveniently located on Talaat Harb (on the 1st floor of the concrete tower block across from the Felfela Takeaway); on Mahmoud Bassiouni, near Thomas Cook; on Qasr al-Ainy (200m south of Midan Tahrir); at the main entrance to the Al-Bustan Centre on Sharia al-Bustan; and in the foyers of all the five-star hotels.

Credit Cards Most hotels, many restaurants and a fair number of upmarket shops accept credit cards, usually one or more of the following: AmEx, Diners Club (less commonly accepted), MasterCard and Visa. The latter two cards can be used for cash advances at Banque Masr and the Banque al-Ahli, as well as at Thomas Cook offices. Banque Masr does not generally charge commission for cash advances, but does set a limit of E£1500.

If you lose your card in Cairo, phone AmEx on ☎ 570 3411; MasterCard and Visa on ☎ 357 1148/9; or Diners Club on ☎ 333 2638. AmEx also operates a 24-hour helpline (☎ 569 3299). Thomas Cook has an emergency hotline (☎ 010 140 1367), which operates from 5pm to 8am daily.

AmEx offices in Cairo are open from 8.30am to 5pm Saturday to Thursday and include the following:

Downtown (Map 2, #80; ☎ 574 7991, fax 578 4003) 15 Qasr el-Nil; (Map 2, #65; ☎ 578 5001/2) Nile Hilton
Giza (Map 4, #30; ☎ 570 3411) Nile Tower Building, 21–23 Sharia Giza
Heliopolis (☎ 290 9158) 72 Omar ibn al-Khattab

Thomas Cook offices in Cairo are open from 8am to 5pm daily and include the following:

Downtown (Map 2, #59; ☎ 574 3776) 17 Mahmoud Bassiouni
Giza (☎ 382 2688) Forte Grand Pyramids Hotel, Cairo-Alexandria Desert Hwy
Heliopolis (Map 9, #26; ☎ 417 3511) 7 Sharia Baghdad
Mohandiseen (Map 3, #4; ☎ 346 7187) 10 Sharia 26th of July

International Transfers Western Union, the international money-transfer specialist, operates jointly in Egypt with Masr America International Bank and IBA business centres. It has the following offices in Cairo:

Downtown (Map 2, #87; ☎ 393 4906) 19 Qasr el-Nil
Garden City (Map 5, #4; ☎ 357 1385) 1079 Corniche el-Nil
Heliopolis (☎ 249 0607) 67 Sharia Hegaz; (☎ 258 8646) 6 Sharia Boutros Ghali
Mohandiseen (Map 3, #5; ☎ 331 3500) 24 Sharia Syria

Backhand Economy – The Art of Baksheesh

Tipping in Egypt is called *baksheesh*. It's a word you'll become very familiar with very quickly. It is more than just a reward for services rendered. Salaries and wages in Egypt are much lower than in Western countries, so baksheesh is often an essential means of supplementing income. To a cleaner in a one- or two-star hotel who might earn only about E£150 per month, daily tips can be the mainstay of his or her salary. It's far from a custom exclusively reserved for foreigners. Egyptians have to constantly dole out the baksheesh too – to park their cars, receive their mail, ensure they get fresh produce at the grocers and to be shown to their seat at the cinema.

For travellers who are not used to continual tipping, demands for baksheesh for doing anything from opening doors to pointing out the obvious in museums can be quite irritating. But it is the accepted way in Egypt. Just use your discretion and don't be intimidated into paying baksheesh when you don't think the service warrants it. At the same time, remember that more things warrant baksheesh here than anywhere in the West.

In hotels and restaurants, a 12% service charge is included at the bottom of the bill, but the money goes into the till; it's necessary, therefore, to leave an additional tip for the waiter. Services such as opening a door or carrying your bags warrant 50pt. A guard who shows you something off the beaten track at an ancient site should receive a pound or two. Baksheesh is not necessary when asking for directions.

One tip is to carry lots of small change with you and also to keep it separate from bigger bills; flashing your cash will only lead to demands for greater baksheesh.

The opening hours for these offices are the same as those of the banks. For more details, you can call the Western Union hotline on ☎ 355 5023.

It is also possible to have money wired from home through AmEx. This service operates through most of its branches, and can be used by anyone, regardless of whether you have an AmEx card or not. The charge is about US$80 per US$1000, payable in the country from which the money is sent.

Black Market The black market for hard currency is negligible and few travellers can be bothered hunting it out for the fraction of a difference it makes.

Security

With the growing proliferation of ATMs and increasing acceptance of credit cards, it is no longer necessary to carry large amounts of cash. Whenever we travel to Cairo we take just enough to cover the first day or two then top up via the plastic whenever necessary. If you do come armed with a wad of notes, then do not leave it in your hotel room (see under Theft in Dangers &

Annoyances later in this chapter for more information). Instead, carry your money on your person, preferably in a moneybelt or pouch. Keep a small stash of cash in your wallet or purse for immediate use.

Costs

By international standards Cairo is still fairly cheap. It is possible to get by on US$15 a day or maybe less if you are willing to stick to the cheapest hotels (you can get a bed for as little as E£7 or US$1.80), eat the staple snacks of *fuul* and *ta'amiyya* (for more details of these dishes, see the Places to Eat chapter), and limit yourself to one historic site per day. At the other end of the scale, Cairo has plenty of accommodation where you can pay upwards of US$100 a night for a room, and some of the better restaurants will set you back US$20 per person or more.

Taking a middle route, if you stay in a modest hotel and have a room with a fan and private bathroom, eat in the type of low-key restaurants locals frequent, with the occasional splurge, and aim to see a couple of sites each day, you'll be looking at between US$20 and US$30 per person per day.

To give some indication of daily costs, a fuul or ta'amiyya sandwich costs about 35pt (around US$0.10), while a Big Mac goes for E£5.95 (US$1.75). A meal in a cheap restaurant will set you back around E£15 (US$4) but if you prefer to go a little up-market you can eat very well for E£20 to E£35 (US$5.50 to US$10). A cup of coffee is anything between 50pt and E£2 (US$0.14 to US$0.50), a beer retails for around E£6.50 (US$1.70), and a bottle of mineral water is E£1.50 (US$0.40).

Getting around town is cheap – most metro rides cost 50pt (US$0.40), while a quick hop across town in a taxi is about E£3, or less than a dollar.

The major expense is admission fees to tourist sites. Foreigners are seen as dollars on legs so places where they flock tend to be pricey. A complete visit to the Pyramids will cost E£120 (US$32) in admission charges, and if you want to see the mummies at the Egyptian Museum as well as the rest of the site, the combined fee is E£60 (US$16).

A service charge of 12% is applied in restaurants and hotels to which a 5% to 7% sales tax is added. In other words, the price you are quoted at a hotel or read on a menu could be almost 20% higher when it comes to paying the bill.

Bargaining

Bargaining is part of everyday life in Cairo and almost everything is open to haggling, from hotel rooms to the price of a packet of imported cigarettes. Even in shops when prices are clearly marked, many Egyptians will still try to shave something off the bill. Of course, when buying in souqs such as Khan al-Khalili, bargaining is unavoidable unless you are willing to pay well over the odds – see the boxed text 'The Art of Bargaining' in the Shopping chapter later in this guide for more details.

POST & COMMUNICATIONS
Post

Cairo's main post office (Map 2, #31), on Midan Ataba, is open from 7am to 7pm daily. Poste restante (Map 2, #34) is down the side street to the right of the main entrance, opposite the Express Mail Service (EMS) office; it's open from 8am to 6pm Saturday to Thursday, 10am to noon Friday. Mail is held for three weeks.

There are also post office branches in the grounds of the Egyptian Museum (Map 2), at Ramses train station (Map 8) and Sharia Brazil (Map 3, #55) in Zamalek. Branch post offices are generally open from 8.30am to 3pm Saturday to Thursday.

Postcards and letters up to 15g cost E£1.25 to send to most countries and take about five days to Europe and a week to 10 days to the USA and Australia. Stamps are available at post offices, some souvenir kiosks, shops, newsstands and the reception desks of major hotels.

Sending letters and postcards from the post boxes at major hotels seems to be quicker than sending mail from post offices. If you use the post boxes, blue is international air mail, red is internal mail and green internal express mail.

Sending Parcels If you want to send a package outside Egypt, go to the Post Traffic Centre (Map 8, #2) on Midan Ramses, which is open from 8.30am to 3pm Saturday to Thursday. Bring your passport. You'll need to go to the first big room to the left on the 2nd floor. At the counter get form No 13 (E£5), have the parcel weighed and pay for it. Customs will probably have a look at it. After it has been inspected, someone will wrap it for you, for which there's a small charge.

Express Mail This can be sent through the EMS main office (Map 2, #35; ☎ 390 5874) down the side street beside the Ataba post office. It's open from 8am to 7pm Saturday to Thursday. Most branch post offices also have an EMS counter.

In addition to EMS, Cairo also has a full complement of international courier services on offer, including the following:

DHL (☎ 393 8988) 34 Abdel Khalek Sarwat, Downtown; (Map 2, #129; ☎ 795 7118) 20 Gamal ad-Din Abu al-Mahasin, Garden City; (☎ 636 0324) 35 Ismail Ramzy, Heliopolis

Federal Express (general inquiries ☎ 268 7888); (Map 5, #4; ☎ 794 0520) 1079 Corniche el-Nil, Garden City; (☎ 331 3500) 24 Sharia Syria, Mohandiseen; (☎ 639 0607) 21 Mohammed Ghuneim, Heliopolis
TNT Skypak (Map 4, #14; ☎ 748 8204) 33 Sharia Doqqi, Doqqi

Telephone

Two companies are currently engaged in a battle to plant international-call cardphones on every street corner in Cairo. Leading the contest by a clear mile is Menatel (a subsidiary of France Telecom), with its distinctive yellow-and-green booths. Cards are sold at a multitude of shops and kiosks bearing the little Menatel sticker and come in units of E£10, E£20 and E£30.

Rates for calling Europe via Menatel are E£4.40 (US$1.20) for the first minute and then E£4.80 (US$1.25) for each additional minute. Calls to the US are slightly cheaper, while to Australia it's about 25% more expensive. Using a 20-unit card gives a 20% discount on all calls.

The old central telephone and telegraph offices, known as *centrales*, still exist. At these places you give the number you want to call to an operator behind a desk, tell them how long you want (there is a three-minute minimum), and pay upfront. You then wait your turn to be connected. It's a slow process and also very frustrating as Egyptian minutes always seem to be far shorter than the international norm. Added

Telephone Numbers

The country code for Egypt is ☎ 20, while the international access code (to call abroad from Egypt) is ☎ 00. The city code for Cairo is ☎ 02, but omit the zero if you are calling from abroad.

Other useful numbers include the following:

General inquiries	☎ 140
Inquiries outside Cairo	☎ 10
International inquiries	☎ 144

See Emergencies later in this chapter for some other important numbers.

to this, using a centrale is no cheaper than using a cardphone.

Collect Calls Collect (reverse charge) calls can be made from Cairo but only to countries – such as Canada, Italy, South Korea, the UK and the USA – that have set up Home Country Direct phones. With this service, you can get through to an operator and then reverse the charges or, depending on the service, charge the call to a credit card. At the time of writing, this service was offered by only a few places, such as the Cairo Marriott or Semiramis Inter-Continental hotels, the telephone office in the departure hall at Terminal II at the airport, or at the British Airways office (calls to the UK only) on Midan Tahrir.

International Calling Cards These cards can be accessed through the following Cairo numbers: AT&T ☎ 510 0200; MCI ☎ 355 5770; Global One & Sprint ☎ 356 4777.

Mobiles Egypt's mobile phone network works on the GSM system, as does Europe but not North America. If your phone works on GSM and your account allows you to roam, you can use it in Egypt. Keep in mind, though, that anyone trying to contact you from within Egypt will have to make an international call. Check with your mobile phone company back home to find out what they charge for roaming.

There are two mobile phone companies in Egypt: Mobinil and Click. The latter is a joint venture with Vodaphone and has better coverage internationally.

Mobile rates are more expensive in Egypt than in most European countries. Getting a permanent line is tricky without a work permit but you can rent temporary mobile phone lines from both Mobinil and Click, although only the former is good for short-term use. There are supposedly Mobinil agents at the airport. If not, you can go to any Mobinil shop and rent a line (but not the phone itself). The service is called Allo Hallo and the line costs about E£50. It is good for a maximum of 20 days and includes a E£10 phone credit. For more

Phonophobia

It is tough to get phone numbers in Cairo. According to a report in a local paper, in one year the phone numbers in a particular part of the city were changed three times. Even more astounding is that the subscribers weren't always informed that they had new numbers. There is also a random element in making connections – just because you've dialled the right number it doesn't mean you're going to end up on the right line.

If you are sure that the number we have listed is inaccurate then you could try dialling directory inquiries, but even if you get through – the lines aren't busy and they decide to pick up – there's still no guarantee that you'll be given the correct number.

credit, simply buy a card available at shops all over town. For more information call Mobinil customer service on ☎ 302 8004 or 575 7100. Mobinil customer service centres include the following:

Heliopolis (☎ 417 2054) 110 Sharia Mirghani
Ma'adi (☎ 516 3019) 49 Sharia al-Lasliky
Mohandiseen (☎ 302 8004/7) 39 Sharia Shehab

Click does not have cheap short-term rental and charges a whopping E£675 to rent a line for a maximum of 120 days (but for the last 30 you can only receive calls); E£80 of the line rental is a calling credit. To increase this amount you buy cards, which are widely available. For more information call Click customer service on ☎ 336 4591 or 293 1170.

Fax & Telegraph

Faxes can be sent to/from the telephone centrale on Midan Tahrir (Map 2, #69; fax 578 0979) and Sharia Alfy (fax 589 7662). A one-page fax to the UK or USA costs about E£14, and to Australia about E£20. Rates from hotels are quite a bit more. The minimum from the Nile Hilton to the UK is E£38.50, and E£51.25 to Australia. Receiving a fax message costs E£6 at a telephone centrale or E£5.50 at an EMS office.

Telegrams in English or French can also be sent from the centrales. The rates to the UK, USA and Europe are 67pt per word and to Australia 84pt per word. Each word in an address is also counted. Major hotels also offer this service but rates vary.

Email & Internet Access

Travelling with a portable computer is a great way to stay in touch with life back home, but unless you know what you're doing it's fraught with potential problems. If you plan to carry your notebook or palmtop computer with you, remember that the power supply voltage in Cairo may vary from that at home, risking damage to your equipment. The best investment is a universal AC adaptor for your appliance, which will enable you to plug it in anywhere without frying the innards. More problematic is the issue of phone plugs. There is a mind-boggling variety of these in use in Cairo, and in some cases the phone cable is wired straight into the wall. All we can recommend is that you come with a selection of adaptors, including a US RJ-11 telephone adaptor that works with your modem. You can almost always find an adaptor that will convert from RJ-11 to the local variety. For more information on travelling with a portable computer see Ⓦ www.teleadapt .com or Ⓦ www.warrior.com.

Other issues are that your PC-card modem may or may not work once you leave your home country – and you won't know for sure until you try. The safest option is to buy a reputable 'global' modem before you leave home.

The good news is that Egypt has taken up the Internet in a big way and there are cybercafes throughout Cairo. In addition, many budget and mid-range hotels provide online terminals for the use of guests, free or otherwise. Unfortunately Internet connections can be infuriatingly slow, a result of too much demand on insufficient international bandwidth.

If you do intend to rely on cybercafes or public access points to collect your mail, you'll need to carry three pieces of information with you so that you can access your

Internet mail account: your incoming (POP or IMAP) mail server name, your account name and your password. Your ISP or network supervisor will be able to give you these. Armed with this information, you should be able to access your Internet mail account from any Internet-connected machine in the world, provided it runs some kind of email software (remember that Netscape and Internet Explorer both have mail modules). It pays to become familiar with the process for doing this before you leave home.

Following is a selection of cybercafes in Cairo:

Buonanno Internet Cafe (Map 2, #39; ☎ 395 6786) 20 Sharia Adly, Downtown. Open from 10am to 9pm daily; E£10 per hour; has the newest hardware and fastest connections.

4U Internet Cafe (Map 2, #57; ☎ 575 9304) 1st floor, 8 Midan Talaat Harb, Downtown. Open from 9am to 10pm daily; E£8 per hour; six terminals.

InternetEgypt (Map 2, #123; ☎ 356 2882) Ground floor, 2 Midan Simon Bolivar, Garden City. Open from 9am to 10pm Saturday to Thursday, 3pm to 10pm Friday; E£10 per hour; 10 terminals.

Mohandiseen Cybercafe (Map 3, #17; ☎ 305 0493), on a side street off Gamiat ad-Dowal al-Arabiyya between McDonald's and Arby's. Open from 10am to midnight daily; E£12 per hour.

Nile Hilton Cybercafe (Map 2, #66; ☎ 578 0444 ext 758) Basement of the Nile Hilton Shopping Mall. Open from 10am to midnight Saturday to Thursday, from 10am to noon and 2pm to midnight Friday; E£12 per hour; eight terminals.

Onyx Internet Cafe (Map 2, #56) Ground floor, 26 Mahmoud Bassiouni, Downtown. Open from 9am to midnight daily; E£6 per hour.

Palm Net Cafe (Map 9, #17; ☎ 415 0685) 1st floor, 12 Sharia Ibrahimy, next to Palmyra, Heliopolis. Open from 10am to 10pm daily; E£7 per hour; six terminals.

St@rnet Cyber Cafe (Map 2, #74; ☎ 391 0151 ext 117) Basement of the Al-Bustan Centre, Sharia al-Bustan, Downtown. Open from 10.30am to 10.30pm daily; E£10 per hour.

Service Providers There are more than 30 Internet service providers (ISPs) in Egypt. Of these, companies that we've had good word on include InternetEgypt (☎ 796 2882, e info@internetegypt.com, w www.ie-eg.com), which is the largest private ISP in the country; Soficom (☎ 342 1954, w www.soficom.com.eg); and Gega Net (☎ 414 9700, w www.gega.net). Account rates used to be expensive but are now becoming much more reasonable. Internet-Egypt, for example, offers unlimited dial-up accounts for E£49 (US$13) a month or E£499 (US$130) a year.

DIGITAL RESOURCES
The World Wide Web is a rich resource for travellers. You can research your trip, hunt down bargain air fares, book hotels, check on weather conditions or chat with locals and other travellers about the best places to visit (or avoid). At the Lonely Planet Web site (w www.lonelyplanet.com) you'll find succinct summaries on travelling to most places on earth, postcards from other travellers and the Thorn Tree bulletin board, where you can ask questions before you go or dispense advice when you get back. You can also find travel news and updates to many of our most popular guidebooks, and the subWWWay section links you to the most useful travel resources elsewhere on the Web.

Alternatively, entering the word 'Cairo' into one of the many Net search engines will result in several thousand links, offering everything from prayer times to current theories on who built the Pyramids. Narrowing the field down a little, here are some of our recommendations:

Al-Ahram Weekly Electronic version of the weekly English-language newspaper. Just about the whole paper is online and the archives are fully searchable and free.
  w www.ahram.org.eg/weekly

Al-Bab An incredible Arab World gateway ('Al-Bab' means 'The Gate') site; the Egypt page includes links to dozens of news services, country profiles, travel sites, maps, people profiles etc. A fantastic resource.
  w www.al-bab.com/arab/countries/egypt.htm

All of Egypt Confusing site that tries to be all things to everybody, from tourist site descriptions to business directories, but well worth a browse to see what you can find.
  w www.allofegypt.com

Cairo Online

In the words of Shaaban Abdel Rahim, the working class singer and self-elected 'voice of the people', *Intahit khalas ayam al-Sitt/Ba'ayna fi asr al-internet*, or 'The days of the Lady (Umm Kolthum) are over/Now we're in the age of the Internet'. Cairo is online in a big way.

The most visible signs of this are the Internet cafes springing up all over town, in every mall and shopping centre. Going online and hanging around chat rooms has replaced lingering over shakes at McDonald's as the favourite pastime for Cairo's Westernised youth. For the more motivated, the Internet is a serious career option. Everyone wants to be the next otlob.com, a hugely successful local site for fast food and pharmaceutical deliveries that was bought out in 2000 by the big boys of global finance. So you have the likes of W netgawez.net (Egypt's online wedding guide), W egymatch.com (helping Egyptians find a partner for marriage), W akhermoda.com (online fashion shopping) and countless other nascent ventures, all taking a gamble on their particular niche markets and hoping to cash in their cyberchips for big bucks.

All this Internet action has been helped out by a surprisingly enlightened attitude of the Egyptian authorities. In contrast to its proclivity for book banning, the government has actively embraced Internet use, seemingly respecting the medium's free-flow of ideas. Most ministries have some kind of online presence, and it's just recently become possible to register an environmental complaint or apply for Egyptian citizenship via the official government Web site (W www.alhokoma.gov.eg), or even to take a tour of the presidential residence (W www.presidency.gov.eg).

However, be advised, the free-flow of information works both ways; W www.gayegypt.com carries the prominent header 'Warning: Egyptian state security police may be monitoring you! Try to avoid always logging on from the same location.' Paranoid? Possibly, but tellingly W www.gayegypt.com is also 'Egypt's last gay Web site'. Nietzsche warned about the dangers of gazing into the abyss lest it then gaze back but he'd never encountered the Internet.

Cairo Cafe Lively site devoted to what's on in the Big Mango. It includes new openings, restaurant reviews and an events calendar, and is particularly good on nightlife. It's updated regularly.
W www.cairocafe.com.eg

Egypt: The Complete Guide The official site of Egypt's Ministry of Tourism is surprisingly good; it's updated regularly with magazine-type features, news and a huge range of resources and links.
W touregypt.net

Egyptian Gazette Nothing to do with the newspaper of the same name, this is an archive of smartly written articles on Cairo's khedival past, the buildings, the districts and the people.
W www.egy.com

The Plateau The official Web site of Zahi Hawass, Undersecretary of State for the Giza plateau, ie, the man who looks after the Pyramids. One of the best places to go for news on recent discoveries and news on what's happening with the Pharaonic sites around Cairo.
W www.guardians.net/hawass

BOOKS

The following is a very short, personal list of recommended reading. Many of these titles can be found at bookshops in Cairo, particularly at the excellent American University in Cairo (AUC) bookshops. Outside Egypt you may have to order them.

Most books are published in different editions by different publishers in different countries. Fortunately, bookshops and libraries search by title or author, so your local bookshop or library is best placed to advise you on the availability of the following recommendations.

Lonely Planet

If you want to see more of the country outside Cairo, Lonely Planet also publishes a guide to Egypt, as well as an *Egyptian Arabic Phrasebook* to help find your way around linguistically. For more information about travel in the region as a whole, pick up Lonely Planet's *Middle East*.

Guidebooks

Numerous locally produced guides are available, some of which usefully supplement the information in this book.

Cairo: The Egyptian Museum & Pharaonic Sites by Mohammed Saleh. A fairly recent publication by the museum's current director focusing on 50 of the most noteworthy exhibits. A good, cheap beginner's guide.

Cairo: The Practical Guide by Claire E Francy. Published locally by the AUC Press, this is aimed at people setting up home in the city and focuses on matters such as finding a flat or a medical centre and a school for the kids, but it also contains a wealth of information of use to the visitor, such as a very comprehensive shopping section.

Islamic Monuments in Cairo by Richard B Parker. Scholarly and comprehensive work on the city's Islamic heritage organised around walks, with accompanying maps.

Royal Mummies in the Egyptian Museum by Salima Ikram & Aidan Dodson. Well illustrated and worth picking up for its explanation of the mummification process, as well as its descriptions of the bandaged, desiccated royals themselves.

Travel

Surprisingly little travel literature has appeared in recent times concerning Cairo, in contrast with the late 19th century when there was a deluge of the stuff. Many of these early accounts are regularly reprinted and make for entertaining reading, so they're worth searching out. The following list runs in roughly chronological order with the earliest travelogues first.

Eothen by Alexander Kingslake. An account of a journey undertaken in 1830 from Constantinople to a Cairo suffering one of its periodic plagues.

Journey to the Orient by Gerard de Nerval. A French eccentric famous for taking his pet lobster for walks around Paris, de Nerval's Orient is a fantastical place embellished with surreal tales concerning the mad caliph Hakim and Solomon and Sheba.

Flaubert in Egypt by Gustave Flaubert. Reprints extracts from diaries Flaubert kept when he visited the country for a few months in 1849. The Pyramids receive short shrift as Flaubert prefers to focus on his exploits in the bathhouses and bordellos.

The Nile: A Traveller's Anthology by Deborah Manley (ed) and ***Egypt: A Traveller's Anthology*** by Christopher Pick (ed). These are collections of literary titbits from some of Egypt's more illustrious visitors, including Lawrence Durrell, EM Forster, Mark Twain and Agatha Christie.

Beyond the Pyramids by Douglas Kennedy. Written in the 1980s, the book is now badly dated, but as one of the very few travel books written exclusively about Egypt in recent years, it's still worth picking up.

Baghdad Without a Map by Tony Horwitz. A novice freelance journalist chasing stories around the Middle East. Horwitz was based in Cairo and his descriptions of the city, its characters and chaos are memorable, entertaining and ring true.

From Giza to Gallipoli by Garrie Hutchinson. An Aussie's account of a pilgrimage to WWI and WWII battlefields throughout the Middle East, which kicks off in Egypt. It's very much a first-impressions book but the research is solid and it's an entertaining read.

The Pharaoh's Shadow by Anthony Sattin. Subtitled 'Travels in Ancient and Modern Egypt' this is travel literature with a twist as Sattin searches for 'survivals' of Pharaonic traditions and practices in the Egypt of today, encountering along the way magicians, snake catchers, mystics and sceptics.

Travels With a Tangerine by Tim Mackintosh Smith. Not strictly about Egypt, this is a modern account of a journey in the footsteps of Ibn Battuta, a 13th-century Arab Marco Polo, which spends a few enjoyable chapters in Cairo.

History

The set text is *Cairo: The City Victorious* (1998) by Max Rodenbeck. If you only read one book on the city it should be this, an entertaining and well researched anecdotal meander through 5000 years of urban history. Beyond that, there are numerous other books that zero in on specific eras and areas of interest.

The Arabian Nights: A Companion by Robert Irwin. Traces the origins of the legendary cycle of stories woven by Sheherezade. Medieval Cairo features as a source of many of the tales, and the descriptions of the city's lowlife types and their scams make fascinating reading.

Cairo by Andre Raymond. Highly scholarly history of the city from the Arab conquest to the end of the 20th century. Facts, figures, dates and statistics are all there but it lacks the lifeblood.

Cairo in the War 1939–1945 by Artemis Cooper. Six heady years in the life of the city at its most glamorous, crowded with soldiers and officers and visited by a who's who of international high society, celebrity and royalty.

The Complete Pyramids by Mark Lehner. Everything you ever wanted to know about pyramids; not just those at Giza but the other 70 or more scattered throughout the country.

Egypt's Belle Epoque by Trevor Le Gassick and ***Lifting the Veil*** by Anthony Sattin. Both deal with Egypt in the late 19th and early 20th century: steamer trunks and dinner dances, big spending and bankruptcy, British rule and nationalism.

Great Cairo: Mother of the World by Desmond Stewart. A lot of condensing has gone on to get all that history into such a slim volume but where Stewart doesn't spare is in the wonderful descriptions of Cairo's various diabolical rulers.

Oleander, Jacaranda by Penelope Lively. Autobiographical account of a Cairo upbringing offering potent glimpses of British colonial Egypt by a bestselling novelist.

Zarafa by Michael Allin. Charming story of a giraffe sent as a gift from the ruler of Egypt to the king of France against a background of Europe in the Age of Enlightenment encountering an Egypt barely out of the Middle Ages.

Culture & Society

There's no one primer on Egyptian culture and society that encompasses strands as diverse as Western educated business communities and Bedouin tribes yet to encounter computers. Bear in mind that the following titles focus only on single aspects and in no way present a particularly full picture.

The Hidden Face of Eve by Nawal al-Saadawi. Considers the role of women in the Arab world, a touchy subject, and consequently the book is banned in Egypt. For more on Al-Saadawi see Arts in the Facts about Cairo chapter.

No God But God: Egypt and the Triumph of Islam by Geneive Abdo. One of the best books on the Egyptian Islamist movements in recent years. Examines the Islamist movement as a response to increased piety and the ineptitude of governance in the post-Nasserist era.

Whatever Happened to the Egyptians by Galal Amin. A collection of insightful essays by an esteemed economist that attempts to trace national social, political, economic and cultural changes (read: 'decline') in Egypt since the heady years of the 1950s. Intelligent and surprisingly readable.

Fiction

With a vivid history stretching back some 5000 years, encompassing pyramid builders, Hammer-horror caliphs, the enchantment of *The Thousand and One Nights*, colonial hi-jinks, wartime romance, and the modern day tinderbox that is the Middle East, little wonder that Cairo has provided a perfect backdrop for the imaginings of writers.

For information about literature by Egyptian writers see Arts in the Facts about Cairo chapter.

Baby Love by Louisa Young. Smart, hip novel that shimmies between Shepherd's Bush in West London and the West Bank of Luxor, as a belly dancer, now single mother, skirts romance and violence. There are also a couple of follow-ups, *Desiring Cairo* and *Tree of Pearls*.

City of Gold by Len Deighton. This thriller set in wartime Cairo brings the city to life in a completely believable manner.

The English Patient by Michael Ondaatje. Although it has a highly impressionistic sense of history, this story of love and destiny in WWII remains a beautifully written, poetic novel. And a bit of it is set in Cairo.

The Eye of Ra by Michael Asher. Indiana Jones meets the X Files–type tale of missing corpses, multiple murders, hidden tombs, psychic Bedouin and other gung ho malarkey. Still, it's fun, and Cairo is well described. Asher's second Egypt novel, *Firebird*, is even more absurd.

The Face in the Cemetery by Michael Pearce. The latest in an ever-expanding series of lightweight historical mystery novels featuring the Mamur Zapt, Cairo's chief of police. A bit like Tintin but without the pictures.

The Key to Rebecca by Ken Follett. Ropey yarn loosely based on the John Eppler story with added kinky sex on a houseboat. It was later made into a dire TV movie starring David Soul.

The Levant Trilogy by Olivia Manning. Cairo during the war serves as the setting for the trials and traumas of a dislikable bunch of expats. It was filmed by the BBC as *Fortunes of War* starring Kenneth Branagh and Emma Thompson.

Moon Tiger by Penelope Lively. This award-winning romance is technically accomplished and very moving in parts, with events that occurred in Cairo during WWII at the heart of the matter.

Proud Beggars by Albert Cossery. Born in Egypt but resident in Paris since 1945, Cossery has written several semi-existential novels set in squalid quarters of Cairo. This is one of the few to be translated into English.

Sands of Saqqara by Glenn Meade. More wartime high adventure as archaeologist friends find themselves on opposing sides in a plot to assassinate Roosevelt at the Mena House. And they both love the same woman. Sounds ripe for Hollywood.

A Woman of Cairo by Noel Barber. One of those historical novels of breathtaking sweep in which dynasties crash and fall about star-crossed lovers. In this, British and Egyptian neighbours are in the run up to the revolution; King Farouk, Nasser and Sadat all get walk-on parts.

FILMS

It's quite some time since Cairo has been seen at cinemas outside the Arab world. True, scenes in the Oscar-sweeping *The English Patient* (1996) took place here but that was silver-screen trickery, achieved with scenic doubles – most Egyptian locations were actually shot in Tunisia and, in the case of some interiors, the stand-in was Venice. Tunisian streets also doubled as an unconvincing Cairo in Steven Spielberg's *The Raiders of the Lost Ark* (1981), while in sci-fi tosh *Stargate* (1994), the US state of Arizona doubled for Giza.

It's not that Cairo is unphotogenic – in fact, it is quite the opposite. It appears beguilingly seductive on the big screen. The problem is a combination of obstructive bureaucracy and extortionate taxes levied on foreign film companies, which has the effect of keeping the cameras away. It wasn't always so, and the 1970s and 1980s, in particular, saw a number of films on location in Egypt, most of which you should still be able to find down at your local video library.

The Awakening (1980) Lame, ineffective horror about an ancient Egyptian queen possessing modern souls, loosely based on Bram Stoker's *The Jewel of the Seven Stars* and starring Charlton Heston. Some scenes were shot in Cairo.

Cairo Road (1950) 'Death and dope, misery and madness, go hand in hand along…Cairo Road. Doublecross road of the world.' Great poster tag line but dull film as Britain's Anti-Narcotics Bureau tackles drug smugglers in Egypt, all shot on location.

Gallipoli (1981) Aussie film about the fateful WWI battle, with an extended middle section devoted to the young soldiers' training in the shadow of the Pyramids.

Malcolm X (1992) During the course of its 3½-hour running time, Malcolm X visits Cairo and patronises the locals before praying in the Mosque of Mohammed Ali up at the Citadel.

The Mummy (1932) The original film, with Boris Karloff as the bandaged, love-lorn monster, had scenes shot in Cairo's Egyptian Museum. The 1999 remake and it's 2001 sequel, *The Mummy Returns*, constructed their Cairos in the CGI labs.

Ruby Cairo (1992) One of the last Hollywood productions to brave the bureaucracy is a limp tale of a wife who tracks down her missing-presumed-dead husband to a hideaway in Egypt. Headlined by Andie MacDowell and Liam Neeson but the real star is Cairo, with no cliche left unshown, including camels, Pyramids, *moulids* (festivals) and feluccas.

Sphinx (1980) Adapted from a best-selling novel by Robin Cook, this is a tale of antiquities smuggling, shot entirely in Cairo and Luxor, from which no-one emerges with any credit except the location scout.

The Spy Who Loved Me (1977) The Pyramids and Islamic Cairo provide Martini-glamorous backdrops for the campy, smirking antics of Roger Moore as James Bond.

NEWSPAPERS & MAGAZINES

The *Egyptian Gazette* is Cairo's awful daily English-language newspaper. It serves largely as a press puff for the office of the president, although it does offer great entertainment for lovers of typos and seriously screwed-up headlines. The Saturday issue is called the *Egyptian Mail*. The French-language equivalents are the daily *Le Progrès Egyptien* and Sunday's *Progrès Dimanche*.

Al-Ahram Weekly, *Cairo Times* and *Middle East Times* all appear every Thursday and do a much better job of keeping English-speaking readers informed of what's going on. Of the three, the *Cairo Times* is the most readable and is great for news analysis but the *Weekly* is the most comprehensive and has particularly good coverage of current events, including restaurant openings, cultural performances and sports. *Al-Ahram* also puts out a weekly French edition, *Hebdo*.

Egypt Today is an ad-saturated, general-interest glossy with excellent listings, but its monthly schedule means that in this most unpredictable of cities, much of the information has a certain hypothetical quality. It also has several associated publications including the monthly *Sports & Fitness* and *Business Today*.

An extremely broad range of Western newspapers and magazines are sold at hotel bookshops and street-side newsstands in town. Papers are a day old and monthly magazines usually make it within a week of their home publication dates, but expect to pay up to twice the cover price. Censorship is still in force and it's not unusual to find a page has been neatly sliced from your copy of *Time* magazine, usually because a model in an ad had a little bit too much flesh on display.

Of the local Arab-language press, the venerable state-owned *Al-Ahram* remains the best known of the national dailies, though the journalism is very stilted and conservative in comparison to some of the newer publications, such as the progressive business-focused *Al-Alam al-Yom* and the Egyptian edition of the Arab world daily *Al-Hayat*.

RADIO & TV

FM95 broadcasts news in English on 557kHz at 7.30am and 2.30pm and 8pm daily. This is the European-language station and, in addition to English-language programs, it has programs in French, German, Italian and Greek. BBC and VOA broadcasts can be picked up on medium wave at various times of the morning and evening. The BBC can be heard on both 639kHz and 1320kHz, and VOA on 1290kHz.

Despite a firm state stranglehold, Egyptian TV is booming. In the last few years the traditional three channels have been supplemented by half a dozen or more, as throughout the country every governorate gets in on the act with their own stations. Nile TV, based in Cairo, broadcasts news and current affairs exclusively in English and French from 7am daily until past midnight. Otherwise, there's little for non-Arabic speakers, apart from the occasional old American movie (the Saturday night Cine Club on Channel One sometimes screens the odd good one) and a nightly English-language news bulletin on Channel Two at 8pm.

Satellite has made a big splash (check the number of dishes on the city skylines), and

cable to a lesser extent. Many hotels have satellite TV, even some of the budget places. MTV seems to be a staple at fast-food joints countrywide.

Check the *Egyptian Gazette* for the day's TV (both local and satellite) and radio program information. There are also a couple of special monthly program-listing magazines for satellite and cable.

PHOTOGRAPHY & VIDEO
Film & Processing

Film generally costs as much as, if not more than, it does in the West. For example, Kodacolor 100/200 (36 exposures) costs about E£22, while for Kodachrome 100 slide film, you'll pay E£24 (36 exposures). Check the expiry dates and don't buy from anywhere that stores the film in direct sunlight.

Colour-print processing costs from E£2 to E£4 depending on whether it's a one-hour or overnight service, plus from 50pt to 135pt per print depending on size. There are plenty of labs Downtown and in Zamalek. One Downtown place we recommend for both quality and price is the Photo Centre (Map 2, #85; ☎ 392 0031) on the 1st floor at 3 Sharia Mahrani, a backstreet off Sherifeen, which itself is a side street off Qasr el-Nil. Also Downtown, there's a Kodak shop (Map 2, #40) on Adly between Sherif and Mohammed Farid, and in Zamalek there's another

Photography & Video Fees

Outrageous fees are charged at many Cairo sites for the use of personal cameras and videos. A charge of E£10 is common if you want to take photos, and it can cost 10 times that or more to use a video. At the Manial Palace Museum the video fee is E£150. If you are carrying a camera or video and baulk at the cost, promising the guards you aren't going to use your equipment doesn't cut the mustard. They will insist that you deposit the gear at the ticket office. If you don't like the thought of leaving possibly expensive equipment in surroundings of dubious security, then leave the stuff at home or at your hotel.

Kodak (Map 3, #63) on Sharia 26th of July and an Agfa outlet at 22 Hassan Sabry.

If you need professional processing, the place to go is Antar Photostores (Map 2, #97; ☎ 354 0786) at 180 Sharia Tahrir, just east of Midan Falaki, Bab al-Luq.

There are numerous places where you can get passport photos done. The cheapest option is to ask one of the photographers in front of the Mogamma. They will use an antique box camera to copy your passport photo or any other photo and make four copies (B&W only and often a bit out of focus) for E£4. For colour shots done quickly, your cheapest bet is the instant photo booth (E£6 for four photos) near the ticket windows in Sadat metro station under Midan Tahrir.

Restrictions

There are several places that are definite no-nos when it comes to taking photos. These include the parliament building, the presidential palace in Heliopolis, Abdeen Palace in central Cairo and any embassies or ministries. Beyond this it's more difficult to predict what you can and cannot point a camera at. A photographer friend had her film confiscated for shooting pictures of public telephones, while another spent a day held at a police station for inadvertently snapping a factory. Always be careful when taking photos of anything other than tourist sites, especially bridges, train stations, anything military, airports and other public works.

Egyptians are also sensitive about the negative aspects of their country. It is not uncommon for someone to yell at you when you're trying to take photos of, say, a crowded bus or a donkey cart full of garbage. Be sure to exercise discretion.

TIME

Egypt is two hours ahead of GMT/UTC and daylight saving time is observed (it begins in late April and ends on 30 September). So, without allowing for variations due to daylight saving, when it's noon in Cairo it is 2am in Los Angeles; 5am in New York and Montreal; 10am in London; 1pm in Moscow; and 8pm in Melbourne and Sydney.

ELECTRICITY

Electric current is 220V AC, 50Hz. Wall sockets are the round, two-pin European type (though for some strange reason the socket holes are often too narrow to accept European plugs). Adaptor plugs are easily found in city shops but bring a transformer if you need one as these are difficult to obtain.

WEIGHTS & MEASURES

Egypt is on the metric system. Basic conversion charts are given on the inside back cover of this book.

LAUNDRY

There are no self-service laundries that we know of but most hotels, even those at the very bottom end of the scale, can arrange to have your washing done. The other option is to find your local *makwagee*, the 'hole-in-the-wall' laundryman, who will wash and iron your clothes by hand for about E£1 or E£1.50 per item.

TOILETS

Public toilets, when they can be found, are bad news: fly-infested, dirty and smelly. Some toilets are still of the 'squat over a hole in a little room' variety. Only in mid-range and top-end hotels will toilet paper be provided; most toilets are simply equipped with a water squirter for washing yourself when you're finished. It's a good idea to adopt this practice if you can as toilets in Cairo are not capable of swallowing much toilet paper and it's not uncommon to find toilets in hotels frequented by Westerners absolutely choked with the stuff. If you do use toilet paper, put it in the bucket that's usually provided.

It's a good idea to make a mental note of all Western-style fast-food joints, such as McDonald's and KFC, and of the five-star hotels, as these are the places where you'll find the most sanitary facilities.

HEALTH

At first sight, Cairo seems a nightmare city for the health conscious: air pollution, leaking sewer systems and dirt everywhere. However, provided you take appropriate precautions before you leave and follow some common-sense measures while you are away, you are unlikely to suffer anything more serious than a bout of diarrhoea.

Before You Go

Before you leave, find out from your doctor, a travel health centre or an organisation such as the US-based Centers for Disease Control (W www.cdc.org) what the current recommendations are for travel to Egypt. Remember to leave enough time so that you can get any vaccinations you need – six weeks before travel is ideal. Discuss your requirements with your doctor, but generally, it's a good idea to make sure your tetanus, diphtheria and polio vaccinations are up to date before travelling. Other vaccinations that may be recommended for travel to Egypt include typhoid, hepatitis A, hepatitis B, rabies and meningitis. Note that if you are coming from a yellow-fever infected area (most of sub-Saharan Africa and parts of South America) you'll need proof of yellow fever vaccination before you will be allowed to enter Egypt, although there is no risk of yellow fever in Egypt.

Cairo is not in a malarial zone but there is a risk of malaria in the Al-Fayoum area from June to October. Get advice on malaria prevention if you intend to travel to this region.

Staying Healthy in Cairo

The main concern in Cairo for most of the year is the heat. Take time to acclimatise to the high temperatures, drink plenty of fluids to prevent dehydration and don't do anything too physically demanding in the first few days. Avoid sunburn by using sunscreen and wearing a hat, and protect your eyes with good quality sunglasses.

The tap water in Cairo is safe to drink but can take a bit of getting used to as it's highly chlorinated. If you are in Cairo on a short-term stay, you're probably better off sticking to mineral water. It's almost inevitable that any newcomer to Cairo will go down with travellers' diarrhoea. If, or more likely when, you get it, drink plenty of water to prevent dehydration. In severe

cases, a rehydrating solution is preferable to replace minerals and salt lost. Commercially available oral rehydration salts, such as Rehydran, are very useful; add them to purified or bottled water and keep drinking small amounts often.

Mosquitoes and other biting insects can be a nuisance in Cairo and may transmit diseases such as dengue fever, so it's worth taking precautions against them. Cover up with light-coloured clothing and use DEET containing insect repellent on any exposed skin.

Schistosomiasis (or bilharzia) is a potentially serious disease carried in fresh water by minute worms and it is prevalent in the Nile Delta area and in the Nile Valley. Do not drink, wash, paddle or even stand in water that may be affected and do not swim in the Nile. Seek medical attention if you think you may have been exposed to the disease.

Beware of stray dogs as rabies is not uncommon. You might consider pretravel rabies vaccination, which involves having three injections over 21 to 28 days. If someone who has been vaccinated is bitten or scratched by an animal, they will require two booster injections of vaccine; those not vaccinated require more.

Hospitals

Many of Cairo's hospitals suffer from antiquated equipment and a cavalier attitude to hygiene but there are several exceptions. Your embassy should be able to provide you with a list of recommended doctors and medical clinics.

Anglo-American Hospital (Map 4, #8; ☎ 735 6162/3/4/5) Sharia Hadayek al-Zuhreyya, to the west of the Cairo Tower, Gezira
As-Salam International Hospital (Map 3, #6; ☎ 302 9091) 3 Sharia Syria, Mohandiseen; (☎ 524 0250) Corniche el-Nil, Ma'adi
Cairo Medical Centre (☎ 258 1003) Midan Roxy, Heliopolis

Pharmacies

There is no shortage of pharmacies in Cairo and almost anything can be obtained without a prescription. Pharmacies that operate 24 hours include Isaaf (Map 2, #5; ☎ 574 3369), on the corner of Sharias Ramses and 26th of July, Downtown, and Zamalek Pharmacy (Map 3, #46; ☎ 736 6424) at 3 Shagaret ad-Durr, Zamalek.

In the city centre, the Anglo-Eastern Pharmacy (Map 2, #47) on the corner of Sharias Abdel Khalek Sarwat and Sherif, is open from 10am to 3pm and 6.30pm to 10pm Saturday to Thursday.

WOMEN TRAVELLERS

Egyptians are conservative, especially about matters concerning sex and women; Egyptian women that is, not foreign women.

An entire book could be written from the comments and stories of women travellers about their adventures and misadventures in Cairo and Egypt. A recent article in the UK's *Guardian* newspaper written by two female travellers reckoned Egyptian men were the 'creepiest on Earth' with incessant chat-up lines such as 'I miss you like the desert misses the rain', which, they wrote, could have been funny had they not been so constant and intimidating. Most of the incidents are nonthreatening nuisances, like a fly buzzing in your ear – you can swat it away and keep it at a distance, but it's always out there buzzing around.

Attitudes Towards Women

Some of the biggest misunderstandings between Egyptians and Westerners occur over the issue of women. Half-truths and stereotypes exist on both sides – many Westerners assume all Egyptian women are veiled, repressed victims, while a large number of Egyptians see Western women as sex-obsessed and immoral.

For many Egyptians, both men and women, the role of a woman is specifically defined: she is mother and matron of the household. The man is the provider. However, as with any society, generalisations can be misleading and the reality is far more nuanced. There are thousands of middle- and upper-middle-class professional women in Egypt who, like their counterparts in the

---

Safety Tips for Women Travellers

- Wear a wedding band. Generally, Egyptian men seem to have more respect for a married woman.
- If you are travelling with a man, it is better to say you're married rather than 'just friends'.
- Avoid direct eye contact with an Egyptian man unless you know him well; dark sunglasses could help.
- Try not to respond to an obnoxious comment from a man – act as if you didn't hear it.
- Be careful in crowds and other situations where you are crammed between people as it is not unusual for crude things to happen in this situation.
- On public transport, sit next to a woman if possible. This is not difficult on the Cairo metro, where the first compartment is reserved for women only.
- If you're in the countryside (off the beaten track) be extra conservative in what you wear.
- Be very careful about behaving in a flirtatious or suggestive manner – it could create more problems than you ever imagined.
- If you need help for any reason (directions etc), ask a woman first.
- Be wary when horse or camel riding, especially at the Pyramids. It's not unknown for a guy to ride close to you and grab your horse, among other things. Riding with a man on a horse or camel is simply asking for trouble.
- You may find it handy to learn the Arabic for 'don't touch me' (*la tilmasni*). Also worth memorising are *ihtirim nafsak* (literally 'behave yourself') or *haasib eedak* (watch your hand). Stronger language will only make it worse.
- Being befriended by an Egyptian woman is a great way to learn more about life in Egypt and, at the same time, have someone totally nonthreatening to guide you around. Getting to know an Egyptian woman is, however, easier said than done. You won't find them in cafes or traditional coffeehouses and fewer women speak English than men.

West, juggle work and family responsibilities. Among the working classes, where adherence to tradition is strongest, the ideal may be for women to concentrate on home and family, but economic reality means that millions of women are forced to work (but are still responsible for all domestic chores).

The discomfiture of many Egyptians at this mixing of roles has been exploited by Islamists, who have politicised the issue of women and the family in their constant battle to undermine the government. Interspersed with the politics is a general wave of conservatism that has swept the country in recent years. The most visible sign of this return to 'traditional values' has been the huge number of women adopting more conservative dress and wearing the *higab* (headscarf). But again, the issue is more complex than first meets the eye. For every woman who adopts the higab for religious reasons, there are many others who wear it because it allows them to walk around freely – not many men would dare hassle a woman wearing the higab! Or because it means they don't have to worry about fashion, or, paradoxically, because it *is* the fashion (check out the different ways to wear a headscarf). It is also a socioeconomic phenomenon; only a fraction of wealthy upper-middle or middle-class women have their heads covered.

Away from dress, the issue of sex is where the differences between Western and Egyptian women are most apparent. Premarital sex (or, indeed, any sex outside marriage) is taboo in Egypt, although, as with anything forbidden, it still happens. Nevertheless, it is the exception rather than the rule – and that goes for men as well as women. However, for women the issue is potentially far more serious. With the possible exception of the upper classes, women are expected to be virgins when they get married and a family's reputation can rest upon this point. In such a context, the restrictions placed on a young girl – no matter how onerous they may seem to a Westerner – are to protect her and her reputation from the potentially disastrous attentions of men.

The presence of foreign women presents, in the eyes of some Egyptian men, a chance to get around these norms with ease and without consequences. This possibility is reinforced by distorted impressions gained from Western TV and by the behaviour of some foreign women – as one young man remarked when asked why he harassed every Western woman he saw, 'For every 10 who say no, there's one who says yes'.

So, as a woman traveller you can expect some verbal harassment at the very least. Sometimes it will go as far as pinching bottoms or brushing breasts but flashing and masturbating in front of women are much less common. Serious physical harassment and rape do occasionally occur, but more rarely than in most Western countries.

What to Wear

Egyptians are quite conservative about dress. Wearing shorts and a tight T-shirt on the street is, in some people's eyes, confirmation of the worst views held of Western women. Generally, if you're alone or with other women, the amount of harassment you get will be directly related to how you dress: the more skin exposed, the more harassment. You'll have fewer hassles if you don't dress for hot weather in the same way you might at home. Baggy T-shirts and loose cotton trousers or long skirts won't make you sweat as much as you think and will protect your skin from the sun as well as from unwanted comments. As with anywhere, take your cues from those around you; if you're in a rural area and all the women are in long, concealing dresses, you should be conservatively dressed. If you're going out to a hip nightspot, you're likely to see middle- and upper-class Egyptian girls in the briefest designer gear and can dress accordingly – just don't walk there.

Unfortunately, although dressing conservatively should reduce the incidence of any such harassment, it by no means guarantees you'll be left alone.

GAY & LESBIAN TRAVELLERS

Homosexuality in Egypt is no more or less prevalent than elsewhere in the world but it's a whole lot more ambiguous than in the West. Men routinely hold hands, link arms and give each other big slobbery kisses on greeting but don't misread the signals – this is not gay behaviour, it's just a local take on male bonding. Beyond this, though, a strange double-think goes on whereby an Egyptian man can indulge in same-sex intercourse but not consider himself gay because only the passive partner is regarded as queer. So it's not uncommon for foreign male visitors to receive blatant and crudely phrased propositions of sex from Egyptian men. It's not for nothing that Cairo has always had more than its fair share of European queens in residence. But if a lot of man-to-man sex goes on, there's not necessarily any sort of gay scene. The concept of 'gay pride' is totally alien and, bar the odd young (possibly foolhardy) crusader, no Egyptian man would openly attest to being homosexual for fear of being shunned by society and labelled as weak and feminine.

While there is no mention of homosexuality in the Egyptian penal code, some statutes criminalising obscenity and public indecency have been used against gay men in the past. Most recently, in May 2001, 55 Egyptian men were arrested when police raided a floating bar/restaurant in Zamalek. They were held and questioned on charges of 'exploiting religion to promote extreme ideas to create strife and belittling revealed religions' – whatever that means. The state prosecutor's office put it more bluntly when it labelled the men 'deviants'. As we went to press, a first verdict on one of the defendants had just been passed, with a 15-year-old boy being pronounced guilty of having committed homosexual acts, earning him a sentence of three years' prison with hard labour. The boy maintained that his confession had been extracted under torture. For the latest information check the excellent W www.gayegypt.com or the Gay in Egypt Private Net Society (W www.geo cities.com/westhollywood/5884/).

Despite governmental persecution there are a few places that are recognised gay hang-outs. Chief of these is the Taverne du Champs de Mars (Map 2, #65), at the Nile Hilton on Midan Tahrir, which has a strong queer element most nights (get here about 11pm), particularly Thursday, some of whom move on later to Jackie's Disco in the same hotel. The Queens Boat (Map 3, #73), moored opposite the Cairo Marriott, also used to be heavily homo but this is the joint that was raided and who knows if the crowd is going to feel safe coming back. There also used to be a lot of activity at certain of the old *hammams* (bathhouses) in Islamic Cairo, particularly Hammam Beshtak (Map 6, #28), on Souq as-Silah, 300m north of Ar-Rifai mosque, but we heard a rumour of a clampdown by the authorities and it now may be closed.

DISABLED TRAVELLERS

Cairo is not well equipped for travellers with a mobility problem; ramps are few, public facilities don't necessarily have lifts, kerbs are high, traffic is lethal and gaining entrance to some of the sites – such as the Pyramids of Giza – is all but impossible due to their narrow entrances and steep stairs. Despite all this, there is no reason why intrepid disabled travellers shouldn't visit Cairo. In general you'll find locals quite willing to help out and assist with any difficulties. Anyone with a wheelchair can take advantage of the large hatchback Peugeot 504s, which are commonly used as taxis. One of these plus driver can be hired for around US$30. Chances are the driver will be quite happy to help you in and out of the vehicle.

Organisations

See the Access-Able Travel Source Web site (W www.access-able.com) for general information for disabled travellers. Before leaving home disabled travellers can also get in touch with their national support organisation, a selection of which are listed here. Ask for the travel officer who may have a list of travel agents specialising in tours for the disabled.

Access – The Foundation for Accessibility by the Disabled (☎ 516-887 5798) PO Box 356, Malverne, NY 11565, USA

CNFLRH (☎ 01 53 80 66 66) 236 Rue de Tolbiac, Paris

Radar (☎ 020-7250 3222, fax 7250 0212, W www.radar.org.uk) 12 City Forum, 250 City Rd, London EC1V 8AF, UK. Produces holiday fact packs that cover planning, insurance, useful organisations, transport, equipment and specialised accommodation.

Society for the Advancement of Travel for the Handicapped (SATH; ☎ 212-447 7284, W www.sath.org) 347 Fifth Ave, No 610, New York, NY 10016, USA

SENIOR TRAVELLERS

Egypt doesn't subscribe to the cult of youth worship that exists in the West, and traditionally its older citizens are accorded great respect. The family remains the single most important thing in the lives of most Egyptians and if you bring along some photos of your children and (even better) grandchildren, they'll act as a great icebreaker.

Respect yes, but concessions no; unlike in many Western countries, there are no discounts on public transport, museum admission fees and the like for senior travellers in Egypt. But when it comes to transport, you may well prefer to hire taxis by the day anyway. This should cost no more than about US$25 per day and is a good way of avoiding the rigours of Egypt's local transport systems. Alternatively, plenty of local tour operators arrange day trips, which can take some of the strain out of sightseeing.

The other major thing to be wary of is the heat. It can be crippling – not just to senior citizens but to travellers of any age. A lightweight folding stool might be a good idea if you are prone to tiring quickly. Some sites such as the Pyramids require a certain degree of fitness. However, the Pyramids are plenty enough impressive without having to go inside. Plan ahead and don't try to do too much in too short a time – advice good for travellers of all ages.

CAIRO FOR CHILDREN

For an Egyptian, the answer to keeping the kids happy is to take them to the club (for more details on this Cairo institution, see The Club under Activities in the Things to See & Do chapter). However, if you don't have membership granting access to one of

these precious swathes of green and you don't want to pay the day fee, there are several other things to do. Although very pricey, Dr Ragab's Pharaonic Village is usually a big hit with kids of all ages; it's fairly educational too and takes up most of a day. Cairo Zoo (Map 4) is good in that it's one of the few zoos where children get to feed the animals – the keepers sell the appropriate foodstuffs. If you are going to the zoo, a fun way of getting there is by river bus, departing from Maspero in front of the TV & Radio building (see under River Bus in the Getting Around chapter for more details).

In Zamalek there's the Fish Garden (Map 3). Never mind that half the fish in question are floating belly-up at the top of the aquariums – the grottoes are great for hide-and-seek and there are some good, tiring, grassy hillocks to run up and roll down. On the fringes of Islamic Cairo is the unusual Sayyida Zeinab Cultural Park (Map 5; ☎ 391 5220), an 8-hectare garden specially landscaped for children. It contains a small mock village and has plenty of other structures for children to clamber over and run around. There are also occasional music and drama activities. Admission is free but two passport photos are required for an identity card. The park is on Sharia Qadry, the street that leads from Sharia Port Said to the Ibn Tulun mosque.

If you have the benefit of a car, Fagnoon (☎ 010-152 6715) is an art centre run by artist Mohammed Allam in the fields between Giza and Saqqara. (The name is a cross between *funoon*, 'arts and crafts', and *magnoon*, 'mad'.) Children can slosh paint around, model clay or hammer together some wood in a farm-type setting. Expect to pay about E£30 for canvases and other materials. You can bring your own food and drink, although coffee and water are usually on sale.

In the same general vicinity is Scoobi-Zoo, at the Pyramids Inter-Continental Resort (☎ 383 8666), Cairo-Alexandria Desert Hwy. It includes a petting zoo with gazelles, a donkey, hamsters and flamingoes; pony rides; caged monkeys; and all kinds of other distractions including face painting, slides, swings, miniature cars, seesaws and a large trampoline. Day use costs E£200 for two adults and two kids.

Swimming is a good way to get rid of excess energy. Most of the Cairo hotels offer day use of their pools, and many have cheap rates for children or families. There are also two water parks on the outskirts of the city. Crazy Water has half a dozen or more water slides, a wave pool, a kiddies' pool, and a playground area with sand, slides and tunnels. Admission is E£15 or E£12 for small fry. It's open from 10am to 10pm daily. To get there, take the Cairo-Alexandria Desert Hwy and then after about 15km (from the Pyramids Rd intersection) turn left on the route to the 6th of October City. Aquapark (☎ 477 088/99) is newer, with much the same facilities, and is 32km out on the Ismailia road.

Toys & Books

The city's best toy shop is reputedly Toys & Joys, which occupies two floors at 3 Mossadeq in Doqqi. It's open from 10am to 10pm Monday to Saturday.

Bookshops at most five-star hotels in Cairo and the major tourist centres stock a wide variety of Egyptology-related children's books that will help children relate to what they're seeing. Locally produced history books, such as Salima Ikram's *The Pharaohs*, are excellent and reasonably priced. (Hoopoe Books is a local children's publisher with a great list of titles that make good souvenirs or presents, too. Visit their Web site at W www.hoopoebooks.com.) For something set in modern Egypt, look for *The Day of Ahmed's Secret*, a wonderful story of a day in the life of a small boy who delivers gas canisters in one of Cairo's poor neighbourhoods.

Children-Friendly Dining

If you're looking for somewhere children-friendly to dine out that isn't McDonald's, then Andrea's and Crazy Fish (for more details, see under Giza & Pyramids Road in the Places to Eat chapter), both open-air restaurants out near the Pyramids, are great.

The kids can roam around the gardens, and there are big climbing frames, swings and donkey rides. Children also enjoy the local chain Felfela – most branches have caged birds and aquariums, and the Ma'adi branch has trampolines.

For little ones, the food court in the basement of the Nile Hilton Shopping Mall (Map 2, #66) has a playroom, as does the Gamiat ad-Dowal al-Arabiyya branch of McDonald's in Mohandiseen (Map 3, #16).

Health & Safety

There are a couple of things to keep in mind while you're out and about with children in and around Cairo. One is that child-safety awareness is minimal. Seat belts are non-existent in the back seats of most cars and taxis; if you're renting a car, remember to specify that you want them. Also, don't expect felucca or other boat operators to have children's life jackets. If you can't do without them, bring your own. Likewise with helmets for horse riding.

Another potential worry is the high incidence of diarrhoea and stomach problems that hits travellers in Cairo. If your children get sick, keep in mind that they dehydrate far more quickly than adults, especially in Cairo's hot, dry climate, so it is crucial to keep giving them liquids even if they just throw them up again. It's worth having some rehydration salts on hand just in case. These are available at all pharmacies (ask for Rehydran) and cost about 90pt for a box of six sachets. They can prevent a bad case of the runs from turning into something more serious. Make up the solution according to the instructions on the packet and keep giving it until the diarrhoea has passed. Get medical advice if you are at all worried.

For a more general discussion of health issues in Cairo, as well as a list of hospitals and pharmacies, see Health earlier in this chapter.

USEFUL ORGANISATIONS

The following organisations might be of interest to anyone in Cairo for an extended stay:

British Community Association (BCA; ☎ 348 1358) 2 Abdel Rahman al-Rifai, Mohandiseen; (☎ 353 8677) 18 Road 10, Ma'adi; (☎ 417 9775) 11 Mohammed Yousef al-Qady, Heliopolis. A social group for British citizens resident in Egypt that organises frequent get-togethers, talks and functions.

Community Services Association (CSA; ☎ 350 5285) 4 Road 21, Ma'adi. Helps newcomers orient themselves. Also offers a library, holds talks and organises trips.

Egypt Exploration Society (Map 3, #20; ☎ 301 0319) British Council, 192 Sharia el-Nil, Agouza. Organises lectures and arranges good guided archaeological tours.

Middle East Wives (☎ 418 3091). A friendship society for non-Arab women married to Egyptian and Arab men.

LIBRARIES

For English readers the best libraries are those at the British Council and American Cultural Center (see Cultural Centres following). Otherwise, there's the new and very grand Greater Cairo Library (Map 3, #30; ☎ 736 2280) housed in a villa at 15 Mohammed Mazhar, Zamalek. It's stocked with a fantastic collection of art, science and other reference books, mainly in English, and it also has newspapers and magazines for browsing. It's open from 9am to 7pm Tuesday to Sunday from September to May, 10am to 8pm from June to August.

CULTURAL CENTRES

Bring your passport as many cultural centres require some ID before they'll allow you to enter. For details of events at the cultural centres, check the local English-language press, particularly *Al-Ahram Weekly* or the monthly *Egypt Today*.

France (Map 5, #6; ☎ 795 3725) Centre Français de Culture et de Cooperation, 1 Madrassat al-Huquq al-Fransiyya, Mounira; (☎ 419 3857) 5 Shafiq al-Dib, Ard al-Golf, Heliopolis. Both centres regularly put on films, lectures and exhibitions, their libraries are open to the public and they screen French-language news from the satellite TV station TV5. The centre at Mounira also runs French and Arabic language courses. Both are open from 9am to 7pm Sunday to Thursday.

Germany (Map 2, #68; ☎ 575 9877) Goethe Institut, 5 Sharia al-Bustan, Downtown. This centre presents seminars and lectures in German on Egyptology and other topics. There are also performances by visiting music groups, special art exhibitions and film screenings. The library has more than 15,000 (mainly German) titles. It is open from 1pm to 7pm Monday to Thursday and from 8am to noon on Friday.

Italy (Map 3, #77; ☎ 735 8791) Istituto Italiano di Cultura, 3 Sheikh al-Marsafy, Zamalek. The centre has a busy program of films and lectures (sometimes in English), it hosts art exhibitions and has a library. It's open from 10am to 1pm Sunday to Thursday.

Netherlands (Map 3, #79; ☎ 738 2522) Netherlands-Flemish Institute, 1 Mahmoud Azmy, Zamalek. This centre hosts art exhibitions and is well known in the Cairo expatriate community for its weekly lectures, usually delivered in English. It is open from 9am to 2pm Monday to Friday.

UK (Map 3, #20; ☎ 347 6118, **W** www.british council.org.eg) British Council, 192 Sharia el-Nil, Agouza. The council carries an assortment of (dated) UK newspapers and has a vast library of books and periodical titles. Library membership costs E£60 but browsing is free. It's open from 10am to 8pm Monday to Thursday and 9am to 3pm Friday and Saturday.

USA (Map 2, #124; ☎ 357 3529, **W** www.usemb assy.egnet.net) American Cultural Center, 5 Latin America, Garden City. Part of the embassy complex, there's an American studies centre and the library is open from 8.30am to 4.30pm Sunday to Thursday.

DANGERS & ANNOYANCES

The amount of crime, violent or otherwise, in Cairo is negligible compared with most Western countries. (Crimes of passion are another thing. The *Egyptian Gazette* carries a column called 'Red Handed', which most days is filled with tales of murderous wives, vengeful jilted lovers, and assorted cases of fratricide, patricide and matricide. It makes fascinating reading.) Most visitors and residents would agree that Cairo is one of the world's safest places, in which pedestrians can walk abroad, anywhere, at any hour of the day or night. Unfortunately, the hassle factor often means that this isn't quite the case for an unaccompanied foreign woman – for more information, see Women Travellers earlier in this chapter.

Scams, Hustles & Hassle

Egyptians take hospitality to strangers seriously. You'll receive a steady stream of *salaams* (hellos) and the odd *ahlan wa sahlan* inviting you to sit and have tea. A lot of this is genuine, particularly out in rural areas, where drink, food and transport are frequently offered with no expectation of remuneration. But in more touristy places – most notably around the Egyptian Museum and the Pyramids – a cheery 'Hello my friend' is doublespeak for 'This way sucker'. You are a magnet attracting instant friends who coincidentally have a papyrus factory they'd like to show you. You are showered with helpful advice such as the museum is closed, take tea with me while you wait – of course the museum isn't closed and refreshments will be taken at a convenient souvenir shop nearby. As an English-speaker you might be asked to spare a moment to check the spelling of a letter to a relative in America, and while you're at it how about some special perfume for the lady or a Tutankhamun hologram lamp…

It's all pretty harmless stuff, but it can become very wearing. Everyone works out their own strategy to reduce the hassle to a minimum. A colleague kept interest at bay by jabbing his finger at his chest accompanied by the words 'Ya Russki' (I'm Russian). Not only would the hustlers be defeated by the language, everyone knew that the Russians had no money. But now that Egypt is a popular holiday destination for newly rich Muscovites, the street entrepreneurs are just as fluent in Slavic sales patter as they are in English, German, French, Dutch and Japanese.

About the only way to deal with unwanted attention is to be polite but firm and when you're in for a pitch cut it short with 'Sorry, no thanks'.

Aside from the hustling, there are countless irritating scams. The most common one involves touts who lie and misinform to get newly arrived travellers into hotels for which they get a commission – for more information, see the boxed text 'Hotel Scams' in the Places to Stay chapter. Hustlers Downtown loiter outside EgyptAir to intercept foreigners and redirect them across the road to a travel agency that they falsely claim is the only place non-Egyptians can buy tickets – and then they collect a commission on the sale. There are well-dressed guys who cruise Midan Tahrir offering their friendship as a smokescreen for whatever they can get out of it. One reader's letter confesses being taken in by a 'schoolteacher' named Omar who helped arrange a camel ride around the Pyramids for E£110 – a fair price would have been E£10.

If you do get stung or feel one more 'Excuse me, where are you from?' will make you crack, simmer down, wise up and beware acting brusquely and offending the majority of locals who would never dream of hassling a foreigner.

Terrorism

Is Cairo safe? Well, there's no absolute answer to that. The country was struck by some particularly horrific acts of terrorist violence back in 1997, which resulted in a great many deaths. For a couple of years tourists stayed away, but since then there have been no further attacks and tourists have returned in greater numbers than ever. Meanwhile security remains at an all-time high and while that in itself is no guarantee of safety from future terrorist atrocities, we'd say that Cairo, and Egypt in general, is at present no more or less dangerous than any other major European city.

Theft

Theft never used to be a problem but it seems to be becoming more so. In the past couple of years we've received a steady stream of letters from readers concerning money disappearing from locked hotel rooms. The obvious conclusion to draw is that staff are involved but in the cases we've been alerted to management have been disinclined to take responsibility until threatened by the tourist police, at which point reimbursements were offered. Money has even 'disappeared' from hotel safes. The advice has got to be to keep your cash and valuables on your person at all times.

Here's a tale in which a bag goes missing from the roof of a taxi:

I was the victim of a well-practised coup which your readers should be on the guard for. Halfway through our journey from Giza to the hotel our taxi driver started tapping the dashboard and feigning irritation. He stopped, got out and went to the back of the vehicle. He opened the boot, thus blocking our view through the back window. It must have been at this point that he transferred one of the bags from the roof into the boot. At the end of the journey in the rush of the traffic and the argument about the fare (he was quite aggressive at this point) we unloaded what there was on the roof, saw that there was nothing left and assumed we had everything. Then with our taxi pulling away swiftly into the traffic we counted the bags. One was missing. Mine! What was in it? Almost everything: air ticket, passport, wallet and nearly all my clothes.

G Bernard

Of course the bag could have fallen off the roof except that two days later, in the early hours of the morning, the thief dropped off the travel documents at the hotel. He kept the money and clothes.

There are also a few areas in Cairo where pickpockets are known to operate, notably the metro and the packed local buses running from Midan Tahrir to the Pyramids. Tourists aren't the specific targets but be careful how you carry your money in crowded places. Most unwary visitors are parted from their money through scams and these are something that you really do have to watch out for – see the boxed text on the previous page.

EMERGENCIES

In case of emergency, call the following numbers:

Ambulance	☎ 123
Fire service	☎ 125
Police	☎ 122
Tourist police	☎ 126, 391 9144

For minor emergencies, such as theft, your first port of call should be the tourist police. You stand a better chance of encountering someone who speaks English than if you go to the regular police. In the case of an acci-

dent and injury call the As-Salam International Hospital (see Medical Services under Health earlier in this chapter). For lost credit cards, see the Money section earlier in this chapter. For anything more serious contact your embassy.

LEGAL MATTERS

Egyptian penalties for smuggling, dealing and even possessing drugs are high (the death penalty can be invoked). Foreign travellers are subject to Egyptian laws – you'll get no special consideration just because you're not Egyptian. If arrested, you have the right to immediately telephone your embassy.

BUSINESS HOURS

Most government offices operate from about 8am to 2pm Sunday to Thursday but tourist offices are exceptions. Shops generally have different hours at different times of the year. In summer (May to September) most shops are open from 9am to 1pm and from 5pm to 10pm or even later. Winter hours are from 10am to 6pm. Hours during Ramadan are from 9.30am to 3.30pm and 8pm to 10pm. There are no real hard and fast rules, however, and even on the holy day of Friday, shops are sometimes open for most of the day. In fact, quite a few shops close Sunday instead, including most of Khan al-Khalili.

PUBLIC HOLIDAYS & SPECIAL EVENTS

Egypt's holidays and festivals are primarily Islamic or Coptic religious celebrations, although all holidays are celebrated equally by the entire population regardless of creed.

The date of Islamic holidays are given according to the Islamic calendar, also known as the Hejira calendar ('hejira' means 'flight', as in the flight of Mohammed from Mecca to Medina in AD 622). As the Islamic calendar is 11 days shorter than the Gregorian (Western) calendar, Islamic holidays fall 11 days earlier each year. The 11-day rule is not entirely strict – the holidays can fall from 10 to 12 days earlier. The precise dates are known only shortly before they fall as they're dependent upon the

Islamic Holidays

Hejira Year	Ras as-Sana	Moulid an-Nabi	Ramadan Begins	Eid al-Fitr	Eid al-Adha
1422	26 Mar 01	3 June 01	16 Nov 01	16 Dec 01	23 Feb 02
1423	15 Mar 02	23 May 02	5 Nov 02	5 Dec 02	12 Feb 03
1424	4 Mar 03	12 May 03	25 Oct 03	25 Nov 03	1 Feb 04
1425	22 Feb 04	1 May 04	14 Oct 04	14 Nov 04	21 Jan 05

sighting of the moon. See the 'Islamic Holidays' table for the approximate dates for the next few years.

The following are public holidays in Egypt:

New Year's Day 1 January – Official national holiday but many businesses stay open.

Christmas 7 January – Coptic Christmas is a fairly low-key affair and only Coptic businesses are closed for the day.

Eid al-Adha (See the 'Islamic Holidays' table for date) – Also known as Eid al-Kebir, the Great Feast, this marks the time of the haj, the pilgrimage to Mecca. Those who can afford it buy a sheep to slaughter on the day of the feast, which lasts for three days (although many businesses reopen on the second day). Many families also head out of town, so if you intend travelling at this time secure your tickets well in advance.

Ras as-Sana (See the 'Islamic Holidays' table for date) – Islamic New Year's Day. The entire country has the day off but celebrations are low-key.

Easter March/April – The most important date on the Coptic calendar although it doesn't significantly affect daily life for the majority of the population.

Sham an-Nessim A Coptic holiday with Pharaonic origins, it literally means the 'Smell of the Breeze'. It falls on the first Monday after the Coptic Easter and is celebrated by all Egyptians, with family picnics and outings.

Sinai Liberation Day 25 April – Official national holiday celebrating Israel's return of Sinai in 1982.

May Day 1 May – Official national holiday.

Moulid an-Nabi (See the 'Islamic Holidays' table for date) – This is the birthday of the Prophet Mohammed. One of the major holidays of the year; the streets are a feast of lights and food.

Revolution Day 23 July – Official national holiday commemorating the date of the 1952 coup when the Free Officers seized power from the puppet monarchy.

National Day 6 October – Official national holiday celebrating Egyptian successes during the 1973 war with Israel. The day is marked by military parades and air displays and a long speech by the president.

Ramadan (See the 'Islamic Holidays' table for date) – Observant Muslims fast for a whole month during daylight hours. Everyone is tired, listless, hungry and bad tempered during the day, but they come back to life again when the sun goes down and they can feast and get festive. Ramadan nights are buzzing. For more information, see Religion in the Facts about Cairo chapter.

Eid al-Fitr (See the 'Islamic Holidays' table for date) – A three-day feast that marks the end of Ramadan fasting.

Special Events

For the casual visitor there's not an awful lot on the annual events calendar that's worth going out of the way for. The biggie is January's book fair, but given that most of the goings-on (talks, seminars, readings) are conducted in Arabic, the appeal is limited for visitors. Any dedicated movie-goer living in the West is also likely to have already seen most of the fare on offer at the film festival. However, the Nitaq Festival brings Downtown to life, imbuing it with an energy and cultural vitality probably not seen since the heady days of the 1950s. Islamic Cairo is riotous during feast times, Ramadan evenings and, if you can catch one, when the moulids hit town (see the boxed text 'Moulids' over the page for more details).

January

Book Fair Held at the Cairo Exhibition Grounds over a two-week period, this is one of the major events on the city's cultural calendar. It draws in massive crowds, most of whom are there for a day out rather than because of any literary leanings.

February/March

Nitaq Festival This excellent arts festival is centred on Downtown Cairo with two weeks of exhibitions, theatre, poetry and music at galleries, cafes and a variety of other venues. It was only in its second year in 2001 but already it is one of the cultural highpoints of the annual calendar.

June

Al-Ahram Squash Tournament International competitors play in glass courts set up for the occasion on the Giza plateau beside the Pyramids.

July

International Festival of Oriental Dance Held at venues throughout Cairo, this is a festival of belly dance in which famous Egyptian practitioners give showcase performances and lessons to international attendees.

September

International Experimental Theatre Festival Held over 10 days, this theatre festival brings to Egypt a vast selection (40 at the last outing) of international theatre troupes and represents almost the only time each year that it's worth turning out for the theatre in Cairo.

October

Pharaohs' Rally This is an 11-day, 4800km motor vehicle (4WDs and bikes) race through the desert beginning and ending at the Pyramids. It attracts competitors from all over the world.

November

Arabic Music Festival This 10-day festival of classical, traditional and orchestral Arabic music is held at the Cairo Opera House. Programs are usually in Arabic only but the tourist office should have details.

December

Cairo International Film Festival This 14-day festival gives Cairenes the chance to watch a vast range of recent films from all over the world. The main attraction, however, is that the films are all supposedly uncensored. Anything that sounds like it might contain scenes of exposed flesh sells out immediately.

Moulids

A cross between a funfair and a religious festival, a *moulid* celebrates the birthday of a local saint or holy person. They are often a colourful riot of celebrations with hundreds of thousands of people. Those from out of town set up camp in the streets close to the saint's tomb, where children's rides, sideshows and food stalls are erected. In the midst of the chaos, barbers perform mass circumcisions; snake charmers induce cobras out of baskets; children are presented at the shrine to be blessed and the sick to be cured. *Tartours* (cone-shaped hats) and *fanous* (lanterns) are made and sold to passers-by, and in the evenings local Sufis usually hold hypnotic *zikrs* in colourful tents.

A zikr (literally 'remembrance') is where the Sufis chant the name of Allah to achieve a trance-like state that brings them closer to God. The *mugzzabin* (literally, the 'drawn-in') stand in straight lines and sway from side to side to rhythmic clapping that gradually increases in intensity. As the clapping gains momentum, the zikr reaches its peak and the mugzzabin, having attained oneness with Allah, awake sweating and blinking. Other zikrs are formidable endurance tests where troupes of musicians perform for hours in the company of ecstatic dancers.

Most moulids last for about a week, and climax with the *leila kebira* (big night). Much of the infrastructure is provided by 'professional' *mawladiyya* (moulid people) who spend their lives going from one moulid to another.

For visitors, the hardest part about attending a moulid is ascertaining dates. Events are tied to either the Islamic or Gregorian calendars, and dates can be different each year. Also, you'll need to be prepared for immense crowds (hold onto your valuables or, better still, leave them behind) and women should be escorted by a man.

The country's biggest moulid, the Moulid of al-Badawi, is held in Tanta in October, but Cairo hosts three major moulids dedicated to Sayyida Zeinab, Al-Hussein and Imam ash-Shafi. You'll need to ask a local for the exact dates in any particular year.

DOING BUSINESS

It will be some time yet before the power breakfast catches on in Cairo. And the idea of log-jamming several appointments into one clock-beating afternoon is unlikely ever to take off. Set a meeting for 2pm and it's likely to be closer to 3pm when your appointment shows. Then allow another half-hour or so for tea or *haga saa* (something cold) and a great deal of informal pleasantries, and you're rolling on for 4pm before the business of the fast-fading day can be broached. Try to speed up the languorous pace and you stand to cause offence and the seeds of noncooperation are sown.

Cultural considerations such as these mean that doing business in Cairo is next to impossible without the aid of Egyptian experience. On a practical level, the laws governing business are changing constantly and a definitive ruling often seems hard to come by. Regulations always seem open to the widest interpretation. To help know what has to be done and then how it can be circumvented, to know who must be tipped and how much, to know what papers to sign and the quickest route from desk A to desk B, you must have a consultant or adviser, preferably one with good contacts.

Where you find your magic worker is another question altogether. Start with the following chambers of commerce:

American Chamber of Commerce (☎ 338 1050) 33 Suleyman Abaza, Mohandiseen
British Egyptian Businessmen's Association (☎ 349 1421, fax 349 1401) 124 Sharia el-Nil, Agouza
Club d'Affaires Franco-Egyptien (☎ 332 2666) 5 Shagaret ad-Durr, Zamalek
Egyptian Businessmen's Association (☎ 572 3855, fax 572 3020) 16th floor, Nile Tower, 21–23 Sharia Giza, Giza

There are also a couple of specialist English-language business monthlies on the newsstands, *Al-Wekallah* and *Business Today*, both of which carry directory sections. You could also try to get hold of the superior *Business Monthly,* which is distributed free by the American Chamber of Commerce – try the commercial section of your embassy.

Other publications worth getting hold of are the *Egypt Almanac*, published locally by Egyptofile (W www.egyptalmanac.com), and *Emerging Egypt 2001*, published by the Oxford Business Group (W www.oxfordbusinessgroup.com), both of which are available at bookshops in Cairo.

One other useful resource might be the commercial library at the USAID office (☎ 354 8211) in the Cairo Centre Building (Map 2), at 106 Qasr al-Ainy, which is open to the public.

WORK

More than 40,000 foreigners live and work in Egypt. That figure alone should give you some idea of the immense presence foreign companies have in the country. It is possible to find work with one of these companies, especially if you begin your research before you leave home. *Cairo: The Practical Guide*, published by the AUC Press, has lists of foreign companies operating in Egypt. Once you have an employer, securing a work permit through an Egyptian consulate or, in Egypt, from the Ministry of the Interior should not be difficult.

Teaching English

The most easily available work for native or fluent English speakers is teaching the language. The best places to do this are at reputable schools such as the British Council (Map 3, #20), the International Language Institute (ILI) in Heliopolis and the Centre for Adult & Continuing Education (☎ 754 2964) at the AUC (Map 2), Sharia Sheikh Rihan, Downtown. However, all these places require qualifications and the minimum requirement is a certificate in CELTA (Certificate in English Language Teaching to Adults). To get the qualification you need to attend a one-month intensive course, which you can do in your home country via an English language training centre. In the UK contact International House (IH; ☎ 020-7491 2598, W www.ihlondon.com), which runs more than a dozen courses a year for about UK£1010. The ILI (☎ 02-291 9295, fax 415 1082, e ili@idsc.net.eg), at 2 Sharia Mohammed Bayoumi, off Mirghani,

Heliopolis, runs several one-month intensive CELTA courses (for about the equivalent of UK£650) each year and sometimes employs course graduates.

If you have no qualifications or experience, you could try one of the 'cowboy schools' such as the International Living Language Institute (ILLI; Map 2, #52) at 34 Talaat Harb, on the top floor above El-Abd bakery, Downtown. These are fly-by-night places (that said, the ILLI has been around for at least 15 years) that take on unqualified staff and work them hard for little financial return. But they do pay enough to allow you to stay on and perhaps earn enough to take the CELTA and gravitate to better-paid employment.

Some travellers also pay their way by offering private tuition, which can be well paid but the difficulty is in finding your students.

Copy-Editing

Another possible source of work for English speakers with a good sense of grammar is in copy-editing for one of Cairo's many English-language publications. *The Egyptian Gazette* and *Al-Ahram Weekly* are probably the best places to try, although new English-language magazines are springing up all the time. The pay is nothing terrific but it could be enough to scrape by on.

Film & TV Extras

Westerners are often in demand to appear as background decoration in local TV commercials, dramas or even films. Australian actress Cate Blanchett age 18 and on vacation in Cairo appeared as an extra in a crowd scene in an Egyptian movie. However, the work is far from glamorous and involves hanging around all day when often you're only required for five minutes of shooting. Still, it pays about E£40 to E£50 per session. Notices for persons wanted are sometimes posted at the hostels in Tawfiqqiya Souq, or more often scouts tour backpacker haunts such as Ash-Shams coffeehouse, just off the souq.

Getting There & Away

AIR

For information about the airport and for details on getting between the airport and central Cairo, see the Getting Around chapter.

Be warned that many travellers arriving at the airport are met by the infamous 'tourist officials'. For more on the tactics of these touts, see the boxed text 'Hotel Scams' in the Places to Stay chapter.

Departure Tax

This tax is factored into the cost of your ticket.

Other Parts of Egypt

Egypt's national carrier EgyptAir (which operates all domestic flights, some under the guise of its subsidiary Air Sinai) is not one of the world's better airlines – departures are too often delayed and in our experience the food is usually poor and the flight attendants often surly. Fares are expensive; however, travellers flying the international sectors of their journey with EgyptAir should receive a 50% discount on internal flights. Check with your travel agency at the time of booking. During the high season (October to April), many flights are full so it's wise to book as far in advance as you can.

Flights between other parts of Egypt and Cairo include Abu Simbel E£822/1645 (one way/return); Alexandria E£197/367; Aswan E£625/1312; Hurghada E£469/938; Luxor E£459/918; Sharm el-Sheikh E£469/938; and Taba E£547/890.

The USA & Canada

The cheapest way from the USA and Canada to Cairo is usually a return flight to London and a cheap fare from there. A round-the-world (RTW) ticket including a stopover in Cairo is also a possibility.

EgyptAir flies from New York and Los Angeles to Cairo. The cheapest advance tickets are for a minimum stay of seven days and a maximum stay of two months.

> ## Warning
>
> The information in this chapter is particularly vulnerable to change: Prices for international travel are volatile, routes are introduced and cancelled, schedules change, special deals come and go, and rules and visa requirements are amended. Airlines and governments seem to take a perverse pleasure in making price structures and regulations as complicated as possible. You should check directly with the airline or a travel agency to make sure you understand how a fare (and ticket you may buy) works. In addition, the travel industry is highly competitive and there are many lurks and perks.
>
> The upshot of this is that you should get opinions, quotes and advice from as many airlines and travel agencies as possible before you part with your hard-earned cash. The details given in this chapter should be regarded as pointers and are not a substitute for your own careful, up-to-date research.

Regular fares from New York/Los Angeles are approximately US$1300/1800 in low season and US$1900/2200 in high season. Lufthansa Airlines has connections to Cairo via Frankfurt from many cities in the USA. Advance fares are available. From Los Angeles, the high season one-way/return fare is US$1750/2200 and from New York it's US$1155/1600.

Discount travel agencies in the USA are known as consolidators. San Francisco is the ticket consolidator capital of the USA, although good deals can also be found in Los Angeles, New York and other big cities. Ticket Planet is a leading ticket consolidator in the USA and is recommended. Visit its Web site at W www.ticketplanet.com.

Council Travel, the USA's largest student travel organisation, has around 60 offices in the USA. Call ☎ 800-226 8624 for the office nearest you or visit its Web site at W www.counciltravel.com. STA Travel

Air Travel Glossary

Alliances Many of the world's leading airlines are now intimately involved with each other, sharing everything from reservations systems and check-in to aircraft and frequent-flyer schemes. Opponents say that alliances restrict competition. Whatever the arguments, there is no doubt that big alliances are the way of the future.

Courier Fares Businesses often need to send urgent documents or freight securely and quickly. Courier companies hire people to accompany the package through customs and, in return, offer a discount ticket which is sometimes a bargain. However, you may have to surrender all your baggage allowance and take only carry-on luggage.

Fares Airlines traditionally offer 1st class (coded F), business class (coded J) and economy class (coded Y) tickets. These days there are so many promotional and discounted fares available that few passengers pay full fare.

Lost Tickets If you lose your airline ticket, an airline will usually treat it like a travellers cheque and, after inquiries, issue you with another one. Legally, however, an airline is entitled to treat it like cash and if you lose it then it's gone forever. Take very good care of your tickets.

Onward Tickets An entry requirement for many countries is that you have a ticket out of the country. If you're unsure of your next move, the easiest solution is to buy the cheapest onward ticket to a neighbouring country or a ticket from a reliable airline which can later be refunded if you do not use it.

Open-Jaw Tickets These are return tickets where you fly out to one place but return from another. If available, this can save you backtracking to your arrival point.

Overbooking Since every flight has some passengers who fail to show up, airlines often book more passengers than they have seats. Usually excess passengers make up for the no-shows, but occasionally somebody gets 'bumped' onto the next available flight. Guess who it is most likely to be? The passengers who check in late. If you do get 'bumped', you are normally offered some form of compensation.

Reconfirmation Some airlines require you to reconfirm your flight at least 72 hours prior to departure. Check your travel documents to see if this is the case.

Restrictions Discounted tickets often have various restrictions on them – such as needing to be paid for in advance and incurring a penalty to be altered or cancelled. Others are restrictions on the minimum and maximum period you must be away.

Round-the-World Tickets RTW tickets give you a limited period (usually a year) in which to circumnavigate the globe. You can go anywhere the carrying airlines go, as long as you don't backtrack. The number of stopovers or total number of separate flights is decided before you set off and they usually cost a bit more than a basic return flight.

Ticketless Travel Airlines are gradually waking up to the realisation that paper tickets are unnecessary encumbrances. On simple one-way or return trips, reservations details can be held on computer and the passenger merely shows ID to claim their seat.

Transferred Tickets Airline tickets cannot be transferred from one person to another. Travellers sometimes try to sell the return half of their ticket, but officials can ask you to prove that you are the person named on the ticket. On an international flight, tickets are compared with passports.

Cairo's awesome urban sprawl is home to some 16.5 million people and over a million vehicles, which jam the roads of the city centre at rush hour. Swelling these numbers, thousands of commuters arrive each day at the city's hectic bus stations.

Downtown (bottom), the commercial heart of Cairo, boasts few sights as such but it's a great place to experience life, Cairo-style: stop for a streetside shoeshine (top left) before hanging out with regulars at one of the many *ahwas* (coffeehouses; top right) around town.

(☎ 800-777 0112) has offices in Boston, Chicago, Miami, New York, Philadelphia, San Francisco and other major cities. Call the toll-free 800 number for office locations or visit its Web site at W www.statravel.com.

Canadian discount air-ticket sellers are also known as consolidators and their air fares tend to be about 10% higher than those sold in the USA.

Travel CUTS (☎ 800-667 2887) is Canada's national student travel agency and has offices in all major cities. Its Web address is W www.travelcuts.com.

Australia & New Zealand

Cheap flights from Australia or New Zealand to Cairo generally go via South-East Asian capitals, involving stopovers at Kuala Lumpur, Bangkok or Singapore. If a long stopover between connections is necessary, transit accommodation is sometimes included in the price of the ticket. If it's at your own expense, it may be worth considering a more expensive ticket.

Expect to pay around A$1700 for a return flight to Cairo from Australia during the low season (May to September) or A$2050 during the high season (October to April). Star Alliance and One World are airline alliances that offer RTW tickets from Australia and New Zealand. Star Alliance has RTW fares from Australia with a stopover in Cairo starting from A$2269 in the low season. Return low-season fares from Auckland start at around NZ$2329, while fares in the high season start at around NZ$2599.

Two well-known travel agencies in Australia offering cheap fares are STA Travel and Flight Centre. STA Travel (☎ 03-9349 2411) has its main office at 224 Faraday St, Carlton, in Melbourne, and offices in all major cities and on many university campuses. Call ☎ 131 776 Australia-wide for the location of your nearest branch or visit its Web site at W www.statravel.com.au. Flight Centre (☎ 131 600 Australia-wide) has a central office at 82 Elizabeth St, Sydney, and there are dozens of offices throughout Australia. Its Web address is W www.flightcentre.com.au.

In New Zealand, Flight Centre (☎ 09-309 6171) has a large central office in Auckland at National Bank Towers (corner of Queen and Darby Sts) and many branches throughout the country. STA Travel (☎ 09-309 0458) has its main office at 10 High St, Auckland, and has other offices in Auckland as well as in Hamilton, Palmerston North, Wellington, Christchurch and Dunedin. The Web address is W www.sta.travel.com.au.

The UK

London is one of the best centres in the world for discounted air tickets. If you start looking early and are prepared to phone around then you shouldn't have to pay more than about UK£240 for a return ticket to Cairo, including all taxes. In recent times Air France, Alitalia and Olympic Airways have all offered fixed-date returns at this price. All these involve a change of flight in the national capital. Only British Airways and EgyptAir offer direct flights; these cost upwards of UK£350.

Start by phoning Suleiman Travel (☎ 020-7244 6855) at 113 Earls Court Rd, London, a long-established Egypt specialist. Its prices are very competitive and staff can sometimes come up with cheaper alternatives to scheduled Cairo flights, such as charters into Luxor or Sharm el-Sheikh. Another good specialist often able to secure the cheapest fares is Egypt On the Go (☎ 020-8993 9993) at 81 Gunnersbury Lane, Acton Town, London W3 8HQ.

Otherwise, popular travel agencies in the UK include STA Travel and Usit Campus. Both these agencies sell tickets to all travellers but cater especially to students and travellers under 26. STA Travel (☎ 020-7361 6262), W www.statravel.co.uk, has an office at 86 Old Brompton Rd, London SW7 3LQ, and branches across the country. Usit Campus (☎ 0870-240 1010), W www.usit campus.com, has an office at 52 Grosvenor Gardens, London SW1W 0AG, as well as branches throughout the UK.

Middle East

Air Sinai (a subsidiary of EgyptAir) and El Al Israel Airlines regularly fly between Tel

Aviv and Cairo, with five flights a week each. Fares are US$185 one way or US$265 return (valid for one month).

There are daily flights with Royal Jordanian and EgyptAir between Amman and Cairo. The fare from Cairo is US$245 one way and US$320 return with EgyptAir, or about US$30 cheaper with Royal Jordanian. There are no student reductions.

Syrian Airlines flies five times a week between Damascus and Cairo for a one-way fare of US$220.

Africa

Despite the proximity, there is nothing cheap about travelling between Cairo and other parts of Africa. In fact, for most African capitals a ticket bought in London will be cheaper than one bought in Cairo. The best bet is to buy your African ticket with a stopover in Cairo.

Ethiopia There are flights from Egypt to Addis Ababa twice a week with a one-way/return fare of US$580/824. However, one-way tickets can only be purchased if you can show a credit card or travellers cheques to cover the cost of a return ticket.

Kenya To Nairobi, Kenya Airways flies three times a week for a one-way fare of US$622. From Nairobi there are onward connections to Rwanda (Kigali), Tanzania (Dar es Salaam), the Democratic Republic of Congo (Kinshasa) and Zimbabwe (Harare).

Sudan EgyptAir and Sudan Airways both have two flights a week between Cairo and Khartoum. The 2½-hour flight costs US$394 one way or US$480 return (valid for one month). One-way tickets will not be sold unless you can show a ticket from Sudan to your home country, and no ticket will be issued until you've got your Sudanese visa.

Airline Offices

Airline office opening hours in Cairo are generally from 8am or 9am until 3.30pm or 4.30pm. Most are closed on Friday and sometimes Saturday too. It is essential that you reconfirm any flights out of Cairo as

overbooking and cancellations are common. Airline offices in Cairo include the following:

Air France (☎ 575 8899) 2 Midan Talaat Harb, Downtown
Alitalia (☎ 578 5823) Nile Hilton, Midan Tahrir
British Airways (☎ 578 0743) 1 Sharia al-Bustan, Midan Tahrir
EgyptAir (☎ 390 0999) general information; (Map 2, #65; ☎ 591 2410) Nile Hilton, Midan Tahrir; (Map 2, #73; ☎ 393 2836) 9 Talaat Harb, Downtown; (Map 9, #22; ☎ 245 0270) 22 Ibrahim Laqqany, Heliopolis
El Al Israel Airlines (☎ 736 1795) 5 Sharia Maqrizy, Zamalek
Emirates Airlines (☎ 336 1555) Batal Ahmed Abdel Aziz, Mohandiseen
Gulf Air (☎ 575 0852) 21 Mahmoud Bassiouni, Downtown
KLM – Royal Dutch Airlines (☎ 574 7004) 11 Qasr el-Nil, Downtown
Lufthansa Airlines (☎ 739 8339) 6 Sheikh al-Marsafy, Zamalek
Middle East Airlines (☎ 574 7372) 12 Qasr el-Nil, Downtown
Olympic Airways (☎ 393 1277) 23 Qasr el-Nil, Downtown
Royal Jordanian Airlines (☎ 575 0875) 6 Qasr el-Nil, Downtown
Syrian Airlines (☎ 392 8284) 35 Talaat Harb, Downtown
Turkish Airlines (☎ 395 8031) 26 Mahmoud Bassiouni, Downtown
TWA (☎ 574 9904) 1 Qasr el-Nil, Midan Tahrir

BUS

The city is in the process of being reordered and part of that process is the relocation of its bus stations. In an attempt to keep the big buses out of the Downtown area, a big new bus station is under construction in the Bulaq district, just north-west of the city centre. Called the Turgoman bus station (Map 8, #7; in Arabic, *mo'af* Turgoman), it lies between Sharias al-Sahafa and Shanan, roughly 1km north of the intersection of Sharias Galaa and 26th of July. It's an awkward location in that it's too far from Downtown to comfortably walk and there are no shuttles of any sort; the only way to get there is by taxi (E£2 from Downtown).

There are other bus stations at Abbassiyya (Map 1, #6), known as the Sinai Terminal because pre-Turgoman this is where the

Sinai buses departed from, and at Al-Mazar in Heliopolis. Hardly any services originate at either of these two stations but some buses call in to pick up additional passengers. To get to Abbassiyya take bus No 983 or 948 or minibus No 32 from the local bus station at Midan Abdel Moniem Riad. Alternatively, a taxi to/from Downtown costs around E£6.

Other Parts of Egypt

Several different companies operate from Turgoman, each with their own ticket cabin. Each company has its own routes, although there is some overlap. Prices for the same route vary according to whether or not the bus has air-con and video service, how old it is and how long it takes to make the journey – the more you pay, the more comfort you travel in and the quicker you get there.

It's advisable to advance-book tickets on popular routes (such as from Cairo to Sinai or Marsa Matruh in the summer) and those with few buses running, but if you're heading to Alexandria, Port Said or Ismailia, just roll up at the station and you'll almost always be able to grab a seat on the next bus out. There are no student discounts on bus fares.

Superjet Luxurious buses with services to Alexandria (E£20 to E£31, every half-hour from 5.30am to 5.30pm, thereafter hourly until 11pm); Hurghada (E£50 to E£55, at 7.30am, 8.30am, 2.30pm and 11.15pm); and Sharm el-Sheikh (E£55, nightly at 11pm).
West Delta Bus Co Good buses with services to Alexandria (E£16 to E£20, hourly from 5.30am to 1.30am); Marsa Matruh (E£28 to E£36, nine times a day June to September, dropping to three a day from October to May).
East Delta Bus Co Covers the Delta region and Sinai with services to Sharm el-Sheikh (E£50 to E£65, 10 buses a day from 6.30am to 11.30pm), some of which go on to Dahab; Nuweiba (E£50 to E£55, at 7am, 9.30am, 10pm), all of which carry on to Taba; St Katherine's Monastery (E£35, daily at 10.30am); Suez (E£6.50 to E£7.50, half-hourly from 6am to 9pm); Ismailia (E£6.50, half-hourly from 6.30am to 8pm); Port Said (E£13 to E£15, hourly from 6.30am to 7pm); Mansura (E£8.50, half-hourly); and Damietta (E£10.50, hourly), among others.
Middle Delta Bus Co Covers the smaller Delta towns such as Tanta (E£6, hourly from 7am to 9pm).

Upper Egypt Travel Luxury buses to Luxor (E£60, 10 to 11 hours, depart daily at 9pm) and to Aswan (E£60, 12 hours, 5pm), as well as services to Hurghada (E£30 to E£50, 18 buses a day between 7am and 1am).
Western Oases Bus Co Several buses a day to Bahariyya, Farafra, Dakhla and Kharga, but check and book in advance; note, there are no direct buses to Siwa – you'll have to go to Alexandria or Marsa Matruh and change there.

Israel & the Palestinian Territories

Since the resurgence of trouble, Travco (Map 3, #71; ☎ 02-735 4650), at 13 Mahmoud Azmy, Zamalek, which used to run daily buses from Cairo to Jerusalem and Tel Aviv in conjunction with the Israeli company Mazada Tours, has stopped all services. It is possible to make your own way via the regular service to Rafah in northern Sinai and from there to cross into the Gaza Strip; however, given the volatile nature of the region at present, we can't recommend this. Instead take a bus to Taba in Sinai and walk across the border, picking up a taxi on the other side to take you the few miles up to central Eilat.

Jordan

Every Sunday and Wednesday Superjet has a bus to Amman (E£180 one way, 20 hours) departing at 5am from Turgoman. On the same days there's also an East Delta Bus Co service for Aqaba departing Turgoman at 10pm; the fare, including the ferry, is E£34 plus US$45.

Libya

Superjet has a daily 8am Libya service departing from the Turgoman bus station. The fare to Benghazi (20 hours) is E£100, while to Tripoli (26 hours) it's E£205. The East Delta Bus Co has slightly cheaper seats to Tripoli (E£180) on its bus, which departs at 8am every Tuesday and Thursday.

TRAIN

Ramses Station (Mahattat Ramses; Map 8), on Midan Ramses, is Cairo's main train station and it's pure confusion. If you need help, there is a tourist office with tourist police just inside the main entrance on the left; it's open from 8am to 8pm daily. In a secondary

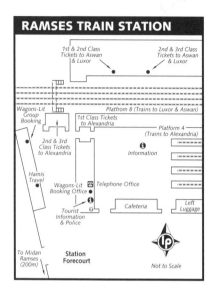

RAMSES TRAIN STATION

1st & 2nd Class
Tickets to Aswan
& Luxor

2nd & 3rd Class
Tickets to Aswan
& Luxor

Wagons-Lit
Group
Booking

Platfrom 8 (Trains to Luxor & Aswan)

1st Class Tickets
to Alexandria

Platform 4
(Trains to Alexandria)

2nd & 3rd
Class Tickets
to Alexandria

❶
Information

Hamis
Travel

Wagons-Lit ☎ Telephone Office
Booking Office ●

❶

Tourist
Information
& Police

Cafeteria

Left
Luggage

To Midan
Ramses
(200m)

**Station
Forecourt**

Not to Scale

entrance to the right of the main entrance is a small post office and next to it is the left-luggage area, which is open 24 hours and charges E£1 per piece.

Although trains travel along more than 5000km of track to almost every major city and town in Egypt, the system is badly in need of modernisation and most of the services are grimy, battered and a poor second option to the deluxe bus. The exceptions are the trains to Alexandria and the tourist trains down to Luxor and Aswan – on these routes the train is preferable to the bus.

If you have an International Student Identification Card (ISIC), discounts of about 33% are granted on all fares except wagon-lit. Some travellers report getting a discount with Hostelling International cards and Youth International Educational Exchange cards.

For travel information call ☎ 579 0767.

Luxor & Aswan

If you can afford it, the wagon-lit sleeper is the way to travel. Wagon-lit trains are 1st-class only, have air-con, are carpeted, and each compartment has towels, coat hangers, hot and cold water and Venetian blinds. There are lounge cars, and dinner and breakfast are served in the compartments. There is one train a day, departing at 7.40pm each evening, arriving in Luxor at 5.30am the next morning (the perfect hour to head off sightseeing) and Aswan at 8.40am. An evening meal and early breakfast are included in the fare of E£362 one way or E£667 return. The same fare applies to both Luxor and Aswan. If you wish to get off at Luxor and continue to Aswan a few days later this must be specified when booking. There's also the option of travelling this luxury service on the cheap by taking a seat rather than a berth; this costs E£125 one way.

The wagon-lit booking office (☎/fax 576 1319) is in the main hall of the train station, beside the tourist police. It doesn't take credit cards or travellers cheques – it's cash only (US dollars or Egyptian pounds). The office is open from 9am to 9pm daily.

Apart from the wagon-lit train, there are only two other services that non-Egyptians are currently allowed to travel on down to Upper Egypt: the No 980, departing daily at 7.30am, and the No 996, leaving at 10pm. Fares on the night train to Luxor are E£60/36 for 1st/2nd class, while to Aswan it's E£73/42. Fares on the morning train are E£4 cheaper. On the night train there's also the option of travelling 'Nefertiti' class, which means newer, cleaner carriages; fares are E£70 to Luxor, E£80 to Aswan. However you go, the journey time is about 10 hours to Luxor and a further five on to Aswan.

Tickets are bought from the ticket office beside platform No 11, that is, on the other side of the tracks from the main hall (see the Ramses Train Station map). At the time of writing, the trains departed from platform No 8. You must buy your tickets at least a couple of days in advance.

Other Destinations

For trains to Alexandria and the Suez towns of Ismailia and Port Said, see the relevant sections in the Excursions chapter later in this book.

Getting Around

Overcrowded buses and minibuses are the most common form of transport for the majority of Cairenes, but for anyone who prefers breathing while travelling, taxis are the only option. By Western standards they're very cheap and there's never one far away. The only time when taxis aren't a good bet is when you are travelling a fair distance, say north to Heliopolis or south down to Ma'adi, in which case they become a little expensive. In such cases, the alternatives are the bus to Heliopolis or the metro to Ma'adi.

It's also wise to avoid taking taxis between about 3pm and 4pm (that's always supposing that you can find one free at this time of day), which constitutes Cairo's rush hour – although to the untrained eye it can appear that rush hour kicks in around 8am and doesn't let up until about 2am.

THE AIRPORT

Cairo international airport (for flight information, call ☎ 291 4288, 291 4299) is 25km north-east of central Cairo. There are two terminals about 3km apart: Terminal II, the new *(gedida)* terminal, services most international airlines, whereas Terminal I, the old *(adimah)* terminal, is mainly used by EgyptAir for both domestic and international flights.

Arriving at Terminal II, you'll pass a couple of duty-free shops, exchange offices and several banks before arriving at customs control. The exchange offices are next to each other and their rates are about the same. They can also issue stamps for a visa (see Documents in the Facts for the Visitor chapter for more information on getting an Egyptian visa). Similar banking facilities are available at Terminal I. There's also a fairly useless tourist information office at Terminal II, which may or may not be open when you pass through.

The departure lounge at Terminal II has a handful of duty-free shops and a post and telephone office. Cardphones and a Home Country Direct telephone are available, as are telex and telegraphic services.

Between the arrival and departure lounges is a left-luggage room, open 24 hours. It charges E£3 for items less than 25kg, and E£6 for those weighing more.

Most major car-rental companies have booths in the arrivals hall. Outside Terminal I is a lost-and-found booth.

TO/FROM THE AIRPORT

Cairo international airport is not the easiest of airports to get away from. Although there are bus services they're far from obvious and it sometimes requires an act of faith to catch one – it's either that or submit to the feeding frenzy of taxi drivers.

Bus

Don't believe anyone who tells you that there is no bus to the city centre, there are two, plus a minibus. The best is the No 356 dedicated airport service. This is serviced by big white, modern, air-con buses that run from Midan Abdel Moniem Riad (Map 2, #60), behind the Egyptian Museum in central Cairo, via Abbassiyya and Heliopolis to Terminal II, where they stop for just a few minutes, then go on to Terminal I. The buses run at 20-minute intervals from 6am to 11pm and the fare is E£2, plus E£1 per large luggage item. To find the buses at either terminal, head out into the no-man's land of the car park and you'll spot the stand and, fingers crossed, before too long a bus.

In addition to the No 356, the same route is shared with local bus No 400 (25pt) and minibus No 27 (50pt).

Taxi

The going rate to central Cairo is around E£30 to E£35, but it takes tenacity to get it. Arrivees are met with a scrum of drivers all volunteering their services and hoping for chumps who'll just pay whatever outrageous fare is proffered. Avoid these guys, they're sharks. It's generally better to get out of the arrivals hall and away from all the touts, finding a lone driver out on the forecourt to bargain with. If these guys quote silly prices then walking away often tends to bring the numbers down. Triple check the agreed fare, as there is an irritating tendency for drivers to nod at what you say and hit you with an out-of-the-world fare later on.

Large 'official' airport taxis, known as 'limousines', have a fixed rate of E£46 (just over US$12) and you might prefer to settle for this and avoid all the aggravation of bargaining.

Heading from the centre of town to the airport there are more taxis around so you can afford to bargain harder – you should not pay more than E£25.

In the traffic-free early hours of the morning (when so many flights seem to arrive) the journey to central Cairo takes 20 minutes, but at other, busier times of the day it can take over an hour.

BUS & MINIBUS

Taking a bus in Cairo is an experience all of its own. First, there's getting on. Cairenes stampede buses, charging the entrance before the thing has even slowed down. Hand-to-hand combat ensues as they run alongside trying to leap aboard. If you wait for it to stop, the pushing and shoving to get on is even worse. Often several passengers don't quite manage and they make their journey hanging off the back doorway, clinging perilously to the frame or to someone with a firmer hold.

The scene inside the bus in this case usually resembles a Guinness World Record attempt on the greatest number of people in a confined space. There are times when, crammed up the back with exhaust fumes billowing around you and ever more people squeezing on, asphyxiation seems perilously close. At some point during the trip, a man will somehow manage to squeeze his way through to sell you your ticket, which is usually 25pt.

Just as the bus doesn't always stop to let people on, it frequently does little more than slow down to let passengers off. In this case you stand in the doorway, wait for the

opportune moment and launch yourself into the road.

Minibuses, which operate exactly like buses but with fewer passengers, are better in that they do at least stop to let people on and off. Plus no standing is allowed.

For all these reasons, we do not recommend travelling around Cairo by bus. The exceptions are the modern airport service (see To/From the Airport earlier), which is also good for travelling to Heliopolis, and the Pyramids bus (No 355/357; see The Pyramids of Giza in The Pyramids & Memphis Necropolis chapter).

If you do want to give the buses a go – if only for the fun of it – then the main central city bus and minibus station is currently at Midan Abdel Moniem Riad (Map 2, #60) behind the Egyptian Museum and under the tangle of flyovers. However, it's slated to move at some stage in the near future, at which point all bus numbers and routes will probably change, which is why we haven't listed any here. The only viable way of finding a bus to where you want to go (and from this station they go just about everywhere in the city) is to ask; locals are only too happy to assist, but always double-check anything you're told by asking more than one person.

MICROBUS

Increasingly, Cairenes are using private microbuses (as opposed to the public minibuses) to get around. These are the little white vans with sliding side doors. Destinations are not marked in any language, so they are hard to use unless you are familiar with the routes. What you do is position yourself beside the road that leads where you want to go and when a microbus passes, yell out your destination – if it's going where you want to go and there are seats free it'll stop.

METRO

The metro system is startlingly efficient and the stations are cleaner than any other public places in Cairo. It's also extremely inexpensive and, outside rush hours, not too crowded. At the time of writing there are two lines in operation. The main line, with 32 stations, stretches for 43km from the

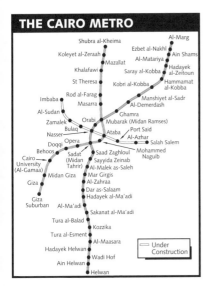

THE CAIRO METRO

Shubra al-Kheima
Al-Marg
Koleyet al-Zeraah
Ezbet al-Nakhl
Ain Shams
Mazallat
Al-Matariya
Khalafawi
Hadayek
al-Zeitoun
St Theresa
Saray al-Kobba
Hammamat
al-Kobba
Imbaba
Rod al-Farag
Kobri al-Kobba
Manshiyet al-Sadr
Masarra
Al-Demerdash
Al-Sudan
Ghamra
Zamalek
Orabi
Mubarak (Midan Ramses)
Bulaq
Nasser
Ataba
Port Said
Doqqi
Opera
Al-Azhar
Behoos
Sadat
Saad Zaghloul
Salah Salem
Cairo
(Midan
Mohammed
University
Tahrir)
Sayyida Zeinab
Naguib
(Al-Gamaa)
Al-Malek as-Saleh
Midan Giza
Mar Girgis
Giza
Al-Zahraa
Dar as-Salaam
Giza
Hadayek al-Ma'adi
Suburban
Al-Ma'adi
Sakanat al-Ma'adi
Tura al-Balad
Kozzika
Tura al-Esment
Al-Maasara
Hadayek Helwan
Wadi Hof
Under
Construction
Ain Helwan
Helwan

southern suburb of Helwan up to Al-Marg in the north. The second line connects the working class district of Shubra with Giza, stopping off at the Opera House complex en route. A planned third line will cross the city from east to west linking Islamic Cairo with Zamalek and Mohandiseen.

Metro stations are easily identified by signs with a big red 'M' in a blue star. It costs 50pt to ride up to nine stops; 70pt for up to 16 stops; 90pt for up to 22 stops; E£1.20 for up to 28 stops; and E£1.50 to ride the length of the line. The service starts at about 5am and stops running about 11.30pm.

The first carriage is reserved for women only. Women who want to ride in this carriage should make sure they're standing at the right place on the platform (near where the front part of the train will stop) as the trains don't hang around in the station for long.

TRAM

Most of Cairo's trams (known to Cairenes, confusingly, as 'metros') have been phased out. One of the few surviving lines is the one connecting central Cairo to Heliopolis. This runs from just north of Midan Ramses up to Midan Roxy on the southern edge of

Heliopolis, at which point the line divides into three, with the final destinations lettered in Arabic in different colours: Nouzha (red), Mirghani (green) and Abdel Aziz Fahmy (yellow). For central Heliopolis catch the red or green; for Merryland, the yellow.

The trams are as cheap and often as crowded as the buses. The fare is 25pt and the trip from Midan Ramses to Heliopolis takes 20 to 30 minutes.

CAR

Driving in Cairo is not for the faint-hearted. It's like the chariot race in *Ben Hur* only with Fiats. The roads are always crowded and heavy congestion is dealt with by flooring the accelerator whenever the slightest opening allows it (the speed limit in urban areas is 40km/h, and 90km/h on expressways). Although road signs conform to international protocol they're brazenly ignored by most drivers, although that is beginning to change with the introduction of harsh new laws – see the boxed text 'Slow Down, Belt Up' over the page. Other vehicles are viewed as obstacles, as on a slalom, and a favourite manoeuvre is to suddenly sweep across multiple lanes of traffic to make a turn on the opposite side of the carriageway. Brakes are scorned in favour of the horn.

Although city driving may seem chaotic, there is one cardinal rule – whoever is in front has the right of way. Even if a car is only 1cm ahead of you and then cuts across your path suddenly, you will be liable if you hit it. As long as you do not assume that anybody looks in their rearview mirror and you use your horn to announce your presence, you'll be fine.

Rental

If you are crazy enough to want to battle the traffic in Cairo, there are a number of car-rental agencies in the city, including the big three of Avis, Budget and Hertz.

You need to be over the age of 25 and have an international driving permit; the rental agencies don't care whether you have a permit or not and will rent you the car regardless, but you could cop a heavy fine if you're caught driving without one.

Slow Down, Belt Up

There is a new regimen being introduced into the anarchy of driving in Egypt, with police cracking down in the wake of recently introduced new traffic laws. Penalties include hefty fines for driving at night without lights, running red lights, unnecessary horn-honking and speeding – all traditionally favourite pastimes of Egyptian drivers.

Apparently, in the first week after the new law was passed on 1 January 2001, more than one million tickets were handed out – including almost 17,000 slapped on cars heading the wrong way down one-way streets. Even if drivers manage to obey all the newly enforced laws, that's still no guarantee of avoiding penalties; one journalist reported encountering a motorist at the traffic department office loudly questioning the legitimacy of a ticket he'd been given for passing a red light. He had a point. On the street where he was accused of committing the offence there were no lights at all. The unimpressed clerk made him pay up anyway.

The new laws also mandate seat belts for front passengers and helmets for motorcyclists. Adjusting to these new regulations has involved plenty of creative interpretations. A good many taxis we've ridden in recently had home-made belts with no buckles – the useless strap is just dangled across the chest in a way that might hopefully fool a traffic officer. And if it seems that half the country has suddenly become employed in the building trade, it's just that bright yellow construction hard hats are considerably cheaper than crash helmets, but just as effective at warding off E£100 on-the-spot fines.

Rates match international charges and finding a cheap deal with local dealers is virtually impossible. No matter which company you go with, make sure you read the fine print. As an indication of prices, a small car such as a Suzuki Swift is about US$40 per day. A Toyota Corolla is about US$60 per day, plus around US$0.25 per kilometre. Remember that a 10% to 17% tax will be added to your bill. It's usually possible to pay with travellers cheques or by credit card.

Avis (☎ 794 7400, fax 796 2464) 16 Mamal as-Sukkar, Garden City
Budget (☎ 735 0070, fax 736 3790) 5 Sharia Makrizy, Zamalek
Europcar (☎ 347 4712, fax 303 6123) 27 Sharia Libnan, Mohandiseen
Hertz (☎ 303 4241, fax 344 6627) 195 Sharia 26th of July, Mohandiseen
Thrifty (☎/fax 266 3313) 1 Sharia al-Entesar, Heliopolis

TAXI

Almost every second car on Cairo's roads is a taxi (black and white and battered) and they are by far the most convenient way of getting about. Stand at the side of the road, stick your hand out and shout your destination at any cab passing in the right direction. It doesn't matter if there is already someone inside because taxis are shared. When a taxi stops, restate where you want to go and if the driver's amenable, hop in.

Do not ask 'how much?'. The etiquette is that you get in knowing what to pay and when you arrive, you get out and hand the money through the window. Make sure that you have the correct money (hoard E£1 bills) because getting change out of drivers is like having your teeth pulled. If a driver suspects that you don't know what the correct fare is then you're fair game for fleecing. If once you get in the taxi the driver starts talking money then just state a fair price (see the list) and if it's not accepted, get out and find another car.

Use the following as a rough guide to what you should be paying for taxi rides around Cairo:

Downtown to the airport	E£30
Downtown to Heliopolis	E£15
Downtown to Khan al-Khalili	E£3.50
Downtown to Zamalek	E£3.50
Midan Tahrir to the Citadel	E£5
Midan Tahrir to Midan Ramses	E£3
Midan Tahrir to the Pyramids	E£15

Taxi!

Taxis are at once a blessing and a curse. They're a remarkably convenient and easily affordable way of getting around the city but they can also be a frequent source of unpleasantness when it comes to paying the fare. The problem comes with the unmetered system of payment, which almost guarantees discontent. Passengers frequently feel that they're been taken advantage of (which they often are), while drivers are occasionally genuinely aggrieved by what they see as underpayment. So why don't the drivers use the meter? Because they were all calibrated at a time when petrol was ludicrously cheap. That time has long passed and any driver relying on his meter would now be out of pocket every time he came to fill up.

Taxi driving is far from being a lucrative profession. Of the 60,000 plus taxis on the road in Cairo it would be a safe bet to assume none of the drivers are yet millionaires. Average earnings after fuel has been paid for are about E£8 per hour. Consider too that many drivers don't even own their car and have to hand over part of their earnings as 'rent'.

Which isn't to say that next time you flag a taxi for a short hop across town and the driver hisses 'Ten bounds' that you should smile and say 'OK', but maybe you can see that from a certain point of view, it was worth his while trying.

Often when you come to paying, a driver will demand more money, sometimes yelling. Don't be intimidated and don't be drawn into an argument. As long as you know you are not underpaying (and the fares we give in this book are generous), just walk away. It's all bluster and the driver is playing on the fact that you are a *khawaga* (foreigner) and don't know any better.

The big Peugeot 504 service taxis charge more than other taxis. The advantage of these taxis is that you can get a group together and commandeer one for a long trip.

HANTOUR

These horse-drawn carriages and their insistent drivers hang around on the Corniche near Helnan Shepheard's hotel and on Gezira near the Cairo Tower. They aren't a feasible means of getting around the city and are there for pleasure rides.

RIVER BUS

The river bus terminal is at Maspero, on the Corniche in front of the big round TV build-

ing. From here, boats depart every 15 minutes or so between 6.30am and 3.45pm for University (Al-Gamaa), a landing over on the Giza side of the river just north of the University Bridge. Every second boat continues south on to Manial, Rhoda, Giza and Masr al-Qadima (Old Cairo). The last stop is convenient for Coptic Cairo. The complete trip takes 50 minutes and the fare is 50pt.

ORGANISED TOURS

Some of the budget hotels in central Cairo arrange tours to various places around the city such as the Pyramids, Saqqara and Memphis. The price is usually about E£20 and includes transport only – there's no guide and admission is extra. The stories about these trips have often been negative, so forewarned is forearmed.

Salah Mohammed Abdel Hafez (☎ 298 0650, 012-313 8446, e samo@intouch .com) runs a full-day excursion to the main sites plus the Wissa Wassef Art Centre for E£18 per person (lunch and admission prices are extra). If you're staying at one of the city-centre hotels, he'll pick you up at around

GETTING AROUND

9am. You'll need to arrange the tour at least one day in advance – leave a message on the answering machine if he's not there.

A third option is to go through a travel agency such as Masr Travel (for contact details, see Travel Agencies in the Facts for the Visitor chapter) or American Express (for contact details, see Money in the Facts for the Visitor chapter). They both do half-day sightseeing tours to the Pyramids and Sphinx, Memphis, Saqqara, Old Cairo and the Egyptian Museum for US$26 to US$30.

Things to See & Do

Cairo is a densely cluttered heap of old and new neighbourhoods. It's as if all the villages that might have dotted Egypt had it not been desert have instead been thrown together in one spot. Each of these neighbourhoods has its own history, character and traditions that define the people who live there.

Encountered for the first time, the city can be a little daunting and after the obligatory visits to the Pyramids and Egyptian Museum it's not always obvious what to do next. Visits to the districts of Old Cairo and Islamic Cairo are good options. The latter covers a vast area and as a pointer for where to begin, take a look at the boxed text 'Mahfouz's Cairo' under Islamic Cairo later in this chapter. This chapter also includes other introductory walks covering the city's legacy of fine 19th-century buildings (see the boxed text 'Paris on the Nile'); modern art and sculpture (see the boxed text 'Art & Artists'); boutique shopping (see the boxed text 'Designer Life'); and a wander around one of the city's most eccentric historical suburbs, Heliopolis (see the boxed text 'Fantasies Set in Stone'). Between them, these excursions could account for several days of exploration.

For more ideas of things to do, there are several lesser-known museums – see the boxed text 'Cairo's (Lesser) Museum Highlights'; some green spaces (see the boxed text 'Precious Parks & Gardens'); and the river (see the boxed text 'Tales of the River Bank'). Beyond that, there are numerous good trips to the Pharaonic sites that stretch south of the city, the highlight of which is definitely Saqqara, easily tied in with visits to the nearby pyramids at Abu Sir and Dahshur – see The Pyramids & Memphis Necropolis chapter for more information.

ORIENTATION

Finding your way about the vast sprawl of Cairo is, remarkably, not as difficult as it may first seem. **Midan Tahrir** is the heart of the modern city. All roads lead here, so

Highlights

No poll was taken and no opinions were canvassed, the following list is completely subjective and in no particular order.

- **The Pyramids (Page 149)** They're what most visitors to Cairo come to see and few go away disappointed.
- **Tut at the Egyptian Museum (Page 84)** They're badly displayed, but the treasures from Tutankhamun's tomb are some of the most magnificent objects held by any museum anywhere.
- **Islamic Cairo (Page 101)** Less well known than the city's Pharaonic crowd pleasers but Unesco rightly recognises this area as a World Heritage Site.
- **Angels in the Architecture (Page 94)** And sphinxes, cherubs, geishas and gods – beneath all that grime Cairo has a stunning legacy of esoteric 19th-century buildings.
- **Coffeehouse Culture (Page 106)** What cafes are to Paris, coffeehouses (or *ahwas*) are to Cairo. Initiate yourself at one of the best, Fishawi.
- **Sunset Felucca Rides (Page 132)** A perfect end to a day's sightseeing; drift along on the Nile and watch the sun sink behind the city skyline.
- **Cairo by Night (Page 199)** Once the sun goes down and the heat of the day is past, the city stirs, stretches and surges into life.

For more of Cairo's best, see the boxed texts on some of Cairo's less well-known museums (page 125), where to go for the best views of the city (page 117) and the highlights of Islamic Cairo (page 101).

expect to spend lots of time observing its motley fringing of architecture from the windows of a gridlocked taxi.

North-east of Tahrir is the heart of **Downtown**. Centred on Talaat Harb, Downtown is a noisy, busy, commercial district which, under all the dust and grime, is full of attractive, turn-of-the-20th-century mansion blocks. Its northernmost extent is marked by **Midan Ramses**, location of the city's main train station. Beyond are the teeming working-class suburbs of Shubra (the true soul of modern-day Cairo), Abbassiyya and Ain Shams. The latter links on to **Heliopolis**, a one-time desert suburb with wonderfully fanciful street facades that has now been swallowed up by the creeping metropolis. Cairo's airport lies on the north-eastern fringes of Heliopolis, some 25km from Downtown Cairo.

Back Downtown, **Midan Ataba**, to the east, marks the abrupt end of modern Cairo and the beginning of what's known as **Islamic Cairo**. This is a blanket term for districts that have existed since medieval times, a compress of narrow winding alleyways harbouring communities whose lives seem to have changed little in centuries. Eastwards, beyond Islamic Cairo, is a string of makeshift shanty towns that have grown up in the shadow of the Muqattam's rocky spurs to accommodate the floods of arrivals that have washed in over the decades from the surrounding countryside.

Immediately south of Midan Tahrir are the curving, tree-lined streets of **Garden City**, prime embassy territory. Once past Garden City you are out of central Cairo and into a vast area of ramshackle neighbourhoods loosely termed **Old Cairo**. Buried in here is the small, tightly defined area of **Coptic Cairo**, a feature on many tourist agendas. Some 8km further south along the Corniche is **Ma'adi**, a very green, very suburban neighbourhood much beloved of American expats.

All the districts described so far are on the east bank of the Nile, but Cairo sprawls across the river, alighting on two sizeable islands on the way. The more central of these, connected directly to Downtown by three bridges, is known as **Gezira**. It has traditionally been a retreat of the Egyptian upper classes and is still home to the city's largest, greenest and most exclusive club and to an opera house which has a strict tie-and-jacket

Misdirections

Beware of asking directions. In their willingness to help out, Cairenes will always oblige, even if they don't have the faintest idea where the place you're asking for is. The response will be delivered with such confidence you won't suspect that it's been made up on the spot. If you do have to ask the way, always ask two or three people and if they all agree then there's a reasonable chance that you're being steered in the right direction.

People tend to drop the word *sharia* (street) in speech and use only the street's name; for example, ask for 'Talaat Harb' not 'Sharia Talaat Harb'. The same goes for *midan* (square) – people will generally just say 'Ataba' when they mean 'Midan Ataba'.

policy. The northern half of Gezira is an affluent, leafy suburb called **Zamalek**, historically favoured by the city's European residents. The southern island is known as **Rhoda**, but, again, its northern part goes by a different name – in this case **Manial**, home to Cairo University's medical faculty and a former royal palace (now a museum).

The west bank is less historical than the east and much more residential. The primary districts, north to south, are **Mohandiseen**, **Agouza**, **Doqqi** and **Giza**, all of which are heavy on concrete and light on charm. Giza covers by far the largest area of the four, stretching some 20km west either side of one long, straight road that ends at the foot of the **Pyramids**.

Downtown

Downtown (Wust al-Balad) can be defined roughly as the area contained within the triangle of Midan Tahrir, Midan Ramses and Midan Ataba. It's the unmistakable commercial heart of Cairo, where the streets are packed with glitzy shops and above which is a beehive of countless thousands of

[Continued on page 91]

Egyptian Museum

EGYPTIAN MUSEUM

More than 100,000 relics and antiquities from almost every period of ancient Egyptian history are housed in the Egyptian Museum. To put that in perspective, if you spent only one minute at each exhibit it would take more than nine months to see everything.

The nucleus of this collection was first gathered under one roof in Bulaq in 1858 by Auguste Mariette, the French archaeologist who had founded the Egyptian Antiquities Service. It was moved to its present purpose-built neoclassical home in 1902. Since then the number of exhibits has completely outgrown the available space and the place is virtually bursting at the seams. A persistent urban legend in Cairo has it that the building's storerooms are piled so high with uncatalogued artefacts that archaeologists will have to excavate their contents when the long-promised new museum (see the boxed text 'The Biggest Museum in the World' in The Pyramids & Memphis Necropolis) is eventually built.

Beyond arranging the exhibits chronologically from the Old Kingdom to the Roman Empire, little has been done to present them in any sort of context or to highlight pieces of particular significance or beauty. In fact, since the museum's foundation a century ago, the displays have never been reorganised, despite the ever-increasing number of artefacts. Labelling is poor or nonexistent, while the manner of display – mostly old wood-and-glass cases with no direct lighting – is hardly the last word in modern museum techniques. But, this is slowly starting to change. Two new galleries opened in 1998 equipped with fibreoptic lighting and – taa daa! – labels. Also, new security and lighting systems have been installed following a sensational attempted robbery in 1996, when the authorities belatedly realised that the outmoded security system (basically barred windows and a dog making the rounds after closing) was insufficient protection for the museum's priceless contents. Still, the museum's eccentricity is part of its charm, and accidentally stumbling across treasures in its sometimes musty rooms is half the fun.

Practicalities

With so much to see, trying to get around everything in one go is liable to induce chronic 'Pharaonic phatigue'. The best strategy is to spread the exploration over at least two visits, maybe tackling one floor at a time. Unfortunately, there's no best time to visit as the museum is heaving with visitors throughout the day, although late afternoons can be a little quieter.

Queues start an hour before opening time and the four-fold admission procedure is as painfully slow as it sounds: 1. queue to pass through a metal detector and have your bags X-rayed; 2. queue to buy a ticket; 3. queue at the automatic ticket barriers to enter the building; and 4. queue to pass through a second metal detector and have your bags searched again.

Title page: The golden funerary mask of Tutankhamun, possibly the best known artefact held by the Egyptian Museum (Photo by Chris Mellor)

Inset: Detail from the back of Tutankhamun's golden throne, depicting the boy king and his wife (Photo by Chris Mellor)

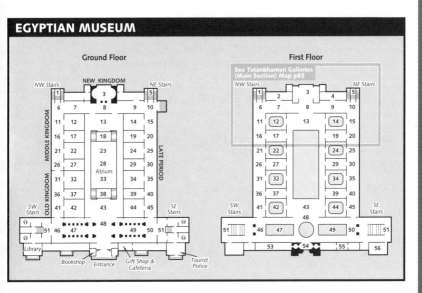

Admission to the museum is E£20 (E£10 for students) plus E£40 for the Royal Mummy Room, and it is open from 9am to 4.45pm daily. The museum (☎ 575 4319) is on Midan Tahrir; the closest metro is Sadat.

Note that the Royal Mummy Room (for which tickets are bought inside the museum) closes a half-hour before the rest of the museum. Permission to use cameras (without flash) costs E£10; otherwise cameras must be left at the entrance. Use of a video camera costs E£100. There are official guides who will take you around for about E£40 per hour.

Highlights of the Egyptian Museum

For those people who do not have nine months to examine everything in the museum, the following is our list of the top 10 mustsee exhibits (also highlighted in the following Museum Tour sections).

1 Tutankhamun Galleries (1st floor; page 84)
2 Royal Mummy Room (1st floor, Room 56; page 90)
3 Amarna Room (ground floor, Room 3; page 82)
4 Graeco-Roman Mummies (1st floor, Room 14; page 88)
5 Royal Tombs of Tanis (1st floor, Room 2; page 88)
6 Old Kingdom Rooms (ground floor, Rooms 42, 37 & 32; page 81)
7 Yuya & Thuyu Rooms (1st floor, Room 43; page 89)
8 Ancient Egyptian Jewellery Room (1st floor, Room 4; page 87)
9 Animal Mummies (1st floor, Rooms 53 & 54; page 89)
10 Pharaonic Technology (1st floor, Room 34; page 88)

Museum Tour: Ground Floor

Before entering the museum, wander through the garden; off to your left is the tomb of Mariette (1821–81), with a statue of the man, arms folded, shaded under a spreading tree. Mariette's tomb is also adorned with an arc of busts of a collection of other famous Egyptologists including Champollion, who cracked the code of hieroglyphs; Maspero, who was successor to Mariette as director of the Egyptian Antiquities Service; and Lepsius, the pre-eminent 19th-century German Egyptologist.

Once, inside, the ground floor is laid out roughly chronologically in a clockwise fashion starting at the entrance hall. Following are a few of the things to look out for.

ROOM 48 – Early Dynastic Period

In glass cabinet No 16 is the near-life-size limestone seated **statue of Zoser (Djoser)**, the 3rd-dynasty pharaoh whose chief architect Imhotep designed the first pyramid, the Step Pyramid at Saqqara. The statue was discovered in 1924 in its *serdab* or stone room in the northeastern corner of the pyramid (a replica now sits in its place) and is the oldest statue of its kind in the museum.

ROOM 43 – Atrium

The central atrium is the part of the museum that really feels like a warehouse, filled with a disordered miscellany of Egyptological finds large and small.

In cabinet No 8, off to the right, is the double-sided **Narmer Palette** which, although you'd never know it from the way it's presented, is one of the most significant artefacts in the whole museum. Dating from around 3100 BC it depicts the pharaoh Narmer (also known as Menes) wearing the crown of Upper Egypt on one side of the palette, and the crown of Lower Egypt on the other side, representing the first uniting of Upper and Lower Egypt under one ruler. This is ground zero – the event Egyptologists believe was the start of ancient Egyptian civilisation. Here begins over 3000 years of Pharaonic history, encompassing 170 or more rulers presiding over 30 dynasties, during which time almost every last exhibit in this building was fashioned. In effect, the Narmer Palette is the keystone of the Egyptian Museum.

At the far end of the atrium is a representation of all that the successors of Narmer would achieve in the form of a huge **colossus of Amenhotep III and Tiy**, his wife, with their small daughters at their feet. This particular pharaoh's lengthy reign, from 1390 to 1352 BC, represented the zenith of ancient Egypt's power and prestige. Among his many projects Amenhotep built Luxor Temple and an even greater temple complex across the Nile on the West Bank – possibly the greatest ever built in Egypt – but one that has long since completely vanished, apart from the two lone guardians now known as the Colossi of Memnon.

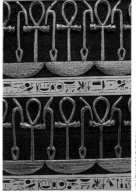

Tutankhamun's treasures at the Egyptian Museum (bottom left) include this painted wooden chest showing Tut as a sphinx trampling his enemies (top) and a wooden statue of the boy pharaoh (middle right). The ankh symbol (bottom right) used on one of Tut's wooden chests denotes eternal life.

CHRIS MELLOR

ANDERS BLOMQVIST

ANDERS BLOMQVIST

One of the great museums of the world, the Egyptian Museum (top) is a must-see for any visitor to Cairo. Its vast collection includes relics from the reign of the 'heretic pharaoh' Akhenaten, such as his statue (bottom left) and the Canopic jar (bottom right) believed to portray Kiya, one of his minor wives.

ROOMS 47, 46 & 51 – Masterpieces of the Old Kingdom

Look for the three matching black schist triads that depict the pharaoh Menkaure (Mycerinus), builder of the smallest of the three Pyramids of Giza, flanked on either side by a female figure. The figure to the pharaoh's right is the goddess Hathor, while each of the figures on his left represents a nome (district) of Egypt, the name of which is given by the symbol above their head. These triads (plus one other that is not held by this museum) were discovered at the pharaoh's valley temple, just east of his pyramid at Giza.

ROOMS 42, 37 & 32 – Old Kingdom Rooms

In the centre of Room 42 is what some consider to be the museum's masterpiece: a smooth, black, dioritic, larger than life-size **statue of Khafre (Chepren)**, builder of the second pyramid at Giza. He sits on a lion throne with the wings of the falcon god Horus wrapped around his head in a protective gesture. From the number of statueless bases discovered, archaeologists believe that this is just one of 23 such pieces that originally lined the hall of the pharaoh's valley temple on the Giza plateau.

Slightly to the left in front of Khafre is the **wooden statue of Ka-Aper** (No 14). Carved out of a single piece of sycamore (except for the arms), he's amazingly lifelike, especially the eyes which, set in copper lids, have whites of opaque quartz and corneas of rock crystal that have been drilled and filled with black paste to form the pupils. When they dug up this statue at Saqqara in 1860, local workmen named him Sheikh al-Balad (Headman), because they thought he resembled their own village chief.

Room 32 is dominated by the beautiful **statues of the royal couple, Rahotep and Nofret**, son and daughter-in-law of Sneferu, builder of some of the pyramids at Dahshur. Almost life-sized with well-preserved painted surfaces, the limestone sculptures' simple lines make them seem almost contemporary, despite having been around for a staggering 4600 years.

Another highlight in here, displayed in a cabinet off to the left, is the slightly bizarre tableau of the 'chief of the royal wardrobe' **Seneb** and his family. Seneb is a dwarf and he sits cross-legged, his two children strategically placed in front where an ordinary man's legs would be. His (nondwarf) wife Senetites has her arms protectively around his shoulders in an immediately recognisable expression of affection. The happy couple and their two children have been used in recent Egyptian family planning campaigns.

Also in here is the panel known as the **Meidum Geese**. This is part of a wall painting that originates from a mud-brick mastaba at Meidum, near the oasis of Al-Fayoum (to this day, the lakes there are still host to a great variety of bird life). Though painted around 2600 BC, the pigments remain vivid and the degree of realism (while still retaining a distinct Pharaonic style) is astonishing – ornithologists have had no trouble identifying the bird types.

Room 37 is entered via Room 32; it contains finds from the Giza plateau **tomb of Queen Hetepheres**, including a carrying chair, bed, bed canopy and a jewellery box. Although her mummy was never found the remains of her internal organs are still inside her Canopic chest. A glass cabinet holds a mini statue of her son Khufu, found at Abydos. Ironically, at just 8cm or so high, it's the only surviving representation of the pharaoh who built Egypt's largest pyramid.

ROOM 26 – Montuhotep II
The seated statue on your right after leaving Room 32, with the black skin (which represents fertility and rebirth) and the red crown of Lower Egypt, is **Montuhotep II**, first new ruler of the Middle Kingdom period and the pharaoh who united the north and south. This statue was discovered by Howard Carter under the forecourt of the pharaoh's temple at Deir al-Bahri in Thebes in 1900 when the ground gave way under his horse – a surprisingly recurrent means of discovery in the annals of Egyptology.

ROOMS 21 & 16 – Sphinxes
These grey-granite sphinxes are very different from the great enigmatic Sphinx at Giza – in fact, they look more like the Lion Man from the Wizard of Oz, with a fleshy human face surrounded by a great shaggy mane and big ears. They were sculpted for the pharaoh Amenemhat III (1855–1808 BC) during the 12th dynasty and were later relocated to the Delta city of Tanis, which is where they were discovered in 1863.

ROOM 12 – Hathor Shrine
The centrepiece of this room is a remarkably well-preserved sandstone chapel with a vaulted roof painted with reliefs of Tuthmosis III and his wife and daughters with the gods. It was part of the pharaoh's temple at Deir al-Bahri in Thebes, complete with the life-size representation of the goddess Hathor in cow form.

Hatshepsut, who was co-regent for part of Tuthmosis III's reign, also built her temple at Deir al-Bahri. She took her position as regent a step further by having herself crowned pharaoh, and there's a life-size pink granite statue of the pharaoh queen to the left of the chapel. She's represented wearing a pharaoh's headdress and a false beard, but the face has definite feminine characteristics. The large reddish-painted limestone head in the corridor outside this room is also of Hatshepsut, and once belonged to one of her huge Osiris-type statues that adorned the pillared facade of her great temple at Deir al-Bahri.

ROOM 3 – Amarna Room
This room is devoted to Akhenaten (1352–1336 BC), the 'heretic pharaoh' who promoted the exclusive worship of the one god, the sun god Aten. A quick glance around the room is enough to see that artistic styles changed almost as drastically as the state religion during his 17-year tenure. Take a look at the great torsos and heads of the pharaoh and compare their strangely bulbous bellies, hips

and thighs, their elongated faces, and thick, Mick Jagger–like lips with the sleek, hard-edged sculpture that you've just seen from the Middle Kingdom. Also worth a look, for their unusual informality, are the stelae of the pharaoh and queen playing with their children, showing an informality and relaxed nature rarely seen in royal Pharaonic art.

Most striking of all is the unfinished **head of Nefertiti**, wife of Akhenaten. Worked in light brown quartzite, it's an incredibly delicate and sensitive portrait and shows the queen to be an extremely beautiful woman – unlike some of the relief figures of her elsewhere in the room, in which she appears with exactly the same strange features as her husband.

ROOM 10 – Ramses II

At the foot of the north-east stairs is a large, grey-granite representation of Ramses II, builder of the Ramesseum and Abu Simbel, but here depicted as a child with his finger in his mouth nestled against the breast of a great falcon, in this case the Canaanite god Horun. The pharaoh's figure actually spells out his name in sculpted form: *ra* (sun disc), *mes* (child) and *su* (the plant he holds).

Right: Pink-granite statue of Ramses II found in Luxor Temple

CHRIS MELLOR

ROOM 34 – Graeco-Roman Room

The lack of any kind of labelling is acutely felt in this room, which is full of fascinating pieces for which there's no explanation or context provided. But what is evident in many of the exhibits is the assimilation by Egypt's Greek, then Roman, overlords of the indigenous Pharaonic style.

This is most obvious in the stelae on the back wall, and on the large sandstone panel on the right-hand wall that is inscribed in three languages: in hieroglyphics (the Egyptian literary language), demotic (the Egyptian popular language; a shorthand form of hieroglyphs) and, at the bottom, in Greek (the official language of the country's then rulers). This trilingually inscribed stone is similar in nature to the more famous Rosetta Stone, now housed in the British Museum in London (although there's a cast replica back near the museum entrance in Room 48). Also, notice the bust immediately to the left as you enter this room: a typically Greek face with curly beard and locks, but wearing a Pharaonic-style headdress.

ROOMS 50 & 51 – Alexander the Great

On the official museum plan this area is labelled 'Alexander the Great' but currently there's nothing here that relates directly to the Macedonian conqueror who became pharaoh. However, there is an extremely beautiful small marble **statuette of the Greek goddess Aphrodite**, who the Egyptians identified with Isis. Carved in the 3rd or 2nd century BC, it was found in Alexandria.

Museum Tour: First Floor

The exhibits up here are grouped thematically and can be viewed in any order, but assuming that you've come up the south-east stairs (through Room 51), we'll go anticlockwise, entering the Tutankhamun Galleries at Room 45. This way, you'll experience the pieces in roughly the same order that they were laid out in the tomb (a poster on the wall outside Room 45 illustrates the tomb and treasures as they were found).

TUTANKHAMUN GALLERIES

Without doubt, the exhibit that outshines everything else in the museum is the treasure of the young and comparatively insignificant New Kingdom pharaoh Tutankhamun.

The tomb and treasures of this pharaoh, who ruled for only nine years during the 14th century BC (1336–1327), were discovered in 1922 by English archaeologist Howard Carter. Its well-hidden location in the Valley of the Kings, below the much grander but ransacked tomb of Ramses VI, had prevented tomb robbers and archaeologists from finding it earlier. The incredible contents of this rather modest tomb displayed here can only make you wonder about the fabulous wealth looted from the tombs of pharaohs far greater than Tutankhamun.

About 1700 items are spread throughout a series of rooms – although most of the 'rooms' are in fact sections of the museum's north- and east-wing corridors, and room numbers are not displayed, which sometimes makes it hard to find what you're looking for.

TUTANKHAMUN GALLERIES (MAIN SECTION)

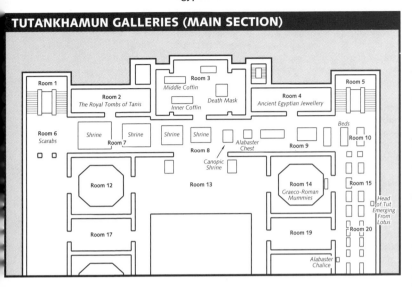

Room 1

Room 2
The Royal Tombs of Tanis

Room 3
Middle Coffin

Inner Coffin

Death Mask

Room 4
Ancient Egyptian Jewellery

Room 5

Room 6
Scarabs

Room 7
Shrine   Shrine

Room 8
Shrine   Shrine

Canopic
Shrine

Alabaster
Chest

Room 9

Beds

Room 10

Room 12

Room 13

Room 14
Graeco-Roman
Mummies

Room 15

Head
of Tut
Emerging
From
Lotus

Room 17

Room 19

Room 20

Alabaster
Chalice

ROOM 45 Flanking the doorway as you enter are two life-size statues of the pharaoh found in the antechamber of the tomb. They served as sentries to the burial chamber (a large black-and-white photo on the wall shows the statues *in situ*). Made of wood, they are coated in bitumen – the black skin, identified with Osiris and the rich black river silt, symbolises fertility and rebirth.

ROOM 40 This area has a beautifully **painted chest** (contained in cabinet No 20) depicting the young pharaoh charging into battle in a chariot, his foes in disorganised chaos before him: Nubians on one side, 'Asiatics' from Syria and Palestine on the other. Although there is evidence that Tutankhamun was planning a foreign campaign just before he died, there's no record of him ever having fought such a battle. However, he did enjoy hunting, as depicted on the chest lid. When this chest was discovered it contained some of the necklaces and belts now displayed in Room 3.

ROOMS 35 & 30 The highlight here is the pharaoh's **lion throne**. Covered with sheet gold and inlaid with glass and semiprecious stones, the wooden throne is supported by spindly lions. The colourful tableau on the back of the chair depicts Tutankhamun's queen placing her hand on his shoulder under the rays of the sun (Aten), the worship of which was a hangover from his father and predecessor, Akhenaten, whose throne this may even once have been, as there is evidence of remodelling of both the figures and the names. Their robes are modelled in beaten silver and their hair is glass paste.

The many **golden statues** found in the tomb were all there to help the pharaoh on his journey in the afterlife. They include a series of 28 gilded wooden deities, meant to protect the pharaoh, and 413 **shabti** (only a selection of these symbolic servants are here) who would perform on behalf of the pharaoh any labours required of him in the afterlife.

ROOM 25 The gold-plated **wooden shrine** exhibited here was found empty, its gold statue having been stolen in ancient times. But it's of great interest for the royal domestic scenes beaten into the gold leaf, all of which are in an unconventional, realistic style evolved from the Amarna period.

ROOM 20 This room contains exquisite **alabaster jars and vessels**, including (just south of the door to Room 19) a lamp in which a small light has been inserted to demonstrate the delicacy of its translucent artwork.

ROOM 15 Intricate rigged **model barques** (ships), designed to be used by the pharaoh on his voyage through the afterlife, are displayed here. Also, almost unnoticeable against the back wall in cabinet No 118, is a small, beautifully rendered **painted wooden head** of the boy pharaoh, complete with pierced ears, emerging as the young sun god from a lotus flower.

CHRIS MELLOR

Left: This elaborate wooden model of a burial boat shows an extraordinary attention to detail. Boats such as these were placed in the tomb of the pharaoh to be used to transport him to the Netherworld.

ROOMS 10 & 9 The northern end of this gallery is filled with the pharaoh's three elaborate **funerary couches**, one supported by two figures of the cow-goddess Mehetweret, one by two figures of the goddess of the underworld Ammut, 'the devourer' who ate the hearts of the damned, and the third by two lionesses. Although their exact purpose is unknown, it has been suggested that the couches would give the dead pharaoh access to the afterlife.

The alabaster chest contains four **Canopic jars**, the stoppers of which are in the form of Tutankhamun's head. Inside these jars were placed the four miniature gold coffins exhibited in Room 3 that, in turn, contained the pharaoh's internal organs. The whole chest and its gory contents was then placed inside the golden Canopic shrine with the four gilded goddesses, Isis, Neith, Nephthys and Selket, all portrayed with protective outstretched arms. If you look closely, you'll see that the alabaster chest is protected by the same four figures at its corners.

ROOMS 8 & 7 These galleries just barely accommodate the four huge **gilded wooden shrines** that fitted one inside the other like a set of Russian dolls, encasing at their centre the sarcophagi of the boy pharaoh.

ROOM 3 This is the room that everybody wants to see. At peak times you'll have to queue, and once inside it feels like you've entered the crush of the Khan al-Khalili bazaar.

The central exhibit is the astonishing **death mask** of Tutankhamun. Made of solid gold and weighing 11kg, the mask was found covering the head of the mummy of Tutankhamun, where it lay inside a series of three sarcophagi. The mask is an idealised portrait of the young pharaoh; the eyes are fashioned from obsidian and quartz, while the outlines of the eyes and the eyebrows are delineated with lapis lazuli.

No less wondrous are the two **golden sarcophagi**. These are the inner two sarcophagi – the outermost coffin, along with the mummified remains of Tutankhamun, remains in place in his tomb in the Valley of the Kings. The smallest coffin is, like the mask, cast in solid gold and inlaid in the same fashion. It weighs 110kg. The slightly larger coffin is made of gilded wood.

ROOM 4 – Ancient Egyptian Jewellery

One of two galleries opened in 1998, this room has finds from sites all over the place, including Saqqara and Giza. The jewellery includes belts, inlaid beadwork, necklaces, semiprecious stones and bracelets. Most beautiful of all the items on display is a diadem of Sit-Hathor-Yunet, a golden headband with a rearing cobra inset with semiprecious stones.

As well as the Pharaonic cache there are also finds from the Graeco-Roman period from the Western Oases and Red Sea areas including bracelets, another diadem and agate bowls.

ROOM 2 – Royal Tombs of Tanis

The second of the new galleries, this room contains a glittering collection of gold- and silver-encrusted amulets, gold funerary masks, daggers, bracelets, collars, gold sandals, and finger and toe coverings from five intact 21st- and 22nd-dynasty tombs found at the site of Tanis in the Nile Delta. Unearthed by the French in 1939, the discovery of these tombs rivalled Carter's finding of Tutankhamun's tomb, but it was overshadowed by the start of WWII and remains largely unknown.

There's also the gold death mask of Psusennes I (1039–991 BC) and his silver inner coffin, with another silver coffin with the head of a falcon belonging to the pharaoh Shoshenq II (c. 890 BC).

ROOM 14 – Graeco-Roman Mummies

This room contains a small sample (over a thousand have been discovered) of the stunning portraits found on Graeco-Roman–period mummies, commonly refered to as 'Fayoum Portraits' after the place in which many were discovered. These images, whose large watchful eyes seem to follow you around the room, were painted onto wooden panels that were then placed over the mummys' embalmed faces; some were even painted directly onto the shrouds themselves, in a fusion of ancient Egyptian and Graeco-Roman funerary practices.

Dating back to between 30 BC and AD 395, the portraits are executed in a technique involving a heated mixture of pigment and wax. As few other painted portraits from the Graeco-Roman era have survived, this collection is unique both for the number of its paintings and the high quality of its images.

Although the cases are barely lit and are piled with dust, the beautiful and hauntingly realistic faces that stare out from behind the glass bring the personalities of their long-dead owners to life in a way that the stylised elegance of most ancient Egyptian art somehow can't. Take a look at the mummy in front of you as you enter the room; the portrait is of a woman with large brown eyes and it's so life-like you'd recognise her immediately if you saw her on the street. Make sure to walk through to area 13, where there's an extremely well-preserved tiny mummy of a young boy.

ROOM 34 – Pharaonic Technology

For gadget buffs, this room contains a great number of everyday objects that helped support ancient Egypt's great leap out of prehistory. Everything from combs and mirrors to fishing tackle, ploughs, hoes (that look exactly like the ones still used by Egypt's *fellaheen*, agricultural workers, today) and serious-looking blades and razors with their cases can be found here. Hunting paraphernalia includes Pharaonic boomerangs that were apparently used for killing birds. (Tutankhamun is depicted using one in the reliefs on the gold shrine in Room 25.)

ROOMS 32 & 27 – Middle Kingdom Models

The lifelike models contained in these rooms were mostly found in the tomb of Meketre, an 11th-dynasty chancellor in Thebes, and together they constitute a fascinating portrait of daily life almost 4000 years ago. The models include fishing boats (complete with fish in the nets), a slaughterhouse, a carpentry workshop, a loom and a model of Meketre's house (with figs on the trees and painted columns). Most spectacular is the 1.5m-wide scene of Meketre sitting with his sons, four scribes and various other hangers-on, counting cattle. Painted wooden servant figures hold the animals by miniature ropes as they pass by the shaded dais on which the boss sits.

ROOM 37 – Model Armies

Discovered in the Asyut tomb of the governor Meseheti and dating from about 2000 BC (the time of the 11th dynasty), these are two sets of 40 wooden warriors marching in phalanxes. The darker soldiers are Nubian archers from the south of the kingdom, each wearing brightly coloured kilts of varying design, while the lighter-skinned soldiers are Egyptian pikemen.

ROOM 43 – Yuya & Thuyu Rooms

Before Tutankhamun, the discovery of the tomb of Yuya and Thuyu (the parents of Queen Tyi, and Tut's great-grandparents) was the most spectacular find in Egyptian archaeology. The tomb was discovered virtually intact in the Valley of the Kings in 1905 and contained a vast number of treasures, including five ornate sarcophagi and the remarkably well-preserved mummies of the two commoners who became royal in-laws. Among the many other items on display here are such essentials for the hereafter as beds, sandals and a chariot, as well as two fabulous gilded death masks – Thuyu's mask is especially beautiful, fashioned with a broad smile.

ROOM 48 – Pyramid Model

There's an excellent large-scale model of one of the Abu Sir pyramids that perfectly illustrates the typical pyramid complex with its valley temple, high-walled causeway, mortuary temple and mini satellite pyramid – it's well worth studying before a trip to Giza.

ROOMS 53 & 54 – Animal Mummies

Before the rise of the Pharaonic dynasties in Egypt, animal cults proliferated, and the results can be seen in the battered and dust-covered little mummified cats, dogs, birds, rams and jackals in Room 53. More of these bizarre little trussed-up packages can be seen just outside in Room 54, where the better-preserved remains of a mummified falcon, a fish, a cat, an ibis, a monkey and a tiny crocodile are on show.

The museum is encouraging people to 'adopt' an animal mummy. On offer via the Internet at W www.animalmummies.com is everything from mummified snakes (donate US$50 to become a co-parent) to ancient crocodiles (US$800). 'Parents' get a special information pack on their chosen animal while the money raised helps to pay for a climate-controlled room and special cases to conserve the poor desiccated beasts.

ROOM 56 – Royal Mummy Room

The Royal Mummy Room houses the bodies of 11 of Egypt's most illustrious pharaohs and queens from the 17th to 21st dynasties, who ruled Egypt between 1650 and 945 BC. They include the brave Seqenre II who died violently during the struggles to reunite the country in around 1560 BC, his arms still twisted by rigor mortis; Seti I; Tuthmosis II; Tuthmosis IV with his pierced ear and beautifully styled hair; Ramses II with his hair-dye job; and the partially unwrapped Ramses III, the model for Boris Karloff in Universal's 1932 version of *The Mummy*. The mummies all lie in individual glass showcases (kept at a constant temperature of 22°C) in a sombre, dimly lit environment reminiscent of a tomb. Talking above a hushed whisper is not permitted (although irreverent tour groups often need to be reminded of this); for this reason, tour guides are not allowed in, making it one of the most peaceful havens in the museum.

Note, taking young children into the Mummy Room could leave them with nightmares for months to come.

ANDERS BLOMQVIST

Left: Detail of hieroglyphs from a painted chest found in Tutankhamun's tomb

[Continued from page 76]

small, dusty businesses. The buildings sag under the weight of peeling signboards and fading placards, and the streets have a typically Egyptian time-worn appearance, which is mildly misleading when you consider that less than 150 years ago there were no buildings here at all.

Before the 1860s the core of the city lay further east, in what is now Islamic Cairo. Between it and the Nile was a swampy plain subject to the annual flooding of the Nile. In 1863, when the French-educated Ismail came to power as khedive, he was determined to upgrade the image of his capital, which he believed could only be done by dismissing what had gone before and starting afresh with a new model. For 10 years the former marsh became one vast building site for a new, Western-style Cairo.

The khedive's inspiration was the Paris of Haussmann, a city of wide, leafy avenues and elegant squares. Stand at one of Downtown's busy *midans* (squares) today and you can still get a sense of the designs of Ismail's chief city planner, Mahmoud al-Falaki Bey. Banks, businesses and rich land owners were offered incentives to build, which they did with the help of architects brought in from Italy, France, Belgium and Germany.

Much grand architecture remains but the character of the area has changed considerably from its cosmopolitan, cafe-society heyday. The money has fled to newer, more chic suburbs, abandoning Ismail's city to the poorer classes. Consequently, buildings are badly maintained, and shops and businesses are aimed at the lower end of the market. The area boasts few sights as such but there is great entertainment to be had window-shopping and crowd-watching.

MIDAN TAHRIR (Map 2)

As the city's main square and focal point, Midan Tahrir (Liberation Square) is badly lacking in splendour. Its original form was a large piazza overlooked by several palaces, but they are long gone and decades of haphazard development has seen the square become little more than a vast, shapeless traffic island with streams of cars and buses as its main feature. Still, most visitors end up spending a lot of time around here because it's home to the Egyptian Museum – the low, dusky-pink building to the north of the square – and central to a great many hotels.

Chief of these is the **Nile Hilton (Map 2, #65)**, a blue-and-white slab that stands between Midan Tahrir and the Nile. It was the first modern hotel to be built in Cairo (in 1959), replacing the Qasr el-Nil army barracks, notorious among the British soldiers bunked there for its vicious bedbugs. Although aged and surpassed in luxury and amenities by the countless five-star hotels built since, the hotel remains vibrant, a favourite with the local high fliers as a place to lunch (especially in the garden courtyard cafe) and as a wedding venue. Visit on a Thursday to see the brides making Broadway entrances down the foyer's central spiral staircase. Attached to the Hilton is a small **shopping mall (Map 2, #66)** with a greenhouse-like design. There's a quiet cafe on the 1st floor which is air-conditioned and a good place to escape the heat. Immediately south of the mall is the drab and very unprepossessing **Arab League Building**, gathering place of the leaders of the Arab world, or at least those who can be persuaded to attend.

Sweeping anticlockwise across Sharia Tahrir, here crowded with passengers preparing to make death-defying lunges for their buses, is the modern **Omar Makram Mosque (Map 2, #114)**, where the funerary receptions for deceased politicians and VIPs are held.

Overshadowing the mosque, the monolithic white, Stalinist structure on the south side of the square is the **Mogamma**, home each working day to thousands of underpaid bureaucrats and the additional tens of thousands of unfortunates who have to chase around its corridors collecting forms, stamps and signatures. (See the boxed text 'The Dreaded Mogamma' over the page.)

East across Qasr al-Ainy is the neo-Islamic facade of the **American University in Cairo (AUC)**, the university of choice for the sons and daughters of Cairo's moneyed

The Dreaded Mogamma

It is totally fitting that the building that dominates Midan Tahrir, the heart of modern Cairo, is a monstrous, 14-storey monument to bureaucracy. The Mogamma, Cairo's central government complex, houses 18,000 bureaucrats from 14 ministries and 65 other government departments, all of whom are seemingly devoted to making life just that little bit more difficult. Add to this some 50,000 visitors each day, condemned to wait and queue and wait some more, and more time must be wasted in the Mogamma than in any other place on earth.

Since the law requiring all visitors to Egypt to register their passports was annulled, foreigners are spared the torture of its Byzantine ways, but for locals the Mogamma remains a place to be approached with trepidation. Legend has it that more than one despairing individual has flung themselves to their death down the well of the huge central stair. In *Irhab wa Kebab* (Terrorists and Kebab), a big hit film of the 1990s, a group of hapless, working-class Cairenes become so frustrated by their Mogamma experiences that they grab the guards' rifles and take the place over. They issue demands for a change in the system, but eventually agree to surrender in exchange for a plate of skewered grilled meat.

classes. The campus has an attractive courtyard, and it's possible to visit the excellent bookshop or go to an exhibition at the university's Sony Gallery. Note that ID (your passport will do) is required to get on to the campus.

About 50m north of the AUC is the **Ali Baba Cafeteria (Map 2, #103)** which, until the 1994 knife attack that almost killed him, was a regular morning stop for Nobel Prize–winning author Naguib Mahfouz. It serves chilled Stella beer and the tables beside the window on the upper floor are a good place to watch the goings-on outside.

The buildings around Midan Tahrir then break for Sharia Tahrir, which leads 250m east to a busy square (Midan Falaki), with

a bus station in the middle, and an area known as Bab al-Luq.

BAB AL-LUQ & ABDEEN (Map 2)

Immediately east of Midan Tahrir, is the small district of Bab al-Luq, centred on **Midan Falaki**. Named for Ismail's city planner, the square has a couple of beautiful, late-19th-century buildings in its north-east corner, but attention is distracted from them by the busy bus station and pedestrian walkways.

On the north side is **Cafeteria Horreyya (Map 2, #98)**, a high-ceilinged *ahwa* (coffeehouse) with tall windows that dates back to 1936. It's one of the few venues for Cairo's chess players and is also unique for an ahwa in that it serves alcohol. South of the square is the **Souq Mansour**, a covered market of vegetable, meat and fish stalls, and a big favourite with the city's cats. The streets either side of the souq are filled with cheap *kushari* (see Egyptian Staples in the Places to Eat chapter for an explanation), pizza and kebab joints.

As you move east from Midan Falaki, Sharia al-Bustan empties into **Midan al-Gomhuriyya** (Republic Square), a sparse empty plaza skirted by speeding traffic. The one time of the year that it livens up is during Ramadan, when a makeshift canteen fills the square, doling out free food each evening at *iftar*, the breaking of the day's fast. For the rest of the year, the only notable activity focuses on the building with the Toytown tower on the midan's north side, the **Cairo Governorate**. The great building over to the east, which dominates the square, is the Abdeen Palace, former residence of the rulers of Egypt.

Abdeen Palace Museum (Map 2, #122)

Commissioned by Khedive Ismail and designed by the French architect Rosseau, the Abdeen Palace (*Mathaf Abdeen;* ☎ *391 0042, Sharia al-Gamaa; Metro: Mohammed Naguib; admission E£10; open 9am-3pm Sat-Thur*) was started in 1863 and completed, 500 rooms later, in 1874. It served as the occasional residence of royalty until the abolition of the monarchy in 1952, when Abdeen became the presidential palace. The presidents have since moved out (Mubarak prefers Uruba Palace up in Heliopolis) and parts of the palace are now open to the public as a museum. Unfortunately, all the glitzy royal chambers are out of bounds and what you get to see instead is a series of halls filled with a vast array of weaponry, from ceremonial daggers to howitzers. One for the boys.

Note, entrance to the museum is via a small gate right round the back of the palace on Sharia al-Gamaa.

MIDAN TAHRIR TO MIDAN TALAAT HARB (Map 2)

Talaat Harb and Qasr el-Nil are Downtown Cairo's two main shop-filled streets. They both run north-east from Midan Tahrir, intersecting at **Midan Talaat Harb**, formerly Midan Suleyman Pasha named after a French colonel who trained Mohammed Ali's armies. His statue was removed to the Citadel (where it stands in a courtyard of the National Military Museum) after the 1952 Revolution and replaced by the current, *tarboosh* (fez)-wearing figure of Talaat Harb, founder of the National Bank. The European influence, however, remains evident in the sublime architecture around the midan and in **Groppi's (Map 2, #58)**, once the most celebrated patisserie and tearoom this side of the Mediterranean. When it opened in the 1920s it was the most fashionable place to be seen in, and attendance at Groppi's society functions and concert dances was *de rigueur*. That was long ago. Today, it's is a sad old place, large and empty, but the entrance still bears a beautiful Italian mosaic, a last bit of sparkle yet to be snuffed out.

Close by, round the corner on Talaat Harb, is another relic of the past, but one that's survived rather better. **Cafe Riche (Map 2, #82)** used to be a hang-out for Egyptian writers and intellectuals. It's claimed Nasser met with his cronies here while planning the 1952 Revolution. Closed all through the 1990s, the Riche reopened in 2000 as an attractive cafe-restaurant (see

under Restaurants in the Places to Eat chapter) trading heavily on nostalgia.

While the Riche was closed a part of its erstwhile clientele migrated into the little alley adjacent where you'll find the **Zahret al-Bustan (Map 2, #83)** coffeehouse. For reasons unknown, the alley and coffeehouse have recently become a bit of a sleazy backpacker flytrap with papyrus sellers and assorted scamsters and hustlers greeting newcomers with 'Hello, my friend I been waiting you', and making offers of visits to villages, papyrus factories, cousins' weddings and whatever else they can improvise on the spot. Short of winning a million on the lottery, never will you receive so many offers of instant friendship. And never will it cost you so dearly if you're suckered along.

One block south on Sharia Hoda Shaarawi (named for one of Egypt's first women's rights campaigners) is **Felfela (Map 2, #76)**, a restaurant which, after the Pyramids and Egyptian Museum, is a must on every tourist's itinerary – see under Restaurants in the Places to Eat chapter for more details.

NORTH OF MIDAN TALAAT HARB (Map 2)

North of the midan, both Talaat Harb and Qasr el-Nil are devoted to shops selling a drag queen's delight of lurid frocks and spangly footwear. Keep looking up above the plate-glass frontages, though, for some rather more tasteful, quite elegant examples of late-19th-century architecture. At No 17 Talaat Harb is **El-Abd (Map 2, #52)**, the city's best and most popular bakery, packed from early morning to midnight with crowds eager for baklava, *kunafe* and all those other sticky, nutty, syrupy pastries.

Across the road is the **Talaat Harb Shopping Centre (Map 2, #45)**, a plasticky, Pharaonic-inspired monstrosity, completely out of scale with its surroundings, the city's most ridiculous bit of modern architecture. Inside are more shoe shops.

On up Talaat Harb, it's worth taking a detour along Sharia Abdel Khalek Sarwat to **Sharia Shawarby**, a pedestrianised shopping street devoted to youthful togs (cut-price

Paris on the Nile

At street level Cairo heaves with pedestrian-crowded pavements and log-jammed traffic, but to experience the far gentler city of a century ago, just look up as you walk this route, which links some wonderful – albeit often woefully neglected – architectural gems.

Hard to imagine it now, but there was a time, and not too long ago, when Downtown was a quarter of extraordinary elegance, with wide, tree-lined boulevards, pleasure parks, tearooms and open-air cafes with dance bands, and grand hotels accommodating the cream of European and American society in Egypt to escape the winter chills of their own more northerly climes.

This was the new city founded by Khedive Ismail in the 1860s, with Paris as his blueprint. Funded by cotton money, what was formerly a flood plain quickly became a boom town. Egypt had no architects of its own so the city was designed and constructed by professionals and labourers drawn from across the Mediterranean. Stand on **Midan Talaat Harb (1)**, formerly Rondpoint Suleyman Pasha, home to a cluster of fine *belle epoque* buildings that still give a flavour of what this 'new' Cairo was like – a city of panache, its buildings fashioned in an eclectic mix of French baroque, neoclassical and faux-Islamic styles, adorned with extensive wrought-ironwork, delicate balconies, plaster mouldings and other flashes of decoration such as the mosaic tiling around the entrance of **Groppi's (2)**, once the most celebrated patisserie and tearoom this side of the Mediterranean.

Follow the gaze of the man up on his plinth and walk down Qasr el-Nil, passing on the left the **Baehler Building (3)**, now a bank but constructed as apartments in typical Parisian-style in 1929–30, replacing the Savoy Hotel where titled lords and ladies once stayed. A contemporary of the Savoy sur-

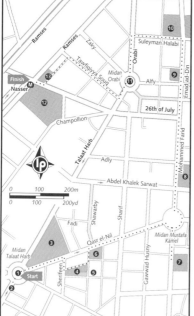

vives, tucked away down the second alley on the right, now known as the **Cosmopolitan (4)** but originally the Metropolitan when it first opened in 1902. The architecture is grand (the renovated interior less so, although the cage-like lift is superb), recently benefiting from a spruce-up of the side streets in this area, which was once the financial heart of Cairo. Next door to the hotel is the **Bourse (5)**. At the time it was built, in the early 20th century, Egypt's stock exchange was rated among the world's top 10. No more, although following decades of centralised government, the trading floor has seen some rejuvenation thanks to a program of partial privatisation initiated in the mid-1990s.

Across from the Bourse, fronting on to Qasr el-Nil, is the splendid **Trieste Insurance Building (6)** designed by Antonio Lasciac, an Italian responsible for a great many of Cairo's most beautiful buildings. Here he grafts Islamic detailing onto a vaguely Florentine design. Walk on east to pretty little Midan Mustafa Kamel and just 100m south is another, similarly styled sparkling example of Lasciac's work, the 1920 headquarters of **Banque Masr (7)**.

Retrace your steps north and continue on up Mohammed Farid, passing the impressive,

Paris on the Nile

brick-red **Davies-Bryan Building (8)**, once a Welsh-owned department store stocking expatriate essentials such as 'helmets, puggarees, mosquito nets and cholera belts'. Notice the lovely plasterwork detailing between the lower arches of the building and the little Gothic-styled arcade above the corner entrances.

Two blocks further, on the corner with Alfy, is the 1930s **Ades Building (9)**, another former department store, this one with a striking Art Deco tower. Further along again is one of the city's meisterworks, the **Khedival Apartments (10)**, a massive commercial and residential complex of four quadrants, each with a grand upper arcade and heavy dome. Sadly, the integrity of the building has been destroyed at ground level by tacked-on shop fronts and clumsy conversions.

Cut west along Suleyman Halabi and then strike south down Sharia Orabi, across **Midan Orabi (11)** – looking quite spruce after a recent whitewash and almost like something that belongs on the French Riviera – and right into Tawfiqiyya Souq, the fruit and vegetable market street. Some of the architecture along here was once quite grand, but neglect has taken its toll. Economics now favour pulling down old buildings rather than restoring them.

At some point before the end of the market, cut left through one of the tight little alleys and onto Sharia 26th of July; cross to stand in the shadow of the unattractive, failed-classical **Law Courts (12)** and look back towards the corner of 26th of July and Sharia Ramses and the **Mohammed Shawarbi Pasha Building (13)**, distinguished by its dome with four Pharaonic heads framed by angelic wings. Ancient Egyptian motifs are surprisingly rare in local period architecture, but this building went up in 1925, three years after the discovery of Tutankhamun's tomb down in Luxor. In the aftermath of the find the whole world went Tut crazy, with cities from London to Melbourne to Los Angeles erecting theatres, cinemas and sundry monuments designed in the style of the pharaohs. Here the Pharaonic touch is very modest, just a little embellishment, but later it would blossom into full-blown pastiche as with the Mausoleum of Saad Zaghloul (see under Qasr al-Ainy, later in this chapter).

From here, it's a short stroll back down to Talaat Harb to where this walk began, or a one-stop metro ride from nearby Nasser station to Midan Tahrir.

For more grand buildings, in particular villas, take a stroll around the backstreets of Garden City or Zamalek. For further information, there's a good photo book *Paris Along the Nile: Architecture of Cairo from the Belle Epoque* by Cynthia Myntti, published by the AUC Press, and a superb Web site (W www.egy.com).

The Baehler Building on Qasr el-Nil, now a bank but originally a typically Parisian-style apartment block

jeans and T-shirts), video and cassette shops, and to lingerie that makes you wonder just what Egyptians get up to in the bedroom: G-strings with faux tiger fur; panties that are no more than two pieces of elastic and a strategically placed sunflower; a velveteen leopard-print bra top and miniskirt linked by chains. You'll never look at a demurely black-cloaked woman the same way again.

Back on Talaat Harb and a little further along on the left is **Cinema Miami (Map 2, #23)**. Its facade is always half hidden under giant hand-painted billboards, executed in a sort of Bollywood-style, advertising whatever film is currently showing. Over the street is the **Metro (Map 2, #24)**, a great 1930s movie palace which when it opened (with *Gone with the Wind*) also had a Ford showroom and a diner attached. That diner is now the Excelsior restaurant; the food is lousy but it does serve cold beers and the view from its large windows is usually every bit as entertaining as whatever piece of Hollywood junk is being screened next door.

One block east of the Excelsior along Sharia Adly, the building that looks like it strayed from the Tomb Raider movie set is the **Shar Hashamaim Synagogue (Map 2, #29)**, the most visible testament to Cairo's once thriving Jewish community. The synagogue can be visited on Saturday, the Jewish holy day, when the caretaker opens up on the off chance that there'll be somebody coming by to pray.

Continuing east along Adly, the next intersection is dominated by the impressive brick-red **Davies-Bryan Building**, a former Welsh-owned department store, now a Kafkaesque warren of small businesses. On the ground floor is the venerable **Anglo-Egyptian Bookshop (Map 2, #38)**, where patrons don't so much browse as excavate. Behind the Davies-Bryan Building is **Groppi's Garden (Map 2, #37)**, sibling to the tearoom on Midan Talaat Harb. English author Penelope Lively, whose childhood was spent in Cairo, writes of this place in her autobiographical book *Oleander, Jacaranda*; she remembers it as a place where you could sit at marble-topped tables in a garden that contained a vine-covered

pergola and have tea and cakes. You really wouldn't want to linger these days.

SHARIA 26TH OF JULY & NORTH (Map 2)

Sharia 26th of July (in Arabic, Sita Wa'shreen Yulyu) cuts right across the city, starting Downtown and slicing west out into the suburbs. Previously it was Sharia Fuad I, named after the father of Egypt's last king, Farouk. After the 1952 Revolution, the boulevard was renamed to mark the date of Farouk's abdication. As Sharia Fuad I it was considered to be Cairo's Oxford St or Champs Élysées. It was home to grand department stores like Cicurel and Chemla, where uniformed Albanian doormen held the doors open for baggage-laden ladies. A few of the names remain, but the businesses were nationalised in the early 1960s and the glamour and grace were dispelled. The biggest store on the street is now the kitsch-filled, state-owned Omar Effendi, the Kmart of Egypt.

One block north of Sharia 26th of July, near Midan Orabi, smoke-filled **Sharia Ezbekiyya** is *the* street for kebabs, while pedestrianised **Sharia Alfy** is Downtown's downmarket nightlife central, with several seedy bars, a couple of ropey belly-dancing joints (see the Entertainment chapter for more details) and a popular 24-hour pit-stop eating place in Akher Sa'a (for more details, see under Fuul & Ta'amiyya Places in the Places to Eat chapter).

Nearby, the **Tawfiqiyya Souq**, a busy squeeze of a fruit and vegetable market filling a narrow street, also stays busy into the early hours. Many traders sleep beside their stalls. There are several interesting ahwas (for more details, see the boxed text 'The Ahwa' in the Entertainment chapter) in the side streets off the market and plenty of cheap eateries. One of the most decrepit buildings is home to a bunch of Cairo's cheapest hostels, so the area has become Cairo's backpacker central.

At its western end, Tawfiqiyya Souq empties into Sharia Ramses, a broad band of tarmac carrying multiple weaving lanes of traffic racing up from Midan Tahrir north to

Midan Ramses. You put yourself at the mercy of God or Allah in trying to cross. Over the other side of the road, 100m to the south, is the **Entomological Society Museum (Map 2, #4)** (☎ *340 2519, 14 Sharia Ramses; Metro: Nasser; admission free; open 9am-1pm Sat-Thur & 6pm-9pm Sat, Mon & Wed)*, a museum that long predates the concept of multimedia and hands-on displays. Dusty wood-and-glass cabinets house a collection of insects and (dead) birds gathered under the British occupation at the turn of the 20th century, a time when the colonial powers were busy collecting and cataloguing the world. It's quirky and a bit of a curiosity, but whether it's worth braving Sharia Ramses for is another matter.

MIDAN OPERA (Map 2)

The opera house that bequeathed its name to this Downtown square was burnt to the ground in 1971. In its place now stands a multistorey car park. That the opera house was burnt so completely was due to its wooden construction, a result of the rush to have it completed in time for the celebrations surrounding the opening of the Suez Canal in November 1869. It was inaugurated with a performance of Verdi's *Rigoletto*, not *Aïda* as is often mistakenly stated, which was the opera that Ismail had commissioned from the composer for the occasion but which wouldn't be ready for another two years.

At the time of the inauguration of the canal, Midan Opera was the grandest of Cairo's squares. It was flanked to the north by the lawns, lakes and tree-lined paths of the Ezbekiyya Gardens; to the east was the Opera House; south was Madam Badia's Casino; and on the west side was the grand Continental Savoy, one of a string of world-famous hotels running north from the square that included the legendary Shepheard's. Tragically, the Ezbekiyya Gardens have been reduced to a modest fenced-off lawn, the Opera House is now a car park, Badia's has been replaced by a concrete office block, Shepheard's has gone and on its site is a petrol station. The Continental Savoy remains but is derelict. It's only a matter of time before that too is demolished.

Observing the changes is an **equestrian statue of Ibrahim Pasha**, father of Ismail, founder of Downtown Cairo, who must feel more than a little despair as he watches the grand urban spaces his son created become ever more ugly.

MIDAN ATABA (Map 2)

Midan Ataba is the chaotic transition zone where the 'modern European' Cairo runs up against the old medieval Cairo of Salah ad-Din (Saladin), the Mamluks and Ottomans. Normally it's one big bazaar, with all its corners filled by traders and hawkers, but for the past year or so it's been more like one massive building site as engineers construct a tunnel meant to take cars under Islamic Cairo. In the south-west corner stands the domed **main post office (Map 2, #33)**, with a pretty courtyard and an attached **Postal Museum (Map 2, #32)** (☎ *391 0011, 55 Abdel Khalek Sarwat; Metro: Ataba; admission 10pt; open 9am-1pm Sat-Thur)* with a vast collection of commemorative stamps and displays on the history of what was one of the world's first postal services.

To the east of the square, immediately behind the big tatty building with the green-painted shutters is the **meat market**, fascinating but not for the squeamish. Just to the north, stalls of cheap clothing mark the beginning of **Muski**, a long market street that leads to Khan al-Khalili. The building with the globe on top supported by four Herculean figures is the former **Tiring department store**, now a decrepit warren of small businesses.

On the north side of Ataba, behind the big white theatre, is the **Ezbekiyya book market (Map 2, #19)** (for more details, see Second-hand Books in the Shopping chapter), and north beyond that Midan Khazindar, where you should take a look in **Sednaoui (Map 2, #18)**, one of Cairo's famous, early-20th-century department stores. Now state-owned and full of tat, the three-storey, glass-atrium interior nevertheless remains glorious.

Ataba to Ramses (Map 8)

Running north from Midan Khazindar, arcing its way over 1.5km up to Midan Ramses, is **Sharia Clot Bey** named for a French physician Antoine Clot who introduced Western ideas of public health into Mohammed Ali's early-19th-century Egypt. By WWI the street had become the heart of the city's red-light district. Known as the Birka, after Wagh al-Birkat, a street running parallel to Clot Bey, it was a quarter of brothels, peep-shows and pornographic cabarets. With Cairo full of Allied troops, no less than seven venereal disease centres had to be set up in the city to deal with the fallout.

These days Clot Bey is a shabby but charming street with stone arcades over the pavements sheltering dozens of sepia-toned coffeehouses and eating places. It has been renamed Sharia Khulud but for most people it's still Clot Bey. At its northern end it connects with Midan Ramses.

MIDAN RAMSES & AROUND (Map 8)

The northern gateway into central Cairo, Midan Ramses is a byword for bedlam. The city's main north-south access collides with flyovers and numerous arterial roads to swamp the square with an unchoreographed slew of minibuses, buses, taxis and cars. Commuters swarm from the minibus ranks while the main train station disgorges carriageloads of passengers, adding to the melee. Hundreds of street vendors take advantage of the pedestrian crush to hawk their shabby goods.

It has been busy here since ancient times when the Nile flowed more over this way and there was a Pharaonic port here. Much later, Salah ad-Din erected an iron gate to the city on this site, which gave the area its name, Bab al-Hadid. The gate came down in 1854 when the railway arrived and the Bab al-Hadid station went up in its place. In 1955 a Pharaonic era **colossus of Ramses II (Map 8, #4)** discovered near Giza was re-erected in front of the station, which henceforth became known as Ramses station (Mahattat Ramses). A colossus still stands, surrounded by multiple lanes of traffic and rendered insignificant by flyovers, but it's not the original, which was wisely removed from all the corrosive pollution, to be replaced by a replica.

The station building comprises an attractive marriage of Islamic styles and industrial-age engineering. At its eastern end it houses the **Egyptian National Railways Museum (Map 8, #1)** (☎ 575 3555, Midan Ramses; Metro: Mubarak; admission E£1.50, Fri & holidays E£3; open 8.30am-1pm Tues-Sun). Egypt had one of the first railways outside Europe. Supervised by Robert Stephenson, son of James Watt, the inventor of the steam machine, work began on the Alexandria-Cairo line in 1852, reaching Cairo in 1856. The museum was inaugurated in 1933. Best exhibit is the Said Pasha Train, a gift from the French empress Eugénie on the occasion of the opening of the Suez Canal in 1869.

On the south side of the midan is Cairo's pre-eminent orientation aid, the **Al-Fath Mosque (Map 8, #8)**. Completed in the early 1990s, the mosque has a toweringly slender minaret visible from just about anywhere in central and Islamic Cairo. Just east of the mosque, where Sharia al-Gomhuriyya joins Ramses, is the ornate **Sabil of Umm Mohammed Ali (Map 8, #9)** built by an Italian architect in 1870. Al-Ahram, Egypt's national newspaper, was founded in this building by a group of Lebanese journalists in the late 19th century.

Sakakini Palace (Map 1, #5)

Count Sakakini Pasha's palace is one of Cairo's greatest architectural follies. It was built in 1897 by a man from humble origins who, legend has it, hit on the path to fame and wealth by exporting a camel caravan of cats to the rat-infested canal then under construction at Suez.

His palace is sited at the junction where eight roads meet, which gives rise to its circular plan. From its base the building rises up like a great rococo wedding cake adorned with frilly buttresses, domes and steeples. The decoration also includes some 300 gargoyles, busts and statues. Unfortunately, after years of service as a rarely visited Museum of Hygiene, the building is woefully neglected and in a terrible state of repair. It's now closed to the public but worth a visit for the exterior alone.

To get to Sakakini take the metro or tram one stop north from Midan Ramses to Ghamra; the palace is about 300m south of the station, visible from Sharia Ramses.

BULAQ (Map 3)

Up until the middle of the 19th century Bulaq was a small port on the banks of the Nile, separated from Cairo by several miles of fields. Before the advent of air travel this was where tourists arrived, brought down by boat from Alexandria. On stepping ashore on 26 November 1849, Florence Nightingale recorded that she needed a servant to keep at bay all the hawkers, a situation still familiar to anyone arriving nowadays at Cairo airport. She writes of then being 'driven up the great valley of acacias from Boulak to the Ezbekeeyah'. The acacias, needless to say, are long gone.

For a time, Bulaq was also the home of the first Egyptian Museum, founded by Auguste Mariette and housed in an old post office building until it outgrew the premises and had to be moved. In 1904 crazed English occultist Aleistar Crowley took an apartment in Bulaq, near the then museum, where he reinvented himself as 'Prince Choia Khan' and claimed to be visited by Satan whose words he transcribed.

These days Bulaq is a sprawling, low-rent district bounded by Sharia Galaa (6th of October Flyover) to the east and the Nile to the west. The major landmark is the **Mosque of Abu al-Ela (Map 3, #75)**, built in 1485 beside the Nile, centuries before the 26th of July Flyover which now passes its door. Directly north of the Mosque of Abu al-Ela (head in beside the orange house with the *mashrabiyya*, or wooden lattice, windows), the alleyways are filled with the **Wikalet al-Balah (Map 3)**, a street market, part of which is devoted to used car spares, part to wholesale cloth and cheap clothing.

At the **Qadi Yahia Mosque (Map 3, #34)** (which dates from 1448), identifiable by its half minaret, take a left and then resume walking north to reach the beautiful **Mosque of Sinan Pasha (Map 3, #35)**. Built in 1571 by Egypt's Ottoman viceroy, the mosque is arcaded on three sides leading

into a small overgrown garden. If the caretaker is around it may be possible to climb the stairs up to the gallery that goes around the inside of the dome to get a better look at the intricate coloured-glass windows.

Over the mosque loom the twin towers of the National Bank. Situated on the Corniche, the bank is part of a scheme to gentrify the Nile-side fringes of Bulaq. Just a little way north is the **World Trade Centre (Map 3, #33)**, which offers office space to international corporations, high finance merchants and the Australian embassy. The lower floors are taken up with an exclusive shopping centre. Next door is the **Conrad International (Map 3, #32)**, one of the newer additions to the city's hotel scene. Guests have unsurpassed views of the slums behind.

GARDEN CITY & MANIAL (Maps 2 & 5)

If you read Olivia Manning's *Levant Trilogy*, a saga of British expat experiences in wartime Cairo, then all life seems to revolve around Garden City. And for many at that time it did. Garden City was Cairo's English suburb. Occupying a plot of agricultural land between two palaces (Qasr al-Ainy to the south, now replaced by a hospital, and Qasr ad-Dubara to the north where the Mogamma now stands), the district was developed in the early years of the 20th century along the lines of an English garden suburb. Its curving tree-lined streets were intended to create an air of tranquility, while the proximity of the **British embassy (Map 2, #125)** no doubt provided a reassuring veneer of security. The embassy, which anchors the north-western corner of the district, originally had grounds that stretched down to the Nile but the lower portion of the lawns was lopped off in the 1950s when Nasser had the riverside Corniche ploughed through.

As well as the embassy, Garden City was home to the headquarters of the British army in Egypt, and was the place where the campaign against Rommel was planned. While many of Garden City's elegant villas have fallen prey to quick-buck developers (including 13 Ibrahim Basha Naguib, wartime

THINGS TO SEE & DO

residence of Olivia Manning) and 21st-century traffic has invaded the narrow avenues, the surviving architecture and the profusion of palm, rubber and mango trees still gives a sense of how things might have been 50 years ago.

Nasser's **Corniche** also makes for a pleasant walk. It's one of the city's main north-south traffic arteries, but with the cars and lorries partially screened from the pavement by trees, and cool breezes coming off the river, it is a popular place for promenading. On the Corniche are the **Semiramis Inter-Continental (Map 2, #106)** and **Helnan Shepheard's (Map 2, #113)**, modern incarnations of hotels that, in their time, were as famous as the London Ritz or Singapore's Raffles, and attracted a similar class of international high society.

Walking south beside the river soon brings you to Manial, the northern end of Rhoda, the southern of Cairo's two inhabited Nile islands. It's separated from the Corniche by just a narrow channel of water, the Sayalit al-Rhoda. It's largely a middle-class residential district, but it's also home to one of Cairo's most eccentric sights, the Manial Palace Museum.

Manial Palace Museum (Map 5, #19)

The palace *(Mathaf Manial; ☎ 368 7495, Sharia al-Saray, Manial; admission E£10; open 9am-4.30pm daily)* was built in the early part of the 20th century as a residence for Prince Mohammed Ali Tawfiq (1875–1955), the uncle of King Farouk. Inside a walled compound are five buildings, all executed in pastiches of Islamic styles of architecture, ranging from Moorish to Persian, and set among luxuriant banyans, palms and rubber trees.

Closest to the gate and ticket office, off to the right as you enter, is the palace mosque, which unsuccessfully marries a Turkish-tiled interior with a crudely done Moorish tower. In even more dubious taste is the nearby Hunting Museum, with a menagerie of shot and stuffed animals including the mounted heads of more than 300 gazelle, all bagged by Farouk and his gun-happy cronies – did they hunt with machine guns? It's no place for animal lovers.

The main palace building, the prince's residence or *haramlek*, has some wonderfully overblown interiors, including a Turkish room covered in Iznik tiles and a Syrian room with an exquisitely painted wooden ceiling. Oriental paintings, ceramics and carpets further decorate the salons. French composer Camille Saint-Saens (1835–1921), perhaps best known for his *Danse Macabre*, was a sometime house guest here and entertained the prince's circle with private recitals. He is said to have composed his Piano Concerto No 5, *The Egyptian*, while in residence.

To the rear of the residence is the prince's own private Throne Hall – compensation perhaps for never attaining the crown of Egypt – complete with red carpet, gilt furniture and the ranked portraits of his illustrious forebears.

Self-appointed guides like to show you around. If you don't want their services, just let them know right from the start. You won't be missing anything.

The easiest way to get here from Midan Tahrir is to head down the Corniche and take the third bridge you come to – it's a very pleasant, 20-minute walk. Alternatively, a taxi from Tahrir (ask simply for Al-Manial) should cost no more than E£3.

QASR AL-AINY (Maps 2 & 5)

Demarcating the eastern side of Garden City, Sharia Qasr al-Ainy (Street of the Palace of the Spring) is the main road running south from Midan Tahrir down to Old Cairo. It takes its name from a former Mamluk palace. During the early 19th century a hospital was established within the palace, visited by French writer Gustave Flaubert and colleague Maxime du Camp in 1850. Dutiful tourists, the pair visited the Pyramids, mosques and bazaars, but much preferred the Cairo brothels and sexual encounters in bathhouses. Flaubert's diary records the trip to the hospital as noteworthy for the 'pretty cases of the pox' they saw displayed. The palace is long gone and in its place is the modern Qasr al-Ainy Hospital.

THINGS TO SEE & DO

There's little of interest along the street, but east of its southern end is the old slaughterhouse district of **Zein al-Abdeen** where there are several good offal restaurants (see Sayyida Zeinab under Restaurants in the Places to Eat chapter); east of its northern end are several government ministries all clustered around the majestically domed **People's Assembly** (Maglis ash-Shab), the Egyptian parliament building. Do not try taking photographs anywhere around here.

A little to the south of the People's Assembly is the **Mausoleum of Saad Zaghloul (Map 2, #128)** *(Sharia Mansour; Metro: Saad Zaghloul; admission free; open 9am-4pm daily)*, resting place of one of Egypt's prime movers for independence during British rule, and a one-time prime minister. His striking mausoleum is fashioned in Pharaonic style with a sculpted cornice and an entrance flanked by two great lotus pillars.

Islamic Cairo

Islamic Cairo is almost another city altogether, distinct from its 20th-century incarnation to the west. Like Alice passing through her looking glass, as the visitor heads east from Downtown's Midan Ataba all the familiar trappings of the modern world drop away to be replaced by chaos and curiosities of a completely different nature.

This is the old medieval metropolis, stretching from the northern walls and gates of Al-Qahira down to Fustat in the south, the site of the first Islamic city (for more information, see History in the Facts about Cairo chapter). Unchanged over the centuries to an astonishing degree, Islamic Cairo's neighbourhoods are full of twisting alleyways so narrow that the houses seem to touch at the top. Splendid mosques and crushes of medieval facades hedge in rutted streets on which little Suzuki vans compete for right of way with donkeys and carts and boys with impossibly laden barrows. The sweet, pungent aromas of turmeric, basil and cumin mix with the odours of livestock

Highlights of Islamic Cairo

It would take weeks, if not months, to thoroughly explore all the districts that together comprise Islamic Cairo. For anyone with slightly less time, here is a rundown of what we consider some of the highlights of this historic district.

- **Beit as-Suhaymi (Page 108)** Slump on floor cushions and languidly admire the incredibly high ceilings and wooden-lattice windows in the reception rooms.
- **Gayer-Anderson Museum (Page 120)** The only fully furnished medieval house in the city, worth visiting to see what one of these places would have looked like when lived in.
- **Haush al-Basha (Page 124)** Cramped burial place of 19th-century royals for whom black was definitely not funerary fashion.
- **Madrassa & Mausoleum of Qalaun (Page 110)** A profusion of gilding and multihued marble adorns one of the most lavishly decorated of Mamluk interiors.
- **Mosque of Qaitbey (Page 122)** The mosque on the E£1 note has to be visited for its exquisitely carved dome – climb up onto the roof for a good look.
- **Mosque-Madrassa of Sultan Hassan (Page 118)** Minimal decoration but simply awesome architecture, especially in the early morning with the sun streaming into the tomb chamber.
- **Northern Gates (Page 107)** Access permitting, look for the carved hippopotamus on a recycled ancient Egyptian stone block at the foot of a short stair on top of Bab al-Futuh.

and petrol. It's a maze-like area that is completely disorienting; the casual visitor easily loses not just any sense of direction but also any sense of time.

The term 'Islamic Cairo' is a bit of a misnomer – the area is no more or less Islamic than any other part of the city, but perhaps the profusion of minarets and domes on the skyline give the impression of piety.

Information

With more than 800 listed monuments and few signposts or other concessions to the visitor, Islamic Cairo can be a fairly daunting place. We've broken it down into nine main sections, each one of which makes for a half-day's outing.

Appropriate dress is necessary for visiting this part of Cairo – legs and shoulders should be decently covered, otherwise custodians may baulk at allowing you inside mosques. Shoes have to be taken off before entering prayer halls, so it might be wise to have footwear that can be easily slipped off and on but is also robust enough for rutted and rubble-strewn alleyways. Since a visiting official Pakistani delegation complained about having to pay money to get into mosques (being Muslims), many admission charges have been dropped. You will, however, be expected to tip guardians and caretakers, so carry lots of small change; E£2 is sufficient.

Also note that any given opening times should be interpreted as a rough guide only; caretakers are usually around from 9am until early evening but they follow their own whims. Most mosques are closed to visitors at prayer times, especially during the noon prayer on Friday.

If this whets your appetite you can find out much more in *Islamic Monuments in Cairo: A Practical Guide* by Caroline Williams or *Historic Cairo: A Walk Through the Islamic City* by Jim Antoniou, both published by the AUC Press. The Society for the Preservation of the Architectural Resources of Egypt (Spare) also puts out four semipictorial maps that are excellent tools for exploration; all are available from most Cairo bookshops.

Getting to Islamic Cairo

Islamic Cairo covers a vast area, but the heart of it is Khan al-Khalili and Al-Azhar, which are easily reached from Downtown. By foot, head for Midan Ataba then bear east along Sharia al-Azhar or Muski. Alternatively, it's a short taxi ride; ask for 'Al-Hussein' – the name of both the midan and the mosque at the mouth of the bazaar. The fare should be no more than E£3.50 from Downtown. Get out at the Al-Azhar mosque where a pedestrian subway burrows under the busy road to surface just off Midan Hussein. Almost all the places we describe in the following pages can be reached from this point.

AL-AZHAR & KHAN AL-KHALILI (Maps 6 & 7)

By far the best place to start becoming acquainted with Islamic Cairo is the area around the great bazaar, Khan al-Khalili. It's a place that panders to preconceptions – this is what everybody always imagines the 'East' to be like. Although most people are in a rush to dive into, or at least dip a tentative foot into, the teeming passageways of the bazaar, there are several major Islamic monuments on the fringes of the bazaar that shouldn't be missed.

Mosque of Al-Azhar (Map 7, #23)

Founded in AD 970 as the centrepiece of newly created Fatimid Cairo, Al-Azhar *(Sharia al-Azhar; admission free; open 24 hr)* is not only one of Cairo's earliest surviving mosques, it's also the world's oldest surviving university. At one time it was the pre-eminent centre of learning, drawing scholars from Europe as well as all over the Arab world. It continues to play a dominant role in Egyptian theological life to this day, with the Sheikh of Al-Azhar being the country's ultimate religious authority. However, students are no longer taught in the mosque's courtyard, they attend one of nine campuses around the country.

Architecturally, it's a mixture of styles, the result of frequent enlargements over its long history. The central courtyard is the earliest part while, from south to north, the three minarets date from the 14th, 15th and 16th centuries – the latter, with its double finial was added by Sultan al-Ghouri, whose mosque and mausoleum complex stands nearby. The tomb chamber, through a doorway on the left just inside the entrance, has a beautiful mihrab (a niche indicating the direction of Mecca) and should not be missed.

Ottoman Houses

Leaving the mosque and turning left and left again brings you into an alley squeezed between the southern wall of Al-Azhar and a row of tiny shops housed within a 15th-century merchants' building. At the top of this alley is **Beit Zeinab al-Khatoun (Map 6, #12)** *(House of Zeinab Khatoun; ☎ 735 7001, Sharia al-Sheikh Mohammed Abdo; admission E£10; open 9am-9pm daily)*, a restored Ottoman-era house that now serves as a cultural centre and sometime exhibition space. Across a small garden is **Beit al-Harrawi (Map 6, #14)** *(Harrawi House; ☎ 735 7001, Sharia al-Sheikh Mohammed Abdo; admission E£10; open 9am-9pm daily)*, another fine piece of 18th-century vernacular architecture, but too sparse inside to really warrant the admission charge – however, it's worth turning up on the first Thursday of every month for the free music recitals (for more details, see under Opera, Music & Dance in the Entertainment chapter). Between the two houses is **Al-Khatoun Gallery (Map 6, #13)** selling an assortment of local crafts – for more details see under Arts & Crafts in the Shopping chapter.

Wikala of Al-Ghouri (Map 7, #21)

Coming left out of Al-Azhar and then turning right, past the fruit and vegetable market, you reach the *wikala (☎ 511 0472, Sharia al-Azhar; admission E£6; open 8am-midnight daily)* or caravanserai, dedicated by Sultan al-Ghouri. Built in 1505 this is an excellent example of what was in essence a medieval motel, warehouse and shopping centre rolled into one. Wikalas provided for the needs of the merchant caravans rolling into Cairo from Africa, Arabia and India. Big rectangular or square buildings, their outwardly blank walls had one

main entrance – wide and tall enough to admit heavily laden camels and horses – that led through to a central courtyard, usually open to the sky and surrounded on four sides by two storeys of small rooms. On the ground floor these would serve as storage bays, stabling, shops and maybe even a coffeehouse, while the upper floor provided accommodation for the merchants.

The building form reached its apogee during the reign of the Mamluks, who had a virtual monopoly on East-West trade. By the time of Al-Ghouri, last of the Mamluks, Cairo's power was waning, but this is a beautiful building, nonetheless, reaching several storeys high and studded with mashrabiyya screens. The former merchants' quarters now serve as artist ateliers, while the courtyard is occasionally put to use as a theatre and concert venue.

Midan Hussein (Map 7)

This was one of the main squares of medieval Cairo, stretching between the two highly venerated mosques of Al-Azhar to the south and Sayyidna al-Hussein to the north. Truncated as it now is by the four lanes of Sharia al-Azhar, it's still an important space, particularly at feast times, on Ramadan evenings, and during the *moulids* (festivals) of Al-Hussein and An-Nabi Mohammed. At such times the midan is filled with vast crowds, bright lights and loud music, and the partying goes on until early morning.

On the northern side, the **Mosque of Sayyidna al-Hussein (Map 7, #3)** is one of the most sacred Islamic sites in Egypt. It contains a shrine under which is reputedly buried the head of Al-Hussein, grandson of the Prophet, brought here in a green silk bag in 1153 (almost 500 years after his death) out of reach of the Crusaders rampaging through Islamic sites in Palestine.

Al-Hussein was killed by the Umayyads who assumed control of the Muslim world after the Prophet Mohammed had died without naming a successor. Ali, the husband of the Prophet's daughter Fatima, challenged their legitimacy, claiming the mantle of successor, or caliph, by marriage. He took up arms against the Umayyads but

THINGS TO SEE & DO

Mahfouz's Cairo

Islamic Cairo is a world unto itself, a crush of narrow zigzag streets packed with activity. It's easy to get lost, easy to lose yourself. One way to experience this world is through the works of Nobel laureate Naguib Mahfouz (for more details on Egypt's best-known author, see Literature under Arts in the Facts about Cairo chapter), pre-eminent chronicler of life in these cramped, close quarters. This walk acts both as an introduction to the alleys and monuments of the old Islamic city, and to the works of its bard.

Mahfouz was born in Gamaliyya in the heart of Islamic Cairo and though his family moved away to the Abbassiyya district before the boy reached his teens, in his writing he never left. Throughout his life, until his failing health prevented it, he would return regularly, haunting the coffeehouses *(ahwas)* of the area. No coffeehouse is more associated with Mahfouz than **Fishawi (1)**, where for much of his life the author would meet with fellow literati in a small interior room. It's a good place to start a walk, perhaps lingering over a mint tea and getting into the mood with the first couple of chapters of one of the author's books.

Leaving Fishawi, walk north to the very end of the alley, turning left and then right to snake northwards before passing under a great tunnel-like arched gateway into **Midan Beit al-Qadi (2)**. This was formerly the garden to a palace belonging to a Mamluk commander under Sultan Qaitbey (who ruled for 28 years from 1468 to 1496). On the south side of the square is a huge five-arched arcade, the partial remains of the palace that during the Ottoman era served as a seat of the governor's court, hence the name of the square, Midan Beit al-Qadi, which means 'Square of the House of the Judge'.

Off the north-east corner of the midan is the short alleyway called **Darb Qirmiz**, which is where Mahfouz was born in 1912. His early childhood here was to provide the images and impressions that informed almost 60 years of writing. This is transparently so in his early novels, such as *Khan al-Khalili* (which is yet to be translated into English) and *Hikayat Haretna* (the title literally means, 'Tales of Our Quarter' but it is published in English as *Fountain and Tomb*), which begins with the narrator as a child telling how much he enjoys playing 'in the small square between the archway and the *takiyya* (monastery)'. But also in his later, more experimental novels, such as *Children of the Alley* and *Harafish*, the whole world is narrowed down to a microcosm of one alley and its inhabitants, with a largely unknown and infinite world beyond it – a world view such as might have been experienced by a child growing up in the security and neighbourliness of early-20th-century Darb al-Qirmiz.

At the top of the alley turn left and head west along Darb at-Tablawi, emerging onto busy **Bein al-Qasreen**. This historic main thoroughfare gives its name to the first volume in Mahfouz's

Mahfouz's Cairo

Cairo Trilogy, which is published in English as *Between the Palaces*. The family of the trilogy's best-known character, the tyrannical Us-Said who dominates his fearful wife and children and has become a part of Egyptian lore, live within sight of the **Sabil-Kuttab of Abdel Katkhuda (3)**, in front of which you should now be standing.

The other two titles in the trilogy are also rooted in local geography: *As-Sukuriyya* (Sugar Street) is down near Bab Zuweila, while *Qasr as-Shuq* (Palace of Desire) is the name of a street just east of Sharia al-Gamaliyya.

After perhaps visiting one or more of the imposing madrassa and mausoleum complexes lining the west side of Bein al-Qasreen, walk due south, passing copper workshops and then the ranks of gold and silver jewellers, across Muski, past a couple of spice vendors and take the next left; just 10m or so along is a tiny stepped alley running up to your left that terminates in three stubby dead ends. This is **Zuqaq al-Midaq (4)**, or Midaq Alley, immortalised by Mahfouz in his book of the same name.

In the book he focuses on the lives of a mixed bunch of people (fictional) who inhabit this small cul-de-sac. It's perhaps his best-known work (and a good one to read if you're new to Mahfouz), teetering on the edge of soap opera, but with such widespread appeal that it was even filmed in Mexican as *El Callejon de los Milagros* (1994) starring Salma Hayek. Such is the alley's fame that the street sign is kept in the coffeehouse at the foot of the steps and is produced only on payment of baksheesh.

From here, you can backtrack to Al-Muizz li-Din Allah; straight ahead you can see Sharia al-Azhar, the best place to flag down a taxi heading back to town.

Alternatively, Fishawi is just five minutes' walk away east along Muski, offering the opportunity of another mint tea and the perfect setting to tackle another few chapters and revisit in print what you've just experienced with your feet.

Sugar Street in Islamic Cairo, made famous through the writings of Mahfouz

was assassinated. His son Al-Hussein then led a revolt, only to be killed at the battle of Kerbala.

This schism between the followers of the Umayyads – known as Sunnis – and the followers of Ali and Al-Hussein – known as Shiites – continues today. Egypt and 90% of the Islamic world are Sunni Muslims; Iran is one of the few Shiite states. Despite being a Shiite martyr, Al-Hussein was a blood relative of the Prophet and as such is regarded as a saint in Egypt.

Because of the importance of the holy head (not on display but buried beneath a cenotaph) non-Muslims are not allowed inside the mosque. The building itself dates only from about 1870 (it replaces an earlier 12th-century mosque) and is not of great interest in itself.

Khan al-Khalili (Map 7)

Jaundiced travellers have been known to glibly dismiss Khan al-Khalili as a tourist trap, and it's true that the tour-bus-pleasing, travellers-cheque-pulling element is well and truly present. But that's just a veneer and the grain of this bazaar, perhaps the Middle East's largest, runs much deeper. Generations of Cairenes have lived their lives in these narrow, canvas-covered alleys, plying their trades, carving, sewing, beating, shaping, engraving, blowing and, of course, buying and selling.

Khan al-Khalili began as a single caravanserai built in 1382 by Garkas al-Khalili, who was Sultan Barquq's master of horses. It was rebuilt by Al-Ghouri some 130-odd years later on a much grander scale but it was Khalili's name, however, that stuck.

Today the Khan is an immense conglomeration of markets and shops. Within the labyrinth of squeezed shop fronts you'll find everything from glassware, leather goods and brasswork to books of magic spells and prayer beads as well as, of course, plenty of stuffed camels and alabaster pyramids. The clumsy 'Hey mister, look for free' touts aside, the merchants of Khan al-Khalili are some of the greatest salespeople and smooth talkers you will ever meet. Almost anything can be bought

in the Khan, and if one merchant doesn't have what you're looking for, then he'll find somebody who does. For the complete rundown on shopping in the bazaar, see the special section 'Shopping Khan al-Khalili' in the Shopping chapter.

Shopping aside there are few specific things to see in the Khan. Several huge, carved **stone gates** survive in the part of the bazaar called the Badestan, which date from the era of Al-Ghouri, and there's **Fishawi (Map 7, #10)**, Cairo's most famous coffeehouse. Hung with huge, ornately framed mirrors and packed day and night for the last 200 years, entertainment at Fishawi comes in the form of roaming salespeople, women and children who hawk wallets, cigarette lighters in the form of pistols, canes with carved tops, *sheesha* (water pipe)-style cigarette holders, and packet after packet of tissues. It's easily found; it fills a narrow alleyway with rickety tables and chairs just one block in off Midan Hussein.

Muski (Map 6)

A congested market street that runs parallel to Sharia al-Azhar from Midan Hussein all the way to Midan Ataba on the edge of Downtown, Muski is less overtly 'Oriental' than Khan al-Khalili but all the more vivid and boisterous for it. The goods on sale range from plastic furniture and party toys on a little midan 200m beyond the Barsbey mosque junction, to items such as wedding dresses and great mounds of bucket-sized bras at the western end.

The chants of the hawkers are fun, often sung to popular tunes, and many shops have their young male staff and friends stand outside hollering discounted prices at the press of shoppers struggling by.

To walk from Ataba to Hussein, or vice versa, takes about 20 to 30 minutes depending on how ruthless you are with your elbows.

NORTH OF KHAN AL-KHALILI (Map 6)

From Midan Hussein take the road that leads up along the western side of Sayyidna al-Hussein mosque. Stick to it as it dog-legs left and enters the district known as Gama-liyya. Sharia al-Gamaliyya, the main street you are following, was the second most important of medieval Cairo's thoroughfares. Today, it has the appearance of a back alley, rutted and unsealed, barely squeezing between the buildings. These buildings include some fine clusters of Mamluk-era mosques and madrassas, though many of them are partly obscured by forests of crude wooden scaffolding, there to shore up damage from the 1992 earthquake. Tragically, one of the district's most impressive monuments, the Musafirkhanah Palace, survived the earthquake only to be burnt to the ground in 1998.

Easily identified by its blindingly white new stone, the **Mosque of Gamal ad-Din (Map 6, #8)** *(Sharia al-Tombakshiyya, Gamaliyya; admission E£10; open 9am-7pm daily)* is one of the monuments that has been subject to the dubious attentions of the restorers (for more details on the conservation project, see the boxed text 'Fatimidland' later in this chapter). It's raised above a row of shops, the rent from which would have paid for the mosque's upkeep.

Next door is the **Wikala of Bazara (Map 6, #7)** *(Sharia al-Tombakshiyya, Gamaliyya; admission E£10; open 9am-7pm daily)*. Until very recently the building lay in ruins but in recent years it has been almost completely rebuilt from scratch, opening to the public in early 2001. While undoubtedly attractive, there's little to see beyond a succession of small, empty rooms. The place cries out to be put to use. A boutique hotel perhaps? Unfortunately, but somewhat predictably, rumour is that it will become another 'cultural centre', similar to the underused Wikala of Al-Ghouri, Beit al-Harrawi, Beit Sennari…

The Northern Walls & Gates (Map 6)

The square-towered **Bab an-Nasr** (Gate of Victory) and the rounded **Bab al-Futuh** (Gate of Conquests) were built in 1087 as the two main northern entrances to the walled Fatimid city of Al-Qahira. Walk along the outside and you'll see what a hugely imposing bit of military architecture they form – though the defences were never put to the test as Cairo was never besieged.

Until recently visitors could access the top of the walls and explore inside the gates via the roof of the neighbouring Mosque of Al-Hakim, but on our last visit this was no longer the case. Perhaps once restoration work in the vicinity has finished the walls may be open again and you can look for the inscriptions above the doorways which read 'Tour Lascalle' and 'Tour Milhaud', evidence that Napoleon's troops of occupation were once garrisoned here. You'll also be able to find the carved animals and Pharaonic figures adorning the inner passages, evidence that stone for Al-Qahira's fortifications was scavenged from the ruins of the ancient Egyptian city of Memphis.

Mosque of Al-Hakim (Map 6, #1)

One of Cairo's older mosques, this place is as notable for its founder as its architecture. Al-Hakim was only 11 years old when his father died and he became the third Fatimid ruler of Egypt. His tutor nicknamed him 'Little Lizard' because of his frightening looks and behaviour. Hakim later got his revenge by having the tutor murdered. During his 24-year reign those nearest to him went in constant fear of their lives. A victorious general who rushed unannounced into the royal apartments was confronted by a bloodied Hakim standing over a disembowelled page boy. For his impetuosity, the general was beheaded.

Hakim took a great interest in the affairs of his people and would patrol the city's streets on a donkey called Moon. He received petitions and complaints from the city folk and punished dishonest merchants by having them sodomised by a large black servant who accompanied him for this purpose. His death was as bizarre as his life. On one of his solitary nocturnal jaunts on Moon up onto the Muqattam Hills, Hakim disappeared and his body was never found. To one of his followers, a man called Al-Darizy, this was proof of Hakim's divine nature. Al-Darizy travelled widely preaching, and founded the sect of the Druze which continues to this day.

Completed in 1010, Hakim's mosque has rarely been used as a place of worship, instead it was used as a prison to hold Crusaders, as a stable, as a warehouse by Napoleon, and Nasser made it into a boys' school. Most fittingly of all, it also served for a time as a madhouse.

In 1980, in exchange for a large donation made to the Egyptian antiquities people, the mosque was handed over to the Bohras, an Ismaili Shiite sect from India. Their treatment of the mosque – adding chandeliers and other fixtures that are out of keeping with local traditions – has outraged purists.

Sharia al-Muizz li-Din Allah (Map 6)

Al-Muizz li-Din (as it's often shortened to), which takes its name from the Fatimid caliph who conquered Cairo in AD 969, is the former grand thoroughfare, or Qasaba, of medieval Cairo. It runs from Bab al-Futuh, one of the two northern gates, down to Bab Zuweila, the remaining southern gate. Despite the best part of a thousand years in service as the city's main axis, Al-Muizz li-Din today remains narrow to the point where the attempted passage of one car can cause untold chaos and pedestrian congestion.

As late as the mid-19th century, the portion of Al-Muizz li-Din outside Al-Hakim's mosque was a slave market; these days, when they're in season, it's a garlic and onion market with sacks of the two piled high on the pavements.

As you head south, the produce gives way to a variety of small places selling the metalworked accoutrements for coffeehouses and *fuul* vendors – sheeshas, braziers and big, pear-shaped cooking pots. On the right, after about 200m, is the **Mosque of Suleyman Silahdar (Map 6, #3)**, built comparatively late in 1839 during the reign of Mohammed Ali and distinguished by its drainpipe-thin minaret. Reflecting the ruler's wider aims of grafting European ideas onto those of traditional Egypt, the mosque mixes a Mamluk-style facade with rococo and baroque forms.

Over the street from the mosque is a 19th-century house occupying a corner site; turn left here onto Sharia Darb al-Asfar and walk along to No 19, Beit as-Suhaymi.

Beit as-Suhaymi (Map 6, #4)

Tucked down a small whitewashed alley off Al-Muizz li-Din Allah, Beit as-Suhaymi *(Suhaymi House; 19 Darb al-Asfar; admission E£20; open 8am-8pm daily)* is Islamic Cairo's finest example of the traditional family mansion built throughout the city from Mamluk times to the 19th century. The house presents a typically blank facade to the street but once through the tunnel-like entrance you emerge into a beautiful inner courtyard. Guests were received in an impressive *qa'a,* or reception room, left off the courtyard, graced with a polychrome marble fountain inset in the floor and a high, painted wooden ceiling. Upstairs are the family quarters, with the wooden-lattice windows known as mashrabiyya, which allowed the women to observe the goings on below without being seen themselves. The rooms are kept cool by devices called *malqaf*, angled wind-catchers on the roof that direct the prevailing northerly breezes down into the building. The admission fee may seem a little steep but if you only shell out for one Islamic monument, then this should be it.

Mosque of Al-Aqmar (Map 6, #5)

Back on Sharia Al-Muizz li-Din, just 50m south of the junction with Darb al-Asfar, is this petite mosque, the name of which means 'the Moonlit'. Built in 1125 by one of the last Fatimid caliphs, it's important in terms of Cairo's architectural development because it's distinguished by being the oldest stone-facaded mosque in Egypt. Here, for the first time, appear several features that were to become part of the mosque builders' essential vocabulary: the stalactite carving, for instance, and the ribbing in the hooded arch. Note that at the time it was built the mosque was at street level.

Sabil-Kuttab of Abdel Katkhuda (Map 6, #6)

A *sabil* is a fountain or tap from which passers-by can take a drink; a *kuttab* is a

Fatimidland

Unesco, the cultural wing of the United Nations, includes Islamic Cairo on its select World Heritage list, which also includes tourist hot spots such as the Pyramids, the Great Wall of China and Venice. But, the shopping bazaar area of Khan al-Khalili aside, Islamic Cairo is an area that sees relatively few visitors. Why? Because unlike historic districts elsewhere in the world, which have been preserved, sterilised and pickled, existing seemingly to provide sales opportunities for fast-food outlets, Islamic Cairo has in the past made few concessions to the visitor. It could hardly do so given that it's home to a dense 21st-century population still living in what are essentially medieval quarters. As a consequence, Islamic Cairo retains a vital human presence that lifts it above being more than a mere open-air museum.

Recently, however, the attentions of Egypt's Ministry of Culture have turned to this neglected area. At the time of writing no less than 60 conservation projects are being carried out in the core of the medieval city, an area now officially designated 'Fatimid Cairo' by authorities worried that the word 'Islamic' (as in Islamic Cairo) might frighten away the tour buses. Results of the work can most clearly be seen around Beit as-Suhaymi, where the surrounding buildings and alley now positively gleam. If all goes to plan, the 21st-century version of Islamic Cairo, sorry, Fatimid Cairo, should see record numbers of visitors flocking to its streets. But it's a scheme not without controversy.

For a start, the actual treatment of the monuments has been criticised as extreme, particularly in instances like the work on the northern walls, which aren't so much being restored as rebuilt from scratch. There's also the question of reintegration; previously restored structures have remained empty and unused, quickly sliding back into disrepair. Ultimately, there is the worry that the upgrading, refacing and repackaging may result in the removal of the people and activities that give character to the area. In fact, just such a plan to relocate 50,000 residents elsewhere has already been unveiled. Should this go ahead, critics say, the authorities might be advised to consider a further rebranding, not Fatimid Cairo but 'Fatimidland', a more suitable name for what sounds suspiciously like the process of turning a living neighbourhood into a theme park.

Quranic school. So, a *sabil-kuttab* provides the two things commended by the Prophet: water for the thirsty and spiritual enlightenment for the ignorant. The building of a sabil-kuttab was a popular way for wealthy people to atone for their sins. This particular example, imposingly placed at a point where Al-Muizz li-Din forks, was built in 1744 by a Mamluk *emir* (lord) well known for his debauched behaviour. It has some nice ceramic work inside and it's worth finding the caretaker who has the key. He sits in the **Qasr Beshtak (Map 6, #9)** (*Beshtak Palace*), which is found down the little alley that runs to the east (the one with the orange seller on the corner), and right through the archway at the bottom. The ticket for the sabil-kuttab is E£6, which also gets you admission to the palace – largely ruined but with splendid rooftop views from the top floor.

Bein al-Qasreen (Map 6)

The part of Al-Muizz li-Din immediately south of the sabil-kuttab is known as Bein al-Qasreen, which translates as 'Between the Palaces', a reference to two great royal complexes that flanked the street here during the Fatimid era (969–1171). The palaces fell into ruin following the fall of the Fatimids but Bein al-Qasreen remained a great public space, a thriving marketplace filled with entertainers and stalls serving food, off which ran dozens of alleys containing more specialised markets wholly devoted to knives, books or candles. As such, the area remained a favourite building place for subsequent rulers whose monuments rose out of the rubble of the former palaces. Today, three great abutting Mamluk complexes line the west of the street, providing one of Cairo's most impressive assemblies of minarets, domes and towering facades.

Madrassa & Mausoleum of Barquq

(Map 6, #10) Barquq seized power in 1382 as Egypt was reeling from plague and famine. His great monument was completed four years later. Although often not noticeably different from a mosque from the outside, this is a madrassa, or theological school. A bold, black-and-white marble entrance opens to a vaulted passageway leading to a main courtyard with four wooden doors with elaborate bronze decoration. Behind these are four separate sets of classrooms and student cells, one for study in each of the four main schools of Islamic law. Most impressive of all is the mausoleum, off the prayer hall, which is like a precious jewellery box with walls of polychrome marble panelling beneath a gilded dome supported by four Pharaonic columns made of red porphyry. Within the cenotaph lies Barquq's daughter, while the sultan himself was interred in the Northern Cemetery – see that section later in this chapter.

Mausoleum of An-Nasir Mohammed

(Map 6, #11) Abutting Barquq's complex is this lower, more modest mausoleum belonging to a sultan who was twice deposed but who regained the throne on each occasion to string together a reign that totalled some 42 years. In this time he endowed Cairo with over 200 buildings, the best known of which is his mosque at the Citadel. This monument on Bein al-Qasreen is fronted by a finely detailed Gothic doorway, removed from a church in Acre (now Akko in Israel) after An-Nasir and his Mamluk army winkled out the Crusaders in 1290. It also possesses some beautifully intricate, North African–styled stuccowork on the minaret. But behind the facade very little survives, just a ghost of a building.

Madrassa & Mausoleum of Qalaun

(Map 7, #1) The southernmost (and earliest) of the three great Bein al-Qasreen complexes, Sultan Qalaun's is the most splendid. A massive fortress of a place, it has echoes of the grand European cathedrals, explained perhaps by the involvement of some 300 Christian Crusader prisoners in its construction. Chroniclers record that it was built in just 13 months, and that to achieve this feat the sultan's soldiers forced hapless passers-by to join the labour gangs. The city's religious authorities were so outraged that they at first declared prayer here unlawful. However, such is the magnificence of Qalaun's legacy that his ill-deeds are forgotten and he is praised as one of the greatest Mamluks of all – which was undoubtedly his intention in the first place.

Entry is through an imposing bronze door. Inside, a long, dark corridor separates the madrassa, on the left, from the mausoleum, on the right. The latter is a highlight, and one of the most stunning spaces in all Cairo. With a plan inspired by Jerusalem's Dome of the Rock, it has an octagonal arrangement of columns, two pairs of which are enormous granite affairs that originated in some Pharaonic structure. The walls are covered in marble panels spelling out the name of Mohammed, and gold is everywhere, glinting in coloured rays of sunlight filtered through countless stained-glass windows.

Qalaun's complex also included a *maristan*, or hospital, which according to the Moroccan traveller and historian Ibn Battuta, visiting Cairo in 1325, contained 'an innumerable quantity of appliances and medicaments'. If such historical accounts are to be believed then the hospital treated up to 4000 patients a day in its prime. Incredibly, an eye clinic still occupies a part of the site, maintaining an unbroken tradition of more than 700 years of medical care.

Madrassa & Mausoleum of As-Salih Ayyub

(Map 7, #2) Opposite Qalaun is a protruding sabil-kuttab which belongs to a complex founded by the last sultan of Salah ad-Din's Ayyubid dynasty.

As-Salih Ayyub died before his complex was finished, so it was completed (in 1250) by his wife, Shagaret ad-Durr, who seized power for herself to become one of Egypt's few female rulers – for more details, see the Mausoleum of Shagaret ad-Durr under Ibn Tulun to Sayyida Zeinab later in this chapter.

Back to Town

Want to buy a minaret top? South of As-Salih Ayyub's complex the monuments give way to a ramshackle string of shops filled with pots and pans and crescent-shaped finials, which is why this area is popularly known as Souq an-Nahaseen or the Coppersmiths' Street. After a short stretch, copper gives way to gold signifying that you have re-entered the precincts of Khan al-Khalili. At the junction with Muski, beside the two mosques, left leads to Midan Hussein, and right leads to Midan Ataba and Downtown (a 20- to 30-minute walk away). Straight ahead is Sharia al-Azhar, the best place to find a taxi, and a footbridge providing a thin link between the bisected parts of Al-Muizz li-Din Allah.

AL-AZHAR TO THE CITADEL (Map 6)

South of Sharia al-Azhar, Al-Muizz li-Din continues as a busy market street running down to the twin-minareted gate of Bab Zuweila. It's a leisurely 15-minute walk. From the gate there are then two possible routes to the Citadel – east along Darb al-Ahmar or south through the Street of the Tentmakers (Sharia al-Khayamiyya). Either way it takes about another 20 minutes of uninterrupted walking to reach the Citadel.

Al-Ghouriyya (Map 7)

The grand pair of black-and-white buildings (dating from 1505) facing each other across the market street on the south side of Sharia al-Azhar form an exquisite monument to the end of the Mamluk era. Qansuh al-Ghouri, the penultimate Mamluk sultan, ruled for 16 years, before, at the age of 78, riding out at the head of his army to do battle with the Ottoman Turks in Syria.

The Mamluks were trounced, and soon after the Ottomans began their 281-year rule of Egypt. The head of the defeated Al-Ghouri was sent to Constantinople; his body was never recovered and his Cairo mausoleum instead contains the body of Tumanbey, his short-lived successor, who was captured by the Turks and hanged at Bab Zuweila.

The building to the west, with its red-chequered chimney-pot minaret, is the mosque-madrassa (Map 7, #19) while to the east is the mausoleum (Map 7, #20) with its missing dome, which collapsed in 1860. Two rooms of the mausoleum now serve as a cultural centre and theatre where twice-weekly performances of Sufi dancing are held – for more details, see under Opera, Music & Dance in the Entertainment chapter. At other times the mausoleum may be closed, but the mosque is generally open to visitors and it's possible to ascend to the roof and climb the minaret.

Gamal al-Ghitani's excellent novel *Zayni Barakat* is set during the last days of Al-Ghouri. The Ghouriyya is portrayed as it was in 1839 in an often-reproduced lithograph by Scottish artist David Roberts entitled *The Silk Market*, which shows a wooden canopy between the two buildings forming a covered market.

Carpets, Hats & Lizards

The passageways behind Al-Ghouriyya (slip down the side) are filled with rug and carpet sellers, although their wares are no longer made of silk as in Roberts' day, but of wool or synthetics. Back on the main market street, south of Al-Ghouriyya, clothes mix with household goods and cloth. On the right, just 50m down, are two of Cairo's last tarboosh (fez) makers (Map 6, #16). You can watch them shaping the hats on their heavy brass presses. Once worn by every respectable *effendi* (gentleman), the tarbooshes are mainly bought now by hotels and tourist restaurants. They sell for E£5 to E£30. Further along, on the opposite side of the street, is a herbalist (Map 6, #15) whose shop front is hung with bunches of dried hedgehogs and lizards, and a small wizened alligator too, and stacked with jars of pods and twigs. All this stuff is used in the preparation of healing compounds. Quite how, we've no idea.

Mosque of Al-Muayyad (Map 6, #18)

Al-Muayyad was a great intriguer, for which he was arrested and thrown into a

THINGS TO SEE & DO

lice-infested prison that stood on this site. While incarcerated he vowed that if he were to survive his ordeal he would replace the prison with a 'saintly place'. On coming to power he did just that; Al-Muayyad's mosque was completed in 1422.

The entrance leads into the mausoleum where Al-Muayyad and his son lie in two cenotaphs. Beyond is the mosque itself, an extremely tranquil place with the prayer hall opening on to a large tree-filled garden courtyard. In the far corner of the prayer hall is a small door leading to the mosque's two minarets which sit on top of Bab Zuweila (added 330 years after the gate was built, how on earth did the master masons know that the gate could take the extra weight?). The view from the top of the minarets is about the best in Cairo, offering a panorama of rooftops used as chicken runs, goat pens, pigeon lofts, rubbish dumps and even workshops. Note that the caretaker will probably insist on baksheesh to open the door up to the minarets.

Bab Zuweila (Map 6)
Built at the same time as the northern gates, Bab Zuweila is the only remaining southern gate of the old medieval city of Al-Qahira. Until the late 19th century it was still closed each evening. The area in front of the gate

was one of the main public gathering places in Mamluk times. It was also the site of executions, which were a highly popular form of street theatre. A particularly vicious bunch, the Mamluks used to execute victims by publicly sawing them in half or crucifying them on the great gates. The last Mamluk sultan, Tumanbey, was spared this indignity. He was sentenced to be hanged from the gate's vaulted ceiling; however, it took three attempts to kill him as the rope snapped the first two times. After the massacre of Mamluks at the Citadel (see the boxed text 'The Massacre of the Mamluks' later in this chapter) the heads of the 500 slain were exhibited in front of the gate on spikes.

The gate gained a slightly better reputation in the 19th century when it became associated with Metwalli, a local saint who lived nearby. People in need of healing or divine intercession would leave a lock of hair or piece of clothing nailed to the gate in the hope of attracting his attention. It's a practice continued to this day – look carefully and you will see fresh nails hammered into the great wooden doors.

Around Bab Zuweila
Just inside the gate, opposite the towering walls of the mosque, is the tiny **Sabil-Kuttab of Nafisa al-Beida (Map 6, #20)**, an

City of the Thousand and One Nights

Ever since the first English and French translations appeared in the 19th century, the tales contained in *The Thousand and One Nights* (in Arabic, Alf Layla wa Layla) have influenced the way in which the West imagines the East. Cairo has a strong claim to being the home of these fantastical tales. Although Sheherezade and her nightly stories have their origins in pre-Islamic Persia, successive storytellers over the ages have added new exploits, relocated the action and generally reshaped the material to suit their audience. In the version passed down to this day, the adventures, enchantments and lowlife goings-on described in *The Thousand and One Nights* take place in the semi-fabled Baghdad of Harun ar-Rashid and in the Cairo of the Mamluks.

Anyone reading one of the more comprehensive editions of *The Thousand and One Nights* can locate the action for themselves, as the authors have provided a wealth of topographical detail. We're told that Marouf the Cobbler, who features in a cycle of tales, lives on Darb al-Ahmar, and there are numerous mentions of places like Bab Zuweila and Bein al-Qasreen, along with descriptions of the things that go on there. And if the physical sites are still there to be seen, you only have to fall into conversation with a local to learn that even in this day there's no shortage of hidden treasures, wicked robbers and evil djinn. In Islamic Cairo the Thousand and One Nights are far from being at an end.

The old medieval metropolis of Islamic Cairo contains an astonishing wealth of Islamic architecture. Highlights include the splendid Mosque of Ibn Tulun (top left), the intricate detailing in the Mosque of Ar-Rifai (top right) and a skyline of towering minarets and bulbous domes (middle right & bottom).

SARA-JANE CLELAND

CHRISTOPHER WOOD

SARA-JANE CLELAND

SUNA KANGA

Unlike some historic districts elsewhere in the world, Islamic Cairo is not merely an open-air museum, it's home to a dense population; while tourists mingle outside the Mosque of Mohammed Ali in the Citadel (bottom right), the streets are full of people going about their daily lives.

ornate, rounded kiosk of a structure dating from 1796, recently restored by a Polish team. The intention was that it should serve as an information centre for the historic old city, but as yet it remains unoccupied.

Outside the gate are several other minor Islamic monuments, including the free-standing **Mosque of Salih Talai (Map 6, #21)** (1160), built over a lower storey of shops whose rent paid for the mosque's upkeep. Over the centuries the ground has risen and today the shops are 3m below street level. This caused problems with flooding (rising ground water is a big problem in Islamic Cairo), but after many years of work by the American Research Centre the building seems to have been made safe and the mosque is once again back in use; the former shops, while vacant, are at least accessible.

To the Museum of Islamic Art & Downtown (Map 6)

Sharia Ahmed Mahir, which runs west from Bab Zuweila, is lined with shops selling striped cotton and canvas, and tin-plate workshops turning out ducting, funnels, scuttles and cages. In the run-up to Ramadan they also make *fanous*, the special ornate lanterns that are hung in most streets and households for the month of fasting. Ramadan is a great time to wander down here because the whole street is lit up like a fairy grotto. The street finishes at Midan Bab al-Khalq, also known as Midan Ahmed Mahir, with the Museum of Islamic Art (see that section later in this chapter) just across the road. Downtown is a further 20 minutes' walk west past the museum.

Street of the Tentmakers (Map 6)

This is Cairo's only remaining medieval covered market, built in 1650 by Radwan Bey, the commander in charge of the annual pilgrimage to Mecca. It takes its name (in Arabic, Sharia al-Khayamiyya) from the artisans who traditionally worked here producing the brightly printed fabrics once used to adorn caravans but nowadays used to form the ceremonial tents that are set up for funerals, wakes, weddings and feasts. There's also a lot of applique work done

here in the form of wall panels, cushion coverings and so on (see also Arts & Crafts in the Shopping chapter).

Continuing south beyond the covered market, Sharia al-Khayamiyya runs for about a kilometre before intercepting Sharia Mohammed Ali; a left turn from this point will take you to the great mosque of Sultan Hassan and to the Citadel. There's an alternative and more interesting route if you backtrack from the Tentmakers' market and follow Darb al-Ahmar.

Darb al-Ahmar (Map 6)

This district, which takes its name from its main street, Darb al-Ahmar or the 'Red Road', was the heart of 14th- and 15th-century Cairo. During these centuries Cairo had a population of about a quarter of a million, most of whom lived outside the city walls in tightly packed residential districts like this where over half the narrow and twisting streets ended in cul-de-sacs. As the walled inner city of Al-Qahira was completely built up, patrons of new mosques, grand palaces and religious institutions were forced to build outside the city gates and most of the structures around here date from the late Mamluk era.

Mosque of Qijmas al-Ishaqi (Map 6, #22) Qijmas was master of the sultan's horses and took charge of the annual pilgrimage to Mecca. His mosque, completed in 1481, is one of the finest examples of architecture from the late Mamluk period. The plain exterior of the building is quite deceptive, as inside there are beautiful, stained-glass windows, inlaid-marble floors and stucco walls. The floor in the eastern *iwan* (vaulted hall) is particularly fine. It's usually covered by prayer mats, but ask the caretaker to lift them. Note that, as at the Salih Talai mosque, there are workshops sunk below street level, and in this case they're still in use.

Mosque of Al-Maridani (Map 6, #23) Built in 1339, this mosque is one of the oldest buildings in the area. Several styles of architecture were used in its construction:

eight granite columns were taken from a Pharaonic monument; the arches were made from Roman, Christian and Islamic designs; and the Ottomans added a fountain and wooden housing. There are several other decorative details inside. The lack of visitors, the trees in the courtyard and the attractive mashrabiyya screening make it a peaceful place to rest for a while.

Back on Darb al-Ahmar, known as Sharia at-Tabana at this point, across from the mosque is a small **carpet-weaving workshop (Map 6, #24)**. As it's open to the street, you can see the great wooden loom inside on which they weave rag rugs from colourful off-cuts. They weave to specification: choose your colour and name the size. It's about E£8 for an item 1m by 1.5m. A little further on, where the road splits, is a small, friendly open-air **coffeehouse (Map 6, #25)**. It's a good place to take a break with an iced *limoon* (lemon juice).

Blue Mosque (Map 6, #27) Properly known as the Mosque of Aqsunqur, this building gets its more popular name from the combination of blue-grey marble on the exterior and the flowery tiling on the interior. The tiles, imported from Syria, were added in 1652 by a Turkish governor, Ibrahim Agha, but the original and much plainer structure dates from 1347. The minaret affords an excellent view of the Citadel, while over to the east, just behind the mosque, you can see the remains of Salah ad-Din's city walls, now largely covered with rubbish and the detritus of collapsed buildings.

From this mosque it's about another 400m up the slightly inclining street to the Citadel.

THE CITADEL (Map 6)

Sprawling over a limestone spur on the eastern edge of the city, the Citadel *(Al-Qalaa; ☎ 512 1735, Sharia Salah Salem; admission E£20; open 8am-5pm daily Oct-May, 8am-6pm daily June-Sept, museums open 8.30am-4.30pm daily)* was home to Egypt's rulers for some 700 years. Their legacy is a collection of three very different mosques, several palaces housing some fairly indifferent mu-

seums, and some impressive fortifications offering superb panoramas of the city.

Salah ad-Din began building the Citadel in 1176 to fortify the city against the threat of the Crusaders, who were rampaging through Palestine. His son Al-Kamil subsequently strengthened the fortifications by enlarging some of the existing towers and adding new ones. Following the overthrow of Salah ad-Din's Ayyubid dynasty, the Mamluks took over the Citadel, adding sumptuous palaces and harems, and extending the walls south to embrace a royal polo field and a stockade where 2000 cattle were kept.

Under the Ottomans (1517–1798) the fortress was extended westwards and a new main gate, the Bab al-Azab, was added, but the Mamluk palaces were allowed to deteriorate. Even so, when Napoleon's French expedition took control of the Citadel in 1798, the emperor's scholars regarded these buildings as some of the finest Islamic monuments in Cairo. Sadly, that didn't stop Mohammed Ali, who rose to power when the French left, from demolishing them. The only Mamluk structure left standing was one mosque, which was used as a stable. He completely remodelled the rest of the Citadel and crowned it with the Turkish-style mosque that currently dominates Cairo's eastern skyline.

After Mohammed Ali's grandson and heir Ismail moved the royal household out of the Citadel (to the new Abdeen Palace), it was used as a military garrison. The British army was barracked here in WWII to be replaced by Egyptian soldiers after 1952. The soldiers still have a small foothold, but the Citadel has now almost entirely been given over to the tourists.

Anyone interested in knowing more should pick up William Lyster's locally published *The Citadel: A Guide* or a map called *The Citadel to Ibn Tulun* published by Spare; both are widely available in Cairo's bookshops.

The Citadel is divided into the Lower, Southern and Northern Enclosures. Entrance is either from the midan below the Citadel, in which case walk up the hill with the walls on your right and loop around to the Bab

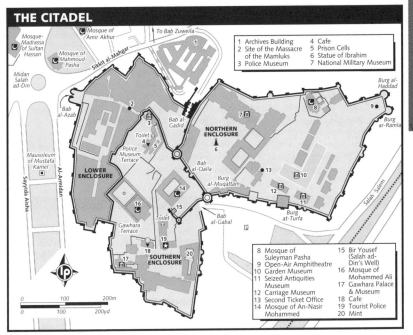

THE CITADEL

Mosque-Madrassa of Sultan Hassan
Mosque of Mahmoud Pasha
Mosque of Amir Akhur
To Bab Zuweila
Sikkit al-Mahgar
Midan Salah ad-Din
Bab al-Azab
Toilet
Police Museum Terrace
Mausoleum of Mustafa Kamel
Al-Amidan
Sayyida Aisha
LOWER ENCLOSURE
Bab al-Gadid
Bab al-Qalla
Burg al-Muqattam
NORTHERN ENCLOSURE
Bab al-Gabal
Gawhara Terrace
Toilet
SOUTHERN ENCLOSURE
Tourist Police
Burg al-Haddad
Burg ar-Ramla
Burg at-Turfa
Salah Salem

1 Archives Building
2 Site of the Massacre of the Mamluks
3 Police Museum
4 Cafe
5 Prison Cells
6 Statue of Ibrahim
7 National Military Museum

8 Mosque of Suleyman Pasha
9 Open-Air Amphitheatre
10 Garden Museum
11 Seized Antiquities Museum
12 Carriage Museum
13 Second Ticket Office
14 Mosque of An-Nasir Mohammed
15 Bir Yousef (Salah ad-Din's Well)
16 Mosque of Mohammed Ali
17 Gawhara Palace & Museum
18 Cafe
19 Tourist Police
20 Mint

0 100 200m
0 100 200yd

al-Gadid (New Gate), or from the car park at the back, which is where taxis drop off.

Lower Enclosure
The lowest part of the Citadel complex, this area has long been closed to the public. No great loss really, as it contains very little of historical interest, mostly just old, badly dilapidated warehouses and vast empty storage sheds. In recent years there have been proposals to turn the area into a shopping mall with attached hotel, but there's no sign of anything happening.

Southern Enclosure
This is the main tourist area, presided over by the **Mosque of Mohammed Ali**. Modelled along Turkish lines, it took 18 years to build (1830–48) and then the domes had to be demolished and rebuilt. It's a building that has never found much favour with those who have written about Cairo, variously described as unimaginative, lacking in grace

and resembling a great toad. In 1873 Amelia Edwards, author of *A Thousand Miles up the Nile*, noted that the interior was carpeted and 'hung with innumerable cut-glass chandeliers so that it looks like a huge vulgar dining room from which the furniture has been cleared out for dancing'. Oblivious to the criticism, the mosque's patron Mohammed Ali lies in the marble tomb on the right as you enter.

Note the chintzy clock in the central courtyard, a gift from King Louis-Philippe of France (in thanks for the obelisk that adorns the Place de la Concorde in Paris), damaged on delivery and never yet repaired.

Dwarfed by the ungainly bulk of Mohammed Ali's mosque, the **Mosque of An-Nasir Mohammed** (1318) is the Citadel's sole surviving Mamluk structure. The interior is a little sparse because the Ottoman sultan Selim I had it stripped of decoration, but the twisted finials of the minarets are interesting in that they are covered with glazed tiles,

The Massacre of the Mamluks

In addition to effacing almost all of the Mamluk structures from the Citadel, Mohammed Ali also had a damn good try at effacing the Mamluks themselves.

On 1 March 1811 he invited 500 Mamluk leaders to attend a grand day of feasting and revelry at the Citadel in honour of his son's imminent departure for Mecca. When the feasting was over, the Mamluks mounted their lavishly decorated horses and were led in procession down a narrow, high-sided, rocky defile towards the Bab al-Azab. But as they approached, the great gates swung closed before them. Gunfire rained down from above. After the scything fusillades, Mohammed Ali's soldiers waded in with swords and axes to finish the job. Not one Mamluk escaped alive. The Citadel, according to one contemporary account, looked like a slaughterhouse.

A popular legend beloved of tour guides has it that one Mamluk survived by jumping his horse over the Citadel walls, fabulously depicted in a painting by Henri Regnault, which now hangs in the Manial Palace. In fact the character in question saved his life by not turning up for the feast that bloody day.

---

something rarely seen in Egyptian mosques. The artisan responsible was from Tabriz (now in north-western Iran) which attests to the close commercial links between Persia and Mamluk Egypt.

Facing the entrance of the An-Nasir Mohammed mosque is a mock Gothic gateway leading out onto a **terrace** that has superb views across Islamic Cairo to the tower blocks of Downtown and, on a clear day, the Pyramids at Giza. At the northern end of this terrace the small building housing the **Police Museum** sits on the foundations of the Mamluk 'Lions Tower', evidence of which survives in a couple of carved lions at the base of the steps. Before entering the museum, if you look down on the Lower Enclosure, you are above the narrow road where the infamous massacre of the Mamluks took place. Inside, the museum has an intriguing Assassination Room, with text and photos telling the stories of the shooting of the British commander in chief of the Egyptian army Sir Lee Stack and the attempt on President Nasser's life. Curiously, the somewhat more successful assassination of Sadat fails to get a mention. In fact, Sadat's assassin was one of the last prisoners to be incarcerated in the alley of small cells that now also forms part of the museum.

South of Mohammed Ali's mosque is another terrace with good views and, off it, the **Gawhara Palace & Museum**. The Gawhara

(or Jewel) was where Mohammed Ali resided and received guests, and its rooms have been reconstructed and filled with costumed dummies in a lacklustre attempt to evoke 19th-century court life.

Northern Enclosure

Entry to the Northern Enclosure is through the 16th-century Bab al-Qalla, which faces the side of the An-Nasir Mohammed mosque. This brings you through to a large area of lawn which, at its centre, contains a replica of the equestrian statue of Ibrahim that stands in Midan Opera. Beyond the statue and the motley assortment of tanks and planes remaindered from the Arab-Israeli wars is Mohammed Ali's one-time Harem Palace, now the **National Military Museum**. It's largely devoted to displays of ceremonial garb, but on the top floor is an excellent scale model of the Citadel.

East of the lawns a hidden narrow road leads to another part of the enclosure where you'll find a further couple of half-hearted collections. The **Carriage Museum** contains several 19th-century, horse-drawn carriages which might occupy 10 minutes of your time, while next door is the pointless **Seized Antiquities Museum** (signposted in Arabic only) with a random and unconnected assortment of sarcophagi, jewellery, icons and other antiquities confiscated from would-be smugglers.

Cairo from High

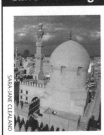

SARA-JANE CLELAND

The obvious vantage point for panoramic city views is the top of the Cairo Tower (see under Gezira later in this chapter), but there are other options, which we have listed below.

Minarets
Many of the minarets attached to Islamic Cairo's mosques can be climbed, especially if you grease your way up with a little baksheesh; try at the Mosque of Ibn Tulun (left), Al-Ghouriyya, Bab Zuweila, the Blue Mosque and, in the Northern Cemetery, the Mosque of Qaitbey and the Khanqah-Mausoleum of Ibn Barquq.

Citadel Terraces
From these ramparts on the eastern edge of the city it's possible to see right over the city to its western edge, signalled by the distinctive punctuation of the Pyramids.

Windows on the World
Take in blazing sunsets while sipping a Stella at the 36th-floor bar at the Ramses Hilton, but beware the dress code restrictions and the minimum charge, which may deter some (see under Bars in the Entertainment chapter for more details).

Fontana Roof Bar
Not quite in the same league as Windows on the World, but this mid-range hotel has a rooftop bar (see the Mid-Range section of the Places to Stay chapter) overlooking the madness of Midan Ramses – you can wear what you like and there's no minimum charge.

The Virginian
This terrace bar is tucked away high on the Muqattam Hills and a pain to get to but worth it at night for the cool evening breezes and the swirling lights of the city laid out below (see under Bars in the Entertainment chapter for more details).

Admirers of Islamic architecture might find more joy at the **Mosque of Suleyman Pasha** (1528), an elegant little Ottoman-era structure topped by a cluster of domes. It has a beautiful interior with painted woodwork lovingly restored during the 1990s by a local art student.

From a point just behind the mosque it may still be possible to get up onto the wall ramparts and walk east towards the **Burg al-Haddad** (Blacksmith's Tower). If the way is now blocked, walk across the rather pointless – and completely hideous – concrete 'amphitheatre' towards the tower and its companion, the **Burg ar-Ramla** (Sand Tower). These are two of Salah ad-Din's towers that were subsequently enlarged by his son Al-Kamil; they can be entered at ground level. Although it is not officially permitted, it is still physically possible to walk either through the walls or along the ramparts right around to the large, square **Burg at-Turfa** (Masterpiece Tower).

Getting to/from the Citadel
It is a good 3km walk from Downtown to the Citadel. From Midan Ataba go straight down Sharia Mohammed Ali, while from Midan Tahrir the best route is via Midan Falaki to Midan Bab al-Khalq and then down Mohammed Ali. Bus No 174 from Midan Ramses passes through Midan Salah ad-Din in front of the Citadel as does bus No 173 which starts and terminates at Midan Falaki.

AROUND THE CITADEL (Map 6)

One of the most disappointing aspects of the Citadel is that its grand main gate, the catamaran-styled Bab al-Azab, is out of use, locked for decades. When it was built, the gate fronted onto the Qara Midan (Black Square), the hippodrome, a great parade and polo ground, where the Mamluks used to show off their renowned horseback skills. That former parade ground is now a large traffic island (Midan Salah ad-Din). On its west side, facing the Citadel, are two enormous mosques, Sultan Hassan and Ar-Rifai, while on the north side are two more modest places – the little mosque with the typically Turkish pencil minaret is the Ottoman **Mosque of Mahmoud Pasha (Map 6, #35)** (1567); beyond it, north of the grassy area, on a sloping site is the **Mosque of Amir Akhur (Map 6, #34)** (1503), a building of the late Mamluk era. Its facade is enlivened by the banding of different coloured stones, a technique typical of the era and known as *ablaq*. Like Al-Ghouri's minaret at Al-Azhar, with which Amir Akhur's mosque is contemporary, it also has a double finial.

Directly behind, down the little alley beside the mosque, is an **18th-century house (Map 6, #33)**, lived in by the internationally renowned architect, Hassan Fathy. He died in the early 1990s and ever since there has been talk of turning the house into a memorial to his life and work, but nothing has happened to date.

Mosque-Madrassa of Sultan Hassan (Map 6, #31)

Equal in scale to the great Gothic cathedrals of Western Europe, Sultan Hassan's hulking creation *(Midan Salah ad-Din; admission E£12; open 8am-5pm daily Oct-May, 8am-6pm daily June to Sept)* is regarded as the finest piece of early Mamluk architecture in Cairo. Hassan became sultan in 1347, at the age of 13. He was deposed four years later in favour of an even younger brother, but was restored to power in 1354. Work on his mosque began two years later. The site was a prestigious one, overlooking the hippodrome at the foot of the royal Citadel. Such a colossal project was expensive, but the population of Cairo had recently been decimated by the Black Death, and the properties and wealth of those who died intestate were used to bolster the royal treasury. Even so, the construction of the mosque nearly bankrupted the state. It continued for seven years, which proved to be too long for Hassan, who was assassinated in 1362.

Tragedy clung to the mosque. While under construction a minaret collapsed and reportedly killed 300 onlookers. Once finished, its monumental scale and location opposite the Citadel proved a liability. During the frequent Mamluk skirmishes in pursuit of power it was used as a fortress, with soldiers on its roof firing catapults at the sultan in his palaces in the Citadel. The battering continued right up until the 19th century when Napoleon turned his cannons on the mosque while quelling one of the frequent popular uprisings that took place against his occupation of the city. The facades still bear the scars. Battle damage might also be the reason why one of the minarets toppled in 1659 and, for safety's sake, was replaced by a structure of a much more modest height.

Possibly the single most impressive element of the mosque is the soaring, sunken entrance portal, the highest in Cairo. Once inside, a dark bent passageway leads to the sudden brightness and humbling dimensions of the main courtyard. It has a central fountain for washing before prayers, and four large iwans, where the Quran would have been taught. The many long hanging chains once held decorated glass lamps, which now can be seen at the nearby Museum of Islamic Art.

At the rear of the eastern iwan is an especially beautiful mihrab flanked by scavenged Crusader columns; to the right is the bronze door which leads through to the sultan's mausoleum.

Mosque of Ar-Rifai (Map 6, #32)

Built on a similarly immense scale to neighbouring Sultan Hassan, this mosque *(Midan Salah ad-Din; admission E£12; open 8am-5pm daily Oct-May, 8am-6pm daily June-*

Sept) appears to be a close sibling, but, in fact, more than 600 years in age separates the two. The dowager princess Khushyar, mother of Khedive Ismail, had the mosque begun in 1869, although it wasn't completed until 1912. It was intended to serve as a tomb for herself and other members of Egypt's royal family. Ismail and King Farouk are buried here, as is the Shah of Iran. The Shah sought asylum in Egypt in 1979 and, after his death in 1980, his casket was paraded through the streets of Cairo from the Abdeen Palace to the mosque with his family, President Sadat and Richard Nixon leading the cortege.

The Mamluk-inspired motifs that decorate the interior were designed by European architect Max Herz who also designed the Museum of Islamic Art and the Shar Hashamaim Synagogue in Downtown. Baksheesh is required to view the tombs of the royals, which lie off to the left of the entrance.

Madrassa of Sunqur Sadi (Map 6, #30)

Also known locally as Hassan Sadaqa (after a local sheikh), this is a rather decrepit old monument (dating from 1321) that has some wonderful carved stucco decorating its minaret and dome. In the 19th century, an order of Mevlevi dervishes (better known as whirling dervishes in the West) extended the madrassa to include a hostel and theatre in which to perform their *zikr* – the dancing, chanting and swaying carried out to achieve oneness with God. Although the madrassa is in a terrible state, the **Dervish Theatre** with its circular, polished-wood stage has been beautifully restored by an Italian team of conservators. There's also a pleasant garden with benches. To get access to the theatre and garden look for the green door just to the right of the madrassa's facade and ring the bell.

The madrassa is on Sharia Suyufiyya; from the back of Sultan Hassan walk north along Sharia Mohammed Ali and take the first left, then left again at the T-junction.

Sharia Saliba (Map 6)

The Citadel has always contained a jail or two, but as you can't have emaciated inmates upsetting the tourists, these days the prison is outside the walls in the triangular white building on the south-west corner of Midan Salah ad-Din. It's necessary to pass by the row of barred windows to enter Sharia Saliba which (under the name Abdel Meguid) runs up to Midan Sayyida Zeinab, passing another of Cairo's must-see monuments, the Mosque of Ibn Tulun, on the way.

Just past the prison, on the left, is the 15th-century **Sabil-Kuttab of Qaitbey (Map 6, #36)**, closed to the public but notable for the intricate inlaid-marble decoration on its western facade. A short distance further the street passes between the twin sentinels of the **Mosque of Sheikhu (Map 6, #37)** (right) and the **Khanqah of Sheikhu (Map 6, #39)** (left), both dating from the mid-14th century. Despite being in bad shape both are still in use.

Beyond the Sheikhu complex Saliba intersects with Sharia Suyufiyya; turning right will take you up to the Madrassa of Sunqur Sadi (see earlier) and then on to Sharia Mohammed Ali, while continuing straight along Saliba brings you after a further 200m to the Mosque of Ibn Tulun.

IBN TULUN TO SAYYIDA ZEINAB (Maps 5 & 6)

About a kilometre or so west of the Citadel, Ibn Tulun's mosque is one of the city's oldest and most splendid – although whether it remains so after the current round of renovations remains to be seen. It can be visited by walking from the Citadel or by taking the metro to Sayyida Zeinab and heading for Midan Sayyida Zeinab, up Port Said (Bur Said) and taking a left down Sharia Qadry, a walk in all of about 20 to 25 minutes.

Mosque of Ibn Tulun (Map 5, #16)

Ibn Tulun was sent to rule Cairo in the 9th century by the Abbasid caliph of Baghdad. He had the mosque *(Sharia Ibn Tulun; admission E£6; open 8am-5pm daily Oct-May, 8am-6pm daily June-Sept)* that bears his name built between AD 876 and 879, making it one of the city's oldest intact functioning Islamic monuments. It's quite unlike any other mosque in Cairo mainly because the inspiration is almost entirely Iraqi, especially the highly distinctive spiralling minaret. The closest thing to it are found at the ancient mosques of Samarra.

To the original Iraqi model, Ibn Tulun added some innovations of his own. According to architectural historians this is the first structure to use the pointed arch – a good 200 years before Christianity adopted it for the European Gothic arch. Constructed entirely of mud-brick and timber, the mosque covers about 2.5 hectares in area, large enough for the whole community to assemble for Friday prayers. Although the mosque is still in use, these days the congregation is much more modest and is usually accommodated in just the southeastern arcaded sanctuary.

After wandering around the massive courtyard, you should climb the spiral minaret reached from the outer, moat-like courtyard. Although originally created to keep the secular city at a distance, this outer courtyard was for centuries filled with shops and stalls. The top of the minaret is the best place to appreciate the grandeur and geometric simplicity of the mosque, and the views of the Citadel to the east and of Cairo in general are magnificent.

Gayer-Anderson Museum (Map 6, #41)

This museum (*Beit al-Kretliyya;* ☎ *364 7822, Sharia Ibn Tulun; admission E£16; open 8am-4pm Sat-Thur, 8am-noon & 1pm-4pm Fri*) is almost an annexe of the Ibn Tulun mosque, reached via its outer court through a gateway to the south of the main entrance. The museum is actually two 16th-century houses joined together. It takes its name from a British major, John Gayer-Anderson, who restored and furnished the houses between 1935 and 1942 and filled them with antiquities, artworks and Oriental artefacts that he acquired on his travels in the region. But the real attraction is the adjoined houses themselves, their puzzle of rooms and the decor. There's a Persian room with exquisite tiling and a Damascus room with its walls and ceiling patterned with lacquer and gold. There's also an en-

chanting mashrabiyya gallery that looks down upon a magnificent *qa'a*, or reception room, with a central marble fountain, decorated ceiling beams and carpet-covered alcoves. It is a complete Orientalist fantasy, and as such provided an excellent setting for sequences in the James Bond movie *The Spy Who Loved Me*.

There are some great legends connected with the house, particularly concerning the well around which it was built (it's still there under an arch in the far right-hand side of the courtyard). This well is said to give access to the underground palaces of Sultan al-Watawit, ruler of the bats and king of the djinn. This and other tales are recounted in the beautifully illustrated *Legends of the Beit Kretliyya*, published by the AUC Press.

On leaving Ibn Tulun and the Gayer-Anderson, immediately across the street is the **Khan Misr Touloun (Map 6, #40)**, a good handicrafts emporium – see under Arts & Crafts in the Shopping chapter for more information.

Mausoleum of Shagaret ad-Durr (Map 6, #42)

Shagaret ad-Durr (Tree of Pearls) was a slave of Turkish origin who managed, albeit briefly, to become the only female Muslim sovereign in Egyptian history. Her husband Salih Ayyub, the last ruler of the Ayyubid dynasty, died of cancer while the Frankish soldiers of the 7th Crusade were occupying Damietta in the Nile Delta, making ready to move on Cairo. Ayyub's son was off fighting in Iraq, and so in order to preserve the throne for him Shagaret ad-Durr hid his father's corpse and for three months managed to pretend that Ayyub was still alive and passing on orders to his generals through her. Unfortunately, the plan was scuppered when the son returned home to receive his inheritance only to be immediately assassinated by a rival. Shagaret ad-Durr herself then assumed the throne.

To forestall Islamic prejudice against the idea of a woman ruler, she married her Mamluk lover Aybek, the leader of her slave warriors, and ruled through him. Looking for a way to strengthen his own position, her husband decided on a strategic second marriage to the daughter of a powerful Syrian. Shagaret ad-Durr put an end to that by having him murdered in his bath. She offered to marry the new chief Mamluk but, probably wisely, he had her imprisoned instead. The son of Aybek by a former marriage became the next sultan and, as a suitable punishment, he handed Shagaret ad-Durr over to his mother who had her beaten to death with wooden bath-clogs. Her bloody corpse was thrown over the Citadel walls as food for the dogs and what they left was collected up and entombed in this small single-domed mausoleum that Shagaret ad-Durr had built for herself during her brief 80-day reign.

Neglected and surrounded by garbage, the tomb is permanently locked, but if the care-taker is around with the key you might be able to gain access and admire the Byzantine glass mosaics gracing its prayer niche.

Sayyida Zeinab (Map 5)

The district of Sayyida Zeinab (St Zeinab), centred on the midan of the same name, commemorates the sister of the Prophet's grandson Hussein who, legend has it, was with him at the battle of Kerbala when he fell (for more details, see under Midan Hussein earlier in this chapter). She's buried in the **Mosque of Sayyida Zeinab (Map 5, #10)** which in its present incarnation dates from 1885. Non-Muslims are not allowed inside.

On the north side of the midan, across from the Sayyida Zeinab mosque, is the gar-ish **Sabil of Sultan Mustafa (Map 5, #9)**, an Ottoman-era public drinking fountain that makes much use of coloured marble. If you take the side street squeezed down the west side of this building, you pass a good late-night kebab place, **Abu Rifai (Map 5, #8)**; turn left here and follow the street around to the right, then take another right through an arch, which brings you to **Beit as-Sennari (Map 5, #7)**. This 18th-century house was one of two requisitioned by Napoleon in 1798 for his Institut de l'Egypte, an aca-demic centre employing 167 scientists, scholars and artists brought to make the first European study of Egypt, which was later published as the *Description de l'Egypte*. At the time of writing, the house was under-going restoration (under the direction of a French team), but by now it should have re-opened as an arts and crafts centre.

NORTHERN CEMETERY (Map 6)

The Northern Cemetery is one half of a vast necropolis inhabited by hundreds of thou-sands of Cairenes, both dead and alive, hence its popular name, the City of the Dead.

It began as an area of desert outside the city walls which offered the Mamluk sultans and emirs the unlimited building space

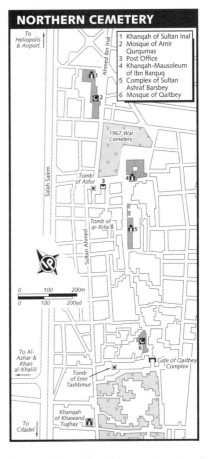

NORTHERN CEMETERY

1	Khanqah of Sultan Inal
2	Mosque of Amir Qurqumas
3	Post Office
4	Khanqah-Mausoleum of Ibn Barquq
5	Complex of Sultan Ashraf Barsbey
6	Mosque of Qaitbey

To Heliopolis & Airport

Ahmed Ibn Inal

1967 War Cemetery

Salah Salem

Tomb of Asfur 3

4

Tomb of ar-Rifai 5

Sultan Ahmed

0   100   200m
0   100   200yd

To Al-Azhar & Khan al-Khalili

6

Gate of Qaitbey Complex

Tomb of Emir Tashtimur

Khanqah of Khawand Tughay

To Citadel

denied them in the already densely packed city. The vast mausoleum complexes they built were more than just tombs, they were also meant as places for entertaining. This is part of an Egyptian tradition which has its roots in Pharaonic times: holiday picnicking among the graves. Even the humblest of family tombs were designed to include a room where visitors could stay overnight. Naturally, the city's homeless took to squatting in the tombs. This phenomenon has been going on since the 14th-century, leading to the situation today where the living and dead coexist comfortably side by side. In some tomb-houses cenotaphs serve as tables and washing is strung between headstones. The municipality has run in water, gas and electricity, and there's a local police station and even a post office. On Fridays and holidays visitors flock here to picnic and pay their respects to the dead.

The easiest way to get to the Northern Cemetery is to walk east along Sharia al-Azhar from the Khan al-Khalili area. As you breast the top of the hill bear right,

Rubbish to Roses

En route to the Northern Cemetery from Al-Azhar the road climbs sharply. No natural phenomena cause this, the road is simply hiccupping over an enormous mound of centuries of accumulated rubbish that has long divided Islamic Cairo from its burial grounds. As part of the scheme to renovate the old medieval city (see the boxed text 'Fatimidland' earlier in this chapter), a part of this great heap – just to the south of the road – is being landscaped into a park. To be known as the Al-Azhar Park, it will be planted in a manner reminiscent of traditional Islamic gardens with a lake, trees, flowerbeds and a very non-traditional 2km running track. In addition there's to be a chichi restaurant, with a design inspired by Fatimid architecture, and a lakeside cafeteria. Work was definitely progressing when we last passed by, with the project scheduled to be completed by the end of 2002. Sounds worth a look if you're in the area.

under the overpass and straight on along the dusty road between the tombs. Follow this road to the left then right. You'll pass by a large crumbling domed tomb off to your left and then about 100m beyond a narrow lane goes off to the left passing under a stone archway. This stone archway is the gate to the former compound of Qaitbey whose splendid mosque is immediately ahead.

Mosque of Qaitbey

Sultan Qaitbey was the last Mamluk leader with any real power in Egypt. He ruled for 28 years (1468–96) and during this time, trade with European mercantile states, such as Venice, Genoa and Catalonia, was at its peak. From the proceeds of exorbitant taxes the sultan completed some of the most impressive buildings, including a sabil-kuttab near the Citadel, a harbourside fortress at Alexandria, and this mosque, arguably the most perfect of all Cairo's Islamic buildings.

The interior has four iwans around a central court suffused with light from large, lattice-screened windows. An adjacent tomb chamber contains the cenotaphs of Qaitbey and his two sisters, as well as two stones that supposedly bear the footprints of the Prophet. The true glory, however, is above, in the interlaced star-and-floral carving adorning the stone dome, which in its intricacy and delicacy was never surpassed in this city or anywhere else in the Islamic world. Climb the minaret for the best view.

From Qaitbey cross the square and continue north. The cemetery has an almost village-like feel with small shops and street sellers, and sandy paths pecked by chickens and nosed around by goats. After about 250m the street widens out and on the left a stone wall encloses a large area of rubble-strewn ground that was formerly the Complex of Sultan Ashraf Barsbey.

Complex of Sultan Ashraf Barsbey

The Complex of Sultan Ashraf Barsbey originally combined a *khanqah* (Sufi monastery), two sabils, two *zawiyas* (schools) and a hostel. The hostel is the long, partially built facade in front of the Khanqah of Barsbey, the only remaining

complete structure, which was finished in 1432. Though not as sophisticated as the one topping Qaitbey, the dome on the khanqah is carved with a beautiful star pattern. Inside, there is some fine marble flooring and a beautiful minbar (pulpit) inlaid with ivory. Look for the guard or have one of the children in the area find him; he'll let you in for baksheesh.

The two small mausoleums to the north of the khanqah are put to excellent use as goalposts by the local boys.

Khanqah-Mausoleum of Ibn Barquq

Ibn means 'son of', and this is the mausoleum of Farag, son of Barquq, the sultan whose great madrassa and mausoleum stands on Bein al-Qasreen at the heart of Islamic Cairo. His tomb is the small mausoleum standing alone in the garden. The khanqah is an imposing, fortress-like building with high sheer facades, and twin minarets and domes. If you go through into the interior courtyard you can see the small monastic cells off the arcades. There's a tomb chamber under each dome, one for the women, one for the men. Both ceilings have been repainted in recent years and look great. It's also possible to get up onto the roof and climb the minarets. The area of surrounding greenery is a cemetery for some of the many Egyptians killed in the 1967 Arab-Israeli war.

Back to Hussein

North of Ibn Barquq are two large adjacent complexes, the **Mosque of Amir Qurqumas** (1507) and the **Khanqah of Sultan Inal** (1456). Both are undergoing extensive restoration work by a Polish team and are currently closed to the public.

Rather than just retracing your steps, to get back to Hussein from Ibn Barquq, walk straight ahead from the entrance of the khanqah-mausoleum, passing the post office on your left, until you come to a small, elongated mausoleum; turn left immediately after this and a walk of a straight kilometre will bring you back to the road leading to the underpass.

SOUTHERN CEMETERY (MAP 1)

The Northern and Southern Cemeteries are separate entities which developed at different times and are divided by the rocky outcrop on which the Citadel is built. The Southern Cemetery is the older of the two, with its beginnings in the Fatimid era – a time before the grand tradition of funerary architecture had taken hold. It's also less accessible and doesn't contain as much to see. Neither does it possess the almost rural charm that makes the Northern Cemetery such a pleasure to explore. However, if you have the time, it is worth taking the trouble to visit the Mausoleum of Imam ash-Shafi, one of Cairo's most venerated shrines. If you visit on a Friday morning, the fringes of the Southern Cemetery are host to a sprawling animal and bric-a-brac market, the Souq al-Gamaa – see under Souqs & Markets in the Shopping chapter for more details.

Mausoleum of Imam ash-Shafi (Map 1, #11)

This is the resting place of Imam ash-Shafi, a descendant of an uncle of the Prophet, and the founder of the Shafiite sect, one of the four major schools of Sunni Islam. Regarded as one of the great Muslim saints, he died in AD 820. In the 12th century, Salah ad-Din founded the first mausoleum on the site of the Imam's grave. The complex has been added to over the centuries – the neighbouring mosque dates from 1891 – but the teak cenotaph in the tomb is original. Around this cenotaph visiting pilgrims circumambulate, while tearful black-robed women are often pressed against the lattice screen whispering implorations to the long-dead sheikh.

Non-Muslims are permitted to enter (men and women through separate doorways) and while there is no admission fee, baksheesh will be requested.

The mausoleum is 2km south of Midan Salah ad-Din. To get there, walk south along Sharia Sayyida Aisha to Salah Salem. Across the junction a dusty road continues and almost immediately forks – take the right-hand branch and the mausoleum is about 1km further on, easily identifiable by its domed lead roof, topped by a small copper boat.

Haush al-Basha (Map 1, #12)

Right behind Imam ash-Shafi is this modest tomb complex *(Southern Cemetery; admission E£10; open 9am-6pm daily)*, constructed by Mohammed Ali in 1820 as his family mausoleum, although he had himself buried in his mosque at the Citadel. From outside it's drab, dull and seriously dilapidated but inside it's a riot. 'All the tombs of Mohammed Ali's family are in deplorable taste – rococo, Canova, Europo-Oriental, appointed and festooned like cabarets, with little ballroom chandeliers', wrote Gustave Flaubert visiting in December 1849. The chandeliers are gone, but the ceilings are still painted like circus tents, while the cenotaphs still look as though they've been decorated by kids in time for Christmas.

To get to the Haush al-Basha take the first left after leaving the Imam ash-Shafi compound and then left again at the junction and it's 50m ahead on the left.

Aqueduct of An-Nasir Mohammed (Map 5)

Running alongside Salah Salem, the six-lane highway that sweeps down behind the Citadel and brushes the edge of the Southern Cemetery, is this impressive stone construction. Built between the 12th and 16th centuries to supply water to the Citadel, it stretches for a length of 5km. Unused for centuries, and buried to half its height, the aqueduct is still largely intact and, in fact, the Supreme Council of Antiquities has recently earmarked E£40 million for its restoration.

MUSEUM OF ISLAMIC ART (Map 2, #121)

Overshadowed by the Pharaonic crowd-pulling power of the Egyptian Museum, this museum *(☎ 390 9930, Sharia Port Said; Metro: Mohammed Naguib; admission E£16; open 8am-4pm daily)*, which has one of the world's finest collections of Islamic applied art, receives undeservedly few visitors. It's hindered by an out-of-the-way location and a complete lack of publicity. Neither does the museum do itself any favours. As in the Egyptian Museum the labelling leaves a lot to be desired – 'Statue

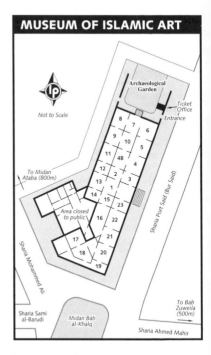

in the shape of a lion painted blue' reads the printed card beside a statue of a lion painted blue. We recommend that you spend some time walking around Islamic Cairo and visit one or two mosques before coming here to help supply the missing context.

Historically, the interpretation of a Quranic injunction against the representation of Allah led Muslims to reject figurative forms and instead develop exceptional skills in floral, geometric and epigraphic forms, applying fantastic patterning to wood, glass, metal, stone, textiles, ceramics, bone and paper, all of which are represented here.

Entry is through the garden door off Sharia Port Said. This brings you into the central hall containing some of the most beautiful exhibits. The collection is arranged by type with only the loosest attempts at imposing any chronology, so it does not matter in which sequence the rooms are visited. We suggest you immediately bear

Cairo's (Lesser) Museum Highlights

Obviously, there's the Egyptian Museum, which cannot be missed, along with the Islamic and Coptic Museums, which together make up the trinity of compulsory, look-and-learn cultural storehouses. In years to come, these are set to be joined by a new antiquities museum planned for Giza (see the boxed text 'The Biggest Museum in the World' in The Pyramids & Memphis Necropolis chapter), a museum of Egyptian civilisation at Fustat and a museum devoted to diva Umm Kolthum on Rhoda, all of which are on the drawing board. But in the meantime the city has literally dozens of other lesser collections, many of them worth a visit if only for their curiosity value. We particularly used to enjoy the Museum of Hygiene with its terrifying models of decaying dentures. That's gone but plenty remains to entertain, amuse – even revolt – if not educate. Following are a few highlights.

- **Abdeen Palace Museum (Page 92)** Daggers, swords, pistols and muskets, medals and decorations, royal silverware and ceramics are on display but all pales before the presidential set of gold-plated machine guns.
- **Agricultural Museum (Page 137)** Unfortunately, some of the more enticing galleries – such as the onion and garlic rooms – are closed but among the wax fruit and veg displays are oddities such as a mummified bull and giant fibreglass strawberries.
- **Egyptian National Railways Museum (Page 98)** Not just a place for trainspotters, this place has some sleek models of 1930s cutting-edge station architecture, ace 1930s travel posters, and a royal locomotive that's more *Thomas the Tank Engine* than *Flying Scotsman*.
- **Entomological Society Museum (Page 97)** Pinned bugs and stuffed birds are displayed but the museum itself is the real period-piece, and deserves to be encased in perspex and preserved whole for posterity.
- **Helwan Wax Museum (Page 144)** A wax museum in Egypt with no air-conditioning? The great figures of Egyptian history wilt and slump, while Nasser with arms outstretched leading his people looks like a refugee from *Night of the Living Dead*. Excellent.
- **Manial Palace Museum (Page 100)** Those easily outraged might want to avoid this museum with its portraits coloured with butterfly wings, an elephant's foot stool, a hermaphroditic goat and an astounding testament to excess in the form of the mounted heads of more than 300 gazelles.
- **Police Museum (Page 116)** Unfortunately presented in Arabic only, but there's a display in here devoted to Egypt's most infamous criminals, Alexandrian sisters Raya and Sakina, tried and hanged in 1921 for the murders of 17 young women.

right, ignoring for now the exhibits in the main hall. Rooms 8 and 9 contain woodwork, including some nice coffered ceilings. Room 11 contains metalwork and Room 12 contains Mamluk weaponry. Room 13 is for 'masterpieces', which include a great door that originally belonged to the Sayyida Zeinab mosque. Beyond are Rooms 14 to 16 which are given over to ceramics. There is no tradition of glazed tile making in Egypt so most of what's on display here comes from Persia (modern-day Iran). The cone-topped fireplace in Room 16, however, is from Anatolia (now central Turkey).

Walk through Rooms 21 (glass) and 20 (Ottoman era) to Room 19, which contains a small collection of illuminated manuscripts and ornate Qurans formerly owned by King Farouk. Now make your way back to Rooms 4 and 4B which are divided by a row of carved Mamluk columns. The museum's centrepiece is in 4B: an Ottoman fountain combined with beautiful mashrabiyya and a carved wooden ceiling. There's another, more elaborate sunken fountain in Room 5 dating from the time of the Mamluks.

The upstairs rooms containing textiles and carpets from Iran and Central Asia were closed for renovations on our last visit – as they have been for several years now.

Getting There & Away

The museum is about a 10-minute walk from Midan Ataba, straight down Sharia Mohammed Ali. Midan Tahrir is 1.5km west along Sharia Sami al-Barudi (passing the Mohammed Naguib metro station en route). Alternatively, a taxi to/from Downtown should cost no more than E£3.50.

Old Cairo

Broadly speaking, Old Cairo **(Map 5)** *(Masr al-Qadima)* incorporates the whole area on the east bank of the Nile south of Garden City and Sayyida Zeinab down to the quarter known to foreigners as Coptic Cairo. Most people visiting this area head straight to the latter, from where it is possible to explore sights further to the north-east, such as the Mosque of Amr ibn al-As and the archaeological site of ancient Fustat. The early-Islamic-era Nilometer on the island of Rhoda is also best visited from Coptic Cairo.

This is a very traditional part of Cairo and appropriate dress is essential. Visitors of either sex wearing shorts or having bare shoulders will not be allowed into churches or mosques.

Getting There & Away

By far the easiest way of getting to Old Cairo is by metro: the Mar Girgis metro station is right outside the Coptic compound. The ride costs 50pt from Midan Tahrir (Sadat station) and takes around 15 minutes. There are also buses running between Tahrir and Old Cairo, but they are incredibly crowded. However, the bus trip back to Tahrir isn't as bad, as you can get on at the terminal, beside the Amr ibn al-As mosque, before the bus has had a chance to fill up.

Slower but far more pleasant is the river bus. These depart central Cairo from the Maspero terminal in front of the TV & Radio building, just north of the Ramses Hilton. Check that it's going to Masr al-Qadima as not all do. The ride takes about

50 minutes and costs 50pt. The last boat back to Maspero leaves at 4.15pm. From the landing at Old Cairo, cross the Corniche and head down the street with the Marlboro-emblazoned shop on the corner; at the end of the street turn left and walk straight along Athar an-Nabi for about 250m until you come to the footbridge over the metro line.

COPTIC CAIRO

Coptic Cairo is the heartland of Egypt's Christian community, as well as being the oldest part of present-day Cairo. Seemingly oblivious to the growth and chaos which it has spawned, the tightly walled enclave remains a haven of tranquillity and peace. Well, not quite; at present the entire site is undergoing massive reconstruction with a USAID-funded project assisting the government's efforts to halt damage from rising groundwater. This project is scheduled for completion in early 2002 but until then many of the monuments are in complete disarray.

Archaeologists believe that there was a small Nile-side settlement on this site in the 6th century BC around which the Romans later established a fortress, called Babylon-in-Egypt, early in the 2nd century AD. The same archaeologists speculate that the name Babylon is most likely a Roman corruption of 'Per-hapi-en-on' (Estate of the Nile God at On), a Pharaonic name for what was the former port for On (ancient Heliopolis).

Predating the arrival of Islam in Egypt, Babylon has always been a stronghold of its precursor, Christianity. At one time there were more than 20 churches clustered within less than a square kilometre, although the number is down to only five today. The area also has strong Jewish traditions, and the country's oldest existing synagogue is found here.

There are two main entrances to the Coptic Cairo compound: one, a sunken staircase beside the pedestrian bridge over the metro, gives access to most churches and the synagogue, while the other, the main entrance, is for visiting the Coptic Museum and the Hanging Church. Eventually, when ongoing restoration works are finished, the two parts of the compound will be reconnected.

COPTIC CAIRO

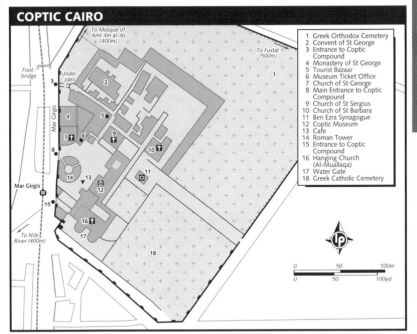

To Mosque of
Amr ibn al-As
(400m)

To Fustat
(500m)

Foot-
bridge

Under-
pass

Mar Girgis

Mar Girgis

To Nile
River (400m)

1 Greek Orthodox Cemetery
2 Convent of St George
3 Entrance to Coptic
   Compound
4 Monastery of St George
5 Tourist Bazaar
6 Museum Ticket Office
7 Church of St George
8 Main Entrance to Coptic
   Compound
9 Church of St Sergius
10 Church of St Barbara
11 Ben Ezra Synagogue
12 Coptic Museum
13 Cafe
14 Roman Tower
15 Entrance to Coptic
   Compound
16 Hanging Church
   (Al-Muallaqa)
17 Water Gate
18 Greek Catholic Cemetery

0   50   100m
0   50   100yd

Because all the churches are still used as places of worship, there are no set opening hours and no admission fees, although donations are appreciated.

Roman Towers

The main entrance to the compound is between the remains of the two round Roman towers of Babylon's western gate. Built in AD 98 by Emperor Trajan, these were part of the waterside battlements and before it shifted course half a kilometre to the west, the Nile would have lapped up right against them. Excavations on the southern tower have revealed part of the ancient quay, several metres below street level. The Greek Orthodox Church of St George has been built on top of the northern tower.

Coptic Museum

Founded in 1908, this museum (☎ 363 9742, Sharia Mar Girgis; Metro: Mar Girgis; admission E£16; open 9am-4pm daily Oct-May, 9am-5pm daily June-Sept) houses Coptic art from Graeco-Roman times to the Islamic era in a collection drawing not just from Cairo but also from the desert monasteries and Nubia. It's split into two wings, the old and the new, but unfortunately the old wing is currently closed while damage sustained in the 1992 earthquake is repaired.

Objects here provide the link between the Pharaonic artefacts in the Egyptian Museum and the collection at the Museum of Islamic Art. Some of the earliest Coptic items display motifs and symbols that are recognisably ancient Egyptian such as ankhs and Horus-like falcons. Elsewhere, carved capitals from an early Coptic cathedral in Alexandria display a mastery of stone carving that would later come to fruition during the era of the Mamluks. A 6th-century Coptic stone pulpit resembles the stairs and shrine of the Heb-Sed Court at Saqqara, and at the same time prefigures the minbars found in all Cairo mosques.

Even more fascinating are the crudely painted depictions of Mary suckling Jesus, which directly echo images found all over Egypt of Isis nursing Horus.

In the new wing the exhibits (stonework, woodwork, manuscripts, glass and ceramics) are housed on two floors and arranged in chronological order anticlockwise. Explanations are in French and English. The rooms themselves are very much part of the attraction, adorned with elaborately painted ceilings, fountains and mashrabiyya screens.

The old wing was due to reopen in 1999, but when we visited, it remained off limits. However, the door to the wing from the museum entrance hall (right as you enter) is often unlocked and ajar; hover around and chances are a custodian will appear and lead you across the courtyard and down the stairs to view the flooded **Water Gate**. This was the southern gate of Roman Babylon, on top of which the Hanging Church was built.

Hanging Church

Dedicated to the Virgin Mary, this church is, nevertheless, more popularly called the Hanging Church (or Al-Muallaqa, 'the Suspended') because it is built on top of the Water Gate of Roman Babylon. Although not the oldest Christian place of worship in Cairo (it dates back to the 9th century), it is arguably the most attractive.

A flight of stairs leads up to a passage through a twin-towered, 19th-century facade into an interior courtyard festooned with icons where there are also several stalls selling cassettes and videos of Coptic sermons. The interior of the church, renovated many times over the centuries, has three barrel-vaulted, wooden-roofed aisles. Ivory-inlaid screens hide the three altar areas, but in front of them, raised on 13 slender pillars that represent Christ and his disciples, is a fine pulpit, used only on Palm Sunday each year. One of the pillars is darker than the rest, symbolising Judas.

In the baptistry off to the right a panel has been cut out of the floor through which you can look down on the Water Gate below; however, it's hard to make anything out in the gloom so also look out of the window

for a good view of one of the gate's twin towers and the violently green water stagnating about its foundations.

There is no admission fee because the church is still in use. Coptic mass is held from 8am to 11am on Friday and from 7am to 10am on Sunday. The ancient, liturgical Coptic language is still used in most of the services.

Monastery & Church of St George

Back on Sharia Mar Girgis, the first doorway north of the garden entrance leads through to a compound dedicated to St George (in Arabic, Mar Girgis), one of the most popular Christian saints in the Middle East. He was a conscript in the Roman army who was executed in AD 303 for tearing up a copy of the Emperor Diocletian's decree that forbade the practice of Christianity. European Crusaders adopted him, leading to George becoming the patron saint of England. There has been a church dedicated to him in Coptic Cairo since the 10th century but this particular one dates from 1909. The interior is a bit gutted from past fires, but the stained-glass windows are bright and colourful. The monastery next door is closed to the public.

Convent of St George

If you descend the sunken staircase off Sharia Mar Girgis by the footbridge, then the first doorway on your left along the alleyway leads into the courtyard of the Convent of St George. The convent is closed to visitors but you can step down into the main hall and the chapel. Inside is a beautiful, wooden door, 8m high, behind which is a small room still used for the chain-wrapping ritual which symbolises the persecution of St George during the Roman occupation. Visitors wishing to be blessed are welcome to be wrapped by the patient nuns present who will then intone the requisite prayers.

Churches of St Sergius & St Barbara

Perhaps the most famous church in all Egypt, St Sergius *(open 8am-4pm daily)* owes its reputation to the widely held belief that the

The Northern Cemetery is a repository of some of Cairo's finest Islamic architecture (bottom); due to population pressures, it is also home to thousands of urban poor who have lived among the old funerary monuments for centuries (top & middle).

EDDIE GERALD

EDDIE GERALD

ANDERS BLOMQVIST

Coptic Cairo is the heartland of Egypt's Christian community (bottom left), as well as the oldest part of the city. Although at one time there were 20 or more churches clustered in this small area, the number is down to only five today, including the Hanging Church (bottom right) and St George's Church (top).

Holy Family took shelter in a cave on this spot during their Flight into Egypt. The cave is preserved in the form of a crypt reached by stairs beside the altar, but the rising water table has caused it to become flooded and it is now inaccessible. Whatever the truth of the Holy stopover, the church is the oldest in the area, with foundations going back to the 5th century AD. Rebuilt and reconstructed many times, most of the fabric of the building dates from the Fatimid era.

Further along the alley is the Church of St Barbara (open 8am-4pm daily), dedicated to the daughter of a merchant beaten to death by her father when she tried to convert him to Christianity. Her relics supposedly rest in a small chapel to the left of the nave. A series of striking icons dating to around 1750 depict Jesus, Mary, two archangels and various saints and apostles.

If you walk on past the church, an iron gate on the right leads through to a large **Greek Orthodox cemetery**, the peace of which is usually shattered by the shouts and cheers from a neighbouring football pitch and sports field.

Ben Ezra Synagogue

Egypt's oldest synagogue occupies the shell of a 4th-century Christian church which the Copts were forced to sell in the 9th century in order to meet the tax demands of Ibn Tulun who was indulging in a bit of mosque building. In the 12th century the synagogue was restored by Abraham Ben Ezra, rabbi of Jerusalem, from whom it takes its name.

Several legends are connected with the synagogue. It is said that the temple of the prophet Jeremiah once stood on the same spot and that this is where he gathered the Jews after they fled from Nebuchadnezzar, destroyer of their Jerusalem temple. There is also a spring which is supposed to mark the place where the pharaoh's daughter found Moses in the reeds, and where Mary drew water to wash Jesus.

The Jews of Cairo

From an all-time peak of 80,000, Egypt's Jews now number no more than 200, almost all of whom are elderly women. Contemporary sources show that as far back as 1168 there were 7000 Jews living in Fustat, who would have formed the backbone of the congregation at the Ben Ezra Synagogue. We know this for sure because of an amazing 19th-century discovery. According to Jewish tradition any document that might bear the name of God could not be idly discarded and instead would be deposited in a special chamber known as a *geniza*. Renovations at Ben Ezra in the 1890s unearthed such a cache containing more than 10,000 documents that dated back to the earliest years of the synagogue. Included were items such as wills, bills of sale, letters of credit and even laundry lists, all of which contributed enormously to historians' knowledge of day-to-day life in medieval Cairo. The geniza documents are now scattered throughout academic institutions, libraries and museums worldwide.

As Cairo extended north so did the Jewish community and in Mamluk times there was a Jewish quarter, Haret al-Yahud, in the vicinity of the Al-Azhar mosque. The first four decades of this century constituted something of a golden age for Jews in Cairo as their numbers expanded and they came to play a bigger role in society and the affairs of state. Jews were responsible for the modernisation of Egypt's finances, including the founding of the national bank, the opening and running of most of the city's department stores, and major financial involvement in new urban developments.

The reversal began with the creation of Israel in 1948. Not long afterwards, the exodus received further impetus with the nationalisation that followed Nasser's seizure of power. In the present climate of media-led anti-Israeli hysteria, mention of the 'J' word in connection with Cairo's history has been all but banished, but the evidence is there in Ben Ezra, Downtown's Shar Hashamaim Synagogue, and in the Bassatine Jewish cemetery just north of the southern suburb of Ma'adi.

Clean-up work in the late 19th century revealed the synagogue's intact *geniza* – for more details see the boxed text 'The Jews of Cairo'. In the 1980s the American Jewish Congress funded extensive repairs and, though no longer used for prayer, the synagogue is in pristine condition.

FUSTAT (Map 5)

Fustat was founded in AD 642 as a garrison for the conquering armies of Amr ibn al-As. It gradually took on a more permanent aspect and became a thriving commercial city and the first Islamic capital of Egypt. Fustat was razed during the reign of the Fatimids. Under the Mamluks it became a rubbish dump and it has remained an uninhabited wasteland ever since.

The fact that Fustat has lain dormant and largely uninhabited for the 600 years since its destruction makes it one of the most important Islamic archaeological sites in the world. It was first excavated in the early 20th century and most of the finds, predominantly pottery, are on display in the Museum of Islamic Art. Excavations are still ongoing.

But while the site is fascinating to the archaeologists, for the layperson it's little more than a vast dusty wasteland pocked with holes and trenches and roamed by feral dogs. That may change in the future. The culture ministry has great plans, including for an ambitious new Museum of Egyptian Civilisation. Whether that happens or not, it's years off. In the meantime, early 2001 saw the opening of an **Arts & Crafts Arcade (Map 5, #27)**, intended to provide workshop and sales space for local artisans. At the time of our last visit it hadn't really got off the ground but all being well it should be up and running by now. It's just to the north of the Coptic Cairo compound.

MOSQUE OF AMR IBN AL-AS (Map 5, #26)

Although hardly any of the original structure remains, this place can claim direct descent from the first mosque ever built in Egypt. It was founded in AD 642 by the victorious invader Amr (the general who conquered Egypt for Islam) on the site where he'd first pitched his tent. The original is said to have been made of palm trunks thatched with leaves, but it was rebuilt and expanded until it reached its current size in 827. The reconstruction didn't end there and the mosque has continued to be amended and reworked until as recently as 1983. There's little of interest to see inside, although of the 200 or so columns supporting the ceiling no two are said to be the same. To the left of the entrance there's a pair of columns extremely close together which, according to a tale told to Gustave Flaubert when he visited in 1849, only a man who has never told a lie can pass between.

MONASTERY OF ST MERCURIUS (Map 5, #25)

Continue along the main road north of the mosque and take the next left, Sharia Ali Salem. About 100m along on the right is a small wooden doorway that leads to a narrow cobbled alley and a compound of three churches and a convent. The foundation is dedicated to a martyred Roman legionary, celebrated in the **Church of St Mercurius** *(open 8am-4pm daily)*, which in its current form dates to around the 10th century. It is a repository of fine early Coptic art with unique wall paintings, an extraordinary collection of icons and a fine wooden altar canopy. A flight of stairs in the north aisle of the church leads down to a small crypt in which the eccentric 4th-century figure of St Barsum the Naked is supposed to have spent 20 years with only a snake for company. The Church of St Shenouda and Church of the Holy Virgin may also be visited, but the convent is still inhabited by nuns and is off limits.

TOMB OF SULEYMAN AL-FARANSAWI (Map 6, #28)

The metro line runs beside the monastery – follow this south to the first footbridge. Cross and continue south on the other side of the tracks, taking the first right and then the second left. This should bring you into a large square at the centre of which is a bedraggled garden and one of the most unusual little monuments in Cairo – a small, cast-iron tomb built in the 19th century in honour of an extremely unusual man.

Suleyman 'the Frenchman' was originally a soldier named Joseph Seves, a veteran of Napoleon's campaigns who came to Egypt to train the armies of Mohammed Ali. He was reputedly so despised by his conscripts that they would shoot at him during target practice. He later converted to Islam, taking the name Suleyman, and became one of the most powerful men in Egypt. The main street of Downtown was originally named after him until, following the 1952 Revolution, it became Talaat Harb. The area surrounding the tomb, now occupied by shops and houses, was once the site of Suleyman's palace and gardens. All that remains is the tomb, designed by Carl von Diebitsch, the German architect responsible for the ornate iron arcades at the Cairo Marriott.

RHODA (Map 5)

Unlike the alluvial island of Gezira, which was formed within the last thousand years, Rhoda is solid bedrock and was around during Pharaonic times when it was part of the territory of ancient Heliopolis. In the Roman era it was the site of a fortress, twin to that at Babylon. In the 13th century, Sultan as-Salih Ayyub quartered his Mamluk guard here and the island contained palaces, mosques, more than 50 towers and extensive gardens; the name Rhoda means 'Garden' in Arabic. The place frequently pops up as an exotic setting in the tales of *The Thousand and One Nights*.

When power later shifted away from the island's Mamluks, Rhoda was abandoned and later quarried for stone. Until the middle of this century the island remained undeveloped and largely agricultural, but during the post-Revolution period it experienced a building boom. Today it's an extremely drab and shabby residential district notable only for the Manial Palace Museum at the northern end and the Nilometer at the south. The distance between the two is quite substantial – a 45-minute walk at least.

Manial is best visited from Garden City (see earlier in this chapter) while the Nilometer is best reached from Old Cairo.

Nilometer (Map 5, #33)

Until the building of the dams at Aswan in the 19th and 20th centuries, Egyptian life had been for millennia governed by the annual flooding of the Nile. Its waters rose most years to swamp the river valley, then retreated, leaving richly fertile deposits of alluvial soil. Occasionally, however, the floods failed to come, resulting in low crop yields and famine. In order to predict what a particular year might bring, the ancient Egyptians constructed a series of Nilometers, the best known of which is on Rhoda (*Sharia al-Malek as-Salah, Rhoda; admission E£8; open 9am-6pm daily*). It takes the form of a deep square pit containing an octagonal column, marked off with graduations. Water was let in through three channels, now blocked up but still visible. At the annual meter-reading ceremony a sufficiently high level of water would be greeted by festivities, while a shortfall would trigger anxious prayers. Although there has been a Nilometer here since Pharaonic times, in its existing form it dates from the 9th century, hence the Islamic inscriptions adorning the walls. The kiosk over the Nilometer, with its distinctive conical cap, dates from the 19th century.

Beside the Nilometer, a former royal residence is slated to open as a museum (Map 5, #32) dedicated to the revered Egyptian singer Umm Kolthum some time whenever.

Gezira & Zamalek

Uninhabited until the mid-19th century, Gezira (meaning 'Island') was a 3.5km by 1km strip of alluvial land rising up out of the Nile opposite Bulaq. After Ismail had created modern-day Downtown on the flood plain of the river's west bank, he built a great palace on the island and had much of it landscaped as a vast royal garden. In the early years of the 20th century, as Cairo was experiencing a land development boom, the

Tales of the River Bank

If it wasn't for the Nile, you'd go mad in Cairo. Cutting a swathe through the city north to south, the river ventilates a channel through the heart of the metropolis, free of the buildings that otherwise stifle breezes. It creates room to breathe, like a vast natural firebreak halting the smoky, choking urban sprawl and keeping it at bay. At the same time, it shows the city off at its best, allowing for miles of dramatic skyline along its banks.

The main place to appreciate all this is the waterside **Corniche (Map 2)** on the east bank. Planted with trees and set with benches it's the favourite spot for evening promenading. Any night of the week it will be crowded with families, kids licking ice cream, father cracking sunflower seeds bought from the roaming vendors; gangs of young students indulging in horseplay; and young lovers dangling their legs over the embankment wall, backs discreetly to the passers-by.

Across on Gezira, starting at the Qasr el-Nil (Tahrir) Bridge and running north to Zamalek is a new **pedestrian corniche (Map 2)**. Opened in 1998, it's a fine addition to the city – a smart, wide, paved area down at water level. However, when it immediately proved such a big hit with promenaders, the authorities decided it was becoming untidy and promptly closed it to the public. Instead, strollers have to make do with the narrow strip of greenery up beside the road known as the **Andalusian Gardens (Map 2)**, a small park, complete with Pharaonic obelisk, that costs 50pt to enter.

South of the Andalusian Gardens is the **Casino el-Nil (Map 2, #107)**, not a casino at all but a cafe-restaurant with plenty of riverside seating. Or if you have the cash, there are also several hotel restaurants at which you can take a table at the water's edge (such as the Nubian Village at Le Méridien Cairo – see Restaurants in the Places to Eat chapter for more details), not to mention the floating restaurants moored off Zamalek and Giza (including TGI Friday and the Fish Market – see Restaurants in the Places to Eat chapter for more details) and several cruising restaurants (see Cruising Restaurants in the Places to Eat chapter for more details).

But absolutely the best way to appreciate the Nile is to take a **felucca**. From several landing stages on the Corniche it's possible to hire one of these graceful lateen-sailed boats, a type that has been plying the Nile since antiquity. Watching the sun set over the city skyline while languidly drifting on the river makes for a fantastically stress-relieving and cool end to a busy day's sightseeing. The best spot for hiring is the **Dok Dok landing stage (Map 2)** on the Corniche at Garden City just north of Le Méridien Cairo. A boat and captain should cost about E£15 per hour irrespective of the number of people on board. This rate is, of course, subject to haggling. Other felucca mooring points are opposite the **Helnan Shepheard's hotel (Map 2)** (captains here tend to be more voracious in their demands for money) and down in Ma'adi, just north of the Felfela restaurant.

palace grounds were partitioned, sold off and built upon. The island today divides almost equally into two: the southern part is largely green and leafy and retains the name Gezira, while the north is an upmarket residential district known as Zamalek.

GEZIRA (Map 2)

Gezira is best approached across the Qasr el-Nil (Tahrir) Bridge from Midan Tahrir, which brings you to Midan Saad Zaghloul, presided over by a statue of a stout man in a tarboosh – Saad Zaghloul, a nationalist leader of the 1930s. To the right of the

bridge is the new Nile-side pedestrian corniche, closed to the public. Between the promenade and the main road is a narrow strip of greenery known as the **Andalusian Gardens**. Immediately south of the midan is the **Casino el-Nil (Map 2, #107)**, a riverside cafe-restaurant and one-time weekly hangout of writer Naguib Mahfouz. The road south beside the Casino leads down to the Gezira Sheraton.

Cairo Opera House (Map 2, #111)

Immediately west of Midan Saad Zaghloul are the immaculately groomed Gezira Exhibition Grounds, dominated by the centre-piece of the Cairo Opera House (☎ 739 8144, Gezira Exhibition Grounds; Metro: Opera; open for performances only), one of the city's few credible examples of modern architecture. Opened only in 1988, it's a modern take on traditional Islamic design, designed and built by the Japanese. You can only enter during performances, but the grounds are pleasant to walk around.

National Museum of Egyptian Modern Art (Map 2, #109)

Across from the Opera House is the National Museum of Egyptian Modern Art (☎ 736 6665, Gezira Exhibition Grounds; Metro: Opera; admission E£10; open 10am-1pm & 5pm-9.30pm Tues-Sun), home to a fairly limited collection of 20th-century Egyptian painting, some of which is certainly worth seeing. There are also two galleries in the grounds, both of which host ever-changing temporary art exhibitions: the **Hanagar Art Centre (Map 2, #110)** (☎ 735 6861, Gezira Exhibition Grounds; Metro: Opera; admission free; open 10am-10pm Tues-Sun), behind the Opera House, and the **Arts Palace (Map 2, #108)** (☎ 736 7627, Gezira Exhibition Grounds; Metro: Opera; admission varies according to the exhibition; open 10am-1pm & 5pm-10pm Tues-Sun), just to the right of the main gate.

Mahmoud Mokhtar Museum (Map 4, #9)

If you leave the Opera House grounds by the rear entrance, on the west of Gezira, near the Galaa Bridge, you'll see across the road a modest gate with a sign for this museum. Mokhtar (1891–1934) was the sculptor laureate of Egypt, responsible for Saad Zaghloul on the nearby midan and for the Mother of Egypt statue outside the entrance to the Cairo Zoo. Unfortunately, the museum has been closed for some years now and is unlikely to reopen during the lifetime of this edition.

Cairo Tower (Map 2, #63)

The story has it that the tower (Burg al-Masr; ☎ 735 7187, Sharia Hadayek al-Zuhreyya, Gezira; Metro: Opera; admission E£30; open 9am-midnight daily), completed in 1961 and looking like a 185m-high wickerwork tube, was built as a thumb to the nose at the Americans who had given Nasser the money used for its construction to buy US arms. After the Pyramids it's now the city's most famous landmark. The view from the top is excellent – clearest in the early morning or late afternoon. There's an expensive revolving restaurant on top as well as a cheaper cafeteria. You may well be greeted with quite a long queue at dusk.

Gezira Club (Map 3)

Carved out of the former Khedival Botanical Gardens, the Gezira Club was established in the 1880s by Egypt's ruling Anglo elite. On its 60 hectares, adorned with acacias and jacarandas, Hussars and Lancers sparred at polo, wagered bets on the Cairo Derby and sipped whisky sours on the terrace. There was no ruling specifically excluding Egyptians, but they were not made welcome. More than a century on, slightly reduced in size but still occupying the whole central area of the island, the club retains an air of exclusivity. These days its membership is wholly Egyptian and the class divide is maintained by annual fees of around US$1000 a year, putting the club beyond the reach of all but the most well off. Nonmembers can pay an E£20 day fee to take advantage of the facilities.

ZAMALEK (Map 3)

Occupying the northern part of the island of Gezira, Zamalek is an attractive residential district with a Continental European tinge. It has few tourist sites but it's a pleasant place to wander around and an even better place to eat (try L'Aubergine, Abu as-Sid, La Bodega, Maison Thomas or Hana) or drink (L'Aubergine, Deals or the Cairo Marriott garden).

The main street is **26th of July**, which cuts south-east to north-west across the island. The junction of Sharias Hassan Sabry and Brazil is the focal point of the area. There's good shopping around here, and three of the city's best newsstands are located at the crossroads. Just a couple of

THINGS TO SEE & DO

Designer Life

Even if you're not buying, this walk by the boutiques of the city's most chic neighbourhood offers Nile views, leafy scenery and stops for decent coffee. Quite a few of the places mentioned close on Sunday; for more details on shop opening hours, see Business Hours in the Facts for the Visitor chapter earlier in this guide and for more information on the Cairo shopping experience, see the Shopping chapter later in this guide.

The city is far from a shopper's paradise. Khan al-Khalili is a hassle and overloaded with tourist tat, while the shops Downtown lean towards trashy clothes and dodgy electronics. When the novelty of haggling starts to pale and the amusement value of the grotesque lingerie stores around Talaat Harb has faded, there's only one place to head and that's Zamalek. Forget necessities, shopping in this privileged island neighbourhood is all about indulgence.

Start by walking past the front of the **Marriott (1)**, once the royal palace of Khedive Ismail, where there's a small retail mall with branches of Daniel Hechter and Safari for cheap cotton clothing. Then continue by heading south along Sharia Saray al-Gezira. The mansion blocks overlooking the river are some of the most sought after in town and a favourite with international correspondents, who no doubt appreciate being able to keep an eye on goings-on at the towering white Foreign Ministry directly across the water.

At No 14 Sharia Saray al-Gezira, up on the 1st floor is **Nomad (2)**, a beautiful little Aladdin's cave of a shop specialising in Bedouin and traditional garb and jewellery.

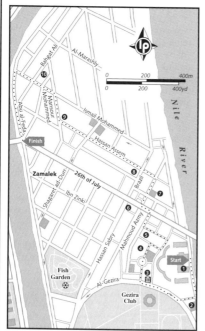

From Nomad backtrack slightly and cut through alongside the Marriott to come out opposite the Gezira Club, and then follow the road round. Opposite the club entrance is the **Gezira Centre of Arts (3)**, once a villa belonging to a member of Egypt's royal family, now a museum of Islamic ceramics that sometimes has sales exhibitions in the basement galleries.

North of the arts centre is a small midan overlooked by Beano's coffeehouse, which serves good coffee and snacks, and next door **A Touch of Glass (4)** (☎ 736 2392), at 8 Sheikh al-Marsafy, selling locally produced sets of glasses and bowls etc in unusual designs. The huge mansion block immediately north of the glass shop, inscribed round the front with the name 'Gezirah Mansions' was designed by Ernest Jaspers the architect responsible for Heliopolis and erected in 1908–09, making it (as far as is known) Zamalek's oldest surviving apartment block.

Directly ahead is All Saints Anglican Cathedral in the grounds of which is the **Tukul Craft Shop (5)** selling handcrafted African items. Cairo is home to large numbers of refugees from Ethiopia and West Africa but mainly from Sudan where war still rages in the south. In fact, the Sudanese form by far the largest

Designer Life

non-Egyptian group in Cairo – not that you are likely to encounter many around affluent Zamalek unless they're maids, cooks or cleaners. All the goods at this particular craft shop were made by Sudanese refugees to whom all profits go.

Continue on to Sharia 26th of July, the neighbourhood's main street, and turn left (west) passing two or three large **antique emporiums (6)**; these are fun to browse in but the pieces are big, blowsy and pricey. Take a right onto Yehia Ibrahim, where at No 27, on the 1st floor of an apartment block, is **Marketing Link (7)**, an excellent place for gift shopping.

Carry on along this quiet, leafy street then take the first left to reach Sharia Brazil, where just off to the left at No 6 is the small arts and crafts gallery **Safar Khan (8)**. This gallery plays host to regularly changing exhibitions of local artists and, as well as paintings, it also carries items of pottery and sculpture.

From Brazil continue west across the island along Hassan Assem, crossing Shagaret ad-Durr to arrive at **Mameluke (9)**, an antiques store and craft emporium full of furniture, ceramics, rugs, paintings and plenty of other useless but vaguely appealing items.

At the end of this street, turn right onto Mansour Mohammed, then left onto Ismail Mohammed and just ahead, second right, at the bottom of Bahgat Ali is **Beit Sherif (10)**, a shop that feels like it might be a museum. Covering four storeys, it's filled with furniture and architectural fittings, presented as if for a fashion photo shoot. A place beloved of interior designers, you may not find anything to buy here but it's certainly fun to browse.

From Beit Sherif it's a short walk back to 26th of July, where taxis are plentiful for the bag-laden shopper. Even better, walk back east along the main street to the junction of 26th of July and Hassan Sabry where you'll find Simonds; lucky types might get to snag a seat at the counter to enjoy the city's best cappuccino.

MELISSA KIRKBY

Housed in a beautiful neo-Islamic villa, the Gezira Centre of Arts is now a museum of ceramics.

doors east of Hassan Sabry on 26th of July is **Simonds (Map 3, #64)**, the best cafe in town at which to read your papers – if you can get a seat.

At the eastern end of 26th of July, beside the bridge over to Bulaq, is the **Akhenaten Centre of Arts (Map 3, #59)** housed in a luxurious European-style villa built in the early 20th century by an Egyptian aristocratic family. There are always several different exhibitions on, so it's worth dropping in; for more details, see Art Galleries under Activities later in this chapter.

Immediately south of 26th of July, overlooking the Nile, is the salmon-pink **Cairo Marriott (Map 3, #76)**, occupying the premises of Ismail's former royal palace. It has a good bakery and an attractive garden, which is a good place for a beer. Behind the Marriott is a beautiful little neo-Islamic villa that opened in spring 1999 as the **Gezira Centre of Arts (Map 3, #80)** (☎ 736 8672, 1 Sheikh al-Marsafy, Zamalek; admission free; open 9am-1pm Sat-Thur), housing a permanent exhibition of Islamic ceramics plus several galleries for temporary art exhibitions.

The Nile-side road on the west of the island is Sharia Umm Kolthum (formerly Sharia Gabaleyya), named after the legendary singer. When she died in 1975, the beautiful villa in which she'd lived was hastily demolished by rapacious developers while parliament was discussing a bill to safeguard its preservation. So, instead, she's now commemorated by a strip of asphalt.

Lying between Sharia Umm Kolthum and Hassan Sabry is the **Fish Garden (Map 3)** (Sharia Umm Kolthum; admission 50pt; open 9am-7pm daily), once part of the grounds of Ismail's Gezira palace (now the Cairo Marriott). It's a small area of grassy hillocks and tree-shaded lovers' benches with an aquarium grotto where the fish swim (or float belly up) in tunnels that resemble bomb shelters.

The view north from the 15th of May Bridge is beautiful. The Nile here is lined with houseboats, with the **Kitkat Mosque (Map 3, #23)** behind them, named for an infamous WWII-era nightclub.

Mohandiseen, Agouza & Doqqi

A map of Cairo in Baedeker's 1929 guide to Egypt shows nothing on the west bank of the Nile other than a hospital and the road to the Pyramids. The hospital is still there, set back off the Corniche in Agouza, but it's now hemmed in on all sides by an unsightly rash of mid-rise housing blocks that shot up during the 1960s and 1970s when Mohandiseen, Agouza and Doqqi were created as new suburbs for Egypt's emerging professional classes. The three districts have remained bastions of the middle classes, home largely to families who made good during the years of Sadat's open-door monetary policy.

Unless you happen to find concrete and traffic stimulating, the sole attraction of these areas is that they contain many of the city's better eating places.

MOHANDISEEN (Map 3)
Cross the 15th of May Bridge heading west out of Zamalek and the broad sweep of the flyover gently slides down to deposit you at **Midan Sphinx**, the starting point of Mohandiseen and its main fast-food-lined thoroughfare **Gamiat ad-Dowal al-Arabiyya** (Arab League St). With its wide roads and roundabouts, this place is all about modern living with supermarkets, cosmetic surgery clinics, discreetly chic restaurants (such as Flux, Kandahar and Maroosh), video clubs, Mercedes showrooms and all the other conveniences you might expect to find in the more affluent suburbs of any international big city. It may make for comfortable living, but for the visitor there's little to do or see; around **Sharia Shehab** is fine for window-shopping but otherwise Mohandiseen tends to be somewhere seen in passing from the window of a taxi.

AGOUZA (Map 3)
What little history there is here is on the river in the form of the **houseboats (Map 3, #22)** moored off Sharia el-Nil just north of

the 15th of May Bridge. Known as *da-habiyyas*, these floating two-storey wooden structures used to line the banks of the Nile all the way up from Giza to Imbaba forming an extensive waterborne neighbourhood. During the 1930s they were something of an interwar tourist attraction, especially when some of the boats were converted into casinos, music halls and bordellos. It was on one of them, owned by the belly dancer Hekmat Fahmy, that the German spy John Eppler was arrested in 1943 (for more background information on this, see The British in Cairo under History in the Facts about Cairo chapter). Many of the houseboats continue to be rented out and they're popular with teachers at the British Council, which is just a few hundred metres south down the street.

DOQQI (Map 4)

Boundaries are ill-defined but Doqqi is roughly the area on the west bank of the Nile lying south of the 6th of October Bridge and north of University Bridge; between Agouza to the north and Giza to the south. It's modern and residential and yields little to exploration by foot. The most interesting parts are the affluent streets around the **Shooting Club** (Nadi as-Seid), dotted with some choice eateries (such as Tia Maria, Map 4, #2), bars (including Le Tabasco, Map 4, #7, and Absolute, Map 4, #6) and boutiques (Al-Ain Gallery, Map 4, #3). Cairo-born, but London-based, author Ahdaf Soueif keeps a flat around here. **Sharia Suleyman Gohar** and the side streets between it and the Nile are also pleasant, quite 'villagey' with lots of small local shops and coffeehouses.

Agricultural Museum (Map 4, #4)

It sounds dull but this place (☎ *360 8682, Sharia Islah al-Ziraa; admission 10pt; open 9am-2pm Tues-Sun)* is actually quite fascinating, verging on the bizarre. It comprises several different museums including one on cotton and one devoted to the 'plant kingdom'. Apart from stuff on life in Egyptian villages, it has giant plastic fruits, glass cases packed full of stuffed birds, and a mummi-

fied bull from Saqqara. The gardens are quite relaxing. It's off Sharia Wizaret al-Ziraa, to the west of the 6th of October Bridge.

Mahmoud Khalil Museum (Map 4, #22)

This museum (☎ *336 2358, 1 Sharia Kafour, Doqqi; Metro: Doqqi; admission E£25; open 10am-5.30pm Tues-Sun)* houses one of the Middle East's finest collections of 19th- and 20th-century European art, including numerous sculptures by Rodin and a rich selection of French works by the likes of Delacroix, Gauguin, Lautrec, Monet and Pissaro. There are also some Reubens, Sisleys and a Picasso. The paintings are housed in a renovated, temperature-controlled (and what a pleasure that is on a hot summer's day) villa that used to be the home of Mohammed Mahmoud Khalil, a noted politician during the 1940s, and was later taken over by President Sadat. It's on Sharia Giza, just a few minutes' walk south of the Cairo Sheraton.

Giza

A former village on the west bank of the Nile, Giza **(Map 4)** is now a vast governorate in its own right. It stretches from the Nile 18km westwards to the Pyramids, adjoining Doqqi to the north and petering out into fields then desert to the south. To Cairenes it's best known as the home of their largest academic institution, **Cairo University**. The plaza in front of the domed main building is a favoured gathering point for demonstrations, directed more often than not against Israel which has an embassy about 500m east of here.

CAIRO ZOO (Map 4)

Though bedraggled and short on funds, Cairo's zoo (☎ *570 8895, Midan al-Gamaa, Giza; admission 10pt; open 8.30am-5pm daily)* has managed to struggle through more than 100 years of existence – it celebrated its centenary in 1994. It was a legacy from Khedive Ismail, a part of his former Harem Gardens passed over to the state in

Art & Artists

This walk acts as an introduction to the Cairo art scene, old and new, taking in two (possibly three) art museums, a couple of commercial galleries, and ending up at a Downtown bar/restaurant favoured by artistically inclined boozers. Along the way it also takes in some wonderful Nile-side scenery. It's best done late afternoon/evening, any day bar Monday or Friday.

Start in Doqqi at the **Mahmoud Khalil Museum (1)** on Sharia Giza; get there by taxi. Aim to arrive around 3pm, which allows a good couple of hours to explore one of the city's best kept secrets – for more details, see this entry in the main text.

On leaving the museum, head away from the traffic of Sharia Giza by cutting east to the river and walking north along its bank, past the rowing clubs and riverside casinos. Cross **Galaa Bridge (2)** and admire the view north, where the Nile narrows to a straight-sided, canal-like strip, perfectly suited to racing sculls. Continue onto the island of Gezira and across the traffic junction; on the right-hand side you'll see a gate with a signboard reading **Mahmoud Mokhtar Museum (3)**. If by chance the museum is open, visit; if not, cross over the road and enter the Gezira Exhibition Grounds. Pass around the magnificent **Opera House (4)** to reach the **National Museum of Egyptian Modern Art (5)**, which opens its doors for the evening at 5pm.

Contrary to popular belief, Egypt's artistic legacy to the world did not end with the pharaohs. There is such a thing as Egyptian modern art. It has its beginnings in the late 19th/early 20th century, when the influence of Europe was seeping into the country during the reigns of the Mohammed Ali dynasty. Looking around the museum, the European influence is readily discernible, but by the 1920s and 1930s some artists were forging their own indigenous styles. Chief of these was

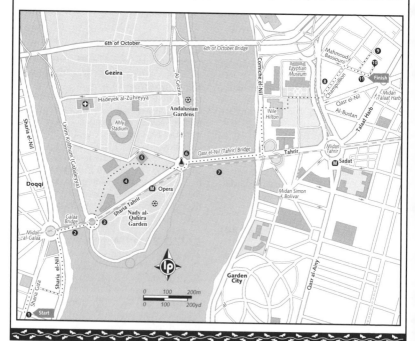

Art & Artists

Mahmoud Said (1897–1964), an Alexandrian son of a former prime minister, who painted only as a sideline while pursuing a career as a judge. His use of luminous colour and subject matter of dignified, proud peasants is reminiscent of the Mexican artist Diego Rivera. Even more distinctive are the works of Abdel Hady al-Gazzar, a true one-off who painted Egypt as a kind of colourful but slightly freakish circus. For more information on these and other artists look in the museum bookshop for Lilliane Karnouk's *Modern Egyptian Art*, or pick up Fatma Ismail's *29 Artists in the Museum of Egyptian Modern Art*.

From the museum head east for the main gate, possibly passing along the way a large woman with a handkerchief – this is a statue of Umm Kolthum, the legendary Egyptian singer and icon of the Arab world. If she's no longer around that'll be because she's been relocated to her museum on the island of Rhoda.

As you negotiate the traffic circling Midan Saad Zaghloul, glance up at the **statue (6)** on the plinth, a pleasingly chunky creation of sculptor Mahmoud Mokhtar, whose museum you may have visited earlier. More sculptures in the form of a pair of regal lions flank elegant **Qasr el-Nil Bridge (7)**, originally built in 1871 but completely overhauled in 1931 by Dorman Long & Co, the British firm responsible for the Sydney Harbour Bridge. The lions belong to the original crossing. Depending on the time of year and time taken in the museums, the sun may already be sinking. If so, you're in luck; Cairo looks its most gorgeous at sunset and Qasr el-Nil Bridge offers some of the best views of the city whatever the time of day.

Once across the bridge we recommend heading north up to the Nile Hilton and taking a shortcut through the hotel – cheeky, but it avoids the worst of the traffic around Midan Tahrir – to pass by the front of the Egyptian Museum, leaving just one main road to cross to reach Sharia Champollion and **Mashrabia (8)** (down the alley with the sheesha smokers) and, a few streets away, **Townhouse Gallery (9)**. These are just two of a surprising number of excellent little, privately run galleries that act as a showcase for the city's vibrant contemporary art scene. Exhibitions change regularly, opening parties are well attended and, generally speaking, the work finds buyers.

Finish up by visiting the **Atelier du Caire (10)**, a block east of the Townhouse, base for the artists' union, with a lively cafe. Better still, cross over to the south side of the street and look for the narrow alley with a small sign for **Crillion (11)**; if you can find it, this is the hidden heart of the contemporary Downtown art scene, a discreet garden bar/restaurant beloved of boozy bohos and their acolytes. It's open until very late, so take a seat, order a Stella, and behold the future of Egyptian art.

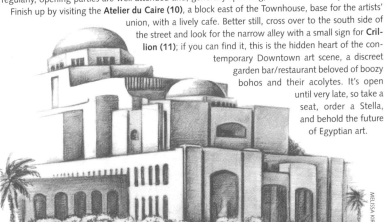

MELISSA KIRKBY

Opened in 1998, the Opera House is a modern take on traditional Islamic designs.

partial settlement of his debts. The backbone of the animal collection was made up of his private menagerie.

The only present-day survivors of the original gardens include a giant banyan, planted around 1871, and the light suspension bridge, built by Gustave Eiffel, that links two artificial hills. It remains a popular excursion for local families and couples, especially on Friday and Saturday. It's not, however, a good place for anybody who cares about animals.

DR RAGAB'S PHARAONIC VILLAGE

This 'village' (☎ 571 8675, 3 Sharia al-Bahr al-Azam, Giza; adult/child E£40/20; open 9am-5pm daily Oct-May, 9am-10pm daily June-Sept) is the city's sole shot at a Pharaonic theme park. Visitors get to float down the 'Canal of Mythology' and try to imagine that they've been thrown back a millennium or three. Actors and actresses in Pharaonic costume play out the fantasy by performing Pharaonic tasks. At the end of the journey, there are several small museums, including an absorbing mock-up of Tutankhamun's tomb as it was discovered by archaeologist Howard Carter, and a new collection devoted to Alexander the Great and Hellenistic Egypt. Dr Ragab is no Disney, but after paying the hefty admission you're probably going to be eager to encourage the illusion to work to get your money's worth. The village is about 20 minutes' walk, or a short taxi ride, south of the Giza Bridge.

PYRAMIDS ROAD

Known as Sharia al-Haram by the locals (even though al-haram means 'pyramid' and the plural, 'pyramids', is al-ahram), this road starts just south of Midan Giza and runs more or less 10km south-west to reach the site of the ancient monuments. It was laid down in the 1860s for the benefit of the Empress Eugénie of France, who was visiting Egypt for the inauguration of the Suez Canal. Wayside houses and places of refreshment sprang up along the route to cater to the carriageloads of tourists that fol-

lowed. These were soon joined by the nightclubs and casinos for which the Pyramids Rd has long been notorious. The most famous were burnt down in the 1972 riots but they were replaced and in the 1970s the strip boomed, providing girlie entertainment for the oil-rich Arabs from the Gulf who began to flock over every summer. The Gulfies still come and Pyramids Rd is still full of dodgy nightclubs, but the shows these days are less risque, more rip-off.

North-Eastern Cairo

HELIOPOLIS (Map 9)

By the beginning of the 20th century the number of Europeans flooding into Egypt was so great that they undertook the building of their own suburb. Underwritten by a Belgian company and figureheaded by Baron Edouard Empain, a Belgian industrialist, Heliopolis was intended to be a garden city, isolated from the squalor of Cairo, which would house the European officials who ruled Egypt.

Construction on a desert site north-east of the city began in 1906. The architectural style was an odd European-Moorish mix of wide avenues with grassy central strips, arcaded pavements, a racecourse, a club and a grand hotel.

In addition to Europeans, the new suburb, known in Egyptian as Masr al-Gedida or 'New Cairo', attracted the Egyptian upper classes and spawned large Coptic, Jewish and Islamic communities. In the 1950s, however, overcrowding in Cairo caught up with this not-so-distant neighbour and the former desert barrier was breached by a creeping tide of middle-income high-rises.

These days Heliopolis is still a fairly up-market address. The president resides here as do most of his ministers and the odd deposed head of an African state. The ranks of apartment buildings festooned with satellite TV dishes now greatly outnumber the graceful, old villas, but Heliopolis still has an urbane charm. Were it to stand alone as a town apart from Cairo it would be considered a gem of northern Africa; as it is, it's an elegantly faded suburb well worth the brief tram ride from Downtown. For more information, see the boxed text 'Fantasies Set in Stone' on the following page.

The best way to get to Heliopolis is to take the airport bus (No 356) from Midan Abdel Moniem Riad, behind the Egyptian Museum. The ride takes about 30 minutes. Get off outside the Heliopolis Club (the first stop after hitting the street with the tram tracks – watch for a Pizza Express on the left. The fare is E£2 and buses are every 20 minutes. Alternatively, there's the tram which goes from just north of Midan Ramses – for more details, see under Tram in the Getting Around chapter.

OCTOBER WAR PANORAMA & SADAT'S TOMB (Map 1)

Built with help from North Korean artists, this memorial (Map 1, #7) (Sharia al-Uruba, Heliopolis; admission E£10; open 9am-9pm Wed-Mon) to the 1973 'victory' over Israel is quite an extraordinary propaganda effort. Contained within the purpose-built, cylindrical structure is a large combined 3-D mural and diorama depicting the breaching of the Bar Lev Line on the Suez Canal by Egyptian forces and the initial retreats by the Israelis. A stirring commentary (in Arabic only) recounts the heroic victories but is short on detail on the successful Israeli counterattacks that pushed the Egyptians back before both sides accepted a UN-brokered ceasefire. Sinai was eventually liberated by negotiation six years later. The exhibition is about 2km south of the Baron's Palace, on the same main road; walk or get a taxi.

About a kilometre or so away, under the pyramid-shaped Victory Memorial, is the Tomb of President Sadat (Map 1, #9) who was assassinated as he sat in the reviewing stand opposite, observing a 6th of October anniversary parade in 1981.

MEDINAT NASR (Map 1)

A thoroughly unappealing place, Medinat Nasr (Nasr City; named for Nasser's success in standing up to Britain, France and Israel during the 1956 Suez Crisis) is a modern, concrete, high-rise suburb that took root in the 1960s on the extreme north-eastern desert edge of the city. Grim though it looks, it's the most progressive and flourishing part of town, neighbourhood of choice for young professionals, and a prime real-estate centre with an ever-escalating number of malls, multiscreen cinemas and slick US-style food outlets. It's badly served by public transport and really you need a car to get up here – but why would you want to?

Southern Cairo

MA'ADI

A gracious garden suburb where high-rises have yet to supplant the villas, Ma'adi developed in the early years of the 20th century as an exclusive suburb populated by bankers and brokers. Wild hedgerows and dust-greyed trees still separate the smart houses and tasteful apartment blocks, all set back a discreet distance from the narrow meandering streets. The abundant greenery and tranquillity make the place a big favourite with expats, particularly Americans. Hence, down here you get malls with bowling alleys, bagel bakeries, softball in the park on Friday, the Cairo American College and numbers instead of street names. For the casual visitor there's absolutely nothing to see, but if you fancy a look around anyway, take the metro to the Al-Ma'adi stop and start your wandering there.

HELWAN

About 25km south of central Cairo and the southern terminus for the metro, Helwan was founded in the 1890s as a luxury spa resort, complete with healing baths, a Japanese garden and sumptuous accommodation. But, from being a spot valued for its clean air and healthy vapours, Helwan is now notorious as the site of Egypt's cement capital, home to some of Cairo's biggest polluting industries – the belching chimneys are visible to tourists across the valley at the ancient site of Saqqara. The Japanese Garden (Geneina Yabaniya; Metro: Helwan; admission 50pt) remains but in a

THINGS TO SEE & DO

Fantasies Set in Stone

While there are few must-see sights, Heliopolis does make for a great place to stroll, free of the dense crowds of Downtown, with a backdrop of charming buildings, plenty of greenery, and some fine places to eat and drink. It's at its best around dusk, when pinking skies add atmosphere, and the bats start to flit between the trees. Arriving from Downtown by bus, you alight opposite the **Uruba Palace (1)**, formerly the Heliopolis Palace Hotel, which at the time it was built was one of the biggest hotels in Africa; it's now occupied by the office of the Egyptian president.

Running up the side of the palace is the main street, **Sharia al-Ahram**. At the first intersection, detour left along **Sharia Ibrahim Laqqany**, lined with fantastical architecture – European architects' fantasies of the Orient set in stone complete with elegantly arched arcades, lacy balconies and teardrop turrets. On the corner of Al-Ahram and Ibrahim Laqqany is an open-air cafeteria, the **Amphitrion (2)**, as old as Heliopolis itself and a popular watering hole for Allied soldiers back during WWI and WWII when troops were stationed up here. Along with the **Palmyra (3)** a little way up the street, it's one of the very few places in Cairo where it's possible to drink a beer without having to skulk in some dingy room away from public eyes. Both terraces serve food and are great places to relax and people-watch on a balmy evening.

At the top end of Al-Ahram is the **Basilica (4),** designed as a pint-sized version of Istanbul's soaring Aya Sofya cathedral, and known locally as the 'jelly mould' because of its distinctive shape. Baron Empain, the Belgian industrialist who founded Heliopolis, is buried in the crypt. Unfortunately, the place is usually kept locked.

Across the road, the best thing that can be said about the brutal and sterile **Horreyya Mall (5)**, full of trashy shops and fast-food concessions, is that its air-conditioned galleries offer respite from the heat outside.

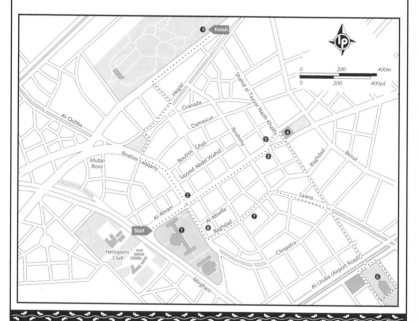

Fantasies Set in Stone

From the Basilica head south (right) down Sharia al-Shahid Tayyar Nazih Khalifa, which will bring you to the Airport Rd (Al-Uruba) and, across it, a bizarre and incongruous sight, a Hindu-style temple looming up among the faceless apartment blocks. This is the **Baron's Palace (6)** (Qasr al-Barun), the former residence of Baron Empain. Built in 1910, it was commissioned from a French architect, Alexander Marcel, and is modelled for no known reason on the temples of Angkor Wat. Three generations of the Empain family inhabited the palace until it was sequestered by the state in the 1950s and allowed to fall into ruin. While a rich collection of sandstone Buddhas, temple dancers, elephants and serpents still adorns the exterior, the interior has been gutted and is now home to large colonies of bats. Entry is not permitted but if you tip the *bawwab* (the caretaker who lives in a shack in the grounds) a couple of pounds, he'll let you walk around the outside.

From the palace retrace your steps north until you reach the point at which the road forks and bear left along Sharia Sawra until Sharia Baghdad; turn left down Baghdad and 200m further on is **Le Chantilly (7)**, about the best place up here to eat or, if you prefer, to take a beer in the garden out back. Continue on down Baghdad, turning right at the bottom; two or three doors along on your right are the former **offices of the Heliopolis Company (8)**, the founders and developers of Heliopolis. Just inside the entrance is the beautifully restored main chamber; the attendants are usually happy for visitors to poke their heads in.

If you haven't already eaten at Le Chantilly then cut across town – on up Ibrahim Laqqany, left onto Granada, over to Hegaz and then to **Merryland (9)**. Originally built as a racecourse, the park has recently been transformed into a large open-air dining and entertainment complex, complete with numerous eateries, kiddie rides, an artifical lake, shops and a couple of discos. Tacky but fun. Large green trams rattle and buckle by outside the main gate heading down to Midan Ramses and central Cairo.

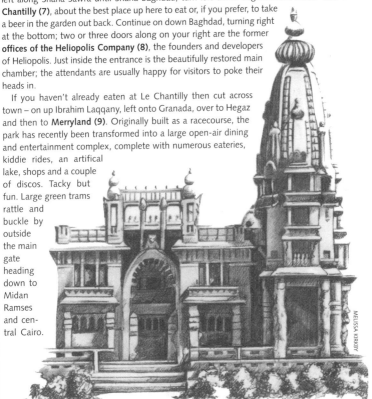

MELISSA KIRKBY

The Baron's Palace, built to resemble a Hindu temple, is Heliopolis' most extraordinary sight.

much reduced and scruffy form, although it does still boast a row of red Buddhas. To get to the gardens head east (left as you exit the metro station).

If you do happen to be down this way then make time for the **Helwan Wax Museum** (☎ 575 4267; Metro: Ain Helwan; open 9am-5pm Sat-Thur) where re-creations of figures and scenes from Egyptian history are gradually losing the struggle against the heat. Salah ad-Din slumps, Nefertiti slouches, Cleopatra looks like she's on drugs. Give it a few more summers and they could consider changing the name to the Helwan Chamber of Horrors. Note that for the museum you get off the metro one stop before the end of the line and it's just outside to your left.

Activities

For more details of activities in Cairo check *Al-Ahram Weekly* or the monthly *Egypt Today* magazine.

ART GALLERIES

In addition to the National Museum of Egyptian Modern Art (see the Gezira section earlier this chapter) there are numerous small galleries around town where contemporary local and foreign artists and sculptors exhibit. The following places tend to show the most interesting work.

Akhenaten Centre of Arts (Map 3, #59; ☎ 735 8211) 1 Maahad al-Swissry, Zamalek. Open from 10am to 1.30pm and 5.30pm to 9pm Saturday to Thursday. These official Ministry of Culture exhibition halls are housed in a grand villa on the banks of the Nile.

Atelier du Caire (Map 2, #55; ☎ 574 6730) 2 Karim ad-Dawla, Downtown. Open from 10am to 1pm and 5pm to 11pm Saturday to Thursday. Official artists' union exhibition halls, off Mahmoud Bassiouni, one block west of Midan Talaat Harb.

British Council (Map 3, #20; ☎ 303 1514) 192 Sharia el-Nil, Agouza. Open from 9am to 9pm daily. A small, one-room gallery that usually features artists from abroad.

Cairo-Berlin (Map 2, #101; ☎ 393 1764) 17 Yousef al-Guindi, Downtown. Open from noon to 3pm and 5pm to 8pm Monday to Saturday.

Along with the Mashrabia, this place consistently hosts the most exciting works in town.

Espace Karim-Francis (Map 2, #84; ☎ 391 6357) 1 Sharia Sherifeen, Downtown. Open from 10am to 2pm and 6pm to 9pm Saturday to Thursday, 6pm to 9pm Friday. This small gallery on the 3rd floor of a side-street apartment block, off Qasr el-Nil, is very hit-and-miss in terms of the shows.

Extra (Map 3, #24; ☎ 735 6293) 3 Sharia al-Nessim, Zamalek. Open from 10.30am to 2pm and 5pm to 8pm Monday to Saturday. An intimate place, tucked away right up at the northeastern tip of the island.

Khan al-Maghreby (Map 3, #45; ☎ 735 3349) 15 Al-Mansour Mohammed, Zamalek. Open from 10.30am to 9pm Monday to Saturday. This modestly sized basement gallery, just north of Sharia 26th July, has a leaning toward retrospectives of the old guard.

Mashrabia (Map 2, #62; ☎ 578 4494, 8 Sharia Champollion) Open from 11am to 8pm Saturday to Thursday. Off Midan Tahrir, this is Cairo's most attractive gallery and one of the best in terms of its stable of artists.

Sony Gallery (Map 2; ☎ 794 2964) AUC Campus, Sharia Sheikh Rihan, Downtown. Open from 9am to noon Sunday to Thursday. Part of the AUC's Adham Centre for Journalism, the Sony focuses on photography. Bring your passport to get admission to the campus.

Townhouse Gallery (Map 2, #54; ☎ 575 5901) Sharia Hussein Pasha, Downtown. Open from 10am to 2pm and 6pm to 9pm Saturday to Wednesday, 6pm to 9pm Thursday and Friday. Occupying three floors of an old townhouse, off Mahmoud Bassiouni, this is Cairo's most exciting gallery, showing two or three exhibitions at any one time and with a small sales space selling art and books.

BELLY DANCING

Whether for health, fun, self-esteem or better sex, if you've ever fancied baring your midriff and making it ripple then there is no shortage of belly-dance teachers around town. One recommended name is that of Foufa al-Faransawi, who leads classes twice a week (currently from 10.30am to 11.30am, Sunday and Wednesday) at the **Creative Dance & Fitness Centre** (☎ 519 6575, 13B Road 254, Digla, Ma'adi). Foufa also runs evening classes on demand and is soon to begin classes at the Mohandiseen branch (☎ 302 0572) of the Creative Dance

& Fitness Centre at 6 Sharia Amr, off Sharia Wadi el-Nil. Classes are geared to amateurs and dancing is done barefoot, wearing leotards or shorts – anything comfortable and close-fitting – with skirt and hip-belt provided. The cost is E£30 per class or E£200 for eight classes over a two-month period.

Another established name is **Mahmoud Reda** (☎ 393 562250, 3rd floor, Qasr el-Nil, Downtown), who offers classes to order for individuals or groups, amateurs or professionals, at his studio. Phone to organise class times and inquire about fees.

BILLIARDS & BOWLS
Billiards (pool), snooker and tenpin bowling have really taken off in Cairo in a big way in the last few years. Most of the venues are in the more wealthy suburbs such as Ma'adi and Medinat Nasr, away from the city centre, but there are a couple of venues Downtown.

Billiards 101 (Map 2, #74; ☎ 391 0151 ext 80) 2nd floor, Al-Bustan Centre, 18 Yousef al-Guindi, Downtown. Open from noon to 2am, it costs E£20 per hour.

Cairo Bowling Centre (Map 3, #33; ☎ 578 2323) World Trade Centre Annexe, 1991 Corniche el-Nil, Bulaq

Misr Bowling Centre (Map 2, #74; ☎ 395 0100) 9th floor, Al-Bustan Centre, 18 Yousef al-Guindi. Open from noon to 2am daily; it has 10 lanes at E£12 an hour as well as pool tables (E£20 per hour).

Ramses Hilton Annexe (Map 2, #2) Off Midan Abdel Moniem Riad, Downtown. Open from 11am to 3am daily. On the top floor is a snooker hall (E£25 per hour) and a separate pool hall (E£20 per hour), both with lots of tables, and both serving beer.

THE CLUB
For those who can afford it or have the right connections, the club (al-nadi) is social centre and sports centre rolled into one.

Precious Parks & Gardens

Interviewed in the *Cairo Times*, novelist Ahdaf Soueif said that she would be prepared to lay down her life to preserve the Gezira Club. Not that this great, fenced, grassy playground of the rich and privileged is under any sort of threat, but so short is Cairo of any kind of greenery that people tend to get very passionate about the little they've got. The sporting club aside, Gezira has a lot of the little green that there is. On the west side of the island is the **Fish Garden (Map 3)**, a small but pretty landscaped park with hills, a banyan grove and bats but no fish. There are also lovely gardens either side of Sharia Hadayek al-Zuhreyya, the road leading to the Cairo Tower, complete with vine-covered arbours. South of the Opera House Grounds (which themselves have well-kept lawns) is the **Nady al-Qahira Garden (Map 2)**. Only recently opened to the public, this is a large park with meandering paths and trees; the entrance is off Midan Saad Zaghloul and there's a small admission fee of a couple of pounds.

Down in Giza there's the immaculately kept **Orman Botanical Gardens (Map 4)** with beds of roses and other blooms. Across the road is the **zoo (Map 4)**, which also began life as a botanical garden and still remains one of the largest green spaces in the city (and it costs just a few piastres to get in). The gardens surrounding the **Manial Palace (Map 5, #19)** on nearby Rhoda are magnificent and wild with luxuriant banyans, palms and rubber trees – remainders again of what was once an extensive royal botanical garden.

Ma'adi is the greenest of the Cairo suburbs. There aren't any parks as such but dense foliage shades the streets. The variety of trees is wonderful and includes jacaranda, poincianna, bougainvillea, palms, bombax and mulberry, all providing inspiration and sustenance for the Ma'adi Tree Lovers Association (call Asma al-Halwagi ☎ 358 0099). Even further afield are the various golf courses (see Golf under Activities later in this chapter), the rather sad **Japanese Gardens** in Helwan, and perhaps best of all, the barrages at **Qanater** (see the Excursions chapter), but here you've really left the city behind and entered the lush vegetation of the Delta.

Membership means access to a private swathe of the city's precious greenery, fenced or walled around and equipped with swimming pools, football pitches, stadiums, tennis courts and sundry other sports facilities, as well as food outlets and cafes.

Being a member of a club is a status symbol; membership of certain clubs (notably the Gezira) is more sought after than others. Thursday night and all day Friday are the big club days, when families pitch up en masse and the kids are let loose on the fields and playgrounds while the adults set to schmoozing.

Annual fees are stratospheric, but anyone may enter most of the clubs for a day fee of around E£10 to E£20. However, this doesn't necessarily entitle you to the use of all facilities (for example, at the Gezira Club the swimming pools and tennis are off limits to day users).

The three main clubs in Cairo are as follows:

Gezira Sporting Club (Map 3; ☎ 736 5270) Sharia Saray al-Gezira, Zamalek
Heliopolis Sporting Club (Map 9; ☎ 291 0065) Sharia Mirghani, Heliopolis
Shooting Club (Nadi as-Seid; Map 4; ☎ 337 4535) Sharia Nadi as-Seid, Doqqi

GOLF

Bizarrely, given the desperate lack of usable land, the shortage of water and the blistering temperatures that Egypt endures for most of the year, the Ministry of Tourism is actively promoting the country as a golfing destination. It's a sport introduced by the British in the 19th century during their occupation of the country but never taken up by Egyptians. Until, that is, 1996 when the first of the modern clubs opened its doors. Since then seven more resort courses have opened around the country, with another four in preparation.

Egyptians have yet to take to the golfing greens in any significant numbers (mainly because it's too expensive), but the idea is that these golf courses will broaden the appeal of Egypt as a tourist attraction beyond ancient monuments, museums, beaches and scuba diving.

Dreamland Golf and Tennis Resort (☎ 20 11 400 577, ⒲ www.dreamgolf.com) 6th of October City Rd, Dreamland City, Cairo. Sports resort on the outskirts of Cairo that also includes a theme park, shopping centre, 16 cinema screens, equestrian riding centre, nine hotels and the worlds largest clubhouse. The 18-hole, par-72 course designed by golf architect Karl Litten has spectacular views of the Pyramids.
Mena House Golf Course (☎ 383 3222, fax 383 7777, Ⓔ obmhobc@oberoi.com.eg, ⒲ www .oberoihotels.com/mena) Pyramids Rd, Giza. The course (18 holes, par 68, 5250 yards, rating 66) lies directly beneath the Giza plateau, with the Pyramids looming up above. Great sport used to be had teeing off from the very top of the Great Pyramid but it's no longer allowed of course. Spoilsports.
Mirage City Golf Course (☎ 408 5041, fax 408 5040) Intersection of Cairo Ring Rd and Cairo-Suez Hwy. An adjoining Marriott (under construction at the time of research, but should be operating by the time you visit) houses resident golfers at this 18-hole, par-72, rating-73 course.
Pyramids Golf & Country Club (☎ 049-600 953, fax 600 954, Ⓔ amn-golf61@hotmail .com) Cairo-Alexandria Desert Hwy. Part of a giant project intended to have no less than 99 holes, the first 27 are open for play, including the championship 18-hole course. The rest should be fully operational by the time you visit.

CYCLING

High temperatures and bad, bad drivers mean that Cairo and its environs are not the ideal place for cycle touring. However, if this hasn't put you off, there's also a club, the Cairo Cyclists (☎ 519 6078) that meets at 7am Friday and Saturday at the front gate of the Cairo American College on Midan Digla down in Ma'adi. The club also organises long-distance rides.

FELUCCA RIDES

Feluccas are the ancient broad-sail boats that are seen everywhere up and down the Nile. For information on where and how to hire them see the boxed text 'Tales of the River Bank' earlier in this chapter.

HORSE RIDING

Horse riding is possible around the Pyramids, at Saqqara and at a few other stables dotted around the fringes of the city. If you are riding at one of the tourist sites, beware; a letter we had from a British veterinary surgeon who had just holidayed in Egypt reckoned that perhaps only 30% of the horses he saw were fit to be ridden.

The following is a simple guide to hiring healthy horses that we advise prospective riders to observe for their own sake (a healthy horse is a better ride) and for the sake of the animals (if stable owners realise tourists will not ride neglected animals they may look after them better). If the answer to any of these pointers is yes, then pass on the horse and request another.

- Is the horse too thin? Are the ribs visible? Are the pin bones prominent? These are the bones on either side of the rump behind the saddle. In a healthy horse they appear as a rounded bump; if a horse is too thin then muscle wastage will cause them to look angular and prominent.
- Is the horse limping/lame? Ask the owner to walk then trot the horse up and down.
- Does the horse have diarrhoea? Is there staining on the back of its legs?
- Does the horse have respiratory problems? Is it coughing? Does it gurgle when it breathes? Is there pus showing at its nostrils?
- Are there any obvious wounds? If they are healing then this shouldn't be a problem, but also check under the saddle for open or weeping sores.

Horses at the following stables are reportedly well looked after.

AA Stables (☎ 385 0351) Pyramids, Giza
Al-Ferousiyya (☎ 735 6000) Gezira Club, Zamalek
MG Stables (☎ 385 3823) Pyramids, Giza
Al-Zahra Stud Farm (☎ 243 1733) Heliopolis

SWIMMING

Finding a place to cool off is not easy in Cairo. Sporting clubs, the places where most Cairenes who can afford it go to swim, restrict access to members only, for insurance reasons. The only option is to make for a hotel, most of which allow day use for nonguests at a price.

Use of hotel pools is generally restricted to 10am to 6pm, or similar.

At the cheaper end of the scale the Atlas Zamalek has a high-rise, postage-stamp sized plunge pool which costs E£30 per day. Even cheaper is the rooftop pool at the Pyramisa in Doqqi, which charges E£20 per person. More expensive but worth splashing out for, Le Méridien Cairo has a fantastic Nile-side pool, open to all-comers at E£65 per day. The Semiramis Inter-Continental charges nonguests E£84, while at the Gezira Sheraton it's E£89. Both the Marriott (which has a lovely pool in the garden) and Conrad ask US$85 per person per day. Gulp.

There are some excellent pools out at the hotels around the Pyramids, including at the Forte Grande, which has a big pool with island patio, which costs E£80 per day. To use the garden pool at the Mena House Oberoi, with its fantastic Pyramid views, you need to reserve a cabana (E£170 for two), and you can swim until sunset. The nearby Pyramids Park Inter-Continental (☎ 383 8666) on the Cairo-Alexandria Desert Hwy has what's claimed to be the largest pool in the Middle East but it comes with the most expensive fee in town: E£256 per person or E£306 for two. Ask about discounts for kids or family packages.

Courses

ARABIC

Several institutions in Cairo offer Arabic courses. The full-blown option is to sign up at the *Arabic Language Institute* (☎ 797 5055, fax 795 7565, W http://bdingana.aucegypt.edu/ali.htm, e alu@aucegypt.edu) (Map 2), a department of the AUC (postal address: PO Box 2511, Cairo 11511). It offers intensive instruction in Arabic at elementary, intermediate and advanced levels. The courses incorporate both Egyptian colloquial Arabic and classical Arabic – in other words, as well as learning to speak, you learn how to read and write. The intensive, full-time course costs US$11,710 for a full year's tuition or US$5905 per semester (20 hours per week over 14 weeks). The institute also offers intensive summer programs (20 hours per week for six weeks) for US$2920.

The *Arabic Department* (☎ 347 6118, fax 301 8348) **(Map 3, #20)** at the British Council (W www.britishcouncil.org.eg), at 192 Sharia el-Nil, Agouza, also does colloquial and classical courses. Courses in the former are 12 hours a week (four mornings) over four weeks for E£1200, or six hours a week (two mornings) over four weeks for E£600. Classical Arabic is taught for eight hours a week over four weeks for E£800. There are also summer programs of two successive three-week terms costing E£1200 for 48 hours of tuition in colloquial Arabic or E£800 for 32 hours classical.

The third and cheapest option is to study at one of the two (unconnected) *International Language Institutes* (ILI) in Mohandiseen (Map 3, #2; ☎ 746 3087, fax 703 5624, e ili@starnet.com.eg, W www.ili.com.eg), at 4 Sharia Mahmoud Azmy, Sahafayeen; or in Heliopolis (☎ 291 9295, fax 415 1082, e ili@idsc.net.eg), at 2 Sharia Mohammed Bayoumi, off Mirghani, a few minutes' walk east of the Baron's Palace. The Heliopolis school offers intensive courses with four sessions a week for four weeks or regular courses of two sessions a week spread over eight weeks. Costs in both cases are E£475 for colloquial Arabic and E£500 for classical. Private tuition can also be arranged from E£35 per hour.

STUDYING AT THE AUC

The AUC is one of the premier universities in the Middle East. In 2000 there were some 4900 students, the bulk of whom are Egyptian, studying at its cluster of campuses just off Midan Tahrir in the heart of Cairo. The curriculum, and a third of the full-time faculty of over 300, are American and accredited in the USA.

The AUC offers degree, nondegree and summer-school programs. Any of the regular courses offered can be taken. Popular subjects include Arabic Language & Literature, Arab History & Culture, Egyptology, Islamic Art & Architecture, Middle East Studies and Social Science courses on the Arab world. Up to 15 unit hours can be taken per semester at the undergraduate level.

Summer programs offer similar courses. The term lasts from mid-June to the end of July. Two three-unit courses can be taken and several well-guided field trips throughout Egypt are usually included.

Applications for programs with the Arabic Language Institute (see the previous section) and undergraduate and graduate studies at the university are separate. Specify which you want when requesting an application form. A catalogue and program information can be obtained from the Office of Admissions (☎ 212-730 8800, fax 730 1600), The American University in Cairo, 420 Fifth Ave, New York, NY 10018-2719; or in Egypt you can contact the AUC (☎ 754 2964, fax 795 7565, W www.auc egypt.edu) at PO Box 2511, Cairo 11511.

OTHER CAIRO UNIVERSITIES

Apart from the AUC, it's also possible to study at other universities such as Al-Azhar, Ain Shams (just south of Heliopolis) and Cairo (in Giza). Courses offered to foreign students include Arabic Language, Islamic History, Islamic Religion and Egyptology. For information on courses, tuition fees and applications contact the Cultural Counsellor (☎ 202-296 3888), The Egyptian Educational Bureau, 2200 Kalorama Rd NW, Washington DC 20008. In London, contact the Cultural Affairs Office (☎ 020-7491 7720).

The Pyramids & Memphis Necropolis

While the world is familiar with the Pyramids of Giza, what is less well known is that these are just three of approximately 70 ancient pyramids spread throughout the country. The majority of these pyramids are concentrated south-west of Cairo, stretching from the outskirts of the capital down to the oasis of Al-Fayoum (see the Excursions chapter). They were all part of a massive necropolis, or 'city of the dead', attached to the ancient capital of Memphis, a city that predated the founding of Cairo by more than 3500 years. While there is sadly next to nothing to see of Memphis itself, the monuments in which its dead kings and nobles were buried (grouped at Giza, Abu Sir, Saqqara and Dahshur) remain hugely

impressive. For details of how best to visit these sites see the South of Giza section later in this chapter.

THE PYRAMIDS OF GIZA

The sole survivors from the Seven Wonders of the World, the Pyramids of Giza are the planet's oldest tourist attraction. Built by successive generations of kings (father, son and grandson), they were already more than 2500 years old at the time of the birth of Jesus Christ.

Orientation & Information

There are two entrances to the Pyramids site, which is open from 8am to 6pm daily. The main entrance is via a continuation of Pyramids Rd, which runs up past the Oberoi Mena House to the foot of the Great Pyramid of Khufu. If you come by public bus or by taxi, this is the way you'll probably approach the site. As you follow the road up to the plateau you'll pass the tourist office on your left, where you can check on the official rates for horse and camel rides. If anyone around here starts steering you towards the unmistakable stench of a stable, backtrack fast and ignore all the jabbering about them being able to get you onto the plateau area without a ticket. Just keep following the tarmac road as it climbs and curves and you'll see the ticket office (a hut) off to your right. Only general-site admission tickets are sold here; tickets to enter the Pyramids are sold at a separate office within the site.

Admission costs E£20 to enter the site plus E£40 to enter the Great Pyramid, E£20 to enter Khafre's pyramid, E£20 to enter Menkaure's pyramid and E£20 for the Solar Boat Museum. The Solar Boat Museum is open from 9am to 4pm October to May and 9am to 5pm June to September. Note that the number of people allowed inside the two larger pyramids (Khufu and Khafre) is now limited to just 300 per day, with tickets

THE PYRAMIDS

Nahya   Al-Mu'tamidiya
Doqqi
Kerdassa   Saft al-Laban   Giza   CAIRO
To Wadi Natrun   Old
& Alexandria   Cairo
(Desert Rd)   Pyramids Rd (Al-Haram)
Al-Kunayesa   Al-Basatin
Giza Pyramids   Ma'adi
See The Giza
Plateau Map p150   Harraniyya
To   To Helwan
Al-Fayoum   (7km)
Al-Manawat
Al-Hawamdiya
0   2   4km   Abu Sir
0   1   2mi   Saqqara
To   Memphis
Al-Fayoum
(Desert Rd)   Al-Badrashein
Shinbab
See Abu Sir &   To Medinat
Saqqara Map p159   al-Fayoum
Dahshur   Dahshur

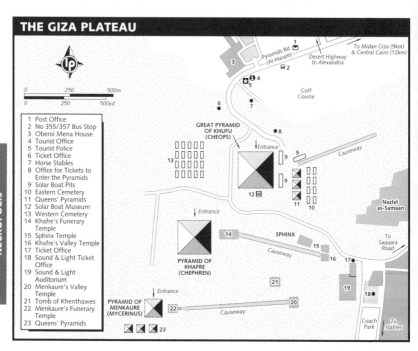

THE GIZA PLATEAU

0   250   500m
0   250   500yd

1 Post Office
2 No 355/357 Bus Stop
3 Oberoi Mena House
4 Tourist Office
5 Tourist Police
6 Ticket Office
7 Horse Stables
8 Office for Tickets to
  Enter the Pyramids
9 Solar Boat Pits
10 Eastern Cemetery
11 Queens' Pyramids
12 Solar Boat Museum
13 Western Cemetery
14 Khafre's Funerary
  Temple
15 Sphinx Temple
16 Khafre's Valley Temple
17 Ticket Office
18 Sound & Light Ticket
  Office
19 Sound & Light
  Auditorium
20 Menkaure's Valley
  Temple
21 Tomb of Khenthawes
22 Menkaure's Funerary
  Temple
23 Queens' Pyramids

THE PYRAMIDS & MEMPHIS NECROPOLIS

issued on a first-come, first-served basis. As it stands, 150 tickets for each go on sale at 8am and another 150 for each are released at 1pm. Note also that if you haven't purchased a photography ticket (E£10) you will not be allowed to take your camera inside the pyramid. As there is nowhere to leave a camera, this could create problems if you're on your own, and might well involve a trek back to the ticket office to get the extra ticket. Readers have also complained of so-called 'officials' asking for additional money once you are inside the Pyramids; this is a scam and you should not hand over any cash.

The other access to the site is via the village of Nazlet as-Samaan and through a gate directly in front of the Sphinx. If you arrive on a private tourist bus (or if your taxi driver's been a bit of a sly dog and brought you via a perfume or papyrus shop), this is the way you'll enter. There's another ticket office here, where you can buy general site admission tickets.

Be aware that the Pyramids close on a rotating basis, and only two are open for the public to clamber inside at any one time. This is to allow for necessary periodic restoration work.

The Hassle Since the time of Mark Twain, who visited in 1866 – and even before – tourists at the Pyramids have 'suffered torture that no pen can describe from the hungry appeals for baksheesh that gleamed from Arab eyes'. Every visitor to the Giza plateau has to run the gauntlet of camel and horse hustlers, souvenir and soft-drink hawkers, would-be guides, agonisingly persistent shop owners and sundry beggars. As writer Tony Horwitz comments in *Baghdad Without a Map*, it's difficult to gaze in awe at these ancient wonders with modern Egypt tugging so persistently at your sleeve.

The good news is that on our last visit the touts were being kept away from the tourists by armies of flustered young policemen armed with big sticks and not afraid of using them. It was actually possible to walk around the Pyramids with next to no hassle. Whether the policing is a permanent measure or not though, one can only hope.

In the event that the scourge has resumed at the time of your visit, all we can say is be firm in your refusals and don't be drawn – 'No' is enough, so don't feel that you have to justify yourself.

Camels & Horses Until very recently, the area in front of the Pyramids resembled a chaotic, sandy paddock full of milling horses and camels and their owners, who had a fine old time reeling in the tourists – a sport on a par with shooting fish in a barrel, but with considerably more profit to be had. But numbers have been drastically reduced, and on our most recent visit there were no more than a handful of animals. Word is that the authorities want to move them out altogether. In the meantime, if you do want to view the Pyramids from an elevated four-legged platform, beware – the camel owners are a pretty unscrupulous lot. Bargain fiercely and be sure of what you have agreed on. A camel should not cost more than E£15 an hour, but more than a few people have found themselves paying ridiculous amounts of money at the end of the ride to be let off their mounts. Women should be particularly careful – do not allow the camel or horse owner to climb on the animal behind you.

Hiring a horse is a better option as once you're mounted you are away and off on your own. There are stables near the tourist office on Pyramids Rd, but the animals here are often not in very good condition. A better option is to head for either MG (☎ 02-358 3832) or AA (☎ 02-385 0531) by the coach park, two stables that look after their horses. Let them know you're an experienced rider and you'll get a better animal. Horses cost E£20 per hour, but you must also have a Pyramids site ticket or you'll be charged E£20 to enter the desert.

It used to be that you could take a horse out any time day or night (moonlight rides around the Pyramids were a big favourite

with the city's expat community), but new regulations only allow riding in the area between 6am and 6pm.

Great Pyramid of Khufu (Cheops)

The oldest pyramid at Giza and the largest pyramid in Egypt, the Great Pyramid of Khufu (Cheops) stood 146m high when it was completed in around 2570 BC. After 46 centuries its height has been reduced by only 9m. About 2.3 million limestone blocks, reckoned to weigh an average of 2.5 tonnes each, were used in the construction of the pyramid.

Although there is not much to see inside the pyramid, the experience of climbing through such an ancient structure is unforgettable, though completely impossible if you suffer even the tiniest degree of claustrophobia. The entrance, on the north face, leads to a descending passage, which ends in an unfinished tomb (usually closed) about 100m along the passage and 30m below the pyramid. About 20m from the entrance, however, there is an ascending passage, 1.3m high and 1m wide, which continues for about 40m before opening into the Great Gallery, which is 47m long and 8.5m high. There is also a smaller horizontal passage from the Great Gallery leading into the so-called Queen's Chamber.

As you ascend the Great Gallery to the King's Chamber, notice how precisely the

Climbing the Pyramid

Climbing the outside of the Great Pyramid was, for centuries, a popular adventure. A 1902 guidebook to Egypt describes how it was correctly done: 'Assisted by two Beduins, one holding each hand, and, if desired, by a third (no extra payment) who pushes behind, the traveller begins the ascent of the steps'. Once up there, many commemorated their climb by carving their names in stone. As early as 1840 one writer was complaining of the excessive amount of graffiti. This is no longer an issue as, since the 1980s, climbing the pyramid has been forbidden.

Pyramids: Some Hows & Whys

Even more than their age, the wonder of the pyramids is in their age-old mysteries – how were they built? And what are they all about?

Why Pyramids?

The earliest Egyptian burial sites were a far cry from their well-known dynastic descendants the pyramids, being little more than shallow pits in the desert containing few, if any, grave goods for the afterlife. Over time, with the desire to create a more protected dwelling for the dead, the graves became deeper and were covered with a mound of rocks and sand. For the majority of the population this continued to be the standard type of burial until modern times. However, with the rise in the belief that the tomb was the 'house of eternity' for the spirit of the deceased, the graves of the wealthy slowly became more and more elaborate in order to create a satisfactory eternal dwelling for their spirit bodies.

In order to protect the body from grave robbers and create a more comfortable abode for the afterlife, the burial pits of wealthy peoples' graves became deep shafts lined with matting, mud brick or wood, and more chambers were added to house the growing collections of grave goods. The simple covering mound also grew greatly in size and developed a low, rectangular mud-brick superstructure which, because of its resemblance to the mud-brick seat found outside many Egyptian peasant houses, was given the name *mastaba*, which means 'bench' in Arabic.

The building of mastabas was well established by the beginning of the 1st dynasty. By this time, the tomb's enclosing mud-brick superstructure regularly rose to a height of 6m and inside contained a labyrinth of storage rooms for burial goods and subterranean burial chambers.

The next step was a product of the technical brilliance of Imhotep, architect to the pharaoh Zoser, who came up with the idea of a series of stone mastabas placed on top of one another in a graduated design – a stepped pyramid. The obvious progression from here was to fill in the steps to achieve a smooth-sided, truly pyramidal structure, of which the earliest surviving example is at Meidum (in Al-Fayoum). However, Egyptologists consider the first pyramid proper to be the Red Pyramid at Dahshur, which did away with the 'steps' altogether, and was built in the same manner as the great Pyramids of Giza – however it was that they were built – where the style attained its highest form.

Pyramid Symbolism

It was neither an obsession with death, nor a fear of it, that led the ancient Egyptians to build such incredible mausoleums as the pyramids. Rather it was their belief in eternal life and their desire to be one with the cosmos. The pharaoh as the son of the gods was also their intermediary, and his

blocks were fitted together at the top. Unlike the rest of the pyramid, the main tomb chamber, which is just over 5m wide and 10m long, was built of red granite blocks. The roof, which weighs more than 400 tonnes, consists of nine huge slabs of granite, above which are another four slabs separated by gaps designed to distribute the enormous weight away from the chamber. There is plenty of air in this room, as it was built so that fresh air flowed in from two shafts on the north and south walls.

Queens' Pyramids

On the eastern side of the Great Pyramid are the Queens' Pyramids, three small structures about 20m high, which resemble little more than pyramid-shaped piles of rubble. They were the tombs of Khufu's wives and sisters.

Solar Boat Museum

Along the eastern and southern sides of the Great Pyramid of Khufu are five long pits, which once contained the pharaoh's boats.

Pyramids: Some Hows & Whys

role was to conduct the gods' powers to his people. He was therefore honoured in life and worshipped in death, and set between the earth and the sky to connect the mortal and divine worlds. The towering pyramid was a fitting tomb for such an individual. A funerary temple attached to each pyramid allowed the pharaoh to be worshipped long after his death, with daily rounds of offerings to sustain his soul. A long covered causeway connected the funerary temple to a valley temple built on the quayside, where the flood waters would reach each inundation season. There's a superb model illustrating all this on the 1st floor of the Egyptian Museum. The whole complex also provided a constant visible reminder of the eternal power of the gods and at the same time the absolute power of the pharaoh for whom it was built.

And the How

We know that the pyramids were massive tombs constructed on the orders of the pharaohs by vast teams of workers tens of thousands strong. This is supported by the recently discovered pyramid-builders' settlement at Giza, complete with areas for large-scale food production and medical facilities. Ongoing excavations at the Giza plateau are providing more and more evidence that the workers were not the slaves of Hollywood tradition, but a highly organised workforce of Egyptian farmers. During the season of the inundation, when the annual Nile flood covered their fields and made farm work impossible, the same farmers could have been redeployed by the bureaucracy to work on the pharaoh's tomb. So the pyramids can almost be seen as a kind of ancient job-creation scheme, with the flood waters also making it easier to transport building stone to the site.

In the case of the Great Pyramid of Khufu, the biggest of the trio at Giza, it supposedly took 10 years to build the causeway and the massive earth ramps used as a form of scaffolding, and 20 years to raise the pyramid itself. The stone was quarried locally and from the Muqqatam Hills. Napoleon calculated that the 2.5 million blocks of stone used in Khufu's pyramid alone were enough to build a 3m-high wall around the whole of France.

Despite all the evidence, there are still those who don't accept that the ancient Egyptians were capable of such astonishing achievements. Pyramidologists – for the study of the vast structures has become a science in its own right – point to the millimetre-precise carving and placement of the stones and argue the cosmological significance of the structures' dimensions as evidence that the Giza Pyramids were variously constructed by angels, the devil or visitors from another planet. It's easy to laugh at such seemingly out-there ideas, but visit the Pyramids on the Giza plateau and you'll immediately see why so many people believe that such awesome structures could only have unearthly origins.

These solar boats (or barques) may have been used to bring the mummy of the dead pharaoh across the Nile to the valley temple, from where it was brought up the causeway and placed in the tomb chamber. The boats were then buried around the pyramid to provide transport for the pharaoh in the next world. One of these ancient cedar-wood vessels, possibly the oldest boat in existence, was unearthed in 1954. It was restored and encased in a glass museum to protect it from damage from the elements.

For the same reason, visitors to the museum must don protective footwear in order to keep sand out.

Pyramid of Khafre (Chephren)

South-west of the Great Pyramid, and with almost the same dimensions (it's 136m high), is the Pyramid of Khafre (Chephren). At first it seems larger than that of his father, Khufu, but this is because it stands on higher ground and its peak is still capped with a limestone casing. Originally all three

THE PYRAMIDS & MEMPHIS NECROPOLIS

What They Said about the Pyramids

We will also mention the Pyramids...that idle and foolish exhibition of royal wealth. For the cause by most assigned for their construction is an intention on the part of those kings to exhaust their treasures, rather than leave them to successors or plotting rivals, or to keep the people from idleness.

Pliny the Elder, circa AD 50

Soldiers, forty centuries of history look down upon you from these Pyramids.

Napoleon, readying his forces for battle at Giza, 1798

Khafre's Pyramid seems to me inordinately huge and completely sheer; it's like a cliff, like a thing of nature, a mountain – as though it had been created just as it is, and with something terrible about it as if it were going to crush you.

Gustave Flaubert, 1849

The Pyramids looked as if they would wear out the air, boring holes in it all day long.

Florence Nightingale, 1840s

The Pyramids were a quarter of a mile away; it felt odd to be living at such close quarters with anything quite so famous – it was like having the Prince of Wales at the next table in a restaurant; one kept pretending not to notice, while all the time glancing furtively to see if they were still there.

Evelyn Waugh at the Mena House Hotel, 1929

I discovered that the marvels of the Pyramids at Gizeh and the Sphinx had been degraded into commodities for an enormous tourist trade.

Cecil Beaton, 1942

Very big. Very old.

camel owner, 1999

pyramids were encased with polished white limestone. They would have gleamed like giant crystals. Unfortunately, right up until the 19th century, successive builders in Egypt stripped away these outer blocks to build their palaces and mosques, exposing the pyramid's softer, inner-core stones to the elements. Had it not been for this, the Pyramids might still stand today exactly as they were built, defying time to shift them.

The chambers and passageways of this particular pyramid are less elaborate than those in the Great Pyramid, but are almost as claustrophobic. The entrance leads down into a passage and then across to the burial chamber, which still contains the large granite sarcophagus of Khafre.

Back outside, to the east of the pyramid are the substantial remains of Khafre's

Funerary Temple and the flagged flooring of the causeway that provided access from the Nile to the tomb.

Pyramid of Menkaure (Mycerinus)

At a height of 62m (originally 66.5m), this is the smallest of the great trio. A deep gash in the north face is the result of an attempt by Malek Abdel Aziz, son of Salah ad-Din Ayyub (Saladin), to dismantle the pyramid in AD 1186. He gave up after eight months, having achieved very little. Inside, a hall descends from the entrance into a passageway, which in turn leads into a small chamber and a group of rooms. There is nothing particularly noteworthy about the interior, but at the very least you can have the thrill of exploring a seldom-visited site. Outside are the excavated remains of Menkaure's

Funerary Temple and, further east, the ruins of his valley temple, still lying beneath the sand.

The Sphinx

Legends and superstitions abound about the Sphinx and the mystery surrounding its long-forgotten purpose is almost as intriguing as its appearance. English playwright Alan Bennett, however, was disappointed, noting in his diary, 'The Sphinx, like a personality seen on TV and then met in the flesh, is smaller than one had imagined'.

Known in Arabic as Abu al-Hol (Father of Terror), the feline man was called the Sphinx by the ancient Greeks because it resembled the mythical winged monster with a woman's head and lion's body who set riddles and killed anyone unable to answer them.

Carved from the natural bedrock at the bottom of the causeway to Khafre's pyramid, recent geological and archaeological survey has shown that the Sphinx most likely dates from Khafre's reign, and it probably portrays his features, framed by the striped *nemes* headcloth worn only by royal personages.

As is clear from the accounts of early Arab travellers, the nose was hammered off some time between the 11th and 15th centuries AD, although some still like to blame Napoleon for the deed. Part of the fallen beard was carted off by 19th-century adventurers and is now on display in the British Museum in London.

One legend about the Sphinx is associated with the fact that it was engulfed and hidden by sand for several hundred years. The sun-god Ra appeared to the man who was to become Tuthmosis IV and promised him the crown of Egypt if he would free his image, the Sphinx, from the sand. The stelae found between the paws of the Sphinx recorded this first known restoration.

These days the Sphinx has potentially greater problems than its ordinance-inflicted injuries of the past. It's suffering the stone equivalent of cancer and is being eaten away from the inside. By what, the experts don't quite know – pollution and rising groundwater are the two likeliest diagnoses. A succession of restoration attempts were made throughout the 20th century, several of which disastrously speeded up the decay rather than halting it. The Sphinx's shiny white paws are the result of the latest effort.

Other Sites

The rarely visited but imposing structure, opposite the Great Pyramid and south of Khafre's causeway, is the **Tomb of Khenthawes**, the powerful daughter of Menkaure. The tomb is a rectangular building cut into a small hill. You can go down a corridor at the back of the chapel room to the burial chambers, but the descent is a bit hazardous.

Private **cemeteries** with several rows of tombs are organised around the Pyramids in a grid pattern. Most of the tombs are closed to the public, but those of Qar, Idu and Queen Merseankh III, in the Eastern Cemetery, are accessible, although it's sometimes difficult to find the guard who has the keys. The Tomb of Iasen, in the Western Cemetery, contains interesting inscriptions and wall paintings that provide a glimpse of daily life during the Old Kingdom.

Sound & Light Show

The Sphinx takes the role of the narrator in this show, which is a little cheesy but worth attending to see the Pyramids by starlight. There are two or three shows an evening, each in a different language, and English features every night except Sunday. Show times are 6.30pm, 7.30pm and 8.30pm from October to May, two hours later in summer (June to September). At the time of writing, the schedule was as follows:

day	show 1	show 2	show 3
Monday	English	French	Spanish
Tuesday	English	Italian	French
Wednesday	English	French	German
Thursday	Japanese	English	Arabic
Friday	English	French	–
Saturday	English	Spanish	Italian
Sunday	Russian	French	German

THE PYRAMIDS & MEMPHIS NECROPOLIS

The auditorium is near the Sphinx, so you need to approach the site through the village of Nazlet as-Samaan. Tickets for the show cost E£33 (no discount for students). Performance times vary during Ramadan. Call ☎ 386 3469 for a current schedule or check it at W www.sound-light.egypt.com.

Getting There & Away

The most comfortable way of getting to the Pyramids is to make use of the No 355/357 service, a big white air-con bus (with CTA written on the side) that runs from Heliopolis via Midan Tahrir, where it picks up from beside the Egyptian Museum (Map 2, #61). There's no bus stand as such but a crowd usually marks the spot, all waiting for various other buses (you should stand across from a sign that reads 'EMS'). Be alert – the bus doesn't automatically stop and you may have to flag it down. It runs every 20 minutes and costs E£2. The bus terminates on Pyramids Rd, about 500m short of the Oberoi Mena House.

Alternatively, you can take a microbus from Midan Abdel Moniem Riad station (Map 2, #60). These depart from near the Ramses Hilton – there are no signs, just ask for 'Haram' and somebody will point you to the right line of vehicles. The fare is 25pt and you'll be dropped off on Pyramids Rd where the No 355/357 bus terminates.

Taking a taxi from Downtown costs E£15 one way. Or, to avoid the worst of the city-centre traffic, take the metro out to the Midan Giza stop (50pt), which lies at the foot of Pyramids Rd, from where a taxi to the Pyramids costs only E£5.

Another option is to visit the Pyramids as part of an organised tour – see under Organised Tours in the Getting Around chapter for more details.

AROUND THE PYRAMIDS
Kerdassa

Many of the scarves, *galabeyyas* (traditional men's robes), rugs and weavings sold in the bazaars and shops of Cairo are made in this touristy village near Giza. There is one main market street along which you'll find all of these items, as well as a hideous collection of stuffed animals such as gazelles, jackals and rabbits. In fact, Kerdassa is almost as well known for its illegal trade in Egyptian wildlife as it is for crafts. The Egyptian Environmental Affairs Agency periodically raids the bazaar to try to halt this.

To get to Kerdassa, head down Pyramids Rd, turn right at the Marioutiyya Canal, and follow the road for about 5km to the village. The minibus from Midan Tahrir to the Pyramids begins and ends its trips at the junction of the canal and Pyramids Rd, and a local microbus does the stretch along the canal for 25pt. You can also get bus No 116 from Midan Giza all the way to Kerdassa; the trip takes 20 minutes and costs 25pt.

The Biggest Museum in the World

It's been a long time coming but following a two-year feasibility study, in September 2001 the Ministry of Culture launched an international competition for a new US$400 million super-museum, meant to take the strain off the existing Egyptian Museum on Midan Tahrir. The ministry boasts that it will be the largest museum in the world. A suitably expansive site has been earmarked 2km north of the Giza plateau at the intersection of the Cairo to Al-Fayoum and Cairo to Alexandria roads. It will have the Pyramids as a backdrop. Plans are that the new museum will display some of the thousands of pieces languishing in storerooms, plus provide a home for the ceaseless flow of new discoveries. Some of the prize pieces from the Downtown museum will also be relocated, including possibly the whole of the Tutankhamun haul. Displays will be thematic and make use of models, videos and other hi-tech presentation techniques. Fingers crossed, they might even have labels. However, given the project's track record – land for the new museum was allocated more than a decade ago now – expect progress to be slow.

Wissa Wassef Art Centre

This tranquil art centre (☎ *385 0746, Saqqara Rd, Harraniyya; admission free; open 9am-7pm daily*) is next to the Motel Salma in Harraniyya, on Saqqara Rd, about 4km south of Pyramids Rd. It specialises in woollen and cotton tapestries, as well as batiks and ceramics, and features a museum, workshops and sales gallery. The indigenous architecture of the complex is also very attractive. A visit here is best combined with a trip out to the archaeological site of Saqqara.

If you particularly want to see tapestries being woven, don't come on Friday when the workshops are closed. To get there, take a microbus for Abu Sir down the Saqqara Rd from Pyramids Rd. It's the same stop as for the Motel Salma.

South of Giza

Strung out due south of the Giza plateau on the line where the desert meets cultivation are several more Pharaonic-era sites, including ancient Memphis and the pyramids fields of Abu Sir, Saqqara and Dahshur. They can be visited in a single day trip, although if you have the money and time we'd recommend spreading the sites over two days.

Getting There & Away

Many of the city-centre hotels in Cairo arrange day-trip packages to Saqqara and Memphis, and occasionally Dahshur, for around E£70 (not including admission fees), split between however many people sign up. Alternatively, you can arrange it yourself. For E£80 to E£100 you should be able to hire a taxi and driver for the day to take you down to Dahshur, visiting Memphis, Abu Sir and Saqqara on the way. If you get four of you together, it's only E£20 to E£25 each.

MEMPHIS
☎ 02

Although the city has almost completely vanished, Memphis was the capital of Egypt for most of the Pharaonic period whereas the southern city of Thebes (present-day Luxor) acted as the ceremonial capital. Memphis is believed to have been founded around 3100 BC, probably by Pharaoh Menes, who is sometimes identified with Narmer. Following his unification of Upper and Lower Egypt, the city's location at the point where the Nile Delta meets the valley was of the utmost strategic importance in maintaining control over the two regions.

Originally called Ineb-hedj, meaning 'White Walls', the modern name derives from 'Men-nefer', meaning 'Established and Beautiful'. Indeed, the ancient city was filled with palaces, gardens and temples, making it one of the greatest cities of the ancient world. As late as the 5th century BC, the Greek historian and traveller Herodotus described it as 'a prosperous city and cosmopolitan centre'. Its enduring importance, even then, was reflected in the size of its cemetery on the west bank of the Nile, an area replete with royal pyramids, private tombs and sacred-animal necropolises. This city of the dead, centred on Saqqara, covers 35km along the edge of the desert, from Dahshur in the south to Giza in the north.

Centuries of annual floods have inundated the city with Nile mud, with the once enormous temple of the creator god Ptah now little more than a few sparse ruins frequently waterlogged due to the high water table. Other ancient buildings have long since been ploughed over so that today there are few signs of the grandeur of Memphis – in fact, it's extremely difficult to imagine that a city once stood where there is now only a small museum and some statues in a garden.

The **museum** (*Al-Badrashein; admission E£14; open 8am-5pm daily*), which is partly open-air, is built around a fallen colossal limestone statue of Ramses II, similar to the one recently moved from Cairo's Midan Ramses. Outside is an alabaster sphinx of the New Kingdom, more statues of Ramses II and the huge travertine beds on which the sacred Apis bulls were mummified before being placed in the Serapeum at Saqqara. There is an extraordinarily overpriced cafeteria across the road.

Getting There & Away

The tiny village of Memphis is 24km south of Cairo and 3km from Saqqara. Getting to it is a pain in the neck – the simplest way to visit is to take a guided tour from Cairo. This solves the transport issue and you have expert help in trying to recreate in your mind's eye, from what is a very disappointing site, what was once one of the world's greatest cities. Memphis can easily be tied in with a trip to Saqqara – see Getting There & Away at the start of the South of Giza section.

Doing it yourself, the cheapest way is to take a 3rd-class train from Cairo's Ramses station to Al-Manashi, and get off at Al-Badrashein village; the trip takes about two hours (to go 24km!) and costs 35pt. From the village, you can then walk for about half an hour, catch a Saqqara microbus for 25pt, or take a taxi. Ask for Memphis and you'll be dropped off at the museum.

Rather than catch the slow train, you could go via Helwan on the metro. From the station there, get a microbus (don't believe it if you're told there are none) to the boat landing (ask for the *markib lil-Badrashein*), then take a boat across the Nile to Al-Badrashein, and then another microbus to Memphis from there. This, however, will still take you a good 1½ hours.

ABU SIR

Lying at the edge of the desert surrounded by sand dunes, the **pyramids of Abu Sir** *(Saqqara Rd; admission E£10; open 8am-4pm daily)* form part of the vast necropolis of Saqqara. Originally there were four pharaoh's pyramids, three more fragmentary pyramids for royal women and an unfinished pyramid possibly for Pharaoh Shepseskare. Most of what exists at the site today is badly worn; the pyramids are slumped and lack the geometric precision of their bigger, older brethren at Giza.

For a long time few visitors ever bothered with Abu Sir, but at the beginning of 1999 the site was officially 'opened' and the enormous asphalt road leading to it is seeing an increasing number of big tour buses detouring by on their Giza, Saqqara and Memphis circuit.

Pyramid of Sahure

This is the most complete of the group. The entrance corridor is only half a metre high and slopes down to a small room, from where you go through a 75m-long corridor before crawling the last 2m on your stomach through Pharaonic dust and spider webs to get into the burial chamber.

The remains of Sahure's once impressive funerary temple complex stand on the east side of the pyramid, its black basalt–paved floors and red granite palm-style columns once embellished with 10,000 sq metres of superbly detailed wall reliefs in painted limestone. Although much is now in the museums of Cairo and Berlin, the scenes included the pharaoh waging war against Asiatics and Libyans, seafaring expeditions and Sahure in the company of the gods. Like most pyramid complexes, Sahure's funerary temple was connected by a long, similarly decorated causeway (almost 250m) which sloped down to his valley temple, built at the edge of the cultivation, bordered by water and again embellished by beautiful relief scenes.

From this pyramid on a clear day, you can see as many as 10 other pyramids stretching out before you to the horizon.

Pyramid of Niuserre

This is the most dilapidated of the three complete pyramids at Abu Sir. Niuserre took over his father Neferirkare's causeway, which you can still see linking up with what's left of Niuserre's funerary temple (built on top of his father's valley temple foundations) to the south-east.

Pyramid of Neferirkare

The pyramid of Sahure's brother Neferirkare now stands 45m high and resembles the Step Pyramid at Saqqara, since the original plans to fill in the steps and make it smooth-sided were never completed. His causeway and valley temple were also taken over by his successor Niuserre, although within Neferirkare's funerary temple were discovered the so-called Abu Sir Papyri in the early 20th century. This highly important archive of Old Kingdom documents is

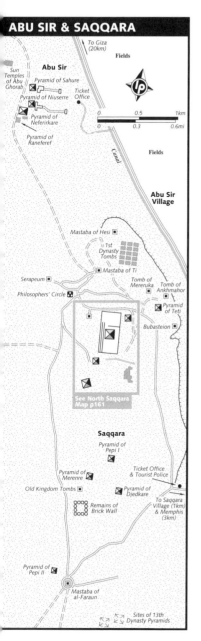

ABU SIR & SAQQARA

To Giza (20km)
Fields
Sun Temples of Abu Ghorab
Abu Sir
Pyramid of Sahure
Ticket Office
Pyramid of Niuserre
Pyramid of Neferirkare
Pyramid of Raneferef
Canal
Fields
Abu Sir Village
Mastaba of Hesi
1st Dynasty Tombs
Mastaba of Ti
Serapeum
Tomb of Mereruka
Tomb of Ankhmahor
Philosophers' Circle
Pyramid of Teti
Bubasteion
See North Saqqara Map p161
Saqqara
Pyramid of Pepi I
Pyramid of Merenre
Ticket Office & Tourist Police
Old Kingdom Tombs
Pyramid of Djedkare
To Saqqara Village (1km) & Memphis (3km)
Remains of Brick Wall
Pyramid of Pepi II
Mastaba of al-Faraun
Sites of 13th Dynasty Pyramids

0   0.5   1km
0   0.3   0.6mi

written in hieratic, a shorthand form of hieroglyphs, and relates to the cult of the pharaohs buried at the site, recording important details of ritual ceremonies, temple equipment, priests' work rotas and the temple accounts.

Pyramid of Raneferef

On a diagonal just west of Neferirkare's pyramid are the remains of the unfinished Pyramid of Raneferef. In its hastily constructed mud-brick funerary temple Czech archaeologists recently found fragments of statuary, including a superb limestone figurine of Raneferef protected by Horus (now in the Egyptian Museum in Cairo), along with papyrus fragments relating to the Abu Sir temple archives.

Other Monuments

To the south of Neferirkare's pyramid lies the **pyramid** recently identified as that built for his wife Queen Khentkawes II, mother of both Raneferef and Niuserre. Although badly ruined, it once stood some 17m tall. In the nearby funerary temple, Czech archaeologists discovered a third set of papyrus archive documents. To the south of the queen's pyramid are two more virtually destroyed pyramids, which may have belonged to queens of Niuserre.

Just to the north-west of the Abu Sir pyramids lie the **royal sun temples** at Abu Ghorab. Although the Abu Sir Papyri describe six such temples, only the two built for Pharaohs Userkaf and Niuserre have been discovered. Both resemble the typical pyramid complex in layout, with a valley temple, causeway and an upper temple. As part of their solar focus they originally featured a large obelisk of limestone blocks, which in Niuserre's case stood some 36m tall on a 20m-high base. In front of the obelisk in the temple's court is the enormous alabaster altar, made in the form of a solar disc flanked by four 'hotep' signs, the hieroglyphic sign for 'offerings' and 'satisfied' – the altar itself reads as 'The sun-god Ra is satisfied'. Although it can easily be reached from Abu Sir, this enigmatic site is somewhat off the beaten track and is very rarely visited.

Getting There & Away

Lying some distance off the main Saqqara road, there's no way to reach Abu Sir by public transport. The only way to visit is as part of an organised tour, in a taxi or in your car. For more details, see Getting There & Away at the start of the South of Giza section.

SAQQARA

The site of Saqqara was one huge cemetery for the inhabitants of the ancient city of Memphis, which was in use for more than 3500 years following the city's foundation. The necropolis is situated high above the Nile Valley's cultivation area, covering a 7km-stretch of the Western Desert. Deceased pharaohs and their families, administrators, generals and sacred animals were all interred here.

Although the Old Kingdom pharaohs were laid to rest within Saqqara's 11 major pyramids, their subjects were buried in the hundreds of smaller tombs that lie beneath the sands of the great necropolis. Apart from the Step Pyramid, most of Saqqara lay hidden until the middle of the 19th century when the great French Egyptologist Auguste Mariette discovered the Serapeum. Even the Step Pyramid's massive funerary complex was unknown until 1924 and is still being restored; the French architect Jean-Philippe Lauer, who began work here in 1926, is still involved in its restoration an incredible 70 years later.

A worthwhile visit to Saqqara will take more than one day. Because of its size it seems that other visitors are few and far between, apart from the organised tour groups, which are rushed through in the mornings. You'll find here, in the middle of the desert, a peaceful quality rarely found at other ancient sites in Egypt.

Orientation & Information

The main places of interest are in the area around the Step Pyramid, known as North Saqqara. Most travellers start their visit here and then, if they are up to it, continue by taxi, donkey or camel north to Abu Sir and/or down to South Saqqara. It's impera-

Saqqara Itinerary

With its vast size and huge collection of monuments and tombs there is too much at Saqqara to be seen in one visit. The following is a sample itinerary that includes the most important monuments:

- Enter through the hypostyle hall and gaze on the **Step Pyramid**, built by the pharaoh Zoser (also rendered Djoser), the world's oldest pyramid.
- Wander around **Zoser's Funerary Complex**, through the huge South Court, into the Houses of the North and South and in front of the eerie serdab (cellar), where you can stare into the stone eyes of Zoser. Continue through the ruins of the funerary temple and around the back of the Step Pyramid.
- Walk south along the hill above the western edge of the funerary complex and down the Causeway of Unas, where you can visit some of the beautiful **tombs** dotted on either side or peer into the huge boat pits.
- Head over to the Pyramid of Teti to see the famous **Pyramid Texts**.
- Descend into the **Serapeum**. Peer through the gloom and into the gigantic sarcophagi of the 25 huge Apis bulls that were entombed in this bizarre place.
- Walk over to the mastaba **tomb** of 5th-dynasty father and son Ptahhotep and Akhethotep, with its beautiful painted reliefs of animals, battle scenes and the two men receiving offerings.
- If you've still got the energy left, visit the wonderful **Mastaba of Ti**, overseer of the Abu Sir pyramids and sun temples, with its fascinating tomb reliefs of daily life in the Old Kingdom showing people trading, building ships, milking cows and rescuing their livestock from the crocodiles.

tive to have some form of transport to get around, as the tombs and sites are spread over a vast distance and walking is not feasible. Make sure you bring some water as it gets very hot. The site's resthouse was

MASON FLORENCE

CHRIS MELLOR

The Pyramids at Giza (top) are the planet's oldest tourist attraction; built by successive generations of pharaohs, they were over 2500 years old at the time of the birth of Jesus Christ. The Sphinx (bottom) dates from the same era; the mystery surrounding its long-forgotten purpose only adds to its allure.

BETHUNE CARMICHAEL

GREG ELMS

The prototype of the Pyramids at Giza, the Step Pyramid of Pharaoh Zoser (top) at Saqqara is the world's earliest stone monument. At Memphis, capital of Egypt for most of the Pharaonic period, the fallen statue of the great pharaoh Ramses II (bottom) is the sole reminder of the city's original grandeur.

recently pulled down because it was leaking water into the surrounding monuments and although another one is planned at a new location, at the time of writing construction had not yet begun and there was nowhere to buy drinks.

Most of the pyramids and tombs at Saqqara can be 'officially' visited between 8am and 5pm. The guards start locking the monument doors at about 4.30pm, although some have been known to lock up even earlier – with tourists inside – in order to extract *baksheesh* (tips). The admission fee for all North Saqqara sights is E£20. There is a E£5 fee for using a camera, collected only at the entrance to the Step Pyramid. Before setting off, check at the ticket office which monuments are open.

Zoser's Funerary Complex

Constructed around 2650 BC by Imhotep, the pharaoh's chief architect who was later deified, the Step Pyramid of Pharaoh Zoser was Egypt's – and indeed the world's – earliest stone monument. It is still the most noticeable feature at Saqqara. Imhotep's brilliant use of stone, and his daring break with the tradition of building royal tombs as underground rooms topped with a mud-brick mastaba, was the inspiration for Egypt's future architectural achievements.

The pyramid began as a simple square mastaba but was transformed into its final form through six separate stages of construction and alteration. With each stage the builders gained confidence in their use of the new medium and mastered the techniques required to move, place and secure the huge blocks. This first pyramid rose in six steps to a height of 60m and was encased in fine white limestone.

The Step Pyramid dominates Zoser's enormous funerary complex, which covers 15 hectares and is surrounded by a magnificent bastioned and panelled limestone wall 1645m long. The enclosure wall survives today at a height of about 5m, and a section at the south-east corner has been restored to its original 10m height. Fourteen false doors carved and painted to resemble real wood, hinges and sockets allowed the pharaoh's

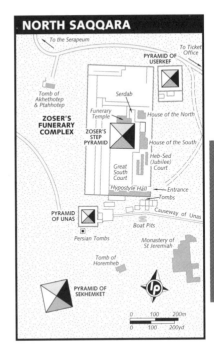

ka, or attendant spirit, to come and go at will. For the living, there is only one entrance, on the south-eastern corner, via a vestibule and along a colonnaded corridor into the broad hypostyle hall. The 40 pillars in the corridor are the original 'bundle columns', ribbed to resemble a bundle of palm or papyrus stems. The walls have been restored, but the protective ceiling is modern concrete. The roof of the hypostyle hall is supported by four impressive columns and there's a large, false, half-open ka door. Here you will be accosted by a bevy of 'guides' eager to show you around.

Great South Court The hall leads into the Great South Court, a huge open area flanking the south side of the pyramid, with a rebuilt section of wall featuring a frieze of cobras. The cobra, or uraeus, was a symbol of Egyptian royalty and represented the goddess Wadjet, a fire-spitting agent of destruction and protector of the pharaoh.

A rearing cobra, its hood inflated, always appeared on the brow of a pharaoh's head-dress or crown.

Near the base of the pyramid is an altar and in the centre of the court two stone B-shaped boundary markers, which delineated the limit of the ritual race the pharaoh had to run in order to demonstrate his prowess and ability to rule. The ceremony was part of the elaborate rituals of the Jubilee Festival or Heb Sed, which usually occurred after 30 years' reign and involved the pharaoh's symbolic rejuvenation and the recognition of his supremacy by officials from all over Egypt. The construction of Heb-Sed features within Zoser's Funerary Complex was therefore intended to perpetuate his revitalisation for eternity.

The buildings on the eastern side of the pyramid are also connected with the royal jubilee, and include the **Heb Sed (Jubilee) Court**, whose sides are lined with dummy structures. Those on the east side represent the shrines of Lower Egypt and those on the west Upper Egypt, all designed to house the spirits of Egypt's gods when they gathered to witness the rebirth of the pharaoh during his jubilee rituals.

North of the Jubilee Court are the **House of the South** and **House of the North**, representing the two main shrines of Upper and Lower Egypt and symbolising the unity of the country. The heraldic plants of the two regions also form the column capitals; those in the House of the North are in the form of papyrus while in the House of the South the capitals are in lotus form.

The House of the South also features one of the earliest examples of tourist graffiti, written during the 47th regnal year of Ramses II, nearly 1500 years after Zoser's reign. The treasury scribe Hadnakhte recorded his admiration for Zoser while 'on a pleasure trip west of Memphis'. His hieratic script, written in black ink, is preserved behind perspex just inside the building's entrance.

Serdab The serdab (cellar), a stone structure right in front of the pyramid, contains a slightly tilted wooden box with two holes drilled into its north face. Look through these and you'll have the eerie experience of coming face to face with Zoser himself. Inside is a life-size, lifelike painted statue of the long-dead pharaoh, gazing stonily out towards the stars. Although it's only a copy (the original is in the Egyptian Museum), it's still quite haunting. Serdabs were designed so that the pharaoh's ka could communicate with the outside world.

The original entrance to the Step Pyramid is directly behind the serdab, and leads down to a maze of subterranean tunnels and chambers quarried for almost 6km through the rock. The pharaoh's burial chamber is vaulted in granite, and some of the other chambers are decorated with reliefs of the pharaoh performing the jubilee race, with some exquisite blue faience tile decoration. Although the interior of the pyramid is unsafe and closed to the public, part of the blue-tiled decoration can be seen in the Egyptian Museum.

Pyramid of Userkaf

To the north-east of the funerary complex is the Pyramid of Userkaf. Although the removal of its limestone casing has left little more than a mound of rubble, this pyramid once rose to a height of 49m. Its funerary temple was decorated with the most exquisite naturalistic relief carvings to judge from one of the few remaining fragments, now in the Egyptian Museum, that shows birds by the river.

Pyramid & Causeway of Unas

What appears to be another big mound of rubble, this time to the south-west of Zoser's Funerary Complex, is actually the Pyramid of Unas, the last pharaoh (2375–2345 BC) of the 5th dynasty. Built only 300 years after the inspired creation of the Step Pyramid, and after the perfection of the Pyramids at Giza, this unassuming pile of loose blocks and debris once stood 43m high. Although it looks nothing special from the outside, the interior marks the beginning of a significant development in funerary practices. For the first time the royal burial chamber was decorated, its ceiling adorned with stars and its white alabaster-lined walls inscribed with beautiful blue hieroglyphs. These are the funerary inscriptions now known as the Pyramid Texts, comprising 283 separate 'spells' chosen by Unas to protect his soul, including rituals, prayers and hymns as well as lists of items such as the food and clothing he would require in the afterlife. Unfortunately, deterioration of the interior led to its permanent closure in 1998.

The 750m-long causeway, which runs from the east side of Unas' pyramid to his valley temple (now marked by little more than a couple of stone columns at the side of the road up to the site), was originally roofed and decorated with a great range of painted relief scenes, including a startling image of people starving, now preserved in the Louvre in Paris.

The two 45m-long boat pits of Unas lie immediately south of the causeway, while on either side of the causeway are numerous tombs, more than 200 of which have been excavated. Of the several better-preserved examples usually open to visitors are the tombs of one of Unas' queens, Nebet, and that of Princess Idut, who was possibly his daughter. There are also several brightly painted tombs of prominent 5th- and 6th-dynasty officials, including the tomb of the vizier Mehu; the tomb of the supervisor of singers Nefer; the joint tomb of Niankhkhnum and Khnumhotep, overseers of the royal manicurists to Pharaoh Niuserre; the tomb of the overseer of the royal hairdressers Neferherenptah, also known as the Bird Tomb on account of its superbly drawn bird-hunting scene; and the tomb of Irukaptah, overseer of the royal butchers, whose appropriate scenes support its title of the Butchers' Tomb.

Persian Tombs

Around the sides of the Pyramid of Unas are several large shaft tombs of the Saite (664–525 BC) and Persian (525–404 BC) eras. These are some of the deepest tombs in Egypt. Although their depth was an attempt to prevent grave robbers stealing their contents, the design failed to protect them, just as it did almost everywhere else. To the north of the pyramid is the enormous tomb shaft of the Saite general Amun-Tefnakht. Around on the south side of the pyramid are a group of three Persian tombs, the entrance of which is covered by a small wooden hut to which a guard in the area has the key.

If you don't have your own torch the guard will lead you down a 25m-deep winding staircase to the vaulted tombs of three officials – the admiral Djenhebu to the west, the tomb of chief royal physician Psamtik in the centre and the tomb of Psamtik's son Pediese to the east. The sheer size of both the tombs and the great stone sarcophagi within, together with their sophisticated decoration, demonstrate that the technical achievements of the later part of Egyptian history were equal to those of earlier times.

Monastery of St Jeremiah

The half-buried remains of this monastery date from the 5th century AD and are up the hill from the Causeway of Unas, south-east of the boat pits. There's not much left of the structure because it was ransacked by invading Arabs in AD 950, and more recently Egyptian antiquities officials took all the wall paintings and carvings to the Coptic Museum in Cairo.

Pyramid of Sekhemket

Although closed to the public because of the danger of a cave-in, the unfinished pyramid of Zoser's successor Sekhemket (2648–2640 BC) is a short distance west of the ruined monastery, near the south-west corner of Zoser's own pyramid.

Although the project was abandoned for unknown reasons when the great limestone enclosure wall was only 3m high, the architects had already constructed the underground chambers in the rock beneath the pyramid, together with the deep shaft of the south tomb. An unused travertine sarcophagus was found in the sealed burial chamber and a quantity of gold and jewellery in the south tomb.

Recent surveys have also revealed another mysterious large complex to the west of Sekhemket's enclosure, but this remains to be excavated.

Tomb of Akhethotep & Ptahhotep

Akhethotep and his son Ptahhotep were top royal officials during the reigns of Djedkare (2414–2375 BC) and Unas at the end of the 5th dynasty. Akhethotep was vizier, judge, supervisor of pyramid cities and supervisor of priests. Most of his titles were inherited by his son, Ptahhotep, along with his tomb – father and son have a joint mastaba with two burial chambers, two chapels and a pillared hall.

The painted reliefs in Ptahhotep's section are particularly beautiful and portray a wide range of animals from lions and hedgehogs to the domesticated cattle and fowl, which are brought as offerings to the deceased. Ptahhotep himself is portrayed resplendent in a panther-skin robe inhaling perfume from a jar, and further on has his wig fitted, his feet massaged and his fingers manicured (although some Egyptologists prefer to interpret this detail as Ptahhotep inspecting an important document, which would be in keeping with his official status).

Philosophers' Circle

On the way to the Serapeum is a group of Greek statues arranged in a semicircle, a collection of philosophers and poets set up as a wayside shrine by Ptolemy I (305–285 BC) as part of his patronage of learning. From left to right are Plato (standing), Heraclitus (seated), Thales (standing), Protagoras (seated), Homer (seated), Hesiod (seated), Demetrius of Phalerum (standing against a bust of Serapis) and Pindar (seated).

Serapeum

The sacred Apis bulls were by far the most important of the cult animals entombed at Saqqara. The Apis, it was believed, was an incarnation of Ptah, the god of Memphis, and was the calf of a cow struck by lightning from heaven. Once divinely impregnated, the cow would never again give birth and her calf was kept in the Temple of Ptah at Memphis and worshipped as a god. The Apis was always portrayed as black, with a distinctive white diamond on its forehead, the image of a vulture on its back and a

scarab-shaped mark on its tongue. When it died, the bull was mummified on one of the large travertine embalming tables discovered at Memphis, then carried in stately procession to the subterranean galleries of the Serapeum at Saqqara and placed in a huge stone sarcophagus.

The first Apis burial took place in the reign of Amenhotep III (1390–1352 BC) and the catacombs were subsequently expanded up until 30 BC. The main corridor contained 28 side chambers for the bulls, which died between the Saite and Ptolemaic periods (664–630 BC). The remaining 25 enormous granite and limestone coffins weigh up to 80 tonnes each, although only one was found intact when the Serapeum was first excavated in 1851.

Up until then, the existence of the sacred Apis tombs was known only from classical references. Having found a half-buried sphinx at Saqqara, and following the description given by the Greek historian Strabo in 24 BC, Auguste Mariette uncovered the avenue of sphinxes leading to the Serapeum. His great discovery sparked the extensive and continuing excavation of Saqqara.

A visit to the Serapeum is one of the definite highlights of Saqqara; it's very eerie to wander along galleries lit only by tiny lanterns that cast barely enough light to illuminate the enormous, macabre black sarcophagi in their chambers. The largest and most elaborate sarcophagus, covered in hieroglyphs, is located at the end of the main gallery on the right. It would be wise to bring a torch, as the lighting has been known to be switched off for no apparent reason, only appearing to work if small change is produced.

Mastaba of Ti

A few hundred metres north-east of the Philosophers' Circle is the mastaba tomb of Ti, discovered by Auguste Mariette in 1865. It is perhaps the grandest and most detailed private tomb at Saqqara and one of the main sources of knowledge about life in Old Kingdom Egypt. Its owner Ti was overseer of the Abu Sir pyramids and sun temples during the 5th dynasty, among other official titles. The superb quality of his tomb is in keeping with his nickname, Ti the Rich. Like Zoser, he has a life-size statue of himself within a serdab in the tomb's offering hall (although, as with Zoser's, the original is in the Egyptian Museum). Ti's wife was the priestess and 'royal acquaintance' Neferhetpes and, together with their two sons Demedj (overseer of the duck pond) and Ti (inspector of royal manicurists), the couple appear throughout the tomb alongside endless scenes of daily life represented in the finest detail. As men and women go about their business working on the land, preparing food, fishing, building boats, dancing, trading and avoiding crocodiles, their figures are accompanied by chattering hieroglyphic dialogue, all no doubt familiar to Ti during his career as a royal overseer: 'Hurry up, the herdsman's coming', 'Don't make so much noise!', 'Pay up – it's cheap!'.

Pyramid of Teti

The avenue of sphinxes excavated by Mariette in the 1850s has again been engulfed by desert sands, but it once extended to the much earlier Pyramid of Teti. Teti was the first pharaoh of the 6th dynasty and his pyramid was built in step form and then filled and encased in limestone. Unfortunately, the pyramid was robbed both for its treasure and its stone and little remains but a mound. However, the inside is well worth a visit and is very similar to that of the Pyramid of Unas (which is now closed), both in plan and also in that its walls are inscribed with Pyramid Texts. Within the intact burial chamber, Teti's basalt sarcophagus is also well preserved and represents the first instance of a sarcophagus with inscriptions on it.

Tombs of Mereruka & Ankhmahor

Near the Pyramid of Teti is the mastaba of his highest official, Mereruka, vizier and overseer of priests. It is an enormous tomb whose 32 chambers covering an area of 1000 sq metres make it the largest Old Kingdom courtier's tomb yet found. The 17 chambers on the east side belong to the tomb owner Mereruka, including a magnificent

six-columned offering hall featuring a life-size statue of Mereruka appearing to walk right out of the wall to receive the offerings brought to him. The other rooms are reserved for his wife, Princess Seshseshat, Teti's daughter, and their eldest son Meriteti (whose name means 'Beloved of Teti'). Much of the tomb's decoration is similar to that of the Mastaba of Ti, with an even greater number of animals portrayed – look out for the wide-mouthed, sharp-tusked hippos as you enter – along with a charming scene of domestic bliss as husband and wife are seated on a bed and Seshseshat plays them music on her harp.

A little further east, the tomb of the 6th-dynasty vizier and palace overseer Ankhmahor contains further interesting scenes of daily life. These include men involved in a manicure and pedicure session and, most unusually, in the surgical procedures that give the tomb its alternative title, the Doctor's Tomb. As two boys are circumcised the hieroglyphic caption says 'Hold him firmly so he does not fall'!

Mastaba of al-Faraun

This unusual funerary complex, known as the Mastaba of al-Faraun or Pharaoh's Bench, belongs to the last 4th-dynasty pharaoh, the short-lived Shepseskaf (2503–2498 BC). Inside an enclosure that once covered about 700 sq metres is the rectangular tomb built of limestone blocks and originally covered by a further layer of fine white limestone and lower layer of red granite. Inside, a 21m-long corridor slopes down to storage rooms and a vaulted burial chamber, which is possible to enter if you can find the guard.

Pyramid of Pepi II

A short distance north-west of the mastaba is the Pyramid of Pepi II (2278–2184 BC), whose 94-year reign at the end of the 6th dynasty must be something of a record. Despite his incredibly long reign, Pepi II's 52m-high pyramid was of the same modest proportions as those of his predecessor Pepi I. Although the exterior is little more than a mound of rubble, the interior is decorated with more excerpts from the Pyramid Texts.

Getting There & Away

Saqqara is about 25km south of Cairo. Although it is possible to get within 1.5km of the Saqqara ticket office using public transport, this is a very time-consuming business and, once there, you'll be stuck for getting around unless you try to hitch a ride up onto the plateau and then haggle for a camel or donkey. The site is best covered in a taxi, combined with a visit to Memphis and Dahshur. You'll have to arrange this option in Cairo as there are no taxis hanging around the site.

If you're coming from Cairo or Giza and are determined to do it on your own you have several options.

Bus One of the cheapest ways of getting to Saqqara without going via Memphis is to take a bus or minibus (25pt to 50pt) to Pyramids Rd (see Getting There & Away under The Pyramids of Giza earlier for more details) and get off at the Saqqara Rd stop. From there you can get a microbus to the turn-off to the Saqqara site (don't ask for Saqqara village as you'll end up in the wrong place), from where you'll probably have to walk the last 1.5km to the ticket office. Once at the ticket office, you'll have to try to hitch.

Train The 3rd-class train from Ramses station in Cairo to the village of Al-Badrashein (see Getting There & Away under Memphis earlier in this chapter for more details) also goes to Dahshur; a taxi from either Al-Badrashein or Dahshur to North Saqqara should cost about E£5. You can arrange a microbus from Memphis to the turn-off to the Saqqara site on the Giza-Memphis road, from where it's about a 1.5km walk to the Saqqara ticket office. There is usually a bit of traffic along the Giza-Memphis road.

From Al-Badrashein, there are sometimes direct microbuses to Giza.

Getting Around

It is not feasible to explore Saqqara on foot and, as there are no taxis near the ticket office, your only option for getting around, if you do arrive independently, is to attempt to hitch or to hire (from near the Serapeum) a camel, horse or donkey. A trip around North Saqqara should cost, after bargaining, E£8 – but don't be surprised if it's more, as the handlers are well aware that you're in need of the extra legs so your bargaining power is diminished.

The only taxis you'll find around here are those coming from Cairo and they're usually already full.

DAHSHUR

Situated some 20km south of Saqqara in a quiet patch of desert, Dahshur *(admission E£10; open 8am-5pm daily)* is an impressive 3.5km-long field of 4th- and 12th-dynasty pyramids. The site was an off-limits military zone until mid-1996, and the camel drivers, guides and other touts who infest Giza and Saqqara have yet to find enough of a market here, so you can enjoy the monuments in peace.

There were originally 11 pyramids at Dahshur, although only the two Old Kingdom ones (the Bent and Red Pyramids) remain intact. Of the three Middle Kingdom pyramid complexes which were built by Amenemhat II (1922–1878 BC), Sesostris III (1874–1855 BC) and his son Amenemhat III (1855–1808 BC), only the oddly shaped Black Pyramid of Amenemhat III is worth much of a look. The tower-like structure appears to have completely collapsed due to the pilfering in medieval times of its limestone outer-casing, but the mud-brick remains contain a maze of corridors and rooms designed to deceive tomb robbers. While thieves did manage to penetrate its burial chambers, they left behind a number of precious funerary artefacts that were discovered in 1993.

However, the site is most famous for being home to Egypt's first true pyramid, the Red Pyramid, and its earlier version, the Bent Pyramid, both of which where built by Pharaoh Sneferu (2613–2589 BC), father of Khufu and founder of the 4th dynasty. It now seems that Sneferu was also responsible for building much of the Pyramid of Meidum further south before moving his court to Dahshur to found a new necropolis and embark on further pyramid building, making him the greatest of all Egypt's pyramid builders.

Bent Pyramid

Experimenting with ways to create a true, smooth-sided pyramid, Sneferu's architects began building with the same steep angle and inward-leaning courses of stone they had been using to create step pyramids. When this began to show clear signs of stress and instability around halfway up its eventual 105m height, they had little choice but to reduce the angle from 54° to 43° and begin to lay the stones in horizontal layers. This explains why the structure has the unusual shape that gives it its name. Together with the Red Pyramid, which is the same height, these two pyramids are the third-largest in Egypt, after the two largest at Giza.

The Bent Pyramid is rare among the pyramids around Cairo in that most of its outer casing is intact. Inside there are two burial chambers, the highest of which retains its original ancient scaffolding of great cedar beams to counteract internal instability (although currently the interior is off limits to visitors). There is a small subsidiary pyramid to the south and the remains of a small funerary temple to the east. About halfway towards the cultivation to the east you can also see the ruins of Sneferu's valley temple, which yielded some interesting reliefs.

Red Pyramid

The world's oldest true pyramid is sometimes referred to as the North Pyramid but more often the Red Pyramid on account of the red tones of the limestone, exposed to weathering when the better-quality white limestone casing was removed. Others say the name derives from the red graffiti and construction marks scribbled on its masonry in ancient times.

Having learnt from their experiences building the Bent Pyramid, the same architects carried on where they left off, building the Red Pyramid at the same 43° angle as the Bent Pyramid's more gently inclining upper section.

Open to the public, the entrance is via 125 stone steps. A 63m-long passage takes you down to three chambers – two antechambers with stunning 12m-high corbelled ceilings and a 15m-high corbelled burial chamber in which fragmentary human remains, possibly of Sneferu himself, were found.

Getting There & Away

The simplest way to visit Dahshur is probably as part of a tour to Saqqara and Memphis; alternatively, you could hire a taxi and driver to take you here, visiting the sites of Abu Sir, Memphis and Saqqara on the way. For more details, see Getting There & Away at the start of the South of Giza section earlier in this chapter.

Places to Stay

The city offers a reasonable array of accommodation, with a good representation of the big international five-star chains and, at the other end of the scale, plenty of flea-ridden dives. What it sorely lacks is any kind of boutique or quirky independent 'hip' hotels, the kind that make the fashionable travel magazines. Other Middle Eastern and North African cities have them – Damascus, Istanbul and Marrakesh all make good use of old properties to create unique, charming places to stay – but it doesn't happen in Cairo. Hotels here are on the whole bland and boring. Shame, because there are plenty of properties with potential if only someone had the vision. If you want a room with character, your only option is to check in at one of the city's historic *belle epoque* hotels – see the boxed text 'Historic Hotels' later in this chapter.

Seasonal Rates & Reductions

In mid-range and top-end hotels, rates often go up by around 10% at peak times, which include the two big feasts (Eid al-Fitr and Eid al-Adha), New Year (20 December to 5 January) and sometimes for the summer season (approximately 1 July to 15 September). As a general rule there is a review of prices each year in October and, on average, prices rise by about 15%. Residents in Egypt are often entitled to something closer to the local rate for rooms in the bigger hotels – yes, there is one rate for overseas travellers and another for locals. If you do have residency, ask about resident rates, as they mean a considerable saving.

One thing that's available to everyone is bargaining. Just because a hotel has its rates displayed in a glass frame on the wall, it doesn't mean they are untouchable. In off-peak seasons haggling will often get you significant discounts, even in mid-range places. That said, at the time of writing the numbers of tourists in Cairo are at an all-time high and hotel rates are at a similar peak.

Best Hotels for...

Views
It has to be the Oberoi Mena House, where you can sit on your balcony, dine in a restaurant and swim in the pool, all the time gazing at the Great Pyramid.

Dining
All the five-star hotels are laden with restaurants but the pick of the crop are The Grill at the Semiramis Inter-Continental, Seasons Restaurant at the Four Seasons and The Moghul Room at the Oberoi Mena House.

Boozing
Arguably the best bar in Cairo belongs to the Windsor Hotel, but for an early evening snifter there's no finer place than the garden at the Cairo Marriott. To see in the dawn, head for the 24-hour rooftop bar at the Odeon Palace Hotel.

Eccentrics
The backpacker dives in the Tawfiqqiya Souq have more than their fair share of oddballs and marooned individuals, including evangelists, wives deserted by Egyptian husbands and grumpy old Japanese men.

Local Colour
For the full-on Oriental experience, go for Al-Hussein Hotel – it's not the cleanest or most comfortable of places, but it's totally Cairo.

PLACES TO STAY – BUDGET

Cairo's budget accommodation scene has seen little development in recent years. Since the demise of the notorious Oxford Hotel in the 1980s, the backpacker ghetto has been focused on one particular block at the top end of Talaat Harb, Downtown (where currently you'll find Hotel Venice, Safary Hotel and Sultan Hotel I-III). For travellers who prefer a modicum of comfort and privacy, the two long-standing favourites are at the bottom of Talaat Harb in the shape of the New Sun and Ismailia House hotels. Lying somewhere between, both geographically and in terms of cost, is the Dahab Hotel. We like the Berlin Hotel for its ultra-helpful manager Hisham, although the rates are really pushing up out of the budget category and into the mid-range. Pick of the crop, however, remains the Pension Roma, but unless you book well in advance you don't stand a chance of getting a room.

There are plenty of other cheapies that are not included in our listings; Cairo is notorious for shyster operators, who enter the backpacker hotel business for the unrivalled opportunities it offers to fleece newly arrived foreigners – see the boxed text 'Hotel Scams' over the page for more information.

Camping

Motel Salma (☎ 384 9152, fax 385 1010, Saqqara Rd, Harraniyya) Camping E£7 per person, 2-/4-person cabin E£30/40, with breakfast E£40/50. Although it's miles and miles from anywhere, this place is the only option when it comes to camping in Cairo. On the plus side, it does have views of the Pyramids from the back of the site. Overland tour companies occasionally stop here. Be prepared for a mosquito attack at sunset.

To get to the Salma, take a microbus for Abu Sir from Pyramids Rd (Sharia al-Haram). It's about a 4km trip; ask the driver about the best place to alight.

Hostels

HI Manial Youth Hostel (☎ 364 0729, fax 398 4107, 135 Sharia Abdel Aziz as-Saud, Manial) **Map 5, #22** 3-bed dorms HI members/nonmembers E£12/16, 6-bed dorms E£8/12. Cairo's only official youth hostel suffers from a lousy location well out of the centre. Neither is it such an attractive proposition that it's worth travelling for – while it's in reasonable nick with clean toilets, the beds are nothing great. Prices include breakfast. It offers dorm rooms only with no provision for couples or families, and there is an 11pm curfew. Expect to spend lots of time in taxis.

Hotels & Pensions

The two-, one- and no-stars form the budget-hotel group. Often the ratings mean nothing at all, as a hotel without a star can be as good as a two-star hotel, only cheaper. You can spend as little as E£10 a night for a clean single room with hot water or E£40 or more for a dirty double room without a shower. Generally the prices quoted include any charges and quite often breakfast – but don't harbour any great expectations about breakfast as it is usually a couple of pieces of bread, a frozen patty of butter, a serving of jam and tea or coffee. If you are staying for more than a week, then it's definitely worth pushing for a discount.

Most hotels will tell you they have hot water when they don't. They may not even have warm water. Before paying, turn the tap on and check for yourself or keep an eye out for an electric water heater when viewing the bathroom. If there's no plug in your bathroom sink and you forgot to bring your own, then try using the lid of a Baraka mineral-water bottle – according to one hip traveller, they fit 90% of the time.

Many budget establishments economise on sheets, putting only one, or sometimes none, between you and blankets that may never have seen the inside of a washing machine. If you aren't carrying your own sleeping sheet, then just ask for clean sheets – most hotels will oblige.

The following list, while far from exhaustive, covers some of the better options. We've listed them in order of ascending cost.

Downtown (Map 2) The inexpensive hotels and pensions are concentrated Downtown, mainly on and around Talaat Harb. This is the most convenient place to stay for getting around, eating and entertainment. Most of the hotels are on the upper floors of old and often fairly decrepit apartment blocks. Rooms tend to be large, but are often also musty and sparsely furnished. In this price range there is rarely air-con, but sometimes there may be a ceiling fan. Shared bathrooms are the norm, usually with a Pharaonic-era plumbing system that delivers a highly erratic water supply.

Hotel Scams

The most perpetrated scam of all in Cairo is the one in which a local convinces the newly arrived traveller that the hotel they are heading for is closed/horrible/very expensive and leads them off to another 'better' place, for which your self-appointed 'guide' earns a commission.

The main culprits are the taxi drivers at Cairo airport. They have fixed commission rates with many of the Downtown hostels and will always take you to whichever is offering the best rate at that time. (Any hostel that refuses to pay the taxi drivers' commission can find itself blackballed and suffer a decline in trade as a consequence.) It's not just the taxi drivers. On arrival at the airport, if you're not with a group, you may be approached by a man or woman with an official-looking badge that says 'Egyptian Chamber of Tourism' or something similar. These people are not government tourism officials, they are hotel touts. There are also a couple of touts who ride the buses from the airport. As a final hurdle, there are also touts who attempt to latch onto new arrivals on the street – they'll offer to lead you to your hotel where they can 'check everything is OK' and, of course, unbeknown to you, claim credit and cash for bringing you in.

The problem with all of this is that, in the worst-case scenario, you could be pressured into checking into some very dodgy fleapit that may be way out of the centre. Added to which, whatever commission was paid out will ultimately find its way onto your bill. Worse still, often your 'local friend' will also negotiate a higher than normal price for the room, thus increasing their own cut.

The simple rule is not to be swayed by anyone who tries to dissuade you from going to the hotel of your choice. Hotels do not open and close with any great frequency in Cairo and if it's listed in this book then it is very unlikely to have gone out of business in the meantime. Some taxi drivers will stall by telling you that they don't know where your hotel is – in that case tell them to let you out at Midan Tahrir (or the Nile Hilton) from where it's a short walk to most of the budget hotels. If you find yourself with a new 'friend' walking you to your hotel, stop them at the door – if they begin to protest, then bear in mind that no decent, ordinary Egyptian would ever dream of accompanying an overseas traveller into their hotel.

Sultan Hotel I-III (☎ 577 2258, *4 Tawfiqqiya Souq, Downtown);* ***Safary Hotel*** *(☎ 575 0752, 4 Tawfiqqiya Souq, Downtown);* ***Hotel Venice*** *(☎ 574 1171, 4 Tawfiqqiya Souq, Downtown)* **Map 2, #10** Dorm beds E£6-9. The three Sultan hotels plus the Safary and Venice hotels all occupy one building on a colourful market street off the top of Talaat Harb. Beds start at E£9 on the 1st floor (Sultan I) and drop to E£6 on the 5th floor (Sultan III and Safary), probably because there's no lift. There's little to choose between the five places; in all cases the word unsanitary springs to mind. Don't expect bed linen, hot water or privacy; do expect plenty of company of the six-legged kind. Venice is marginally better than the rest, with a few private rooms (E£25), but still, it's recommended only for those on the tightest of budgets.

Dahab Hotel *(☎ 579 9104, 26 Mahmoud Bassiouni, Downtown)* **Map 2, #56** Dorm beds E£15, singles/doubles E£20/25, with shower E£30/35. This is a collection of whitewashed huts on a rooftop attempting to recreate the feel of a Sinai beach camp in unremittingly urban Downtown Cairo. It's not a bad attempt, with cushioned communal spaces open to the sky, bamboo screens and Bob Marley on the cassette deck. Totally laid-back.

Hotel Minerva *(☎ 392 0600/1/2, 39 Talaat Harb, Downtown)* **Map 2, #25** Singles/doubles E£16/28, doubles with shower E£32. This hotel has a ground-floor reception hidden down the alley opposite the Al'Américaine cafe, while the hotel itself occupies the 5th and 6th floors. The less than obvious location means this old place is often overlooked, but the rooms are kept clean and it's good value.

Richmond Hotel (☎ *393 9358, 41 Sharia Sherif, 7th floor, Downtown*) **Map 2, #27** Singles/doubles/triples E£25/40/50. The Richmond is a new addition to the scene, with friendly management who are trying hard. Rooms are basic, and perhaps a little gloomy, but the shared showers/toilets are kept serviceable. It's about the only budget hotel to offer a double bed (just the one, mind).

Ismailia House Hotel (☎ *356 3122, 8th floor, 1 Midan Tahrir, Downtown*) **Map 2, #104** Singles/doubles/triples E£25/40/45, doubles with shower E£45. The location is tremendous (west-facing rooms have panoramic views over Cairo's main square and the Nile), but as far as we're concerned, the rooms and bathrooms are prohibitively grubby.

New Sun Hotel (☎ *578 1786,* e *newsun hotel@yahoo.com, 9th floor, 2 Talaat Harb, Downtown*) **Map 2, #70** 4-bed dorm E£15, singles/doubles E£25/40. The New Sun has a good location just off Midan Tahrir but unfortunately no views. Rooms are a decent size but dingy, although the shared bathrooms are commendably spotless.

Magic Hotel (☎ *579 5918, 3rd floor, 10 Sharia al-Bustan, Downtown*) **Map 2, #72** Singles/doubles E£25/40. Formerly run by the same management as the New Sun and Ismailia House, the Magic Hotel's bedrooms (with fans) and bathrooms are that little bit cleaner and the place has a cosier, less traveller-worn feel.

Amin Hotel (☎ *393 3813, 38 Midan Falaki, Bab al-Luq*) **Map 2, #100** Singles without/with bathroom E£26/33, doubles E£37/41. A short distance from the established travellers' areas, the Amin has big and fully carpeted rooms (some with bathrooms) with fans; the shared bathrooms tend to get rather messy.

Pension Roma (☎ *391 1088, fax 579 6243, 6th floor, 169 Mohammed Farid, Downtown*) **Map 2, #30** Singles/doubles/triples E£35/55/70, with shower E£5 extra. Down a side alley next to the Gattegno department store, this hotel is the city's most charming budget option. It has long been popular for its old-world elegance, including shiny hardwood floors, antique furniture, a splendid breakfast room and proprietor Madam Cressaty herself. Reservations are necessary.

Berlin Hotel (☎*/fax 395 7502,* e *berlin hotelcairo@hotmail.com, 4th floor, 2 Sharia Shawarby, Downtown*) **Map 2, #89** Singles/doubles/triples E£77/96/115. It's a little pricier than most other budget options, but you may consider it worth it for clean, air-con rooms all with their own shower cubicles. Rare among Cairo's budget hotels, Hisham Yousef, the English-speaking owner and manager, actually seems to care about keeping guests happy. It's off Qasr el-Nil.

Zamalek (Map 3) Staying in Zamalek gives a different slant on the city. It's more residential, relaxing and greener than Downtown, with lots of good eating and drinking options, yet it's still only a five- or 10-minute taxi ride from most of the sights.

Mayfair Hotel (☎ *735 7315, fax 735 0424,* e *mayfaircairo@yahoo.com, 9 Aziz Osman, Zamalek*) **Map 3, #66** Singles/doubles E£25/30, with air-con & bathroom E£50/60. This is a quiet and tranquil place with a pleasant shady breakfast terrace. Rooms are highly variable so check out a few first before accepting one. Just a minute away is the buzzing shopping street of 26th of July.

Zamalek Pension (☎ *340 9318, 6 Salah ad-Din, Zamalek*) **Map 3, #69** Singles/doubles E£50/70. There are only about five rooms at this pension, where you feel like a house guest rather than a hotel resident. Added to which, it's located on a leafy street in an attractive neighbourhood. Price-wise it's really heading into the mid-range, and there's a supplement for rooms with air-con.

PLACES TO STAY – MID-RANGE

While Cairo has a handful of reasonable budget hotels and a full complement of international five-star hotels, the choices are not as good when it comes to mid-range options. Foreign investment is channelled into top-end accommodation, while local establishments often pitch themselves as mid-range when, through inexperience, lack of

PLACES TO STAY

funds or poor practices, they actually offer no-star facilities at three-star rates. Also, beware the extras. Breakfast is often compulsory and sometimes you are charged for the fridge and TV in your room. You can take an ordinary double room, add E£8 for breakfast, E£2 for the fridge you never used and E£2 for the TV you never turned on, whack 12% service on the whole lot, then 5% sales tax and possibly a government tax on top of that, and your E£50 room is suddenly costing you more than E£70. When checking in, be sure to ask about overheads.

Most mid-range (and top-end) hotels quote prices in dollars, but you can also pay in Egyptian pounds if you'd prefer.

Downtown (Map 2)

What many of the Downtown hotels lack in amenities they more than make up for in character – see, for example, the Carlton, Cosmopolitan, Garden City House and, most splendid of all, the Windsor hotels.

Ambassador (☎ 578 3225, fax 574 3263, 31 Sharia 26th of July, Downtown) **Map 2, #7** Singles/doubles US$40/55. Just west of the Rivoli cinema and opposite the law court building, the Ambassador occupies the upper floors (7th to 10th) of a well-looked-after 1950s block. Carpeted rooms are clean and come with air-con and breakfast. The clientele is largely Egyptian.

Carlton Hotel (☎ 575 5022, fax 575 5323, 21 Sharia 26th of July, Downtown) **Map 2, #8** Singles US$15-25, doubles US$25-30. One for nostalgia buffs, the Carlton, beside the Rivoli cinema, is stuck in a 1950s time warp and shows its age around the edges. But there are some recently renovated rooms with air-con and private bathrooms that are a good deal at the price. There's also a pleasant rooftop cafeteria (no alcohol) overlooking the grand law court building.

Cosmopolitan Hotel (☎ 392 384, fax 393 3531, 1 Sharia ibn Taalab, Downtown) **Map 2, #86** Singles/doubles US$42/54. Off Qasr el-Nil, right at the heart of Downtown, this is a gorgeous old (1910) building with a wedding-cake exterior and, inside, plenty of dark lacquered antique furniture, a wonder-

ful elevator, and rooms with tiled bathrooms with tubs, supplemented by mod-cons such as central air-con. Many of the rooms have also benefited from a recent spruce-up.

Garden City House Hotel (☎ 794 4969, fax 794 8126, **W** www.geocities.com/gard en77house/, 23 Kamal ad-Din Salah, Garden City) **Map 2, #105** Singles US$11-15, doubles US$19-22. Opposite the back of the Semiramis Inter-Continental (look for the small sign at 3rd-floor level) is this long-time favourite among Egyptologists and scholars of the Middle East, now more popular with young students from the nearby American University in Cairo. It's noisy, a bit dusty and definitely overpriced, but a lot of people love it and keep coming back. Prices include breakfast and supper.

Lotus Hotel (☎ 575 0966, fax 575 4720, 7th floor, 12 Talaat Harb, Downtown) **Map 2, #78** Singles/doubles US$20/25, with bathroom US$28/34. The Lotus is an old favourite that's now showing its age. All rooms have air-con and are clean, if a little shabby, but way overpriced. Yet still the place remains popular. The hotel is reached via an elevator at the end of an arcade almost opposite the Felfela Takeaway.

Odeon Palace Hotel (☎/fax 577 6637, 6 Dr Abdel Hamid Said, Downtown) **Map 2, #41** Singles/doubles US$34/43. Don't be put off by the scruffy Downtown surroundings, inside the Odeon is quite comfortable and cosy. Its 24-hour rooftop bar is popular with night owls.

Windsor Hotel (☎ 591 5277, fax 592 1621, **e** wdoss@link.net, **W** www.windsor cairo.com, 19 Sharia Alfy, Downtown) **Map 2, #17** Singles/doubles from US$37/47. This was the British Officers' Club before 1952. It retains a colonial air, particularly in the reception area and the lounge bar, which is one of the best spots in town for a beer. In 1991, former Monty Python member, Michael Palin, stayed here while filming the BBC series *Around the World in 80 Days*; he described the place as possessing an 'almost unreal individuality'. There's a wide variety of rooms with all combinations of bathroom types, cramped or the size of a tennis court, with or without shower/toilet/tub, newly tiled or well-worn antique, hot water or no water.

Around Midan Ramses (Map 8)

Midan Ramses is a little north of the centre, but no more than about 15 minutes' walk or two stops on the metro.

Fontana Hotel (☎ 592 2321, fax 592 2145, Midan Ramses) **Map 8, #5** Singles/doubles US$17/25. On the north-east corner of the midan, high above the traffic and fumes, the Fontana has clean rooms and a pleasant rooftop cafe/bar. The views are good but the location is not really convenient for anywhere except the train station. Some readers have also complained about the noise from the disco on the floor below.

Happyton Hotel (☎/fax 592 8600, 10 Ali al-Kassar, Downtown) **Map 8, #13** Singles/doubles US$16/20. Tucked down a village-like little alley off Emad ad-Din, the Happyton appears a bit grim and utilitarian but rooms are modern(ish), have air-con, are clean and offer value for money. A lack of windows means some rooms are a little gloomy, so you might need to look at a few before accepting. It's halfway between Midan Ramses and Downtown, about a 10-minute walk from the top of Talaat Harb.

Victoria Hotel (☎ 589 2290, fax 591 3008, 66 Sharia al-Gomhuriyya, Downtown) **Map 8, #11** Singles/doubles US$20/25. For the price, the Victoria's air-con, three-star-standard, well-kept rooms are an absolute steal. All have immaculate bathrooms and breakfast is included. It's got to be Cairo's best accommodation bargain. If the hotel seems a little out of the way, remember the Ataba metro station is just a couple of minutes' walk away, and then it's just two stops to Midan Tahrir.

Islamic Cairo (Map 7)

Islamic Cairo is the liveliest and most fascinating part of the city, but noise levels are high and once you have managed to get off to sleep you're almost sure to be woken soon after by the early morning calls to prayer.

Al-Hussein Hotel (☎ 591 8089, Midan Hussein, Khan al-Khalili) **Map 7, #11** Singles/doubles US$12/15, with air-con,

bathroom & midan view US$19/22. It's institutional and grim, but about the only option if you fancy a location right at the heart of the Khan al-Khalili bazaar.

Radwan Hotel (☎ 590 1311, fax 592 5287, Sharia Muski, Khan al-Khalili) **Map 7, #12** Singles/doubles US$13/21. Few overseas travellers seem to stay here; the place is badly maintained and far from clean. We mention it only because options in the Islamic Cairo area are so few. Prices are for rooms with bathrooms.

Zamalek (Map 3)

For a general rundown of the advantages of staying in Zamalek, see under Hotels & Pensions in Places to Stay – Budget earlier in this chapter.

Flamenco Hotel (☎ 735 0815, fax 735 0819, ⓔ sales@flamencohotels.com, Ⓦ www.flamencohotels.com, 2 Geziret al-Wusta, Zamalek) **Map 3, #26** Singles US$38-105, doubles US$43-125. This is the kind of modern three- or four-star hotel you associate with small-town business trips back home. It's modest, a little bland, a little corporate, but comfortable and with excellent facilities. The streets around are quite lively and windows on the west side look down on a sweep of houseboats. It also possesses two OK bars and a good restaurant.

Horus House (☎ 735 3634, fax 735 3182, 4th floor, 21 Ismail Mohammed, Zamalek) **Map 3, #37** Singles/doubles US$38/47. This small, friendly, family-run hotel is in an apartment block a few minutes' walk north of the main street, 26th of July. The place is kept immaculately clean and service is excellent. It's the sort of place that guests return to year after year.

Longchamps Hotel (☎ 735 2311, fax 735 9644, 5th & 6th floors, 21 Ismail Mohammed, Zamalek) **Map 3, #40** Singles/doubles US$36/48. Once notorious for its raucous African disco, the Longchamps is much more sedate these days. Overseen by Heba Bakri and husband Chris, it's highly recommended for its spotless air-con rooms with all new fixtures in the bathrooms, and wonderful, shady terraces. There's also a small bar and restaurant.

PLACES TO STAY

New Star Hotel (☎ 735 0928, fax 735 3424, 34 Yehia Ibrahim, Zamalek) **Map 3, #54** Doubles US$30. Rooms are badly neglected, with peeling wallpaper and leaky toilets, but they are big (some have reception areas and kitchens) and the quiet backstreet location could also be regarded as a plus.

Mohandiseen (Map 3)
There are few advantages to staying over this side of the Nile (and hence the choices are few) and we don't recommend it unless you have a particular reason to.

Atlas Zamalek (☎ 346 6569, fax 347 6958, 20 Gamiat ad-Dowal al-Arabiyya, Mohandiseen) **Map 3, #15** Singles/doubles US$77/96. Far from picturesque, with views limited to one of the city's busiest (and noisiest) roads, the Atlas is typical of Mohandiseen hotels. It scores a little more highly than others for its facilities, which include a bar, popular disco and small rooftop pool.

Heliopolis (Map 9)
As Heliopolis is about 40 minutes north of the city centre by taxi, bus or tram, staying here is not a viable option for a casual visitor to Cairo, but if you have business up here or want to be close to the airport and don't wish to spend big money, then there are a couple of reasonable three-star options.

Baron Hotel (☎ 291 5757, fax 290 7077, e *resvcai@baronhotels.com,* w *www.baron hotels.com, 8 Mahaad as-Sahari, Heliopolis)* Singles/doubles US$120/145. Off the Airport Rd, this modestly sized, smart, modern hotel has a popular nightclub and bar, a very pleasant conservatory cafe, and a good bakery. It overlooks the incredible Hindu-style Baron's Palace.

Hotel Beirut (☎ 415 2347, fax 415 9422, 56 Sharia Beirut) **Map 9, #5** Singles/doubles US$55/69. A fairly sombre place, but it's convenient for exploring central Heliopolis. Its ground-floor bar is popular with Cairo's expat community.

PLACES TO STAY – TOP END
All Cairo's five-star hotels come with all the usual amenities: restaurants, bars, executive suites, business centres, shops and banks, plus a few Egyptian touches, such as belly-dancing nightclubs and weekly wedding receptions in the foyer. The prices given in this section generally don't include breakfast or taxes (typically around 20%).

Central Cairo
Almost all central Cairo's five-star hotels are on or overlook the Nile, so river views are almost a given. For convenience of getting around, the closer you are to Midan Tahrir the better.

Cairo Marriott (☎ 340 8888, fax 340 8240, Sharia Saray al-Gezira, Zamalek) **Map 3, #76** Rooms from US$165. This former royal palace (see the boxed text 'Historic Hotels' on the facing page) has been tastefully extended and added to. Behind a gorgeous neo-Islamic frontage of cast-iron arcades, it boasts a classy reception area, palatial dining areas and a serene garden with bar, cafe, pool and tennis courts. While the location isn't great for sightseeing (you'll need to take taxis), Zamalek is one of the city's most attractive and affluent districts, and just a few minutes' walk away are some of the city's best restaurants and bars, interesting boutiques and lots of greenery.

Cairo Sheraton (☎ 336 9700, fax 336 4601, e *sheratonegypt@starwoodhotels .com,* w *www.sheraton.com, Midan al-Galaa, Doqqi)* **Map 4, #18** Singles/doubles US$152/176. This very soulless hotel has a reception area buried somewhere deep in the middle, similar to the king's chamber in a pyramid. It's also on the wrong (western) side of the Nile, necessitating a long walk or taxi ride to get anywhere. Added to which the building is very 1970s in appearance (ie, ugly), both externally and internally. Not a big favourite with us then, but the Sheraton name ensures that it's busy nonetheless, mostly with package tours.

Conrad International (☎ 580 8000, fax 580 8080, e *reservation@conradcairo .com.eg, 1191 Corniche el-Nil, Bulaq)* **Map 3, #32** Singles/doubles from US$159. This attractive, low-rise, river-front hotel opened in 1999. However, it's somewhat devoid of life courtesy of a location too far north of

Historic Hotels

The inauguration of the Suez Canal in 1869 inspired Ismail, Egypt's reigning khedive, to initiate a flurry of building activity to provide suitable accommodation for the invited heads of state and royalty. The guest of honour was to be the Empress Eugénie of France for whom he constructed the Gezira Palace, a baroque three-winged building modelled on the Alhambra in southern Spain. The building, which originally had two storeys, was painted with yellow and maroon horizontal stripes and was set in gardens that spread over most of the island of Gezira. Today, it has three storeys, is salmon pink and is better known as the Cairo Marriott. To appreciate its former splendour, peer into some of the ballrooms up on the 1st floor or the reception rooms at garden level.

While attending the Suez Canal opening, Eugénie was taken to visit Ismail's hunting lodge, built in the 1860s beside the Pyramids. By the time she revisited Egypt 40 years later, Ismail had lost Egypt and his one-time lodge was now a hotel owned by an English couple. Large terraces and verandas had been added. 'At tea hour', according to a pre-WWI description of the hotel, 'the Mena House terraces are crowded with a gay and brilliant throng'. By this time there was also an open-air pool, tennis courts, a golf course and a croquet lawn. Being so grand and, until the 1960s, the only hotel in the vicinity of the Pyramids, Mena House was host to an array of the great and famous, including Roosevelt and Churchill, who met here in 1943 to hammer out plans for the defeat of Germany.

Since 1952 both hotels have been owned by the Egyptian government, from whom the Marriott and Oberoi chains lease them.

the city centre. On the plus side, the in-house restaurants are very good and next door is the World Trade Centre, containing Cairo's most exclusive shopping mall.

Four Seasons (☎ 573 1212, fax 568 1616, **W** www.fourseasons.com, 35 Sharia Giza, Giza) **Map 4, #27** Singles US$220-300, doubles US$250-330. Cairo's newest luxury hotel (it opened in 2000) is part of the exclusive First Residence Complex, the most expensive real estate in the city. Service is reportedly unnervingly efficient – doors are whisked open by flunkies at your approach – and this has rapidly become the hotel of choice for oil sheikhs, heads of state and stars (Sting recently stayed here) but the location is terrible, convenient for absolutely nowhere except the zoo, which it overlooks.

Gezira Sheraton (☎ 736 1333, fax 735 5056, **e** gzher@rite.com, **W** www.sheraton.com, Sharia al-Orman, Gezira) **Map 2, #131** Singles US$185-210, doubles US$210-250. A choice site on the very southern tip of the island of Gezira ensures that there are superb views from just about every room in this hotel, and from the numerous river-front restaurants and bars. Although it's just that

little bit too far to walk to get anywhere, it does score highly on facilities and activities, with plenty going on in terms of promotions, nightlife and entertainment.

Helnan Shepheard's (☎ 355 3800, fax 355 7284, **e** reshs@helnan.com, **W** www.helnan.com, Corniche el-Nil, Downtown) **Map 2, #113** Singles/doubles US$90/105, with Nile frontage US$135/160. Shepheard's is a gloomy, badly aged place with little to recommend it apart from the good location just south of the Midan Tahrir.

Le Méridien Cairo (☎ 362 1717, fax 362 1927, **W** www.lemeridien-hotels.com, Corniche el-Nil, Manial) **Map 2, #130** Singles US$165-250, doubles US$140-285. A location right on the northern tip of the island of Rhoda ensures that most rooms have excellent views, which may or may not make up for the fact that you're far from the action and have to resort to taxis to get to and from the hotel. A massive new annexe dwarfing the original hotel was due to open, which should improve facilities that are starting to show their age.

Nile Hilton (☎ 578 0444, fax 578 0475, **e** nhilton@brainy1.ie-eg.com, **W** www.hilton.com, Midan Tahrir, Downtown) **Map 2, #65**

Singles/doubles from US$215/250, with Nile views US$25 extra. Cairo's oldest five-star hotel is still a fine place to stay courtesy of the best location in the city – on Midan Tahrir next to the Egyptian Museum. It's very much a hub of social life; the terrace Ibis Cafe is popular with city residents and the hotel's pool is one of the city's best.

Pyramisa (☎ *336 7000, fax 360 5347, 60 Sharia Giza, Doqqi*) **Map 4, #20** Singles/doubles US$100/120. A sort of mini five-star hotel, Pyramisa is considerably more modest in size than the Sheratons, Hiltons and the like, with far fewer amenities. At the same time it is very modern and comfortable and offers a degree of intimacy, with reasonable rates. The location, beside the Cairo Sheraton, is a minus, but the Doqqi metro station is close by.

Ramses Hilton (☎ *574 4400, fax 575 7152,* **W** *www.hilton.com, 115 Corniche el-Nil*) **Map 2, #3** Singles US$88-215, doubles US$111-230. Modern and towering, the Ramses Hilton is also bland and characterless. Worse still, it's surrounded by flyovers and is adjacent to a city bus station – unless you take a taxi from the door of the hotel every time, walking anywhere involves negotiating at least half a dozen of Cairo's most lethal roads.

Semiramis Inter-Continental (☎ *795 7171, fax 796 3020,* **e** *cairo@interconti.com,* **W** *www.interconti.com, Corniche el-Nil, Downtown*) **Map 2, #106** Singles/doubles US$190/220, with Nile views US$210/240. A reasonably attractive, very modern place, with an excellent foyer area filled with cafes and greenery and with large areas of glass overlooking the river. It also benefits from a great location just off Midan Tahrir, so it's close to the Egyptian Museum.

The Pyramids

Where once the venerable Mena House could boast of being the only hotel in the vicinity of the Pyramids, that's now far from the case. The Cairo end of the desert road to Alexandria is fast resembling a Vegas-like strip of large resorts on the fringe of the desert. Most of these places are grand affairs offering all amenities, which

they have to do because apart from the Pyramids there's just nowhere else to go around here, stranded as you are 16km or more out of the city centre.

Cataract Pyramids Hotel (☎ *384 2901, fax 384 2902, Saqqara Rd, Giza*) Rooms from US$90/117. Another recent five-star addition to Cairo, this is an enormous, self-contained resort hotel (400 rooms) on the road between the Giza Pyramids and Saqqara. It has got no fewer than 11 restaurants, numerous bars and an enormous pool, but public transport is rare around here so you need your own vehicle or else you're dependent on organised tours.

Le Méridien Forte Grand Pyramids (☎ *383 0383, fax 383 1730,* **W** *www.lemeridien-hotels.com, Cairo-Alexandria Desert Hwy*) Singles/doubles from US$125/160. It may be almost a kilometre away, but still the views of the Pyramids from this place are wonderful. Best of all are the outdoor pools, which feel pure Caribbean, especially the swim-in bar.

Mövenpick Jolie Ville (☎ *385 2555, fax 383 5006,* **e** *resort.cairo-pyramids@ moevenpick.com,* **W** *www.moevenpick-hotels .ch, Cairo-Alexandria Desert Hwy*) Singles US$100-120, doubles US$139-150. This bungalow village is set among luxuriant gardens a short distance from the Pyramids.

Oberoi Mena House (☎ *383 3222, fax 383 7414,* **e** *obmhofc@oberoi.com.eg,* **W** *www.oberoihotels.com, Pyramids Rd, Giza*) Singles/doubles from US$150/180, with pyramid views US$250/300. A former royal hunting lodge converted into a sumptuous luxury hotel, the Mena House has an unbeatable location right next door to the Pyramids. The interior is an opulent Oriental fantasy, and there are beautiful gardens with a large swimming pool from which you can see the Pyramids while floating on your back. If you can afford it, stay in the main building rather than the garden annexe.

Heliopolis

Most of the trade at these places, all 20km or so north-east of the city centre, comes from business travellers and people who need to remain in the vicinity of the airport.

EDDIE GERALD

BRETT SHEARER

It's only once the sun has gone down and the intense heat of the day has subsided that Cairenes come out to play. The upmarket residential districts of Gezira (top) and Zamalek offer some great places to eat, while Downtown (bottom) is the place to do some late-night shopping.

Cutting a swathe through the city north to south, the Nile creates room to breathe and shows off the city at its best, with miles of dramatic skyline along its banks. Strolling along the river at Gezira (bottom) is a favourite pastime, but the best way to appreciate the river is to take a cruise on a felucca (top).

Mövenpick Hotel & Casino (☎ 637 0077, fax 418 0761, [e] email@movenpickhel .com.eg, [w] www.moevenpick-hotels.ch, *Cairo International Airport*) Singles US$145-170, doubles US$190-265. This big hotel has all the usual amenities and is just a couple of kilometres from the airport. It operates a free shuttle bus service to/from the airport and Downtown.

Novotel (☎ 291 8520, fax 291 4794, *Cairo International Airport*) Singles/doubles US$129/163. The closest hotel to the airport terminals, it's nothing special but does the job.

Sheraton Heliopolis (☎ 290 2027, fax 290 4061, [e] shhelio@gega.net, [w] www .sheraton.com, *Sharia al-Uruba*). Rooms US$136-260. Some 8km or so separates the residential centre of Heliopolis and the airport, and this hotel lies closer to the former. As a result, it's a bit more lively than the other chain hotels up here, with more going on in the way of events and entertainment.

LONG-TERM RENTALS

If you are planning on staying in Cairo for a couple of months or more, it's relatively easy to find a flat to rent. However, if you're on a budget, then a month's rent on the cheapest flat can work out to cost more than 30 nights at a budget hotel. Of course, it depends on the area you're looking at, but the lowest monthly rental you can expect to pay (say, in an area such as Bab al-Luq, which is cheap and close to the centre) is about E£600 per month. This will get you a one- or two-bedroom place, old and none too clean, with a horrible bathroom and kitchen. For the same figure you could perhaps find a room in a more decent two- or three-bedroom shared flat, somewhere like Doqqi, Agouza or Zamalek. A decent flat in any of these three areas with two bedrooms, a good kitchen and bathroom, and a balcony goes for between E£1500 and...well, the sky's the limit. We know of people paying US$1700 a month for three-bedroom flats in Zamalek. Price depends on size, how modern the furnishings are, whether the place has an international phone line or not, the quality of the plumbing, and location.

A Nile view, for example, will add a couple of hundred pounds a month. If you don't mind being out of the centre, flats in Giza and Heliopolis tend to be extremely large, often with spacious balconies, and with lower rents than those Downtown.

Finding a Flat

By far the easiest way to find a flat is to use a *simsar* (flat agent). Every street has one of these guys: he's generally a *bawwab* (doorman) who makes it his business to know who is renting what in his area. Choose the neighbourhood you want to live in and then ask any bawwab for directions to the local simsar. You'll need to speak Arabic or have an Arabic-speaking friend along. The last time we did this we were shown nearly a dozen flats in neighbouring streets in our desired area in the space of just a couple of hours. The finders' fee should be about 10% of the monthly rent. If nothing takes your fancy, a little *baksheesh* (tip) is in order for the simsar's time. In addition to the simsar network, there are also real estate agents, but they tend to deal with the upper end of the market and charge higher commissions. Some agents you could try include the following:

Alfi Doss Services (☎ 418 6516) 63 Osman ibn Affan, Heliopolis
Conserv (☎ 735 1811) 17A Mohammed Mazhar, Zamalek
Excel Services (☎ 290 7882, fax 616 805) 69 Omar ibn al-Khattab, Heliopolis
Sourya Abdel Wahab (☎ 748 2713) 12 Midan al-Missaha, Doqqi
Sunny Home (☎ 358 2278) 35 Road 13, Ma'adi

Many local supermarkets, particularly in areas with a significant foreign presence such as Heliopolis, Ma'adi, Mohandiseen and Zamalek, have boards on which people post notice of flats to let.

There's also an Egyptian real estate Web site, [w] www.e-dar.com, which includes rental listings, although these tend to be at the more expensive end of the market.

For more information on flat hunting pick up *Cairo: The Practical Guide*, which is available from the American University in Cairo (AUC) bookshops.

Places to Eat

For somewhere of its size and cosmopolitan nature, Cairo has little to excite when it comes to dining out. Taste is most definitely the sense least excited by a stay in the city. The large numbers of Armenians, Greeks and Levantines to whom Cairo has traditionally been home are all but invisible when it comes to the restaurant scene, and while the architectural legacies of the French and Italians are omnipresent, their influence on menus is sadly lacking.

As for the local cuisine, while there are many wonderful things about Egypt, none of them are gastronomic. In fact, Egypt can lay claim to having introduced the world to one of the most revolting dishes of all time, *molokhiyya*. Made by stewing the deep green molokhiyya leaf *(Corchorus olitorius)* in chicken stock, the resulting soup looks like green algae and has the consistency of mucus. The 11th-century caliph Al-Hakim found the stuff so repulsive he had the dish banned. Still, it has its fans and ought to be tried at least once, if only for the experience.

Matters are improving, and since the first edition of this guide a number of very commendable restaurants have appeared, including Abu as-Sid, Flux, La Bodega and the Seasons Restaurant. Even so, progress is slow and worthwhile choices remain few. Residents and visitors alike usually find themselves returning again and again to the same tried-and-tested favourites, which are often establishments attached to one or other of the five-star hotels. For this reason, over the following pages we've tried to avoid hotel restaurants, highlighting just a few of the most noteworthy, and instead concentrate on digging out more interesting alternatives, places where the flavour of the locale often goes some way towards compensating for any lack of flavour in the food.

WHEN TO EAT

Restaurants tend to open around noon, or just before, and keep the kitchens going until the last customer leaves, which can be long past midnight. Although we give opening times in our listings, treat them as a guideline, not gospel. Apart from the few cases noted, reservations are rarely necessary. Other than snack joints, few places ever get busy at lunch time and, Egyptians being late eaters, proper restaurants don't fill up until around 9pm or later. Once tables are taken though, they stay taken – the Cairo way is to linger over dinner and make an evening of it.

WHERE TO EAT

In contrast to most cities, where the centre is where it's at, Downtown is not somewhere to dine in Cairo. There's the odd bright spot such as Felfela, and perhaps such lesser lights as Cafe Riche and Estoril, but otherwise Downtown equals downmarket, and the choice rarely extends beyond *fuul*, *ta'amiyya* and *kushari* (see Egyptian Staples later in this chapter). Similarly, Islamic Cairo, where other than a string of overpriced and underwhelming kebab houses facing Midan Hussein, there's only one true restaurant to speak of.

No, the dining scene in Cairo is concentrated where the money is, which means the affluent neighbourhoods of Zamalek, Doqqi and Mohandiseen, plus Heliopolis to the north-east. (The far-flung districts of Medinat Nasr and Ma'adi are also full of restaurants, but they're beyond the geographical scope of this book.) Of these, Zamalek is attractive, which makes dining there a pleasure, and the area is within walking distance of most hotels. By contrast, Doqqi and Mohandiseen are fairly grim and dining there usually involves taking a taxi to and from the restaurant.

Sadly, the option of casually wandering the streets browsing for somewhere pleasant to eat does not exist in Cairo – restaurants are too sparsely scattered and are often well hidden on the upper floors of buildings. Instead, plan in advance – or go hungry.

What Is Egyptian Cuisine?

Much of the food eaten in Egypt is not unique to the country but is shared with other Middle Eastern neighbours and near-neighbours – hardly surprising given Egypt's history of occupation by foreign powers. Trade also had a lot to do with it. Perhaps half the dishes typically passed off as 'Egyptian' can be claimed by the Turkish, while the Lebanese account for much of the rest. There are also Persian, Greek and even English elements in there – the popular dessert Umm Ali (an Egyptian bread-and-butter pudding) is said to have been introduced by a Miss O'Malley, an Irish mistress of Khedive Ismail. In fact, it's near impossible to disentangle what originates where and with whom. However, there are a few specialities that can be upheld as truly Egyptian. Coptic Christians, who claim to be the descendants of ancient Egyptians, claim both fuul and ta'amiyya as their own, as well as *molokhiyya*, the making of which is claimed to be shown in Pharaonic tomb paintings.

But whereas Turkish cooking was raised to high art by the chefs in the sultans' kitchens and, Lebanese cuisine was refined by the influence of the Persians and French, Egyptian cuisine has remained essentially peasant cooking. It's the food of the under-classes: basic, easy to prepare and cheap. So while Turkish, Lebanese and Persian restaurants are found worldwide, true Egyptian restaurants are about as common as Iranian pubs. Most of the so-called 'Egyptian restaurants' in Cairo are also nothing of the sort, they're just generic 'Oriental'. Interestingly, having been stigmatised in the past as beyond the pale, this humble form of cooking is now becoming fashionable; McDonald's Egypt has recently added the McFelafel to its brightly illuminated menu, while Zamalek's Abu as-Sid is the talk of the town, serving refined versions of peasant dishes in ultra-chic surroundings to the city's moneyed classes.

FOOD
Egyptian Staples
What burger and fries are to most of the Western world, fuul and ta'amiyya are to Egypt. Fuul is made from small brown beans, soaked overnight then boiled and mashed. In its most refined form the resulting paste is sprinkled with olive oil and lemon juice and seasoned with salt, pepper and cumin. It's then ladled into a pocket of *shammy*, a pitta-like bread. Ta'amiyya is mashed fava beans and spices fried in a patty and stuffed into a piece of shammy with salad and tahini (sesame-seed paste). It's better known outside Cairo as felafel. Bright pink pickled vegetables, known as *torshi*, are usually served complimentary. The better takeaway joints and sit-down restaurants offer variations on the fuul and ta'amiyya theme, serving them up with egg, garlic, butter, mincemeat or *basturma*, Egyptian pastrami.

Most fuul and ta'amiyya joints also do *shwarma*. Strips of lamb or chicken are sliced from a spit, sizzled on a hotplate with chopped tomatoes, onion and parsley, and then stuffed in a pocket of shammy.

Next in national affections after fuul and ta'amiyya is *kushari*, a mix of noodles, rice, black lentils, fried onions and tomato sauce. The ingredients are served up together in a bowl or spooned into a polythene bag for takeaway. You can recognise kushari joints by the great tureens of noodles and rice in their windows.

Starters
Eating Egyptian often involves starting with an array of small side dishes known as mezze, although these are more limited in variety compared with Lebanese or Turkish cuisine. Most common are hummus, cooked chickpeas (garbanzos) ground into a paste and seasoned with garlic, lemon and olive oil; tahini, a thinner paste made from sesame seeds; and *baba ghanoug*, a rich creamy paste of aubergine (eggplant) baked to impart a smoky flavour then mashed and blended with tahini, lemon juice and garlic.

Also very common is *mahshi*, which is various vegetables, such as vine leaves (in summer), cabbage (in winter), peppers, or white and black aubergines, stuffed with

PLACES TO EAT

Eat Like an Egyptian

Cairene eating habits are not wildly different from those in any city in Europe or America. They, too, consume a standard three meals a day, based largely on vegetables, beans, pulses and meat, with pasta and rice thrown in for variety. However, bread and bread products account for 60% of the average calorific intake. Egyptians consume far less fast food or frozen meals than their Western counterparts (a result of economics rather than health awareness), which might translate into a more life-prolonging diet if it wasn't for the fact that most cooking is slathered in lethal amounts of clarified butter *(samna)*, similar to Indian ghee.

When it comes to breakfast Kellogg has yet to make a great impact – for much of the populace their morning meal consists of bread and cheese, perhaps with some olives, and maybe a fried egg taken at home or a fuul sandwich on the run. Lunch is the day's main meal, taken from 2pm onwards, but more likely around 3pm or 4pm when dad's home from work and the children are back from school. Whatever's served, mama will probably have spent most of her day in the kitchen preparing it (Egyptian cooking always seems to be very labour intensive); it'll be hot and there'll probably be plenty to go round. Whatever's left over will probably be served up again later in the evening as supper.

Although quite happy to patronise the local fuul and ta'amiyya stand, and buy grilled chicken from Am Arabi or baked fish from Fawzi or whoever (the important thing is that they know these characters and will swear that they do the best chicken, fish etc in all Cairo), most Egyptians treat restaurants with suspicion. Why pay hard-earned money when they know mama does it better? Hence the rather disappointing dining-out scene. However, those who do dine out, do so late and wouldn't dream of taking a table before 9pm or 10pm. It's not unusual for families to be out, working their way through dinner, at 1am or 2am.

minced meat, rice, onions, parsley and herbs and then baked. It's good when just cooked and hot, but less so when cold.

Salads tend to be uninventive. Typically, what's offered is a mixture of chopped tomatoes, lettuce and cucumber doused in a fairly overpowering vinegary dressing. You need to visit an upmarket restaurant to get anything more exciting.

Many menus also offer a soup *(shurbah)* or two. The standard is a variation on vegetable broth, often with pearl pasta. Also popular is *hamud*, which is made with chicken stock, strongly flavoured with lemon and garlic. Cooked rice and any green vegetables that are to hand often find their way in too. The other common item, especially in winter, is *shurbat ads*, lentil soup, often spiced with cumin.

Main Dishes

Mains tend to be no-frills platters of meat. Lamb is the favourite and most predominant, the gift of the fat-tailed sheep that you

sometimes see being marshalled through town early in the morning. Beef is much less common and, because of the dietary laws of Islam, pork is a no-no. At restaurants and cheap eateries, the most common serve is *shish kebab*, where the lamb is chopped into small chunks and flame grilled together with tomato and chunks of onion. (The chicken equivalent is *shish tawouq*.) Alternatively, the meat is ground, spiced, squeezed into sausages, then grilled: this is kofta. Kebab and kofta usually come on a bed of *badounis* (parsley) with accompanying bread and perhaps a little salad, and are ideally accompanied with a selection of mezze, ordered separately. Typically, kebab and kofta are ordered in restaurants by weight: 250g *(roba kilo)* is usually sufficient for one person and usually costs from E£9 to E£12.

Chicken *(firekh)* is also popular, commonly sold whole or by the half, crackling off a spit grill at hole-in-the-wall restaurants all over town. Ghanem on 26th of July near the junction with Shagaret ad-Durr in Zamalek is one of our favourites for a hot take-away bird. Here they sprinkle the skin with spices before grilling and the result is gorgeous. Another big favourite is pigeon *(hamam)*. Egyptian pigeons are a totally different variety from the flying rats of European cities. They're a lot cleaner for a start, mostly being bred up in the Delta in the distinctive conical pigeon towers you see out the window on the train up to Alexandria. They can be cooked like chicken, halved over a charcoal grill or, better still, baked and stuffed with spiced rice and giblets.

Egyptians are keen on offal. *Kebda firekh* (chicken livers) are often excellent – if done right they should be beautifully soft with an almost pâté-like consistency. Less appealing is *mokh*, or brain. This is served crumbed and deep-fried, or boiled whole and garnished with salad. Lamb testicles *(beid ghanem)* are another delicacy (try them at the Alfy Bey Restaurant on Sharia Alfy in Downtown), although these are rarely served alone and are usually included within a mixed grill.

All of these dishes are fairly straightforward servings of meat with little invention involved. For something more interesting, look out for *fatta* dishes. These involve rice and bread soaked in a garlicky-vinegary sauce with lamb or chicken, all in a clay pot, which is then cooked in the oven. It's heavy, and not recommended as a lunch unless you have a chaise longue handy, but it can be extremely satisfying.

Molokhiyya (unfairly slandered, some might say, in the introduction to this chapter) is greatly improved by the addition of lamb, duck or rabbit. It's also sometimes ladled over rice as sauce. Much use is made of *bamia* (okra, also known as ladies' fingers), a common component in stews. These also typically involve lamb, and perhaps other vegetables, often potatoes, simmered in a rich tomato sauce and served over rice.

For a wealth of further information together with hundreds of recipes, look out for the superb *A New Book of Middle Eastern Food* by international cook and food writer Claudia Roden.

Desserts & Sweets

Sticky, syrupy pastries have given Egypt a reputation for a sweet tooth, but, traditionally, such things were only bought to mark special occasions. Judging from the profusion of pastry shops and the crowds that continuously throng them, that's no longer the case. The generic term for these sugar-loaded confections is baklava, and it applies to a delicacy constructed of layers of wafer-thin filo pastry filled with crushed nuts and pistachios and drenched in syrup. It is baked in great trays and then typically sliced into small diamond-shaped pieces. *Kunafa* is another generic type; this is made by sieving liquid batter onto a hot metal sheet so it sets in vermicelli-like strands, which are quickly swept off so they remain soft. These are then piled on top of a soft cheese, cream or pistachio base.

When buying from a pastry shop order by weight – a quarter kilo is generally the smallest amount you can buy, and that's probably more than enough for one person.

Apart from pastries, desserts are surprisingly few in number. *Muhalabiyya* is cream thickened with cornflour or ground rice, often flavoured with rose-water, with coconut or chopped almonds sprinkled on top. It looks like blancmange. Umm Ali is layers of pastry, filled with nuts and raisins, soaked in milk, then baked. It's similar to English bread-and-butter pudding, but made more sumptuous with cream, rose-water and nuts. *Roz b'laban* (rice with milk) is completely self-explanatory; it's served cold.

DRINKS
Non-Alcoholic Drinks

Shay (tea) and *ahwa* (coffee) are served strong and sugary. Specify how much sugar you want, otherwise, in most non-Western places, staff will automatically dump three or four heaped teaspoons of the stuff into your glass. To moderate that, order your tea *sukhar shwayya*, with 'a little sugar'. If you don't want any sugar at all, ask for *sukhar minrayer*. If you take your tea with milk, ask for *bi-laban*. Far more refreshing, when it's in season, is tea served with mint leaves; ask for *shay naana*.

Nothing but the Juice

Recognisable by the hanging bags of netted fruit (and carrots) that adorn their facades, juice stands are found throughout the city. An absolute godsend on a hot summer's day, you can get a cool, vitamin-packed drink squeezed out of just about anything that hangs off a tree – provided it's in season. Standard juices *(asiir)* include banana *(moz)*, guava *(guafa)*, lemon *(limoon)*, mango *(manga)*, orange *(bortuaan)*, pomegranate *(rumman)*, strawberry *(farawla)* and sugar cane *(asab)*. Depending on the type of fruit, a glass costs from 50pt to E£1.50. Alternatively, take along an empty mineral-water bottle and get that filled up.

If you ask for coffee, you will probably get Turkish coffee, which comes in a two-sip sized cup. It is gritty and *very* strong. Let the grains settle before drinking it. As with tea, you have to specify how much sugar you want: *ahwa mazboot* comes with a moderate amount of sugar but is still fairly sweet; if you don't want any sugar ask for *ahwa saada*. Coffee is often flavoured with cardamom. If you want something more like Western-style instant coffee, ask for *nescaf*.

The best place to drink tea and coffee is at one of Cairo's multitudinous coffeehouses – see the boxed text 'The Ahwa' in the Entertainment chapter later in this book.

Locally bottled mineral water is available at all restaurants and is perfectly safe to drink. Only the most upmarket of places are likely to have sparkling water.

Alcoholic Drinks

Although the ancient Egyptians are supposed to have invented wine, until recently it was all but absent from contemporary Egypt, at least in any drinkable form – a government-owned company produced a single red, rosé and white, vinegary banquets that went by nicknames such as Chateau Migraine. Most bottles were bought as one-off, never-to-be-repeated experiments by expats and tourists. That situation changed in 1999 with a buy-out and relaunch. The new, revamped trio of Omar Khayyam (red), Rubis d'Egypte (rosé) and Cru des Ptolemées (white), made with grapes from the Delta and with the assistance of a Bordeaux-based winery, are quite drinkable.

Bottles can be bought at Al-Ahram Beverages shops (see under Self-Catering later in this chapter), where they sell for about E£30. The wines are also offered at restaurants frequented by foreigners (Egyptians account for only 20% of wine sales). However, seriously upmarket places usually have the real stuff, imported and subject to outrageous taxes, meaning prices are astronomic. Economics may dictate that you give the local stuff a go.

The local liquor isn't just bad, it's potentially lethal. Egypt produces its own gin, whisky, vodka and brandy. They all taste roughly the same, which is to say dreadful. Amusingly, the spirits are marketed to resemble foreign imports – the whiskies include Johnny Wadie and Robert Horse, while bottles of Garden's Gin used to carry a bold claim to the effect that 'The Queen drinks this'. What's less funny is that some local liquor is truly poisonous. Tales have long circulated among Cairo folk of deaths caused by drinking local spirits. The stories were always apocryphal until the Canadian embassy issued a circular, warning that two deaths had proven to be as a result of drinking local whisky. Leave this stuff well alone.

For the lowdown on Egyptian beer, see the boxed text 'Stella Stuff' in the Entertainment chapter.

FUUL & TA'AMIYYA PLACES

There are fuul and ta'amiyya places on nearly every street, most of which are takeaway only. Some are better than others, with several standing out above the rest. A fuul or ta'amiyya sandwich usually costs about 50pt and two make a substantial snack.

Akher Sa'a *(8 Sharia Alfy, Downtown)* **Map 2, #14** Open 24 hr. The sign is in Arabic only, but look for the Christian bookshop next door. This is a hugely popular fuul and ta'amiyya takeaway joint with a no-frills restaurant next door where you can also get things such as omelettes (with basturma is good) and salads.

Felfela Takeaway (13 Talaat Harb, Downtown) **Map 2, #75** Place your order, pay at the tills, then present your ticket at the busy counter at the back to get your sandwiches. There's standing room only – if you want to sit, try the hugely popular Felfela restaurant round the corner (see under Restaurants later in this chapter).

Al-Halwagy (☎ 591 7055, Midan Hussein, Khan al-Khalili) **Map 7, #13** Dishes E£10-20 (2 people). Open 24 hr. Just along from the Egyptian Pancake House, this is a good ta'amiyya, fuul and salad place that has been around for nearly a century. You can eat at pavement tables or secrete yourself upstairs where one of the tables has a veiled view over the bazaar below.

Na'ama (Sharia el-Nil, Agouza) **Map 3, #84** Open 24 hr. Just north of the 6th of October Bridge, with six lanes of traffic thundering by outside, Na'ama doesn't pick up much pedestrian traffic but it's a big favourite with taxi drivers.

Al-Omda (Sharia Tahrir, Doqqi) **Map 4, #16** As well as good fuul and ta'amiyya, this takeaway-only branch of Al-Omda does a very decent shwarma. There's also a branch in Mohandiseen (Map 3, #14), at 6 Sharia al-Gazayer, near the Atlas Zamalek hotel.

At-Tabei ad-Dumyati (31 Sharia Orabi, Downtown) **Map 8, #15** About 200m north of Midan Orabi, near the Orabi metro station, this is a personal favourite. It serves fuul with tomatoes and onions, egg and basturma, or clarified butter. Also on the menu is a fuul platter with salad, tahini, ta'amiyya and french fries to accompany your beans. As well as the takeaway, it has a sit-down restaurant. There's also a branch in Mohandiseen (Map 3, #7) at Gamiat ad-Dowal al-Arabiyya.

Zamalek Restaurant (Sharia 26th of July, Zamalek) **Map 3, #65** Being an up-market neighbourhood, Zamalek has precious few fuul and ta'amiyya places but this one, on the main street near the junction with Hassan Sabry, is a good 'un.

KUSHARI JOINTS

There are plenty of kushari joints about town, but the best are all Downtown; an exception is Al-Omda in Mohandiseen, which also serves up a decent dish. Kushari serves come in small *(sughayyer)*, medium *(metawasit)* or large *(kebir)*. A medium serve, more than most people can eat, costs from E£1 to E£1.50.

Abu Tarek (40 Sharia Champollion, Downtown) **Map 2, #42** Just a few minutes' walk west of upper Talaat Harb, Abu Tarek is a gleaming two-storey kushari joint that's reckoned to be *the* best. It does a good roz b'laban for dessert.

Lux (Sharia Tahrir, Bab al-Luq) **Map 2, #119** Lux is handily placed not far from Midan Tahrir, on the south side of Midan Falaki, which also makes it a useful place for anyone who gets the munchies part way through a boozy evening at the Cafeteria Horreyya. It also has a branch on Sharia 26th of July.

At-Tahrir (19 Abdel Khalek Sarwat) **Map 2, #46** Holding its own in the fast-food stakes against near-neighbour KFC, At-Tahrir is equally clean, bright and shiny, it's also air-conditioned, and what's more, the food's a damn sight healthier.

RESTAURANTS

The following listings are subdivided by area and for each area the restaurants are given in order of price, with the cheapest first. The prices we quote are for main dishes. No alcohol is served unless otherwise stated. You might also want to check out the regularly updated *Restaurant Guide* published in the monthly *Egypt Today*.

Downtown (Map 2)

Akher Sa'a and *At-Tabei ad-Dumyati*, listed under Fuul & Ta'amiyya Places earlier, both have restaurants where the range of food is limited but they're good for a quick snack.

Gomhuriyya Restaurant (42 Sharia Falaki, Downtown) **Map 2, #99** Dishes E£8-12. Open 2pm-3am daily. You can find pigeon on the menu at any number of restaurants, but this place just off Midan Falaki,

Best Restaurants for...

Something a Bit Different

Try stuffed pigeon at the Gomhuriyya Restaurant; or heaped grilled meats in the old slaughterhouse district at Abu Ramy; or super-filling *fatta moza* (fatta with a shank of lamb) at Abu Shaqra; or the infamous *molokhiyya* at Abu as-Sid; or *beid ghanem* (lambs' testicles) at Estoril...Appetite whetted?

Sumptuous Surrounds

A must-see is the super-chic Orientalism of Abu as-Sid, and the food is just as splendid; nearby La Bodega also made the interior magazines particularly for its lounge; kitschy but dazzling nonetheless, Moghul Room goes over-the-top on Indian.

Starlit Evenings

Take a table beside the Nile at Nubian Village; or a seat in the tree-shaded garden at Andrea; there's rare open-air seating Downtown at Da Mario; in Heliopolis try Le Chantilly or the restaurants at Merryland.

Fine dining

Fish, meat and a fine wine list impress at The Grill; the pan-French cooking at Justine continues to win plaudits; hard-to-find Flux experiments with fantastic fusion cooking; and Seasons Restaurant is simply superb.

Fun dining

Once your plate is cleared, hit the dance floor at Le Tabasco; or book onto the Nile Maxim or any of the Nile cruise boats for a buffet and belly dance; or stay moored but entertained by live music and cheesy antics on board TGI Friday.

Children

Caged birds, tanks of terrapins and tree-trunk tables keep kids happy at Felfela; kids can roam around the gardens, play on frames and ride donkeys at Andrea's and Crazy Fish; the McDonald's on Sharia Gamiat ad-Dowal al-Arabiyya and at the Ramses Annexe both have activity areas.

between Al-Bustan and Hoda Shaarawi, is reckoned to serve the best, delivered to the table piping hot with crisp brown skin. Non-bird-fanciers can order kebab and kofta.

Fatatri at-Tahrir (166 Sharia Tahrir, Downtown) **Map 2, #102** Dishes E£8-16. Open 24 hr. Close to Midan Tahrir, this place specialises in *fiteer*, the Egyptian take on pizza; order savoury or sweet, small, medium or large.

Alfy Bey Restaurant (☎ 577 4999, 3 Sharia Alfy, Downtown) **Map 2, #15** Dishes E£9-16. Open 1pm-1am daily. In business since 1938, but looking spruce after a refurbishment, the Alfy Bey is strictly trad. Food is basic but good and represents excellent value; choose from the like of lamb chops, kebab, grilled chicken or stuffed pigeon.

Felfela Restaurant (☎ 392 2751, 15 Sharia Hoda Shaarawi, Downtown) **Map 2, #76** Dishes E£8-24. Open 8am-midnight daily. Perpetually packed with tourists, coach parties and locals, Felfela deserves its popularity. The quirky decor (tree-trunk tables, stuffed animals, aquariums and lanterns) creates a fun dining environment and, depending on your choices, the all-Egyptian food is excellent and moderately priced. Give the meat dishes a miss, as they are all overpriced and done better elsewhere. Instead, order a selection of fuul, ta'amiyya, salads and other side dishes such as tahini and baba ghanoug. Beer is served. Felfela also has branches at 27 Cairo-Alexandria Desert Hwy, on Sharia Abdel Aziz as-Saud in Rhoda (Map 5, #23) and on the Corniche in Ma'adi.

Cafe Riche (☎ 392 9793, 17 Talaat Harb, Downtown) **Map 2, #82** Dishes E£12-25. Open 8am-midnight daily. A survivor of pre-Revolution days, Cafe Riche was extensively renovated in the 1990s and now serves traditional Egyptian fare in a room hung with portraits of Egypt's revered cultural pantheon. The chicken fatta is recommended. Alcohol is served, and late on in the evening the place reverts to a boozing joint for Cairo's elderly bohos.

Le Bistro (☎ 392 7694, Sharia Hoda Shaarawi, Downtown) **Map 2, #96** Dishes E£14-26. Open 11am-11pm daily. About

200m beyond the Felfela, Le Bistro has cooking that is sufficiently Gallic to ensure that the place is heavily patronised by the city's French-speaking community. The menu features some good salads and lots of beef and chicken-in-sauce dishes. It's busy at lunch, but like a morgue in the evenings.

Abu Shaqra (☎ *364 8602, 69 Qasr al-Ainy, Garden City*) **Map 5, #5** Dishes E£16-30. Open noon-1am daily. Founded in 1947 by Ahmed Shaqra, known as the 'king of kebab', this is a Cairo institution. A front counter does a great trade in takeaways or there's a restaurant at the back. Come for grills and mixed meats and definitely try the *fatta moza*, fatta with a shank of lamb. Abu Shaqra also has branches in Mohandiseen at 17 Gamiat ad-Dowal al-Arabiyya (Map 3, #7) and on Mirghani in Heliopolis.

Da Mario (☎ *578 0444, Nile Hilton, Midan Tahrir*) **Map 2, #64** Dishes E£18-25. Open noon-1.30am daily. Out in the garden courtyard of the Nile Hilton, this is one of the better value five-star hotel restaurants, serving a variety of pizzas and pasta in generous portions. Alcohol is served.

Estoril (☎ *574 3102, 12 Talaat Harb, Downtown*) **Map 2, #79** Dishes E£16-35. Open noon-2am daily. Down the alley next to the DeCastro travel agency, this is a venerable old eatery similar to the Cafe Riche but totally unreconstructed. The menu is limited to grilled meats plus Lebanese mezze and the quality is very variable; however, the place has atmosphere in spades. Alcohol is most definitely served.

Peking Restaurant (☎ *591 2381, 14 Sharia Ezbekiyya*) **Map 2, #16** Dishes E£20-30. Open noon-1am daily. Just north of 26th of July is this very passable Cantonese restaurant. Don't be put off by the shabby exterior, inside the place is smart, if a little dark. The food is reasonably authentic and if you've been in Egypt for any length of time it makes a welcome change from grilled meat. Alcohol is served.

Arabesque (☎ *574 7898, 6 Qasr el-Nil, Downtown*) **Map 2, #67** Dishes E£25-35. Open 12.30pm-3.30pm & 7.30pm-12.30am daily. Between Midan Talaat Harb and Midan Tahrir, the Arabesque scores highly for its decor and surroundings – you enter through a small art gallery into a cosy dining area divided by *mashrabiyya* (wooden lattice) screens and columns with a small gurgling fountain as a centrepiece. Unfortunately the dishes – a mix of traditional Egyptian fare, seafood and steaks – are hit and miss, so it's wise to steer clear of anything too ambitious.

Hard Rock Cafe (☎ *532 1285, Le Méridien Cairo, Manial*) **Map 2, #130** Dishes E£25-40. Open 3pm-3am daily. The second branch of the rock 'n' roll 'n' burgers chain to open in Egypt (first off the mark was in Sharm el-Sheikh) currently has queues round the Méridien foyer most nights wanting in. Visit to view Elton John's cherry-red suit or Michael Jackson's hat, or to tuck into glorified American diner cuisine and giggle over fancy cocktails.

Nubian Village (☎ *362 1717, Le Méridien Cairo, Manial*) **Map 2, #130** Dishes E£25-50, minimum charge E£60. Open 1pm-1am daily. This is one of the better hotel restaurants – expect fancy-fied Egyptian cuisine with a few excellent dishes rarely found in Cairo, such as duck in pastry. Even better, Nubian Village occupies a fine Nile-side terrace, making this one of the most pleasant spots in town for a languorous dinner under the stars.

The Grill (☎ *795 7171, Semiramis Inter-Continental, Corniche el-Nil, Downtown*) **Map 2, #106** Dishes from E£35. Up on the 3rd floor of the hotel with splendid Nile views, The Grill is an exceptional fish and meat restaurant with French overtones courtesy of a head chef from Normandy (it's about the only place in Egypt where you'll find *escargots*, snails). This is dining as fine as it gets in Cairo and the wine list runs to over 100 choices.

Shubra (Map 1)

A real working-class district north of the city centre, Shubra's not a place that many visitors ever see. However, if you want to experience the city as the locals live it, jump on the metro, get off at the Rod al-Farag stop and take a look – and while you're at it, you can visit an excellent fish restaurant.

Asmak ad-Dawran *(125-127 Sharia Shubra, Shubra)* **Map 1, #3** Dishes E£10-30. Open noon-1am daily. A legendary fish restaurant occupying two premises (one rough-and-ready, one glitzy) that's suddenly become a whole lot more accessible with the completion of the Shubra metro line, Asmak ad-Dawran has the absolute freshest of sea creatures fried, baked, grilled, boiled and souped, then served up in mammoth portions. Beer is available.

Islamic Cairo (Map 7)

Now that the authorities are pumping money into the historic old city we may finally get to see some decent places to dine here (one of the many renovated but redundant old houses would make a fantastic setting). For the moment, however, the choice remains chronically limited.

Egyptian Pancake House *(Midan Hussein, Khan al-Khalili)* **Map 7, #14** Dishes E£10-14. Open noon-2am daily. This is a fiteer-only place, specialising in the Egyptian flaky-pastry pizzas. Choose from the following savoury or sweet toppings: cheese, egg, tomato, olives or ground meat (although you'll probably want to give 'turkey cock' a miss), or raisins, coconut or icing sugar.

Naguib Mahfouz Cafe/Khan al-Khalili Restaurant *(☎ 590 3788, 5 Sikket al-Badestan, Khan al-Khalili)* **Map 7, #5** Dishes E£24-40. Open 10am-2am daily. In the heart of the bazaar, this is run by the Oberoi hotel chain, so, while it's certainly classy, the 'Disneyfied Orientalism' of resident musicians and chintzy decor can come across as a bit phoney. The cafe section does shwarma and other sandwiches, while the restaurant menu is an unexciting mix of Middle Eastern and European favourites.

Sayyida Zeinab (Map 5)

This is a district on the very southern fringes of Islamic and Downtown Cairo, reached by heading south from Midan Tahrir along Qasr al-Ainy. It abuts the area where the city slaughterhouses used to be and it's still a great place for no-frills meat eating.

Haram Zeinab *(Cnr Sharia Abdel Meguid & Midan Sayyida Zeinab)* **Map 5, #12** Dishes E£8-12. Open 24 hr. On a busy corner next to a coffeehouse and bakery, this place does arguably the best and cheapest fiteer in town. It's a good fuel stop on a visit to Ibn Tulun mosque.

Abu Rifai *(Zuqaq Gineid, Sayyida Zeinab)* **Map 5, #8** Dishes E£10-14. Open 10pm-6am daily. On the north side of Midan Sayyida Zeinab, opposite the mosque and up the alleyway to the left of the ornate old kiosk, Abu Rifai is a small kebab house well known among Cairo's clubbers and night owls as a place to wolf down grilled meats after a night spent shimmying. It's at its busiest around 4am, when you'll even find the odd feasting family – don't these people ever sleep?

Ouf *(Midan Zein al-Abdeen, Sayyida Zeinab)* **Map 5, #18** Dishes E£10-20. Open noon-4am daily. This dedicated kebab house is distinguished by fine meat and excellent offal, particularly the kidneys *(kellawi)*.

Abu Ramy *(Sharia ibn Yazid)* **Map 5, #24** Dishes E£10-30. Open dusk to dawn daily. At one time Abu Ramy was nothing but benches and tables on open ground beside the old slaughterhouse buildings. Now it has indoor seating, but sheep are still tethered behind the ramshackle kitchens, so there are no illusions about where your supper is coming from. There's no menu, just mounds of meat – order from kofta, kebab, liver *(kebda)*, kidneys or lamb chops *(rayesh)*. Bread, salad and hummus are provided. It's way distant from anywhere – to get here, take a taxi to Midan Zein al-Abdeen, locate Ouf, and then head down the street to the left of it. At the bottom, past the stalls selling butchers' knives, bear left and Abu Ramy is 50m on the right.

Zamalek (Map 3)

For expats, moneyed Egyptians and anyone who eats to be seen, Zamalek is the place to dine.

Al Dente *(☎ 735 9117, 26 Bahgat Ali, Zamalek)* **Map 3, #25** Dishes E£8-14. Open 10am-midnight daily. Only pasta is served at this tiny place, which is popular with students from the nearby American University in Cairo hostel. Choose the pasta type and the sauce and the chef cooks it up while you wait. Portions are generous.

Maison Thomas (☎ 735 7057, 157 Sharia 26th of July, Zamalek) **Map 3, #60** Pizzas E£16-25. Open 24 hr. This is Cairo's only Continental-style deli. It does by far the best pizza in Cairo, and a 'regular' is easily enough for two. It also has excellent, though pricey, sandwiches and salads. You can eat in or take out.

Deals (☎ 736 0502, 2 Sayyed al-Bakry, Zamalek) **Map 3, #58** Dishes E£16-30. Open noon-2am daily. This is a busy little bar serving good food. Check the menu for what's on, but typically it's the likes of burgers, chilli con carne, calamari and large salads. Get here before 8pm to stand a chance of finding some table space. There are also branches in Mohandiseen (☎ 305 7255) at 2 Sharia Gol Gamal and in Heliopolis (☎ 291 0406) at 40A Sharia Baghdad.

L'Aubergine (☎ 735 6550, 5 Sayyed al-Bakry, Zamalek) **Map 3, #56** Dishes E£17-30. Open 10am-2am daily. Among expats and Westernised Egyptians this has long been one of the city's most popular restaurants. The menu is constantly changing, but last time we visited it included items such as blue cheese and leek lasagne, aubergine moussaka and vegetables in coconut, ginger and green coriander sauce. There are also salads and soups, and beer is served. Upstairs is an equally heavily patronised bar (see under Bars in the Entertainment chapter for more details).

Hana (☎ 736 3197, Sharia Brazil, Zamalek) **Map 3, #36** Dishes E£20-30. Open 1am-11pm daily. About 400m north of 26th of July, Hana is an unpretentious, smoky little Korean restaurant that serves up fairly authentic South-East Asian food (the menu includes some Japanese and Chinese dishes). *Kimchi* (fermented pickles) comes complimentary, as does fruit at the end of the meal. Dishes are substantial. Beer is available.

La Piazza (☎ 736 2961, 4 Hassan Sabry, Zamalek) **Map 3, #83** Dishes E£16-35. Open 12.30pm-12.30am daily. Part of a complex of restaurants under the collective title Four Corners, La Piazza has a light and airy dining room with plenty of greenery,

and makes for a good lunch spot. Not everything on the menu is a success (we'd suggest you avoid the pastas), but the onion soup is excellent as is the liver pâté mousse, and the salads are usually a good bet. Alcohol is served.

Abu as-Sid (☎ 735 9640, 157 Sharia 26th of July, Zamalek) **Map 3, #62** Dishes E£24-50. Open 11am-4am daily. One of Cairo's newest and most sumptuous restaurants, Abu as-Sid is decked out in stage-set Orientalia: padded cushions, brass lamps and spangly bric-a-brac. It looks stunning. The food is equally notable, and this is one of the very few restaurants where you can get real home-style Egyptian food, including the likes of *sharkassiyya* (chicken breast with walnut sauce), *sayadiyya* (fish with tomatoes, onions and red rice) and molokhiyya, the green-leaf soup, served here with rabbit. Reservations are necessary. Alcohol is served.

La Bodega (☎ 735 6761, 157 Sharia 26th of July, Zamalek) **Map 3, #60** Dishes E£30-50. Open 7am-1am daily. Another fairly recent addition to the Cairo dining scene, La Bodega is an elegant and unusual restaurant, bar and cocktail lounge combination with fabulous decor. The menu ranges wide and includes Middle Eastern and international dishes. The selection of spirits is possibly the best in town, and the lounge even has its own cigar humidor.

Morocco (☎ 735 3114, 012-390 0256, 9 Saray al-Gezira, Zamalek) **Map 2, #1** Dishes E£40-75. Open 9pm-4am daily. Lodged on the Blue Nile Boat moored off Zamalek, Morocco is flavour of the moment with the city's glitterati – which means by the time you are reading this it'll no longer be quite so hot and you'll have a chance of actually getting a table. It's a restaurant-cum-club with arabesque decor and a North African menu. The food is good but pricey (you're looking at E£100 per person for dinner) and drinks start at E£25. There's a house DJ and breathtaking views from an outdoor lounge, but you've got to dress up and reserve in advance to get in.

Justine's (☎ 737 2119, 4 Hassan Sabry, Zamalek) **Map 3, #83** Dishes E£45-80.

PLACES TO EAT

Open noon-3pm & 8pm-11pm daily. One of the city's top restaurants and a favourite with the diplomatic corps, Justine is buried in an unprepossessing apartment block overlooking the Gezira Club, part of the Four Corners complex of restaurants. The place is a little over-formal, but the dishes – from an all-French menu – are top class. Reservations are advisable. Alcohol is served.

Mohandiseen (Maps 1 & 3) & Doqqi (Map 4)

First impressions are that all dining in these Westernised suburbs goes on in fast-food joints, which are infesting the streets round here like cancerous cells. However, tucked away in the double-parked backstreets are some surprisingly worthwhile restaurants.

Al-Omda (☎ 345 2387, 6 Sharia al-Gazayer, Mohandiseen) **Map 3, #14** Dishes E£8-26. Open noon-2am. Al-Omda serves kebab and kofta, shish tawouq, mixed salads and mezze, plus king-size fiteer, with your choice of fillings. Portions are huge so order sparingly. There is another branch specialising in salads close by.

Prestige (☎ 347 0383, 43 Sharia Geziret al-Arab, Mohandiseen) **Map 3, #11** Dishes E£12-40. Open noon-2am daily. Prestige is two eateries in one – a cheerful, cheap pizzeria and a more expensive international restaurant specialising in steaks and fresh fish, with pavement seating under large sun umbrellas. Beer is served, but only inside.

Maroosh (☎ 345 0972, 64 Midan Libnan, Mohandiseen) **Map 1, #1** Dishes E£8-30. Open 8am-2am daily. Maroosh has excellent mezze, which you can enjoy while lounging in rattan chairs on a street-side terrace. Skip the main meat dishes (which shouldn't be too difficult in the case of the 'lamb scrotum sandwich') and fill the table with bread and dips. For those who don't know their *tabouleh* from their *fattoush*, everything is described in English on the menu.

Tia Maria (☎ 335 3273, 32 Sharia Jeddah, Doqqi) **Map 4, #2** Dishes E£16-30. Open 1pm-1am daily. Don't be put off by the incredibly chintzy interior, all frilly pink curtains and whatnot, because the Italian-ish food here is good. We can thoroughly

recommend the spaghetti carbonara, the seafood pasta, served in an enormous clam shell, and the *crespelle Argentine* (crepes with ice cream smothered in caramel sauce).

Le Tabasco (☎ 336 5583, 8 Midan Amman, Doqqi) **Map 4, #7** Dishes E£25-40. Open 1pm-2am daily. Owned and operated by the same people as Zamalek's L'Aubergine, this place is just as popular. Again, the menu changes regularly, ranging over a wide culinary field, including on past visits dishes from the Mediterranean, Mexico and Eastern Europe. Be warned though, the place gets crowded and loud. What's that? I said IT'S LOUD! Alcohol is served.

Kandahar (☎ 303 0615, 3 Gamiat ad-Dowal al-Arabiyya, Mohandiseen) **Map 3, #19** Dishes E£25-45. Open noon-midnight daily. Despite a lousy location on one of Cairo's most thunderous main drags, once inside Kandahar is all calm and order, with charming decor. Food is Indian with a menu divided between curries and tandooris. The spicing is toned down in deference to Egyptian palates, but the dishes are accomplished. Alcohol is served.

Flux (☎ 338 6601, 2 Sharia Gamiat al-Nasr, Mohandiseen) **Map 3, #8** Dishes E£25-50. Open 7pm-2am daily. At the time of writing, Flux is the city's most stylish and chic restaurant, more Soho/SoHo than Cairo. In fact, it's run by an ex-Londoner and partner, an Australian-Egyptian chef who worked at some of the top restaurants in Sydney. The food is a unique Middle East meets the Pacific Rim fusion – adventurous and most of the time successful. Reservations are recommended. Alcohol is served.

Samakmak (☎ 347 8232, 92 Ahmed Orabi, Mohandiseen) **Map 3, #3** Dishes E£25-50. Open 10am-6am daily. This is a branch of the famed Alexandrian fish restaurant, but one that suffers from a bit of an unfortunate setting between two apartment blocks off a busy road in a concrete suburb with not a glimpse of the Nile let alone a whiff of the ocean. However, the fish and seafood are excellent and that's what counts. Simply point out what you want from the iced display and tell the waiters how you want it cooked. Then tuck in. Beer is served.

Giza (Map 4) & Pyramids Road

There are very few places to eat in Giza itself, while Pyramids Rd is fine only if you're happy to settle for Western fast-food joints. However, at the Pyramids end of the road there are a few options, as well as a branch of the ever-reliable Felfela at 27 Cairo-Alexandria Desert Hwy.

Andrea (☎ 383 1133, 59-60 Marioutiyya Canal Rd) Meals E£20-30. Open noon-12.30am daily. This famed open-air restaurant off Pyramids Rd has seating in a large tree-shaded garden – it's pleasant but take plenty of mosquito repellent. There's no menu, it's spit-roasted chicken only (sometimes quail too) served with a selection of mezze. The restaurant is about 1.5km north of Pyramids Rd; if you're taking a taxi here from Downtown, you can expect it to cost about E£15, or it's about E£2 from the Mena House area.

Crazy Fish (☎ 388 6288, 2 Marioutiyya Canal Rd) Open 9am-1am daily. Opposite the Siag Pyramids Hotel and primarily set up to cater to groups post-Pyramids, Crazy Fish is, nevertheless, a fun place, with terrace dining and charming staff. Fish is sold by the kilo and there are also things like prawn rice and lobster, plus chicken and kofta for any who don't fancy seafood.

TGI Friday (☎ 570 9690, 26 Sharia el-Nil, Giza) Map 4, #26 Dishes E£25-40. Open 12.30pm-2.30am. On a boat moored between the University and Giza Bridges, this is a shamelessly manufactured American feel-good franchise, which the Egyptians love. The menu offers a broad range of American cuisine and reservations are recommended at the weekend when it's at its liveliest and loudest. Alcohol is served.

Fish Market (☎ 570 9693, 26 Sharia el-Nil, Giza) Map 4, #26 Dishes E£30-60. Open 12.30pm-2.30am. Occupying the upper deck, above TGI Friday, Fish Market offers arguably the city's finest seafood dining experience. Fish is selected from an ice-packed display, weighed and cooked; meanwhile you dig into some fine mezze. Enhancing the meal is the lovely view of the Nile and city skyline, which is particularly fine at night. Alcohol is served.

Seasons Restaurant (☎ 573 1212, Four Seasons, 35 Sharia Giza, Giza) Map 4, #27 Dishes E£40-75. Open 11.30am-1am daily. Part of the über-expensive Four Seasons hotel, its flagship restaurant is eclectically elegant and totally swish. Choose from a seafood bar buffet (E£95) or order from a widely roaming menu that's Mediterranean in the widest sense, from Morocco to Italy. Dishes are inventive (duck ravioli, prawn kunafa), even bizarre (tahini ice cream), but reportedly superb. Alcohol is served.

Moghul Room (☎ 383 3222, Oberoi Mena House, Pyramids Rd) Dishes E£45-90. Open 12.30pm-2.45pm & 7.30pm-midnight daily. This is arguably the city's finest Indian restaurant. Not only is the food excellent (the owners Oberoi are, after all, an Indian company), but the dining room is completely and dazzlingly over the top – diners feel as though they're sitting in a jewellery box. Pricey perhaps, but definitely worth splashing out on. Alcohol is served.

Heliopolis (Map 9)

Basic grilled meat dishes can be had at the *Amphitrion* and *Palmyra* (see under Bars in the Entertainment chapter for more details) and there's also *Merryland* (Map 9, #2), an ex-racecourse that is now an entertainment park with a disco, nightclub and children's rides, plus plenty of places to eat, including Lebanese, Egyptian and fish restaurants, a branch of Andrea (see the Giza & Pyramids Road section earlier) and, soon to come, TGI Friday.

Chabrawi (Sharia Ibrahimy) Map 9, #16 Dishes E£4-12. Open 8am-midnight daily. A great budget option, Chabrawi does fuul and ta'amiyya, plus things like omelettes and deep-fried cauliflower (arnabeet). It also has an extensive salad bar. There's a seated dining area upstairs from the takeaway area.

Pizza Express (☎ 450 5871, 19 Sharia Mirghani) Map 9, #11 Pizza E£8.50-17. Open 11.30am-1am daily. On Mirghani, in front of the Heliopolis Club, is this franchise of the London-based chain. It's several cuts above the likes of Pizza Hut, boasting a cool, classy interior and very good food – salads are crisp with good dressings and the pizzas (17 varieties) are made in view of the diners. There is also a branch in Doqqi at 52 Sharia Dr Michael Bakhoum.

Le Chantilly (☎ *290 7303, 11 Sharia Baghdad*) **Map 9, #19** Dishes E£25-35. Open 7am-midnight daily. Despite ever-increasing competition, Le Chantilly remains Heliopolis's most popular restaurant. It's a homely sort of place, fronted by a bakery, that's a source of safe, dependable food, including club sandwiches, pasta and meaty European dishes. There's a pleasant garden out the back with a bar.

Cruising Restaurants

In addition to the restaurants housed on moored boats (such as TGI Friday, Fish Market, Morocco and a whole string of places stretching from the Marriott down to the Gezira Sheraton), there are a few vessels that actually cast off and head for centre stream. While the city drifts by outside portholes port and starboard, guests tuck into a luxurious set dinner (usually a buffet) and are entertained with belly-dance shows, live music and even acrobats. Prices include food and entertainment but not drinks. Reservations are recommended.

Nile Maxim (☎ *735 8888, Saray al-Gezira, Zamalek*) **Map 3, #74** Dinner E£175. Cruises 7pm & 9pm daily. Swankiest of the lot, the *Nile Maxim* is operated by the Marriott. The food is reportedly very good, the entertainment (a live band and a Russian belly dancer) loud.

S/S Nile Peking (☎ *531 6288, 012-216 912, Corniche el-Nil, Old Cairo*) **Map 5, #35** Dinner E£55-80. Cruises 7pm daily, additional cruises 2pm Fri & Sun, 10pm Tues, Wed & Sat. Moored by the Nilometer this boat (part of the Peking chain) houses several restaurants and bars, all with a Far-Eastern theme. Cruise passengers are offered 10 choices of complete four-course dinner menus.

The Nile Pharaohs (☎ *570 1000, fax 570 3737, 138 Sharia el-Nil, Giza*) **Map 4, #28** Cost E£120. Cruises 7pm & 9.30pm daily. Talk about over the top – *The Nile Pharaohs* and its sister ship *The Golden Pharaohs* look like floats made up for some camp

Mardi Gras. Boarding is attended by servants in Pharaonic dress. However, despite the tacky appearance, the two are operated by the Oberoi hotel chain so expect a classy deal once on board.

MS Scarabee (☎ *794 3444, Corniche el-Nil, Garden City*) **Map 2, #112** The *Scarabee*, operated by Helnan Shepheard's hotel, is a much cheaper option than most of its competitors, offering the same ingredients but less slickly packaged.

CAFES, BAKERIES & PATISSERIES

The following are all European-style places, good for coffee, tea, soft drinks, pastries and snacks (though maybe not all of them at each place) and are not to be confused with *ahwas*, the Egyptian coffeehouses, which are a different ball game altogether – see the Entertainment chapter for more details.

Downtown (Map 2)

Once upon a time, Groppi used to be *the* place to take tea and cakes, but that was a long time ago. Now it's dim and dismal, and the offerings are poor and overpriced – a place for nostalgia buffs only (without tastebuds).

El-Abd (*35 Talaat Harb*) **Map 2, #52** Open 8am-midnight daily. This place serves the very best Egyptian pastries in town, as testified by the permanent crowds pushing to be served. It's takeaway only. There's a second Downtown branch (Map 2, #22) on the corner of Sharias 26th of July and Sherif.

Simonds (*Sharia Sherif*) **Map 2, #50** Open 7am-8pm daily. This is a sister outlet to the much better place of the same name in Zamalek, but it still does a tolerable cappuccino even if the surroundings are grim.

Zamalek (Map 3)

In addition to the following places, Zamalek also has a branch of the *Harris Cafe* (**Map 3, #29**) (see under Heliopolis, following, for more details) at 18 Sharia al-Marashly, up near the AUC hostel.

Beano's (*8 Sheikh al-Marsafy, Zamalek*) **Map 3, #78** Open 10am-1am daily. Beano's is a US-style coffee shop along Starbucks lines, except that the coffee's better here. It also serves up pastries, snacks and ice creams. Bright and airy, Beano's is popular with mothers waiting for their kids to come out of the nearby British School.

Cilantro (☎ *736 1115, 157 Sharia 26th of July)* **Map 3, #60** Snacks E£4.50-15.50. Open 9am-2am daily. This is a stylish, new, Continental-type cafe that does a range of healthy sandwiches, salads and pastries, as well as decent coffee.

Marriott Bakery (☎ *735 8888, Cairo Marriott, Saray al-Gezira)* **Map 3, #76** Open 6.30am-9pm daily. This is the place to get croissants, all kinds of breads from walnut bread to toast, quiches, cakes and sandwiches. There are several branches of the bakery around town including on Gamiat ad-Dowal al-Arabiyya in Mohandiseen (Map 3, #18) and on Sharia Baghdad in Heliopolis (Map 9, #18).

Simonds (*112 Sharia 26th of July)* **Map 3, #64** Open 7.30am-9.30pm daily. This is the closest thing you'll find to a real Italian cafe this side of the Mediterranean, so make the most of it. It has been in existence for more than 40 years, serving up the city's best cappuccino, as well as fruit juices and savoury pastries.

Heliopolis (Map 9)
In addition to the Harris Cafe, Heliopolis also has a *Marriott Bakery* **(Map 9, #18)**, similar to the one in Zamalek, at the northern end of Sharia Baghdad.

Harris Cafe (☎ *417 6796, 6 Sharia Baghdad)* **Map 9, #27** Open 24 hr. This is a pleasant Continental-style cafe, with outdoor seating, which, in addition to cappuccinos, hot chocolate and the like, also does decent turkey, roast chicken, smoked salmon and club sandwiches.

FAST FOOD
Fast-food chains are mushrooming in Cairo quicker than you can say 'Big Mac and fries'. There are now over 30 international franchises in town, including Arby's, Baskin-Robbins, Chicken Tikka, Domino Pizza, Hardee's, House of Donuts, KFC,

McFelafel

Apparently, ever since McDonald's first opened in Egypt back in 1994, it had been thinking of introducing a 'local sandwich with a local taste'. Now it's gone and done it. Launched in early 2001 and backed by a giant ad campaign in the local media, the Egyptian franchise holders of the US fast-food company have taken the nation's favourite food, slapped it in a hamburger bun and are selling it back to them as McFelafel. No ordinary felafel (or ta'amiyya, as it's more commonly called in Cairo, except McTa'amiyya doesn't quite have the same ring), this is 'aristocratic felafel'. It's a supersized bean patty garnished with lettuce, tomato and spicy tahini. Is it any good? Well, the jury's still out but the price is right – E£1.50, or about a third the cost of a burger. And why shouldn't it do well? The precedents are there: Japanese McDonald's serves Teriyaki burgers and McDonald's India has substituted the Big Mac with the Big Maharaja, made of lamb not beef. Cairenes are now wondering what can they expect next: McFuul and McKushari? 'We're investigating our options' said a McDonald's spokesman.

McDonald's, Pizza Hut and a whole host of others we've never heard of – and the number is growing all the time. There are far too many branches for us to list, and to be honest, we don't want to encourage the spread. You'll spot them for yourself around town. However, it is always worth noting the location of such places – McDonald's and KFC in particular – because they tend to have clean, well-maintained Western-style toilets. For this reason alone we have marked a few branches on the maps at the back of this book.

Most shopping malls have a slick of franchises as do Midan Tahrir and the area opposite the American University; the square in front of the Sphinx; Pyramids Rd; Gamiat ad-Dowal al-Arabiyya in Mohandiseen; the junction of Ismail Mohammed and Abu al-Feda in Zamalek; and Sharia Sawra and Merryland in Heliopolis.

VEGETARIAN

Being a vegetarian in Cairo is not impossible, just dull. After all, the Egyptian staples of fuul and ta'amiyya are perfect veggie fodder – both are bean dishes – as is kushari, which is pulses and pasta. Most mezze are also meat free, including hummus, tahini, baba ghanoug and other aubergine dishes, and mahshi (although this can just as often be stuffed with mincemeat). But there the list just about ends. Mains are always meat based, even when they're called 'vegetable stew' as a vegetarian friend found out when he ordered this dish at Fefela Restaurant – it came with floating chunks of lamb. The waiter's response was, 'But it does have vegetables in it'. An explanation of vegetarianism resulted in the dish being whisked away and promptly returned minus the meat – never mind that it had probably stewed in the pot along with the vegetables all day. Obviously, vegetarianism is a concept little understood, although there is a word for it in Arabic: say 'Ana nabeti' for 'I'm vegetarian'.

Unsurprisingly, in this highly carnivorous city, there are no dedicated vegetarian restaurants. The closest it gets is L'Aubergine in Zamalek where the menu always includes several veggie dishes. Flux in Mohandiseen also features nonmeat mains included specifically with vegetarians in mind. Places like At-Tabei ad-Dumyati and Felfela Downtown, Maroosh in Mohandiseen and Chabrawi in Heliopolis are all good in that they serve basic, budget food which has no meat in it because generally speaking their clientele can't afford it. Otherwise, stick to hotel restaurants which are well used to Westerners and their magnoon (crazy) eating habits.

SELF-CATERING

The place to shop for supplies is the ba'al, which is the Egyptian equivalent of the corner-shop grocer. Come here for bread and cheese, trays of briny olives and sharp pickled vegetables, yogurts, biscuits, and all manner of tinned and dried goods. You'll find these places all over town and they all carry pretty much the same stock.

Bread & Cheese

The general term for bread is aish. The same word in Arabic also means 'life', which tells you how big a part bread plays in the standard diet. In fact no meal is eaten without bread. The basic form is aish baladi (country bread), coarse, flat and dinner-plate sized. Others include aish faransawi, or French bread, which is a crude baguette, and aish shammy, which is a small pocket of bread-like pitta. Bakeries also often carry simit, which are crusty wreaths of bread covered in sesame seeds, and batusaleeh, cumin- or sesame-flavoured bread sticks. Every area has its bakery, just follow your nose. Bread can also be picked up at the ba'al. For more suggestions, see also Cafes, Bakeries & Patisseries earlier in this chapter.

There are two main types of cheese: gibna beida, a white cheese that's very much like Greek feta, and gibna ruumi (Turkish cheese), which is a hard, sharp, yellow cheese. Most ba'als also stock a fairly bland, European-style cheese, generically known as 'sheedar' (cheddar).

Beer

For the lowdown on Egyptian beer see the boxed text 'Stella Stuff' in the Entertainment chapter. Takeaway booze is best bought from the shops run by Al-Ahram Beverages, brewers of Stella beer and stockists of the full range of beers and wines. Drop in at the outlet on 26th of July in Zamalek (Map 3, #61) or the one on Sharia Ibrahim opposite the Palmyra up in Heliopolis (Map 9, #15), or phone for free delivery: in Downtown and Zamalek call ☎ 738 1694; in Doqqi and Mohandiseen call ☎ 340 3194; in Giza call ☎ 780 1439; and in Ma'adi call ☎ 351 2315.

Otherwise, there are a number of small, seedy, usually Greek-run liquor stores dotted around Downtown, including Nicolakis (Map 2, #11) at the top of Talaat Harb next to the Leyaleena coffeehouse, and another place just round the corner on Sharia 26th of July, near the alley leading to Ash-Shams coffeehouse. In Zamalek there's Ambrosio (Map 3, #53) on Sharia Brazil.

Produce Markets

Fresh fruit and vegetables are generally bought from greengrocers, or, better still, from one of the many small street markets throughout the city.

Downtown there's the *Tawfiqiyya Souq* (Map 2), off the top end of Talaat Harb and the *Souq Mansour* (Map 2), off Midan Falaki in Bab al-Luq; in Islamic Cairo fruit and vegetable vendors line *Souq as-Silah* (Map 6) north of the Sultan Hassan mosque; in Doqqi head for the southern end of *Sharia Suleyman Gohar* (Map 4); in Heliopolis stalls line *Sharia Sayyed Abdel Wahid* (Map 9), one block west of Sharia al-Ahram. At all these places as well as mounds of okra, potatoes, aubergines, mangoes, melons and so on (depending on what's in season), you'll also find bundles of fresh herbs laid out on mats and crates of live chickens and rabbits, sold by the kilo. When buying fruit and vegetables be vigilant for attempts by the vendor to slip in rotten stuff.

Supermarkets

Maybe it's the lack of personal contact or poor opportunities for haggling, but Cairo has been slow to embrace the supermarket. In the late 1990s that all looked set to change with the high-profile arrival of UK supermarket chain Sainsbury's, whose flagship store opened on Pyramids Rd, almost in view of the ancient monuments. However, after a shaky few years during which many Egyptians kept away because of rumours of the company's links with Israel, the experiment has failed and Sainsbury's has now withdrawn from the country. Its stores may or may not be taken over by a local retailing outfit.

In the meantime Cairo does have a few supermarket chains, notably ABC and Alphamarket, which are most commonly found in the more affluent neighbourhoods such as Heliopolis, Ma'adi, Medinat Nasr and Mohandiseen. The most central of the supermarkets is on Sharia Abu al-Feda in Zamalek.

Entertainment

Cairenes tend to make their own entertainment, which largely revolves around simple socialising. For the men this often centres on the *ahwa*, or coffeehouse, which is to Cairo what the pub is to London or cafe to Paris (see the boxed text 'The Ahwa' later in this chapter). Women tend to do their visiting at each others' homes. Family visits also account for an inordinate amount of free time. Beyond that, the city has a vibrant cultural life and entertainment scene.

Cinema-going is hugely popular, with audiences flocking to both locally made films and foreign imports. Theatre thrives, with a plethora of Egyptian playwrights providing fare for the numerous municipal playhouses. Music is slightly disappointing in that opportunities to see live performances – classical or pop – are surprisingly limited, but there's always the belly-dancing nightclubs. Alcohol doesn't play anything like the role it does in the West, but there is a surprisingly diverse bar scene as well as a smattering of discos.

For information about activities such as felucca trips, gallery visits, golf, horse riding, swimming and cycling, see the Activities section at the end of the Things to See & Do chapter. For information on gay venues – such as there are – see Gay & Lesbian Travellers in the Facts for the Visitor chapter.

OPERA, MUSIC & DANCE

Cairo Opera House (☎ 739 8144, ⓦ www.cairooperahouse.org, Gezira Exhibition Grounds) **Map 2, #111** Metro: Opera. This is the city's premier venue for all performing arts. In addition to regularly playing host to famed international names and companies (the Bolshoi Ballet visits almost annually), it's also home to the Cairo Symphony Orchestra, which gives concerts here every Saturday from September to mid-June, and to the Cairo Ballet Company and the Cairo Opera Company. Check *Egypt Today* and *Al-Ahram Weekly* for what's on, or pass by and pick up a program. Jacket

and tie are required by males for main hall performances, but less-well-dressed travellers have been known to borrow them from staff. In addition to a main hall and small hall, the Opera House also has an open-air amphitheatre.

American University in Cairo (AUC; ☎ 797 5020 for information) **Map 2** There are often music recitals and plays of varying quality at the Ewart Hall and Wallace Theatre (Map 2, #118) at the AUC. Events are advertised on boards at the campus entrance on Sharia Mohammed Mahmoud, off Midan Tahrir.

Beit al-Harrawi (☎ 735 7001, Sharia al-Sheikh Mohammed Abdo, Islamic Cairo) **Map 6, #14** Admission free. On the first Thursday of every month at 8pm a free performance of classical Arabic music is given here. At other times, especially during Ramadan, the house, along with neighbouring Beit Zeinab al-Khatoun, is used for theatre, art exhibitions and music performances. If anything is going on during your visit (see the local press) then it's worth attending if only for the setting.

The same could be said of *Aïda*, Giuseppe Verdi's grand opera written in honour of the opening of the Suez Canal. In the past, performances have been held at the temples of Hatshepsut and Karnak in Luxor, but most recently the venue has been the Pyramids, and the authorities are hoping this might become an annual fixture. Egypt's overseas tourist offices will have full details on when the next grand event takes place.

Sufi Dancing

Al-Tannoura Egyptian Heritage Dance Troupe (Mausoleum of Al-Ghouri, Islamic Cairo) **Map 7, #20** Admission free. On Wednesday and Saturday nights from 8pm (8.30pm in winter) this troupe gives a 1½ hour display of Sufi dancing. Sufism is a semimystical branch of Islam and its practitioners aspire, through meditation, recitation and frantic dancing, to attain union with God.

It's an idea that is considered blasphemous by most orthodox Muslims, thus Sufism is something of an underground phenomenon.

The performances here are for tourists and are devoid of religious significance; nevertheless, it's a marvellous sight, watching the dancers with brightly coloured skirts spinning like wurlitzers, while a line of accompanying musicians creates a hypnotic pulse and jerkily sling their heads left to right. It's advisable to come early, especially in winter, as performances are popular and the small auditorium can get quite crowded.

THEATRE

The dramatic tradition is strong in Cairo and there are numerous theatres Downtown, particularly along Sharia Emad ad-Din. Productions are always of local fare, typically slapstick comedy with a bit of belly dancing thrown in. For non-Arabic speakers the AUC's *Wallace Theatre* (☎ 797 5020) **(Map 2, #118)** puts on several student plays and musicals throughout the year, usually in English. See the notice board at the AUC campus on Midan Tahrir for details. Once a year the International Experimental Theatre Festival (see under Public Holidays & Special Events in the Facts for the Visitor chapter for more details) brings in a variety of troupes from around the world, with performances held at a number of venues all over Cairo.

CINEMAS

There was a time, just a few years back, when all that was on offer at Cairo's movie houses were James Bond movies from the Roger Moore era and perpetual reruns of *Predator* and *Rocky*. But the cinema business is now booming and new deals mean that Cairo gets first-run Hollywood blockbusters soon after their US release (and in some cases before they're seen in Europe). Many of the city's cinemas have also recently been refurbished and revamped, and speculators have invested in several new multicinema complexes.

Films are subtitled rather than dubbed, which is both good and bad. Good in that it means that at any given time there are plenty of movies showing with original English-language soundtracks, bad in that

the audience reads the dialogue and doesn't have to listen, leaving everyone free to chatter. Cairo cinema-goers are also big on audience participation, which with the right movie can be great fun, but the whooping, cheering and clapping is a bit distracting if you're trying to settle into something like *Captain Corelli's Mandolin*.

Despite this improvement, the selection of films on offer is limited to international box office heavy hitters. Don't expect Wim Wenders or even the Coen Brothers. Nothing lewd either – all films are subject to censorship. How heavy-handed this is depends on the mood of the moment. Even the most seemingly innocuous movies often have the telltale hiccups that indicate scissor cuts.

Be aware that Egypt's antiterrorism laws mean that no-one is allowed to leave a cinema before the film ends. One sticky summer evening we shelled out a couple of quid just for the relief of the air-conditioned auditorium, but were driven to despair by the sheer awfulness of the film showing – we then had to beg, plead and eventually deposit a business card with security before they would let us out.

Screenings are usually at 1.30pm, 3.30pm, 6.30pm and 9.30pm. A few cinemas also have midnight shows on Friday and Saturday. Tickets range from E£8 to E£18 depending on the venue. Check the daily *Egyptian Gazette* or *Al-Ahram Weekly* for details of what's showing.

The following cinemas regularly screen English-language films:

Cairo Sheraton (Map 4, #19; ☎ 760 6081) Cairo Sheraton, Midan al-Galaa, Doqqi. This is the closest Cairo has to an arthouse cinema, in that it tends to forgo blockbusters for the likes of Merchant Ivory.

Cosmos (Map 8, #17; ☎ 574 2177) 12 Sharia Emad ad-Din, Downtown. Big old cinema recently subdivided into five screens, two or three of which are usually showing English-language movies.

Karim I & II (Map 8, #14; ☎ 592 4830) 5 Sharia Emad ad-Din, Downtown. This refurbished, old cinema typically screens action movies. Cheap tickets make it popular with young Egyptian males and it's not a place for women to go unaccompanied.

ENTERTAINMENT

The Ahwa

The coffeehouse or *ahwa* (the Arabic word means both coffee and the place in which it's drunk) is one of the great Cairo social institutions. Typically just a collection of cheap tin-plate-topped tables and wooden chairs in a sawdust-strewn room open to the street, the ahwa is a relaxed and unfussy place where the average Joe, or Ahmed, will hang out for part of each day reading the papers, meeting friends, sipping tea and whiling away the hours. The hubbub of conversation is usually accompanied by the incessant clacking of slammed *domina* (dominoes) and *towla* (backgammon) pieces, and the burbling of smokers drawing heavily on their *sheeshas*, the cumbersome water pipes.

Traditionally, ahwa-going has been something of an all-male preserve, and older men at that, but in recent years sheesha smoking has become almost fashionable. It's now common to see young groups of Egyptians (men and women) in ahwas, especially around more moneyed districts such as Zamalek.

What to Drink
In the hot summer months many ahwa-goers forgo their regular teas and coffees (see Drinks in the Places to Eat chapter for a description of these beverages as prepared Egyptian style) for cooler drinks such as the crimson-hued, iced *karkadey*, a wonderfully refreshing drink boiled up from hibiscus leaves, *limoon* (lemon juice) or *zabaady* (yogurt). In winter many prefer *sahleb*, a warm drink made with semolina powder, milk and chopped nuts, or *yansoon*, a medicinal-tasting aniseed drink.

Sheesha
Filtered by the water in the glass bowl, sheesha smoke is mild, but the effort required to draw it can leave you quite light-headed. Typically there's a choice of two kinds of tobacco: the standard *ma'asil*,

PATRICK HORTON

The ahwa is where local men while away the hours, sipping tea and enjoying a sheesha.

ENTERTAINMENT

The Ahwa

which is soaked in molasses, or *tofah*, which is soaked in apple juice and has a sweet aroma but a slightly sickly taste. A good sheesha can last 15 to 20 minutes. When the tobacco is burnt out or the coals have cooled, the *raiyis* (waiter) will change the little clay pot of tobacco (known as the *hagar* or 'stone') for a fresh one. Each hagar costs around E£1. Most locals will happily smoke two or three hagars per sitting.

When it's time to pay, catch the eye of the raiyis and shout *Filoos!* (Money!).

Where to Go

With the exception of the newer suburbs such as Mohandiseen, Doqqi and Agouza, nearly every street in Cairo has at least one ahwa. One of the oldest, and certainly the most famous, is *Fishawi* (Map 7, #10), a few steps off Midan Hussein in Khan al-Khalili. Despite frequently being swamped by foreign tourists and equally wide-eyed Egyptians from out of town, Fishawi manages to shrug it all off (no waiters in fancy headgear or Fishawi key rings for sale) and play the role of a regular ahwa, serving up tea, coffee and sheesha to all-comers. The place is open 24 hours, apart from Ramadan, and is especially alluring in the early hours of the morning.

Even more colourful than Fishawi in terms of decor, if not atmosphere, is *Ash-Shams* (Map 2, #9). It's tucked in a courtyard alleyway off the Tawfiqiyya Souq beside piles of onion sacks belonging to a stall in the market, and a blue barrel into which the chopped heads of chickens are thrown by the poultry store on the corner. The ahwa walls are adorned with gilt stucco and kitschy faux-classical paintings. However, because of its popularity with travellers from the neighbouring hotels, waiters have a bad tendency to overcharge and the sheesha here, frankly, is terrible.

Much better is the nearby *Al-Andalus* (Map 2, #21), tucked away behind the Grand Hotel on the corner of Talaat Harb and 26th of July. This place is kept spotlessly clean, prices are displayed (we've never been cheated by staff here) and, most unusually, upstairs is a 'family room' where women can go to smoke sheesha away from masculine eyes. Also good and in the vicinity is *Leyaleena* (Map 2, #11), a new ahwa with rattan chairs and a very cultured, foreigner-friendly feel. It's just around the corner from the eastern end of the Tawfiqiyya Souq.

At the opposite end of Tawfiqiyya Souq, towards Sharia Ramses, in the last alley on the left, is *Al-Agaty* (Map 2, #6), frequented by musicians, actors and journalists. It has a smoky 'Islamic' room with *mashrabiyya* (carved wooden screens) and couches, and a rooftop terrace. It's another of those places that only really gets going after midnight.

After Ash-Shams, the other big backpacker favourite is *Zahret al-Bustan* (Map 2, #83), in the alleyway beside Cafe Riche off Sharia Talaat Harb (for more details, see under Midan Tahrir to Midan Talaat Haab in the Things to See & Do chapter).

Although domina, towla and occasionally cards are the standard games played at ahwas, there are a couple of places popular with the chess crowd, notably *Cafeteria Horreyya* (Map 2, #98), on Midan Falaki in Bab al-Luq, and *Zahret al-Midan* (Map 5, #13) on Midan Sayyida Zeinab at the junction with Sharia Abdel Meguid.

Also in the Sayyida Zeinab district are the *video cofeehouses* (Map 5, #1), four or five large coffeehouses, each with one, two or three TVs, which screen nonstop Arabic movies on video. The deal is that you have to buy at least one tea or coffee for every film you watch. They're all on Sharia Nasriyya which runs from Sayyida Zeinab north towards Bab al-Luq.

Anyone who fancies the idea of a smoke of a sheesha, but finds the idea of entering an ahwa a little intimidating, could try one of the cafes attached to the big hotels. Best of the lot are Abu Ali, the open-air, garden courtyard cafe at the *Nile Hilton* (Map 2, #65), and the garden cafe at the *Marriott* (Map 3, #76).

Metro (Map 2, #24; ☎ 393 7566) 35 Talaat Harb, Downtown. Once Cairo's finest, this cinema is now one of its scruffiest. Its choice of films and clientele are similar to the Karim I & II.

MGM (☎ 519 5388) Ma'adi Grand Mall, Ma'adi. A fine modern cinema for those who live in Ma'adi, but a long way to travel otherwise.

Normandy (Map 9, #13; ☎ 258 0254) 32 Sharia al-Ahram, Heliopolis. This is one of Cairo's older cinemas, with welcome open-air screenings in summer.

Odeon (Map 2, #44; ☎ 575 8797) 5 Sharia Dr Abdel Hamid Said, Downtown. A three-screen cinema just off Talaat Harb, beside the new Talaat Harb Shopping Centre.

Radio (Map 2, #53; ☎ 575 6562) 24 Talaat Harb, Downtown. This place is similar to Karim I & II.

Ramses Hilton I & II (Map 2, #2; ☎ 574 7436) 7th floor, Ramses Hilton Mall, Abdel Moniem Riad, Downtown. These are two relatively new, well-maintained screens, although II is a bit small.

Renaissance (Map 3, #33; ☎ 580 4039) World Trade Centre Annexe, 1191 Corniche el-Nil, Bulaq. Central Cairo's newest, swishest cinema.

Tahrir (Map 4, #13; ☎ 335 4726) 122 Sharia Tahrir, Doqqi. A comfortable, modern cinema where single females shouldn't receive any hassle.

NIGHTLIFE

The best of Cairo nightlife isn't nightlife in the Western sense (bars and clubs) it's just street life that never seems to notice that the sun's gone down and everyone should be thinking about bed. The city just keeps on going – see the boxed text 'Cairo by Night'. What we really love, for example, is how after a party, walking home at 2.30am through residential backstreets, we came across a cassette kiosk, still open, the vendor and friend sitting on roadside chairs shooting the breeze. So we bought a couple of tapes – early morning music shopping, why not?

Bars

There are two distinct types of bar in Cairo: the Western-style bar and the local spit-and-sawdust-type joints, euphemistically known as 'cafeterias', though the only food present is usually a small plate of salty beans to quicken the down-flow of beer. These local places are discreet and don't advertise themselves, but if you know what you're looking for, they're pretty easy to spot – look out for saloon-type doors. Patronised by the more roguish end of Egyptian society and resolutely all-male, these places are not suitable for women on their own (and the toilets are barnyard foul). A beer in these places costs from E£5.50 to E£6.50 and they're open daily from around noon to anywhere between 1am and 4am. They all close completely during the month of Ramadan (see Public Holidays & Special Events in the Facts for the Visitor chapter for dates), as do all the Western-type bars except those in hotels.

Local Bars There are several local bars on and around Sharia Alfy in Downtown, most of which are fairly unwelcoming. Exceptions are *Cafeteria Port Tawfiq* (Map 2, #12), on Midan Orabi, and *Cafeteria Orabi* (Map 8, #16), 150m north on the left-hand side of Sharia Orabi. *Cap d'Or* (Map 2, #48), on Sharia Abdel Khalek Sarwat, is a litle more salubrious and is possibly the best of its type. Staff and regulars here are quite used to seeing foreigners. The same applies to the cramped *Stella Bar* (Map 2, #77), on the corner of Hoda Shaarawi and Talaat Harb. Although primarily a coffeehouse, *Cafeteria Horreyya* (Map 2, #98), on Midan Falaki in Bab al-Luq, also serves Stella.

Up in Heliopolis the *Amphitrion* (Map 9, #12) and *Palmyra* (Map 9, #14) are two excellent terrace bars at which it's possible to enjoy beer and sheesha (not a recommended combination) in a streetside setting.

Western-Style Bars Like any other busy city, bars and hang-outs open and close and go in and out of favour, but the place to go boozing (if you have the cash) is Zamalek, where there are several stylish bars within a short walk of each other.

L'Aubergine (☎ 735 6550, 5 Sayyed al-Bakry, Zamalek) **Map 3, #56** Open until 2am. No longer quite as 'in' as it once was, upstairs at L'Aubergine still gets pretty rammed most evenings with an AUC-type crowd (ie, young, rich and good looking). The atmosphere is cool jazz and candlelight. A beer costs E£12.50.

Cairo by Night

Forget all this guff about New York being the 'city that never sleeps'. Whoever coined that phrase had obviously never been to Cairo. In fact, to get to know this city properly you have to change your sleeping habits because it's only once the sun's gone down that the place really comes to life.

During the summer months, families don't head Downtown to shop until 9pm, when the intense heat of the day has lessened to a simmer. Until well after midnight high-street traders do a roaring business. In the back alleys a thousand little hole-in-the-wall shops, workshops and garages are lit with the blue blur of late night TV, the proprietors glued to their screens.

At 1am or 2am families think about heading home but there are plenty of fathers left behind in the coffeehouses jabbering away between puffs of the sheesha, filling seats that spill out across pavements (forbidden during the day). Elsewhere, while some diners are just leaving their restaurants and look-ing for a taxi (of which there's no shortage whatever the time), it's 2am or 3am before the orchestra gets into its swing and the big-name belly dancers take to their five-star stages. At 4am there are still couples out along the Nile enjoying the early-morning chill. This is the time, too, when delivery lorries take to the roads and the camel traders marshal their animals across town, sometimes by vehicle, some-times in galloping, barely controlled herds. At 5am, finally, the traffic dies down and a brief silence descends only to be broken by the dawn chorus of the muezzin, summoning the faithful to prayer and also a signal for the cars to come creeping back onto the streets again. And that's not to mention Ramadan, when the whole city alters its body clock to sleep late into the day and remain awake through the night, thus neatly getting round the business of fasting during daylight hours.

Some of our favourite all-night haunts include the following:

Coffeehouses
In summer most coffeehouses remain open until at least 2am, many later. There are two (Map 2, #43) next door to each other at the bottom of Sharia Ramses (just north of Midan Abdel Moniem Riad) that remain open 24 hours, as does Al-Agaty at the Sharia Ramses end of the Tawfiqiyya Souq and, most famously, Fishawi in Khan al-Khalili (see the boxed text 'The Ahwa' earlier in this chap-ter for more details).

All-Night Bites
Most restaurants wind up between midnight and 2am but Abu as-Sid and Morocco in Zamalek are open until 4am. Around the corner, Maison Thomas never closes. The Harris Cafe in Heliopolis is the same. Abu Rifai kebab house in Sayyida Zeinab is open until dawn, as is Abu Ramy just to the south in Zein al-Abdeen. For 24-hour *fuul* and *ta'amiyya* head for Na'ama beside the Nile in Agouza.

Bars
Most places kick you out at 2am, but the New Arizona, on Sharia Alfy, doesn't usually stack its chairs on the tables until 4am. Or go straight to the Odeon Palace Hotel, Downtown, which has a rooftop bar that's open all hours.

Cafe Riche (☎ 392 9793, 17 Talaat Harb, Downtown) **Map 2, #82** Open until mid-night. The management would probably pre-fer that you ate, but plenty of people use this nicotine-wreathed cafe-restaurant as a bar.

Deals (☎ 736 0502, 2 Maahad al-Swissry, Zamalek) **Map 3, #58** Open until 2am. A small cellar bar, Deals gets too packed for comfort late on week nights and at week-

ends, but if you like loud, sweaty crowds then suck in your breath and elbow your way to a table. Deals is also in Mohandiseen (Map 3, #12; ☎ 305 7255, 2 Sharia Gol Gamal) and Heliopolis (Map 9, #6; ☎ 291 0406, 40A Sharia Baghdad).

Harry's Pub (☎ 735 8888, Cairo Mar-riott, Zamalek) **Map 3, #76** Open until 2.30am. Harry's is your typical British pub abroad with all the tackiness that implies – karaoke, lounge singers and televised sport.

La Bodega *(☎ 735 6761, 157 Sharia 26th of July, Zamalek)* **Map 3, #60** Open until 2am. Beside the restaurant of the same name is this swish lounge bar. You need to be dressed to impress to get in and a beer is going to set you back E£15, but if you want a glimpse of Cairo's nouveau riche at play, this is the venue.

Odeon Palace Hotel *(☎ 577 6637, 6 Sharia Dr Abdel Hamid Said, Downtown)* **Map 2, #41** Open 24 hr. This is a rooftop bar favoured by Cairo's heavy-drinking theatre and cinema clique for its unsociably good hours.

Pub 28 *(☎ 735 9200, 28 Shagaret ad-Durr, Zamalek)* **Map 3, #48** Open until 2am. One of the oldest Western-style bars in town, Pub 28 has a loyal following of largely middle-aged types, but on a quiet night it can feel like a forlorn lonely hearts club.

Le Tabasco *(☎ 336 5583, 8 Midan Amman, Doqqi)* **Map 4, #7** Open until 2am. Run by Nicha Sursock, the Conran of Cairo (he's also responsible for L'Aubergine), Le Tabasco is smart and hip and draws a similarly styled crowd with good music, fine food and a fizzy pre-club atmosphere. While here check out ***Absolute*** **(Map 4, #6)** just round the corner, another Sursock joint.

Taverne du Champs de Mars *(☎ 578 0444, Nile Hilton, Midan Tahrir)* **Map 2, #65** Open until 1am. A 1920s pub transposed in total from Belgium to Cairo. Major sporting events are shown on the big screen and imported beers are available on tap for the outrageous price of E£24, while Stella costs E£12.

The Virginian *(☎ 506 3923, Sharia al-Ahram, Medinat Muqattam)* **Map 1, #10** Open until 2am. Impossible to get to without your own transport (a taxi will cost E£12), this is a wonderful terrace bar high up on top of the Muqattam Hills. Its excellent decor would be hailed in any other city as retro classic; here, it's just a neglected little-known gem.

Windows on the World *(☎ 577 7444, Ramses Hilton, 36th floor, Downtown)* **Map 2, #3** Open until 4am. Drinks are phen-

Stella Stuff

For beer in Egypt just say 'Stella'. It's been brewed and bottled in Cairo now for more than 100 years. It's a yeasty lager, the taste of which varies enormously by batch. Since 1998, the standard Stella (sold in 75cL dark-green bottles at E£4.50 in shops and anywhere from E£5.50 to E£16 in bars) has been supplemented by sister brews, including Stella Meister (a light lager) and Stella Premium (which tastes like a particularly rough homebrew). Most locals just stick to the unfussy basic brew – it's the cheapest and as long as it's cold it's not bad. Since the late 1990s there's also been a rival brew on the market called Saqqara, brewed at Al-Gouna on the Red Sea coast. It's more reliable in quality than Stella but unfortunately as this book was in production an announcement was made that Saqqara was in the process of being bought by ABC Breweries, producers of Stella, so its future now looks highly uncertain.

Some bars in five-star hotels serve imported beers, but prices are always outrageous. The duty-free shops (for more details, see under Customs in the Facts for the Visitor chapter) often have crates of imported beer.

omenally expensive, there's an E£40 minimum charge, the live music is atrociously cheesy and a dress code is enforced; but, despite all the drawbacks, WoW has to be experienced at least once for the stunning panoramic views over the city. Visit at sundown for best effect.

Windsor Bar *(☎ 591 5277, 19 Sharia Alfy, Downtown)* **Map 2, #17** Open until 1am. Unfortunately, the affable Mahmoud, a former Mr Universe sometime back in the 50s has passed on, but the Windsor bar still remains engagingly eccentric and supremely relaxed. Easily Cairo's best hotel bar. Beer is a reasonable E£7.50.

Casinos

Most of Cairo's five-star hotels have casinos, open to non-Egyptians only (take your passport). All games are conducted in

US dollars or other major foreign currencies, with a minimum stake of US$1. Smart casual attire is required. These casinos are not to be confused with local *casinos*, the name given for certain restaurants popular with families on a day out.

Cairo Sheraton Casino (Map 4, #18; ☎ 336 9700) Cairo Sheraton, Midan al-Galaa, Doqqi. Open 24 hours.
Casino d'Egypt (Map 2, #113; ☎ 792 1000) Helnan Shepheard's Hotel, Downtown. Open 24 hours.
Casino d'Egypte (☎ 383 3222) Mena House Oberoi Hotel, Pyramids Rd, Giza. Open 7pm to 5am.
Casino Ramses Hilton (Map 2, #3; ☎ 574 4400) Ramses Hilton, Downtown. Open 3pm to 9am.
Casino Semiramis (Map 2, #106; ☎ 795 7171) Semiramis Inter-Continental, Downtown. Open 24 hours.
Conrad International Cairo Casino (Map 3, #32; ☎ 580 8325) Conrad International, Bulaq. Open 24 hours.
Kings & Queens Casino (☎ 267 7730) Sheraton Heliopolis, Heliopolis. Open 24 hours.
Le Casino (Map 2, #131; ☎ 736-1333) Gezira Sheraton, Gezira. Open 24 hours.
Nile Hilton Casino (Map 2, #65; ☎ 578 0444) Nile Hilton, Midan Tahrir, Downtown. Open 1pm to 10am.
Omar Khayyam Casino (Map 3, #76; ☎ 735 8888) Cairo Marriott, Zamalek. Open 24 hours.

Discos & Clubs

Apart from the very occasional one-off dance club night, the nightclub scene in Cairo has barely progressed beyond school disco level. There have been some good clubs (we hazily remember eventful nights at the Borsalino and Casanova), where the appeal lay not with the music, but with the fringe crowds these places attracted: tanked-up African students in the case of the former and leather queens, Russians and wide boys in the latter. But such places only ever exist for a short time and once too many people get wind, they're suddenly closed down by the authorities on the grounds of 'licensing infringements' or some such vague reasoning.

Instead, what's left is a limited bunch of sanitised establishments, many attached to hotels, where it's as if the 1970s never went away. Expect high admission fees (typically E£20 to E£40), strict dress policies, pricey drinks and Euro pop. Of course, the situation may improve. To find out what's happening try W www.cairocafe.com.eg or W www.croc.com.eg, two Web sites devoted to the city's entertainment scene.

Africana (Pyramids Rd, Giza) Open 11pm-4am weekends only. It seems impossible that this infamous joint survives; frequented by Cairo's African crowd, it's colourful to say the least, with fast and furious *soukous* and *mbalax* blasting from the speakers, a packed and sweaty dance floor, and the occasional punch-up and high-velocity-chair show. Not easy to find, the club is way down Pyramids Rd on the right-hand side, beyond the Haram Theatre and then one block past the KFC.

Crazy House Disco (☎ 366 1082, 1 Salah Salem) Map 5, #37 Open 10pm-5am daily. Stuck out on the edge of the medieval Southern Cemetery, Cairo Land Entertainment Centre opened in 1999 as Cairo's first purpose-built nightclub. It's actually just a glorified disco with a playlist of international pop from Britney Spears to home boy Amr Diab. To get there you'll have to take a taxi (about E£5 from central Cairo).

Exit (☎ 391 8127, Atlas Hotel, 2 Sharia Mohammed Rushdy, Downtown) Map 2, #95 Open 10am-3am daily. It's a different crowd every night at Exit, where the music ranges from African to rap to pop, but Friday is *the* night, when it doesn't matter what's playing as the place is banging anyway.

Jackie's (☎ 578 0444, Nile Hilton, Midan Tahrir, Downtown) Map 2, #65 Open 9pm-4am daily. There's a strict door policy here and you've got to be smart to satisfy – if the bouncers have really got a strop on then they'll admit couples only. Once in, Jackie's is one of the city's better discos, especially on a Thursday night when you might even get some decent sounds. Boy George DJ'd here in 2001.

Pharaoh's (☎ 361 0871, Pharaoh's Hotel, 12 Lotfy Hassouna, Doqqi) Map 4, #10 Open 9pm-3am daily. This is a fairly downmarket place that pulls a youngish crowd with hip hop and rap.

Upstairs (☎ 578 3334, World Trade Centre, Corniche el-Nil, Bulaq) **Map 3, #33** Open 9pm-4am daily. Tuxedoed monkeys at the door enforce a strict dress policy while inside a posey, no-fun mindset rules the dance floor. This is where the city's seriously rich young darlings come to rattle their jewellery.

U-Turn (☎ 451 2313, Merryland, Heliopolis) **Map 9, #1** Open 10pm-5am daily. A large, new, purpose-built nightclub in the middle of the Heliopolis fun park, this place opened in early summer 2001 as DaKarma and presumably didn't do too well because by August it was set to relaunch as U-Turn. As we go to press the relaunch has yet to happen so check the local press to see the state of play.

Belly-Dancing Nightclubs

Cairo is the world capital of belly dance and what passes for belly dancing in other cities is pastiche. See it here or don't bother at all. For more general background on belly dancing see Arts in the Facts about Cairo chapter.

A 'nightclub' in the Egyptian sense is a place to take a table and spend several hours overindulging in food and booze while watching entertainment that typically features folkloric dancing, singing and – the real crowd puller – belly dancing.

The best dancers perform at nightclubs attached to the five-star hotels, places that include *Abu Nawas (☎ 383 3444, Mena House Oberoi)*, *Alhambra (☎ 336 9700, Cairo Sheraton)* **(Map 4, #18)**, *Haroun al-Rashid (☎ 795 7171, Semiramis Inter-Continental)* **(Map 2, #106)** and *La Belle Epoque (☎ 362 1717, Le Méridien Cairo)* **(Map 2, #130)**, but you'll have to phone around to find out who's currently performing where. Shows are lavish affairs with plenty of preliminaries before the main artist of the night, typically backed by a 30-plus piece band, takes to the stage. They tend to take place at weekends (Friday and Saturday), but sometimes Wednesday and Thursday too, beginning not much before midnight with the main act not taking to the stage until around 2am or later. Admission

charges are steep; expect to shell out upwards of E£150, which will include a three-course meal or buffet but not drinks.

Belly dancing cuts across social divisions and at the other end of the scale, it is possible to go navel gazing for just a few pounds. There are several places Downtown as well as plenty more along Pyramids Rd (generally expensive rip-off joints, although *Parisian* and *Nariman* are said to be reasonable) that cater mainly to locals rather than the oil-rich Gulf Arabs who predominate among the five-star audiences. It has to be said that these places are fairly sleazy, although in a totally nonsexual way – most of the dancers have the appearance and grace of amateur wrestlers, and the addled old gentlemen patrons who step up onto the stage to join in generally out-gyrate the bored performers.

Most entertaining of the lot is *Palmyra* **(Map 2, #28)**, which is just south of 26th of July, 100m east of the junction with Sharia Sherif. Run by a monocled old lady (aptly enough, known as Madame Monocle), it's a cavernous, slightly shabby place that puts on a full nightly show with several belly dancers (from about 1am to 4am) of varying capabilities and, occasionally, other acts such as acrobats. There's a minimal admission fee and a Stella costs E£12.

Other options include *Sheherazade* **(Map 2, #15)**, above the Alfy Bey restaurant on Sharia Alfy, Downtown, and, across the road, *New Arizona* **(Map 2, #13)**.

Live Music

Some days being in Cairo can seem like being an extra in some vast, uncoordinated musical; songs hang in the air, cast out of passing cars or wafted down from apartment windows; boys cycle by crooning endearments at the girls; and car horns beep, parp and honk in a bizarre vehicular symphony. Life in Cairo is lived out to an ever-present soundtrack. Which makes it completely baffling that a city which thrives on song and rhythm has virtually no live-music scene.

The occasional big-name artist gets to play the Pyramids – the Grateful Dead rocked the Sphinx in the late 1970s as did Sting in 2001. Otherwise, only the Interna-

Star Navels

Belly dancing is an art not a sport, and so to the question 'who's the best belly dancer of them all?' there's just no answer. Every dancer has their own individual style, a reflection of their personality as much as their abilities. Unlike other forms of dance where lithe youth reigns supreme, belly dance favours a fuller, more mature figure and experience adds to the allure.

Nagwa Fouad is the Tina Turner of the scene, a glamorous entertainer with a huge fan base, still strutting her ample stuff in her 60s. Her big rival and self-crowned Queen of the Nile is Fifi Abdou, who's certainly no babe but who remains a full-tilt, feisty performer with an earthy sense of humour. A controversial figure, Madame Fifi is rarely out of the gossip columns, whether for the 5000 costumes she reportedly owns, or the US$14.5 million she supposedly paid for her Nile-view apartment or for assaulting police officers who stop her for speeding.

Chasing Fifi's title are a swag of younger (but not necessarily young) dancers including most prominently Dina and Lucy (single, two-syllable names being almost a prerequisite for the modern dancer). Dina is the quintessential belly dancer, with a gypsy-like mane of jet-black hair, voluptuous to the point of caricature, flirty and mischievous. She's pushed the level of sexual expression allowed in the dance up a few notches. Lucy, also an actress of note, is derided by detractors for being too static but having seen her perform we'd have to disagree – she's got hips that gyrate like a tumble dryer on full spin.

One point of agreement for most fans is that foreign dancers just don't cut it. Back in the mid 1990s when Islamic conservatism began to scare away the home-grown talent, their places were taken by an influx of European women who'd studied all the movements – often under Egyptian tutors – and were keen to show what they could do. Some of these women still dance in Cairo's clubs and on the cruise boats, and to the untrained eye they seem to do a pretty fine job. But ask any connoisseur and they'll tell you, no, belly dancing is in the Egyptian blood and only an Egyptian emotionally and instinctively understands the music, the words and the rhythms. 'I'd rather watch an Egyptian who knows three steps', declared one fan, 'than a foreigner who knows a hundred'.

---

tional Conference Centre up in Medinat Nasr is equipped to handle a major concert, something it does only rarely. Most foreign artists hesitate to play in Egypt because of the bureaucracy – the organisation of the Sting concert was an absolute shambles that will probably have the effect of keeping Western stars away from Cairo for years to come.

At a grass-roots level the situation is even worse. It's a bit of a catch-22 situation: there are no live-music venues because there are no bands (Egyptian pop is created in the studio), and there are no bands because there are no live-music venues. The one exception is the **Cairo Jazz Club** (☎ *345 9939, 197 Sharia 26th of July, Agouza)* **(Map 3, #21)**, which is at least suitably dingy, dark and smoky, with jazz or blues every night, reasonably priced drinks and food. It's open from 7pm to 2am daily and the minimum charge is E£30.

Otherwise, the only live music on offer comes courtesy of the cabaret outfits that pedal popcorn ('Careless Whispers', 'I Just Called To Say I Love You', 'Hello') as an accompaniment to meals at numerous restaurants, including TGI Friday, Peking in Zamalek and sundry other places that all who love music should avoid.

SPECTATOR SPORTS

If you're talking sport in Cairo then you're talking football. About 90% of sports coverage in the media is concerned with football, even in the closed season when there are no matches. The other 10% is given over to squash, not because it's a big national sport, but because it's the president's favourite game. It makes for dull viewing, worth watching only during the international Al-Ahram Tournament held each June at the Pyramids.

Football

Football (soccer) has always been by far the most popular sport throughout Egypt, and a big match remains one of the few occasions when the streets of Cairo fall silent – at least until the final whistle, when if the result is right the streets quickly fill with flag-waving, horn-tooting fans. The national side (nicknamed 'The Pharaohs') includes several players who ply their trade at clubs in Europe: Hany Ramzi, Mohammed Emara and Yasser Radwan play in the German leagues; Tarek al-Said is with Belgian champions Anderlecht; Salah Hosni is with Ghent; and young wunderkind, Ahmed Hossam (known as Mido), became the highest paid player in the history of Egyptian football when he joined famed Holland side Ajax Amsterdam for US$4.5 million. The national team also draws on the services of veteran Hossam Hassan who, in 2001, at the age of 34, celebrated his 150th international cap to equal the record set by Germany's Lothar Matthaus.

With its array of international stars, Egypt holds its own in the region and generally performs well in the African Nations Cup. But the team has only qualified once in recent times for the World Cup, in 1990, when it suffered a first-round exit from a group that included England and Holland. Neither will Egypt be going to the 2002 World Cup, having come third in its qualifying group to Morocco and Senegal.

Domestically, Cairo dominates the country's footballing life, hosting its two biggest clubs, Zamalek (club colours, white) and Al-Ahly (red). This may not be healthy for Egyptian football, but it's good news for the visitor hoping to catch a game. Domestic competition focuses on the league championship, which sometimes has a lopsided feel, as little clubs line up for a battering by the Cairo heavyweights. For a really intense atmosphere, try to catch one of the Cairo derbies. Tickets generally go on sale two or three days prior to the match. They range in price from E£15 (3rd class) to E£1500 for box seats – ideally, go for 1st or 2nd class, which are still inexpensive but generally not as crowded as 3rd class. Advance tickets are sold at the box offices of the two teams' home grounds, which are Ahly (Map 2), next to the Cairo Tower on Gezira, and Zamalek (Map 3), south off 26th of July in Mohandiseen, or turn up at the stadium on the day but get there a few hours early. The season runs from September to May. The big matches are held in the Cairo Stadium (Map 1, #8) in Medinat Nasr.

For more information on Egyptian soccer visit W www.egyptiansoccer.com.

Horse Racing

A vestige of the days of British rule, horse racing still takes place once a week, Friday, at the *Gezira Club* (Map 2). It's a pretty poor show and you can't see most of the track from the grandstand, so the race goes on out of view until the horses round the last bend. Most of the attending regulars are taxi drivers, and betting is restrained due to a high incidence of race fixing. Still, it's an afternoon out in the open air.

Shopping

Cairo is both a budget souvenir and a kitsch-shoppers' paradise. Visitors with shelf space to fill back home can indulge in an orgy of alabaster pyramids, onyx Pharaonic cats, sawdust-stuffed camels and the ubiquitous painted papyrus. Hieroglyphic drawings of pharaohs, gods and goddesses embellish and blemish everything from leather wallets to engraved brass tables. Beyond the tourist tat though, there's actually little to tempt, except perhaps the handicrafts (including jewellery, rugs and ethnic clothing) found in the many small boutiques and galleries dotted around town.

For information on food shopping, see Self-Catering in the Places to Eat chapter; for details of boutique shopping see the boxed text 'Designer Life' in the Things to See & Do chapter.

WHERE TO SHOP

There are two main kinds of shopping experiences in Cairo: casual browsing, where the actual purchase of an item is secondary to the search itself, and the more straightforward hunt for something specific. For the former, the most fun places to prowl are the covered alleyways of Khan al-Khalili – for more details, see the special section 'Shopping Khan al-Khalili' later in this chapter.

Otherwise, the main concentration of shops is Downtown, along Sharias Talaat Harb, Qasr el-Nil and 26th of July. Not that there's much of worth to be found – mainly rows of cheap clothing and shoe shops. For better quality, high-street shopping try the following areas: on and off Sharia 26th of July and at the Yamama Centre in Zamalek; along Sharia Shehab in Mohandiseen; around Midan Roxy and Sharias Ibrahim Laqqany and Baghdad in Heliopolis; Road 9 in Ma'adi; and the better malls, such as the World Trade Centre, Arkadia and First Residence (for more details, see Shopping Malls later in this chapter).

Souqs & Markets

Khan al-Khalili is just the largest and best known of numerous souqs (markets) that dot Cairo. Unlike the Khan, most are authentic marketplaces where Egyptians do their household shopping. For the visitor

The Art of Bargaining

Almost all prices are negotiable in Cairo, especially in Khan al-Khalili where there is no such thing as a correct price. Bargaining is a process to establish how much the customer is willing to pay. It can be a hassle, but keep your cool and remember it's a game, not a fight.

The first rule is never to show too much interest in the item you want to buy. Secondly, don't buy the first item that takes your fancy. Wander around and price things, but don't make it obvious otherwise when you return to the first shop the vendor will know it's because they are the cheapest.

Decide how much you would be happy paying and then express a casual interest in buying. The vendor will state their price, grossly inflated, doubly so if it's a foreigner doing the buying. Respond with a figure somewhat lower than that which you have fixed in your mind. So the bargaining begins. The shopkeeper will inevitably huff about how absurd your offer is and then tell you the 'lowest' price. If it is still not low enough, be insistent and keep smiling. Tea or coffee might be served as part of the bargaining ritual – accepting it doesn't place you under any obligation to buy. If you still can't get your price, then walk away. This often has the effect of closing the sale in your favour. If not, there are thousands more shops in the bazaar.

If you do get your price or lower, never feel guilty – no vendor, no matter what they say, ever sells below cost.

SHOPPING

they're worth a visit whether you intend buying anything or not. For information on food markets, see under Self-Catering in the Places to Eat chapter earlier.

Muski Map 6 Stretching between Midan Ataba and Khan al-Khalili is a couple of kilometres or so of small shops selling everything from bridal wear to toys to electronics. Most shops are closed Sunday.

Souq al-Gomaa Map 1 On Friday morning from about 6am to 11am the fringes of the Southern Cemetery are host to a sprawling animal and bric-a-brac market. Among the assorted junk – plus the rare intriguing find – vendors offer budgerigars, cockatiels, canaries and finches, tortoises, guinea pigs, dogs and snakes. For anybody who cares about animals it's a grim place. To get here, head south from the Citadel along the main Ma'adi highway; the market is off to your right after about a kilometre. You'll probably need to take a taxi.

Wikalet al-Balah Map 3 Also known as Souq Bulaq, or the Bulaq Market, this is a whole neighbourhood, just north of Sharia 26th of July and inland of the Nile, dedicated to cheap cloth and fabrics, second-hand clothes and also to spare car parts and tools. Lace curtains and sump pumps – it's an odd mixture. Low prices draw lots of customers, especially on Friday. It's closed on Sunday.

Shopping Malls

These are the souqs of the 21st century. Cairo has turned its back on Khan al-Khalili and, instead, wholeheartedly embraced the blue-collar American way of shopping, complete with food courts, tenpin bowling alleys and piped muzak. Young Cairenes have become happy mall rats, hanging out in the atriums and aisles, enjoying the air-conditioning and hitting on the opposite sex.

The north-eastern suburb of Medinat Nasr is mall city, with no less than three large shopping complexes: **Tiba Mall** (clothes and shoe shops, two-screen cinema and a bowling centre), **Geneina Mall** (shoe shops, six-screen cinema and a roller-skating rink) and **Serag City Mall** (clothes shops and a big gym housed in three hideous pink, maroon and white towers).

However, central Cairo has its share too, with more on the drawing board.

Al-Bustan Centre (Shária al-Bustan, Downtown) **Map 2, #74** Not so much a mall as an old-fashioned shopping centre at the heart of Downtown, with lots of cheap clothing stores, pool and bowling on the upper floors and an Internet cafe in the basement.

Arkadia Mall (Corniche el-Nil, Bulaq) **Map 3, #31** Located just north of the Conrad International hotel and managed by the Hilton corporation, this is currently the biggest mall in town with some 500 shops including a plethora of international franchises (including Toys 'R' Us, Timberland, Adidas, Nike and Habitat). The international food court is distinguished by a branch of the excellent local grilled-meat masters, Abu Shaqra.

First Residence Mall (35 Sharia Giza, Giza) **Map 4, #27** No mall rats, it's too rich for their tastes. Part of the exclusive First Residence apartment complex, this mall welcomes only the most chic of shoppers with the most sterling of credit cards strengthened for use at the likes of Louis Vuitton and Cartier. The atrium cafe is nice, though.

Ramses Hilton Annexe (Midan Abdel Moniem Riad, Downtown) **Map 2, #2** Belonging to the adjacent Ramses Hilton hotel, this is a family-oriented shopping centre on seven levels, filled with lots of cheap clothing and shoes. On the top floor is a two-screen cinema and snooker and billiards halls.

Talaat Harb Shopping Centre (Talaat Harb, Downtown) **Map 2, #45** Opened in 2000, this is a pink-plastic and green-glass monstrosity with seven circular floors largely devoted to shoes. Outside the food court (which includes McDonald's, Hardees and KFC), international franchises are few and most units are occupied by small-time independent retailers.

World Trade Centre (1191 Corniche el-Nil, Bulaq) **Map 3, #33** This is another upmarket shopping mall, but exclusivity works against it and the place is usually empty and echoing. Retailers are largely

[Continued on page 211]

SHOPPING KHAN AL-KHALILI

Khan al-Khalili is the place to head for the Cairo shopping experience par excellence. Beyond the plethora of tacky souvenirs you'll also find copperware, blown glass, gold and silver, perfume, spices, clothing, fabrics, semiprecious stones, antiques, belly-dancing costumes, water pipes and all kinds of stuff that you were never even aware existed, but once you've seen you can't do without.

In the central parts of the bazaar, the hassle factor can be high, with shopkeepers cajoling and entreating in a dozen languages, determined not to let a visitor indulge in such a noncommercial activity as sightseeing. The only way to shop the Khan successfully is to ignore unwanted overtures and, if you have a particular item in mind, to head for the section specialising in what you're after. See Map 7 at the back of this book for guidance on where to find what.

Many visitors fail to realise that many parts of the Khan are multistorey – when you see steps, go up; some of the most interesting shops and workshops are on the 1st floor and rooftops.

Most shops in the Khan are open from around 10am to 9pm Monday to Saturday.

Backgammon Boards & Sheesha

A plain backgammon box with plastic counters, similar to those used in many Cairene coffeehouses, goes for as little as E£20. As the boards get more fancy the price goes up – a board inlaid with bone will set you back more than E£100. The place to look is the Souq an-Nahaseen area and north up Sharia al-Muizz li-Din Allah.

Sheeshas (water pipes) start at around E£30, but if you might actually use it and not just stick flowers in the top you need to buy a supply of the little clay tobacco holders and some tobacco. The entire package is bulky and heavy. Again, look along Souq an-Nahaseen and also on Al-Mashhad al-Husseiny, alongside the Sayyidna al-Hussein mosque.

Inset: Bags of herbs and spices on sale (Photo by Juliet Coombe)
Right: A cluster of *sheesha*, traditional water pipes

Belly-Dancing Outfits

Sequined bras, beaded hip bands, veils and filmy skirts are sold in several specialist emporiums in Khan al-Khalili. There are a couple in the small passageway leading from Muski to Fishawi's coffeehouse, plus another upstairs at the very easternmost end of Muski. Most famous of all is **Al-Wikalah** (☎ *589 7443, 73 Gawhar al-Qaid*) **(Map 7, #18)**, owned by Mahmoud Abdel Ghaffar, which consists of three storeys of sequins, stretch fabrics, chiffons and everything that jingles and spangles. Beaded scarves (E£30 to E£70), coin belts (E£50), finger cymbals (E£20) and candelabra headdresses (E£180) are sold as accompaniment to harem pantaloons (E£60), bra-top-and-belt combinations (E£250 to E£600) and bead-and-sequin top and skirt ensembles (E£650). It's all good-quality stuff at fair prices that are more or less fixed, so bargaining is not necessary. To find the place head down As-Sanadqiyya from Al-Muizz li-Din Allah and take the first main right, then look for the alley with a tailor's counter in front and a sign saying 'Mahmoud Reda' and it's down there.

Brass & Copperware

Brass and copper pans, plates, coffeepots and a variety of other objects are good value. Engraved trays and plates start at around E£15, depending on their intricacy and age. Watch for the quality of any engraving work and be wary of claims that an object is 100 years old – more often than not it rolled off the production line a couple of weeks ago. The best place to browse is Souq an-Nahaseen (which means 'Street of the Coppersmiths') and also on the upper floor of an old *wikala* (caravanserai), reached by a dank stairway just south of the Badestan Gate.

Left: The best place to look for brass and copper pans is Souq an-Nahaseen. They're generally good value but may be hard to fit into your luggage.

ELLIOT DANIEL

Shopkeepers in Cairo's bazaars will expect you to bargain over prices; it's all part of the shopping ritual. A traditional *sheesha* (water pipe; top) is a popular buy but is bulky to take home; spices (bottom) are often sold in small packets and make wonderfully aromatic souvenirs.

ADINA TOVY AMSEL

ANDREW MACCOLL

CHERYL CONLON

IZZAT KERIBAR

In the crush of narrow streets that make up Cairo's great Khan al-Khalili bazaar (bottom), people ply their trades as they have done for centuries. Different areas of the bazaar are devoted to specific wares, including perfumes (top left), copperware (top right) and cloth and clothing (middle left).

Cloth

A small alley off Sharia al-Azhar, one block west of Al-Muizz li-Din Allah, is home to numerous drapers all piled high with bolts of cloth, as well as sheets, blankets, towels etc. Of these, *Ouf* (Map 7, #17) has been recommended to us. For something special visit *Atlas* (☎ 590 6139) (Map 7, #6); a tiny shop, it is stocked with beautiful fabrics made from all-natural fibres such as cotton and silk, including striped *shahi*, a weighty cotton-silk blend traditionally used to make kaftans for sheikhs. Because it is handwoven, it is sold in 0.8m by 6m pieces ranging in price from E£90 to E£150.

Gold & Silver

Gold and silver shops are concentrated along As-Sagha (Gold Market), a part of Al-Muizz li-Din Allah, and up along Sikket al-Badestan. Buying precious metals is always a little fraught. The Assay Office in Birmingham, UK, says that hallmarking for gold of at least 12 carats and silver of 600 parts per 1000 or more is compulsory in Egypt – verifying this is another matter. The hallmark contains a standard mark showing where a piece was assayed and a date mark in Arabic. Foreign goods cannot be resold, in the UK at least, unless they are first assayed there.

Shopkeepers have an irritating habit of weighing the gold out of sight. Insist that they put the scales on the counter and let you see what's happening. This reduces the chances of cheating. Another precaution is to check current gold prices, listed daily in the *Egyptian Gazette*. Much the same cautionary rules apply to silver and other jewellery.

Gold and silver jewellery can be made to specification for not much more than the cost of the metal, although the craftwork is often less than wonderful. Tried-and-tested favourites include personalised cartouches with the name spelt out in hieroglyphs – *Mihran Yazejian*, Map 7, #8, specialises in this – and reproduction Pharaonic jewellery (for this kind of stuff try the Badestan gate area, in front of the Naguib Mahfouz Cafe). For antique silver jewellery and unusual pieces from Yemen and around Africa try *Mohammed Amin Silver* (☎ 592 1214, 70 Al-Muizz li-Din Allah) (Map 7, #7). *George Aziz* (Map 7, #5), with a shop just to the right of the Naguib Mahfouz Cafe, was also recommended to us for silver jewellery.

Muski Glass

Muski glass, hand-blown glassware still produced in the Khan al-Khalili neighbourhood, is distinguished by its vivid, cloudy, green-and-blue hues and, less commonly, deep reds. You can find nice vases, pitchers and glasses. Prices are usually reasonable. The glass merchants are congregated immediately south of the Madrassa & Mausoleum of As-Salih Ayyub, and in the Wikalet al-Mekwa, off to the right, south-west of the Badestan Gate.

Perfume

Egypt is a big producer of many of the essences that make up French perfume, hence it's no surprise that part of Cairo's Khan al-Khalili is devoted to a perfume bazaar. Here you can buy pure essence (from E£8 to E£20 an ounce) as well as cheaper substances diluted with alcohol or oil. Some of the perfume traders have price tags on their goods, but that doesn't mean you can't haggle. Intricate perfume bottles are also popular. Again, there are expensive and cheap varieties. Small glass bottles start at about E£3; the heavier and more durable Pyrex bottles start at about E£10.

Prayer Beads

Wafts of incense drift along Sharia al-Mashhad al-Husseiny, the narrow street alongside the Sayyidna Hussein mosque, creating the perfect ambience for the shops displaying row upon row of multicoloured *sebha* (prayer beads). Muslims use the beads, which come in strings of 33 or 99, to recite the *tasabih*. Materials used for the beads range from plastic, shells and camel bone to precious stones; prices range from E£5 to E£20, or to E£35 per gram for coral. Deeper into the Khan, just west of Fishawi's coffeehouse is **Haj Shaaban Aly (Map 7, #9)**, whose shop sells antique beads fetching prices of up to and over E£1000.

Spices

Every conceivable herb and spice, and many you will never have heard of or seen, are found in the area around the Mosque of Al-Ashraf Barsbey. Not just used for cooking or as scents, the spices sold here have all manner of qualities attributed to them, usually to do with combating ill health, increasing vitality or improving sexual prowess – ask about *nosgha*, which the vendors swear is the natural alternative to Viagra.

Souvenirs

Second only in popularity to papyrus (sold absolutely everywhere from E£1 to E£5 per piece) as souvenir items are the inlaid boxes piled high throughout Khan al-Khalili. They are very inexpensive, a small one selling for as little as E£6. For that price you'll get poor quality (it will not be inlaid with mother-of-pearl, as the shopkeeper may tell you, but plastic), though for a higher price you can buy something beautifully crafted such as a mirror frame or jewellery casket. A mother-of-pearl chessboard together with camel-bone pieces would sell for E£240 to E£300.

[Continued from page 206]

international franchises (including Benetton, Naf Naf and Daniel Hechter) plus luxury-goods stores (such as furniture and diving supplies). The place is also home to several pricey eateries and a couple of nightclubs.

Yamama Centre *(3 Taha Hussein, Zamalek)* **Map 3, #38** One of the oldest malls, the Yamama is a no-frills eight-floor shopping centre, heavy on shoes and women's clothing, with the odd interesting store such as Zoganon, Egypt's answer to Body Shop, and Ad-Dukkan (for more details, see under Clothes later in this chapter).

WHAT TO BUY
Antiques & Auctions

Until recently Egyptians firmly believed that old was bad and new was good, and were in the habit of tossing out all the old stuff. That's changed and now antique is chic. The sudden popularity for period furnishings means there are now few real antique bargains around. Dealers here know what they're about and the latest Sotheby's catalogues are their bedtime reading. It is also illegal to export anything of antique value out of Egypt without a licence from the Department of Antiquities. But if you're interested then the best places to browse include the emporiums (particularly **Hassan & Ali** and **Mahrous**) along Sharia Hoda Shaarawi in Downtown; several places in Zamalek, including **Atrium** *(☎ 735 6869, 4 Mohammed Mazhar)* and **Nostalgia** *(☎ 737 0880, 6 Sharia Zakaria Rizk)*; plus **Clarine** *(☎ 760 8393, 11 Suleyman Abaza)* in Mohandiseen.

For the true connoisseur, **Osiris** *(☎ 392 6609, 15 Sharia Sherif, Downtown)* **(Map 2, #92)** is the city's premier auction house and a place where the occasional genuine bargain can be had, although it's a haunt of avid collectors with well-lined pockets. Auctions are held every few weeks, preceded by three days of viewing.

Kitsch aficionados should check out **Maktab al-Nasr Auctions** *(☎ 575 8063, 5 Dr Abdel Hamid Said, Downtown)*, across from the Cinema Odeon, and **As-Sharq Auctions** *(☎ 393 8599, 44 Qasr el-Nil,*

Downtown), both of which are more like junk warehouses, with most of the items up for sale rather then for auction.

Arts & Crafts

Cairo is excellent for arts and crafts galleries and boutiques that collect together handicrafts and work from all over Egypt, much of it originating in the desert oases and among the Bedouin. For more suggestions, see also the special section 'Shopping Khan al-Khalili' in this chapter.

Al-Ain Gallery *(☎ 349 3940, 73 Sharia al-Hussein, Doqqi)* **Map 4, #3** Open 10am-9pm daily, closed Fri morning. This gallery is known for intricate 'Oriental' metalwork lamps by designer Randa Fahmy, and gorgeous unique items of jewellery fashioned by sister Azza. It also has assorted 'ethnic' clothing and furnishings, fabrics from Akhmim and rugs from Sinai.

Khan Misr Touloun *(☎ 365 2227, Sharia Ibn Tulun, Islamic Cairo)* **Map 6, #40** Open 10am-5pm Mon-Fri. Run by a French lady and her Egyptian husband and located opposite the entrance to Ibn Tulun mosque, this is a beautiful shop that carries wooden chests, bowls and plates, marionettes, blown glass, clay figurines, scarves and woven clothing.

Al-Khatoun Gallery *(☎ 012-226 5329, Sharia al-Sheikh Mohammed Abdo, Islamic Cairo)* **Map 6, #13** Open noon-9pm daily. Lying between Beit Zeinab al-Khatoun and Beit al-Harrawi behind Al-Azhar mosque, this is a small place with an eclectic assortment of new (including glassware, leatherwork, printed fabrics and wrought-iron furniture) and old (including furniture, paintings and cigarette tins).

Marketing Link *(☎ 736 5123, W www .egyptcrafts.com, 27 Yehia Ibrahim, Apt 8, Zamalek)* **Map 3, #57** Open 9am-8pm Sat-Wed, 9am-5pm Thur. This is a fair-trade shop with merchandise produced in income-generating projects throughout Egypt. Items on sale include Bedouin rugs from Sinai and the northern Western Desert, embroidery from Sinai, handmade paper from Muqattam, Bedouin beadwork and Upper Egyptian shawls. Prices are competitive.

Nagada (☎ 792 3249, 8 Sharia Dar al-Shefa, 3rd floor, Garden City) **Map 5, #2** Open 9.30am-3.30pm daily. Beautiful handwoven textiles from the town of the same name (about 28km north of Luxor) are sold here, as well as handmade pottery from Al-Fayoum and clothes, lamps and jewellery. To get here head south along the Corniche and take the left immediately opposite the turn-off on the right for Le Méridien Cairo hotel; follow the street that veers to the right, then take the first right and it's the second or third building along.

Nomad (☎ 341 1917, 14 Saray al-Gezira, Zamalek) **Map 3, #85** Open 10am-3pm Mon-Sat. Up on the 1st floor of an apartment building down the street from the Cairo Marriott hotel, this is a small, well-hidden gem of a place that specialises in jewellery and traditional Bedouin craft and costumes. It's well worth a look. There's also a smaller and much less enticing branch within the Marriott.

Senouhi (☎ 391 0955, 54 Abdel Khalek Sarwat, 5th floor, Downtown) **Map 2, #36** Open 10am-5pm Mon-Fri, 10am-1pm Sat. This is a grotto-like apartment with a horde of antiques (jewellery, silver and miscellanea) and handicrafts; worth a rummage for rugs, traditional clothing and artworks.

Shahira Mehrez (☎ 748 7814, 11 Sharia Abi Imama, 3rd floor, Doqqi) **Map 4, #21** Mehrez works closely with Bedouin women and travels widely to collect the items for her shop, including Bedouin-style costumes and jewellery, kilims from the Eastern and Western Deserts, Siwan bridal wear, embroidered cushions, coin purses, mats, woven textiles, baskets and 100% cotton *galabeyyas* (traditional men's robes).

Sheba Gallery (☎ 735 9192, 6 Sharia Sri Lanka, Zamalek) **Map 3, #81** Contemporary gold and silver designs based on traditional Yemeni jewellery are sold here, along with beautiful necklaces, bracelets, earrings and rings with semiprecious stones that are snapped up by chic Cairenes.

Tukul Craft Shop (☎ 736 8391, All Saints Cathedral, Sharia Sheikh al-Marsafy, Zamalek) **Map 3, #72** Open 9am-4.30pm Mon-Thur & Sat, 11am-3pm Fri & Sun. This shop has bags, clothing and wall hangings made from fabrics printed with original African designs made by displaced Sudanese who keep the profits.

Applique South of Bab Zuweila in Islamic Cairo, *Sharia al-Khayamiyya (Street of the Tentmakers)* **(Map 6)** is where a dozen or more workshops are clustered in a medieval covered market, all specialising in applique work. Colours of the applique work are bright to garish, and designs range from arabesque patterns and calligraphy to the more figurative (such as dervish dancers or Pharaonic motifs). Price depends on the intricacy of the pattern (arabesques and calligraphy cost the most), the quality of the work and the size. As a guide, a small cushion cover costs E£20; a larger one E£40. Wall hangings of about 1.5 sq metres range from E£80 to almost E£200.

Mashrabiyya Virtually nobody these days still makes complete *mashrabiyya* (wooden lattice) screens. What you get are things that look like magazine racks (actually Quran holders) or table bases. It is still possible to find large screens in some of the antique shops, but they'll be prohibitively expensive. The one exception is the *National Art Development Institute for Mashrabiyya (NADIM; ☎ 348 1075, Sharia al-Mazaniyya, off Sharia Sudan, Doqqi)*, a craft shop dedicated to keeping the art of mashrabiyya alive. It has all manner of mashrabiyya products, screens included (from E£2000 to E£3500), and visitors are welcome to watch the artisans at work with no obligation to buy. It's behind the Coca-Cola factory.

Books & Magazines
Cairo's bookshops are, unsurprisingly, excellent for titles relating to Egypt, Egyptology and the Middle East in general, but less good for titles on other subjects.

Anglo-Egyptian Bookshop (☎ 391 4337, 165 Mohammed Farid, Downtown) **Map 2, #38** Open 9am-1.30pm & 4.30pm to 8pm Mon-Sat. Most of the titles are academic, but if you dig around at the back you'll find plenty of classic English literature.

AUC Bookstore (☎ 797 5377, AUC Campus, Mohammed Mahmoud, Downtown) **Map 2, #115** Open 9am-4pm Sun-Thur, 10am-3pm Sat. An academic outlet, it has stacks of material on the politics, sociology and history of Cairo, Egypt and the Middle East, but also plenty of local guidebooks (and Lonely Planet), coffee-table volumes and some fiction. There is also a smaller branch at the AUC hostel (Map 3, #28) at 16 Mohammed ibn Thakeb in Zamalek.

Everyman Bookshop (☎ 417 6064, 12 Sharia Baghdad, Heliopolis) **Map 9, #20** Open 9.30am-2pm & 5pm-9.30pm Mon-Sat. Stationary and newspapers are sold downstairs, but upstairs there's a limited selection of bestsellers (such as Collins, Grisham and King).

Lehnert & Landrock (☎ 393 5324, 44 Sharia Sherif, Downtown) **Map 2, #26** Open 9.30am-2pm & 4pm-7.30pm Mon-Fri, 9.30am-2pm Sat. There are books in both English and German, plus a large collection of historic postcards and prints.

Livres d'France (☎ 393 5512, 36 Qasr el-Nil, Downtown) **Map 2, #91** Open 10am-7pm Mon-Fri, 10am-2pm Sat. This is a French-language bookshop, but it does have in addition a well-chosen selection of English-language titles all concerned with Egypt and the Middle East.

L'Orientaliste (☎ 575 3418, 15 Qasr el-Nil, Downtown) **Map 2, #81** An antiquarian bookshop specialising in dusty, old volumes on Egypt, as well as old prints and maps. However, at the time of writing the shop is closed and its future is uncertain.

Romancia (☎ 735 0492, 32 Shagaret ad-Durr, Zamalek) **Map 3, #49** Open 9am-9pm daily. A tiny place but Romancia is good for newspapers and magazines and carries a small stock of airport novels.

Zamalek (☎ 736 9197, 19 Shagaret ad-Durr, Zamalek) **Map 3, #39** Open 8am-8.30pm Mon-Sat. Opposite Romancia, this bookshop also sells newspapers and magazines and has a similar selection of novels.

Second-hand Books There's a fairly large *second-hand book market* **(Map 2, #19)** on the east side of the Ezbekiyya Gardens, reached from Midan Ataba in central Cairo. Many of its 40 or 50 stalls (cabins, actually) carry English-language books and magazines, but half the stock is piled knee-high on the floor, and much of the rest sits on shelves with their spines to the wall making browsing something of a chore.

Newspapers & Magazines The three best newsstands are right next to each other in Zamalek, at the junction of 26th of July and Hassan Sabry. You can get just about any publication from these guys, provided there are no bare breasts or buttocks involved. The Zamalek and Romancia bookshops on nearby Shagaret ad-Durr are also good.

Downtown, the places with the best selections include the guy on Midan Talaat Harb out the front of Groppi and the newsstand on Sharia Mohammed Mahmoud, opposite the entrance to the AUC. In Heliopolis, try Everyman.

Hotel bookshops also carry a selection of international press, some more than others – best are the Semiramis Inter-Continental, Cairo Marriott and the Nile Hilton (the bookshop in the garden courtyard, not the one in the lobby), in roughly that order.

Of course, there's a premium to be paid on foreign publications, which generally sell for up to twice their home cover price.

Carpets & Rugs
Unlike Morocco, Turkey or Iran, Egypt has no tradition of carpet weaving. What you can find, however, are brown-and-beige striped, hardwearing, camel-hair rugs of Bedouin origin. The biggest selection is in the *Haret al-Fahhamin* **(Map 7, #H)**, a tight squeeze of alleys behind the Mosque-Madrassa of Al-Ghouri, across the road from Khan al-Khalili in Islamic Cairo. In addition, many of the places listed under Arts & Crafts earlier in this chapter also carry Bedouin rugs.

Cotton rag rugs are a great buy: a brightly coloured rug 2m by 1m costs around E£12. The best place to buy is a small *workshop* **(Map 6, #24)** where the rugs are woven, partway along Darb al-Ahmar in Islamic Cairo. Alternatively, try Marketing Link in Zamalek (see Arts & Crafts earlier).

SHOPPING

In the area of the Pyramids, just off the Saqqara Rd, the **Wissa Wassef Art Centre** (☎ 385 0746, Saqqara Rd, Harraniyya) specialises in very distinctive woollen rugs and wall hangings depicting rural and folkloric scenes. Wissa Wassef rugs are now very much imitated and you can buy similar ones at most souvenir shops, but for the greatest choice – and choice pieces – visit the art centre (for more details, see the Around the Pyramids section in The Pyramids & Memphis Necropolis chapter earlier in this book).

Clothes

Although Egypt is a major cotton producer, most of what's best goes abroad, like the oil, the agricultural produce and the brainy university graduates. It is possible to find good-quality cotton clothing, but invariably it is let down by bad finishing – terrible hems and seams, buttons that come off at the first wash and colours that run. Cairenes who can afford it shop abroad. Still undeterred? Then for plain cotton shirts, blouses and khakis try chain stores such as **Daniel Hechter**, **Safari** and **Lifestyle**, branches of which can be found at the five-star hotels and in the malls.

One way of getting good-quality unique clothing is to have it tailor made. This can be fantastically cheap. The best way of doing this is to take along a favourite shirt or dress and have it copied in a fabric of your choosing. For wonderful fabrics go to **Nagada** or **Marketing Link** (see under Arts & Crafts earlier for contact details) or to one of the fabric places in Khan al-Khalili. Recommended tailors include **Amin Ladies Fashions** (☎ 735 2792, 4 Sharia Brazil, Zamalek), which is tucked down an alley off the main street, and **Mohammed Ali Abdel Latif** (☎ 523 6287, Hara al-Gadawy, Sharia Darb Sa'ada, Bab al-Khalq, Islamic Cairo), which is even more difficult to find: cross the road from the Museum of Islamic Arts as though heading for Bab Zuweila, then take the first left, followed by the first right into a small alley and the tailor is down here.

Belly-Dancing Outfits For dance enthusiasts (or kinky dressing-up fun) you could go where Fifi Abdou goes and pay a fortune at **Bekhita** (☎ 735 1094, Cairo Marriott, Zamalek) **(Map 3, #76)**. Alternatively, another prime source of outfits is **Amira al-Qattan** (☎ 349 0322, 27 Sharia Basra, Mohandiseen) **(Map 1, #2)**, a famed designer whose made-to-order handiwork is also highly prized by the great and good of the belly-dance world. For more affordable wear go and haggle in the bazaar – see the special section 'Shopping Khan al-Khalili' for more details.

Ethnic For something different, visit **Ad-Dukkan** (☎ 736 6500, Yamama Centre, 3 Taha Hussein, Zamalek) **(Map 3, #38)**, which has glamorous take-offs of ethnic Egyptian styles. Prices are high but justified. There's also a branch in the Ramses Hilton Annexe. **Nagada** (see under Arts & Crafts earlier for more details) has a range of elegant gowns, pants, dresses, tops and scarves, all cut to traditional patterns and made of a blend of cotton and silk woven in Upper Egypt. If you can't find what you're looking for, owners Michel and Sylva will measure and make to order in about 10 days.

Fine Art

Contemporary art is affordable in Cairo. Check *Al-Ahram Weekly* for notices of exhibition openings. **Mashrabia** and the **Townhouse Gallery** (see under Activities in the Things to See & Do chapter) also have large archives of work that the gallery owners are happy to haul out for serious buyers.

Health Food

Sekem Health Store (☎ 342 4979, 6 Ahmed Sabry, Zamalek) **(Map 3, #51)** stocks organic fruit and vegetables, additive-free jams and honey, herbs and pulses, as well as a range of herbal and homeopathic teas. It's open from 8am to 9pm daily. There are also Sekem stores in Heliopolis and Ma'adi.

Jewellery

Although many head straight for Khan al-Khalili for jewellery, much of the work found there is clumsy and unimaginative. There's better to be found elsewhere: visit **Al-Ain Gallery** to see the work of Azza

Fahmy, *Nomad* for chunky Bedouin pieces, and *Sheba Gallery* for something elegant (for details of addresses, see under Arts & Crafts earlier in this chapter). Other jewellery shops of note include:

Bashayer (☎ 335 3233) 58 Sharia Mossadeq, Doqqi

Kafr al-Nada (☎ 760 0290) 18 Sharia ibn al-Walid, near the Shooting Club, Doqqi

Qasr as-Shouk (☎ 737 2111) 11 Sharia Brazil, Zamalek

Sayyed Mohammed Gomaa (☎ 453 3609) 10 Sharia Haroun ar-Rashid, Midan al-Gamaa, Heliopolis

Musical Instruments

Traditional musical instruments such as an *oud* (lute), *kamaan* (violin), *nay* (flute), *tabla* (drum) and various others are made and sold in about a dozen shops in Cairo on Sharia Mohammed Ali **(Map 2)**, which runs south-east from Midan Ataba to the Museum of Islamic Art. *Gamil Georges (170 Sharia Mohammed Ali, Ataba)* sells ouds, for example, with prices ranging from E£150 to E£300.

Papyrus

You can pick up cheap, poor-quality papyrus all over Cairo for virtually nothing, but many well-heeled visitors continue to part with ridiculous sums of money for garbage. Look long and hard at what you are getting. Is it machine printed? Has it rolled off a sweat-shop production line? Or has it been masterfully hand-painted? And is it papyrus, which will not be damaged by rolling, or is it in fact banana leaf, which will crack?

Dr Ragab's Papyrus Institute (☎ 748 8177, Sharia el-Nil, Doqqi) **Map 4, #23** The 'institute' is a boat on the Nile between the Cairo Sheraton and University Bridge. His stuff is good quality, but it's also expensive.

Said Delta Papyrus Centre (☎ 512 0747, Sharia al-Muizz li-Din Allah, Islamic Cairo)

Map 6, #19 A good alternative to Dr Ragab's, it's on the 3rd floor above a shoe shop: look for a yellow sign at 1st-floor level. Said learnt his craft from the famed Dr Ragab, and some of his work is stunning. The posted prices seem to be negotiable.

Tapes & CDs

Cassette kiosks dot the city, but the highest concentration is along Sharia Shawarby, which runs between Qasr el-Nil and Abdel Khalek Sarwat, Downtown **(Map 2)**. There's also a good kiosk in a little alleyway, west off the top end of Talaat Harb, just a few doors up from McDonald's. As well as cassettes by Egyptian and other Arab artists, most places have a very limited selection of pirated, poor-quality tapes of Western artists, which sell for around E£8 to E£10.

For CDs by both local and international artists, visit *Jukebox (☎ 578 2980, World Trade Centre, 1191 Corniche el-Nil, Bulaq)* **(Map 3, #33)** or *Mirage Megastore (☎ 760 9793, 71 Gamiat ad-Dowal al-Arabiyya, Mohandiseen)* **(Map 3, #13)**; they're not cheap.

Textiles & Egyptian Cotton

For thick, simple, white towels, cotton bedspreads and sheets go to *Salon Vert (☎ 393 1937, 28 Qasr el-Nil, Downtown)* **(Map 2, #90)**. The place looks shabby and the payment process is a drag, but the goods are quality and represent excellent value.

Gallerie Hathout (Sharia Mohammed Farid, Downtown) **(Map 2, #49)** has a sign in its window proclaiming that it sells Egyptian goods only, everything from simple kitchen towels (E£3to E£7) to tablecloth and napkin table sets (E£50 to E£100) and to embroidered bedsheet sets (E£120 to E£220).

For Egyptian-motif cotton, silk and linen try *Tanis (World Trade Centre, Corniche el-Nil, Bulaq)* **(Map 3, #33)**.

SHOPPING

Excursions

Most of the destinations described in this chapter can be visited on day trips from Cairo, although in the case of Alexandria it's definitely worth considering an overnight stay. The destinations in this chapter are described in alphabetical order.

ALEXANDRIA
☎ 03

Founded by Alexander the Great in 331 BC, in classical times this great seaport was a centre of learning and commerce second only to Rome. It was home to the world's greatest library and the fabulous Pharos, a towering lighthouse counted as one of the Seven Wonders of the World. Cleopatra, queen of Egypt, held court here, where she was romanced by Mark Antony. Sadly, the Alexandria of antiquity is long buried, but it has provided the foundations for a modern, 19th-century city, where the Greek and Italian influences still echo in some fine architecture and in the names attached to countless old-world cafes and patisseries.

Cairenes flock here in their thousands every summer to escape the stifling heat of the capital and settle like sea birds on the beaches to the west of the centre. In fact the city's beaches aren't overly enticing and the thing to do in Alex is book a hotel room overlooking the bay, take long breakfasts on the balcony, then while away the days walking the Corniche and idling in cafes.

Orientation & Information

Alexandria is a true waterfront city, nearly 20km long from east to west and only about 3km wide. The focal point of the city is Midan Ramla, also known as Mahattat Ramla (Ramla Station) because this is the central terminus for many of the city's tram lines. Immediately adjacent is Midan Saad Zaghloul, a large square running back from the seafront Corniche and joining Midan Ramla at the corner. Around these two midans, and in the streets to the south and west, are the central shopping area, the tourist office, airline offices, restaurants and most of the cheaper hotels.

The main tourist office (☎ 807 9885) is on the south-west corner of Midan Saad. It's open from 8am to 6pm daily. For changing cash or cashing travellers cheques, the simplest option is to use one of the many exchange bureaus on the side streets between Midan Ramla and the Corniche. ATMs are scarcer in Alex than in Cairo. The most reliable ATM (and the one most likely to accept foreign cards) belongs to the HSBC (☎ 487 2839), at 47 Sultan Hussein, a five-minute walk east of the centre. There are also several ATMs on Salah Salem, including one belonging to the EAB.

Things to See & Do

Places to visit here include the **Fortress of Qaitbey** (☎ 480 9144, Eastern Harbour; admission E£20; open 9am-4pm daily), a 15th-century squatter on the site once occupied by the Pharos; the **Catacombs of Kom esh-Shoqqafa** (☎ 484 5800, Carmous; admission E£12; open 9am-4pm daily), a series of Roman-era burial chambers sunk deep below the surface and adorned with intriguing reliefs in which Pharaonic deities and Roman mythology are merged; **Pompey's Pillar** (☎ 484 5800, Carmous; admission E£6; open 9am-4pm daily), a 30m-high pink-granite column raised in AD 293 in honour of the Roman emperor Diocletian; and the **Graeco-Roman Museum** (☎ 487 6434, 5 Al-Mathaf ar-Romani; admission E£16; open 9am-4pm Sat-Thur, 9am-noon & 1.30pm-4pm Fri), packed with statuary and artefacts relating to the city's classical past, including marble busts of founder Alexander and several impressive mosaics.

Places to Stay

Most hotels are clustered around the Eastern Harbour near Midan Saad Zaghloul.

Hotel Union (☎ 480 7312, fax 480 7350, 164 Sharia 26th of July, 5th floor) Singles/doubles E£35/50, with bath E£45/60. Rooms

Fountain in front of Alexandria's Mosque of Abu Abbas al-Mursi

Colourful fishing boats moored in the Eastern Harbour of Alexandria, a true waterfront city

In Alexandria, Fort Qaitbey was built on the foundations of the ancient Pharos lighthouse.

North-west of Cairo, camel traders tend to their charges at Birqash, Egypt's largest camel market.

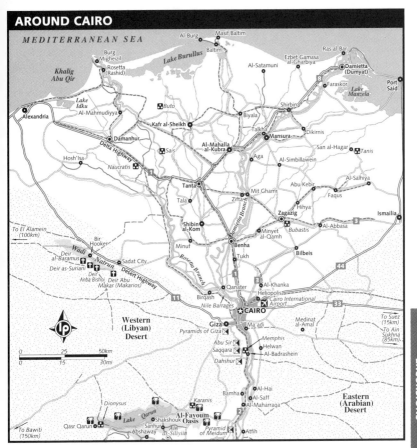

AROUND CAIRO

MEDITERRANEAN SEA

Al-Burg • Masif Baltim

Khalig Abu Qir

Burg Migheizil • Baltim • Ras al-Bar

Rosetta (Rashid) • Lake Burullus • Ezbet Gamasa al-Gharbiya

Al-Satamuni • Damietta (Dumyat)

Port Said

Lake Manzela

Lake Idku • Faraskor

Alexandria • Al-Mahmudiyya • Buto • Shirbins

Kafr el-Sheikh • Biyala • Talkha • Dikirnis

Damanhur • Mansura • San al-Hagar • Tanis

Delta Highway • Sais • Al-Mahalla al-Kubra • Aga • Al-Simbillawein

Hosh'Isa • Naucratis • 1 • Tanta • Al-Salhiya

Tala • Mit Ghamr • Abu Kebir • Ismailia

Zifta • Hihya • Faqus

To El Alamein (100km) • Shibin al-Kom • Zagazig • 3 • Al-Abbasa

Bir Hooker • Minuf • Minyet al-Qamh • Bubastis

Wadi Natrun • Benha • Bilbeis

Deir al-Baramus • Sadat City • Tukh • 44

Deir as-Suriani • Desert Highway

Deir Anba Bishoi • Deir Abu Makar (Makarios) • Qanater • 3 • Al-Khanka

Birqash • Heliopolis • Cairo International Airport • 33

11 • Nile Barrages

To Suez (15km)

Western (Libyan) Desert • CAIRO

Medinat al-Amal • To Ain Sukhna (85km)

Giza • Ma'adi

Pyramids of Giza • Memphis • Helwan

Abu Sir • Al-Badrashein

0   25   50km
0   15   30mi

Saqqara • Dahshur

EXCURSIONS

Bamha • Al-Hai

Dionysus • Karanis • Al-Saff

Eastern (Arabian) Desert

Qasr Qarun • Lake Qarun • Al-Fayoum Oasis • Al-Maharraqa

To Bawiti (150km) • Shakshouk • Sanhur • Ain as-Siliyin • Pyramid of Meidum • Atfih

Abshaway

---

at the Union are some of the cleanest in Alex, with sparkling tiled bathrooms. Some have balconies and harbour views. Reservations are recommended.

Hotel Crillon (☎ *480 0330, 5 Sharia Adib Ishaq, 4th floor)* Doubles with shower E£53, with bath E£67. We like the lovely pre-Revolutionary reception/lounge area, and the rooms with polished wooden floors and French windows that give on to balconies with that great harbour view.

Metropole Hotel (☎ *484 1465, fax 484 2040, 52 Sharia Saad Zaghloul)* Singles/doubles from US$100/120. The Metropole has a good, central location with most rooms overlooking either Midan Ramla or Midan Saad Zaghloul and the harbour. It's a classy, old joint that has been recently renovated, earning itself a four-star rating.

Cecil Hotel (☎ *487 7173, fax 484 0368, Midan Saad Zaghloul)* Singles US$120-150, doubles US$133-168. This is Alexandria's most famous establishment, once patronised by the likes of Somerset Maugham and Winston Churchill and a setting in Lawrence Durrell's *Alexandria Quartet.*

Places to Eat

One of the great pleasures of visiting Alexandria is in sitting around in its various cafes and gorging yourself on the abundant, fresh seafood. The place for cheap eating is around the area where Sharia Safiyya Zaghloul meets Midan Ramla, and along Sharia Shakor Pasha, one street over to the west. There are plenty of little *fuul* (bean puree) and *ta'amiyya* (fried bean patties) places here, as well as sandwich shops.

Mohammed Ahmed (17 Sharia Shakor Pasha) Reckoned by all to be the best of the lot, it specialises in fuul, but also does ta'amiyya, omelettes and fried cheese, plus all the usual salad and dip accompaniments.

Havana (☎ 487 0661, Tariq al-Horreyya) Dishes E£12-24. Opposite the Sednaoui store, this is primarily a bar, but it also does great food. There is a menu with standards such as fried calamari (superb) and pizza, but ask about the specials of the day.

Elite (☎ 486 3592, 43 Sharia Safiyya Zaghloul) Dishes E£4.50-30. Open 11am-late daily. Near the Cinema Metro, this place seems sealed in a 1950s bubble, under the spell of the elderly but formidable Madame Christina, the ever-present proprietress. The menu is displayed outside, beside the door, and ranges from spaghetti bolognese to grilled meats.

L'Osobuco (☎ 487 2506, 14 Tariq al-Horreyya) Dishes E£20-40. Open 11am-3am daily. Run by the same people as Cairo's L'Aubergine, this is a chic bar/restaurant on two floors (boozing downstairs, candle-lit dining upstairs) with a frequently changing, wide-ranging world menu.

Getting There & Away

Train Alexandria's main train terminal is Masr station (Mahattat Masr; general inquiries ☎ 392 0010), although Sidi Gaber (general inquiries ☎ 427 7363), which serves the populous eastern suburbs, is almost as busy.

The best trains running between Cairo and Alexandria are the Turbini, taking 2¼ hours. You can't mistake them, they look a little like the high-speed European TGVs. They depart Cairo at 8am, 2pm and 7pm and tickets for 1st-/2nd-class air-con cost E£30/22. The next best trains are the Espani, the 'Spanish' services, which take 2½

hours, departing from Cairo at 9am, noon, 5pm and 10.30pm. Fares are the same as for the Turbini.

All other Alexandria services (of which there are a further nine between 6am and 8pm) take three hours or more (1st-/2nd-class fares are E£23/14).

Bus Long-distance buses all leave from one garage behind Sidi Gaber train station. This is connected to the Downtown area by tram Nos 1 and 2, which pass in front of the train station. There are Superjet buses to Cairo every 30 minutes from 5am to 10pm. The trip takes 2½ hours and costs from E£20 to E£25. The West Delta Bus Co also has buses to Cairo every 30 minutes between 5am and 2am (5.30am to 1am in winter) and charges E£16 to E£20, with prices rising by E£1 after 5pm, and jumping to E£25 after 11.30pm.

BIRQASH CAMEL MARKET

Egypt's largest camel market *(souq al-gamaal)* is held at Birqash, about 35km north-west of Cairo. Until 1995, this famous market *(admission E£3, plus E£2 for a camera or E£15 for a video)* was located among run-down tenements and overcrowded streets in Imbaba, one of Cairo's western suburbs. But a burgeoning population has made land, even on the city's periphery, a valuable commodity – too precious for camels – and so one of Cairo's age-old institutions was relocated to the edge of the Western Desert, an area deemed more suitable for camel trading.

The market is an easy half-day trip from Cairo, but, like all Egypt's animal markets, it's not for animal lovers or the faint-hearted. Hundreds of camels are sold here daily, most having been brought up the 40 Days Road from western Sudan to just north of Abu Simbel by camel herders. From here, most are sold at the market in Daraw, from where they're hobbled and crammed into trucks for the 24-hour journey to Birqash. By the time they arrive, many are emaciated while others are fit only for the knackery. Traders stand no nonsense and camels that get out of line are beaten relentlessly. The sound of bawling beasts is sickening.

In addition to those from Sudan, there are camels from various parts of Egypt (including Sinai, the west and the south) and sometimes as far away as Somalia. They are traded for other livestock such as goats, sheep and horses, or sold for farm work and for slaughter. If you're interested in buying a camel, smaller ones cost about E£1500 while the bigger beasts fetch E£3000. The market is most lively on Friday and Monday mornings, from about 7am to 9am. As the day wears on, the bargaining activity subsides and by early afternoon it becomes quite subdued.

Getting There & Away

Using public transport, the cheapest way involves getting yourself to the site of the old camel market at Imbaba, from where microbuses filled with traders and potential buyers shuttle back and forth to Birqash. To get to the old camel market take bus No 99 from Midan Abdel Moniem Riad or minibus No 72 from Midan Ramses to Midan Libnan (in Mohandiseen), then catch a microbus from there. Or, easier still, take a taxi from central Cairo all the way to the old site – ask for Imbaba airport *(matar Imbaba)* as it's the closest landmark. Expect to pay about E£5. Microbuses to Birqash (E£1) leave from a cafe (look for the sign 'Modern Cairo House') opposite the old souq site.

From Imbaba, the road winds through fields dotted with date palms, dusty villages and orange orchards before climbing the desert escarpment to the market. In all, it's a 45-minute taste of rural Egypt. Microbuses from Birqash back to Imbaba leave when full so, depending on the time of the day, you may have to wait an hour or so.

Alternatively, on Friday only, the New Sun Hotel (see Places to Stay – Budget in the Places to Stay chapter) organises a minibus tour to the souq, leaving from the hotel at 7am and returning at about noon. The charge is E£20 per person (minimum five people); you must book a day or two in advance.

To hire a taxi yourself to take you all the way there and back, depending on your bargaining skills, is going to cost around E£70.

AL-FAYOUM OASIS
☎ 084

About 100km south-west of Cairo, Al-Fayoum is Egypt's largest oasis, covering an area about 70km wide and 60km long, including Lake Qarun (Birket Qarun). Home to more than two million people, it is an intricately irrigated and extremely fertile basin watered by the Nile via hundreds of capillary canals.

The region was once filled by Lake Qarun and during the reign of the 12th-dynasty pharaohs Sesostris III and son Amenemhet III a series of canals was built linking the lake to the Nile. It was a favourite vacation spot for pharaohs of the 13th dynasty, and many fine palaces were built in the area. The Greeks later called the area Crocodilopolis, because they believed the crocodiles in Lake Qarun were sacred. A temple was built in honour of Sobek, the crocodile-headed god, and during Ptolemaic and Roman times pilgrims came from all over the ancient world to feed the sacred beasts.

These days, the region is revered as the 'garden of Egypt' for its lush fields of vegetables and sugar cane, and groves of citrus fruits, nuts and olives, all of which produce abundant harvests. The lake, canals and vegetation support an amazing variety of bird life. There isn't a whole lot to do here – and the grimy **Medinat al-Fayoum** (Fayoum City) is a place to be avoided at all costs. However, a couple of the archaeological sites (notably **Qasr Qarun** and the **Pyramid of Meidum**) are worth a visit, the vicinity of the lake is attractive, and the desert scenery around **Wadi Rayyan**, just beyond Al-Fayoum, is gorgeous.

Getting There & Away

Given that the oasis is so spread out, you really need your own transport. Ideally, you want to hire a taxi for a day in Cairo to bring you down here and chauffeur you around (expect to pay around E£100 for the day). Alternatively, get a bus to Medinat al-Fayoum from a small station in the vicinity of Midan Giza. To get to the station, take a Pyramids minibus from Midan Abdel Moniem Riad and get off just after Midan

EXCURSIONS

Giza, immediately after passing under a railway bridge, then walk north along the canal; the bus station is 500m ahead. Another option is to take the metro to the Giza stop. Al-Fayoum buses go every 15 minutes and the fare is E£3.50 on the newer air-con buses or E£2.50 on the old heaps (no air-con). Once at Medinat al-Fayoum hire a taxi locally, where you can expect to pay maybe E£40 to E£50.

ISMAILIA
☎ 064

Ismailia was founded by and named after Pasha Ismail, khedive of Egypt in the 1860s while the Suez Canal was being built. Ferdinand de Lesseps, the director of the Suez Canal Company, lived in the city (his house is preserved here but closed to the public) until the canal was completed. A stroll around the elegant colonial streets of Ismailia can be an unexpected pleasure. We're not talking great monuments, but there are some beautiful old villas laid out in a shady, Western-style grid. The small but interesting **Ismailia Museum** (*☎ 322 749, Mohammed Ali Quay; admission E£6; open 9am-3pm Sat-Thur*) has more than 4000 objects from Pharaonic and Graeco-Roman times.

There are also several good beaches around Lake Timsah, 12km south-east of town, but as these have become highly popular among middle-class Cairenes, using them involves paying to get into one of the clubs and hotels that dot the shore. Admission fees vary but on average they are E£20, and some include a buffet lunch as part of the admission price. All include access to a private beach.

We recommend paying a visit to ***George's*** (*☎ 337 327, 11 Sharia Sultan Hussein*), a Greek-run restaurant that's been around since 1950 with few changes in the intervening half-century. Pick your fish from an iced display in the back kitchen or order meat from the menu. It also includes a wonderful old bar area.

Getting There & Away
Ismailia is served by a large new bus station some 3km north-west of the old quarter. Taxis between the bus station and the town

centre cost about E£3. From the station both West Delta Bus Co and East Delta Bus Co have frequent departures to Cairo (E£6, 2½ hours). Service taxis also depart from the bus station for Cairo (E£5), but given the poor safety record of these things we really wouldn't recommend you use them except as a last resort. Similarly, although there are about 10 trains a day between Ismailia and Cairo services are slow, slow, slow, and for rail enthusiasts only.

PORT SAID
☎ 066

The main attraction of Port Said, and the reason it was established on the Mediterranean, is the Suez Canal. The spectacle of the huge ships and tankers lining up to pass through the northern entrance of the canal is something to be seen.

The central district around the canal is full of five-storey buildings with wooden balconies and high verandas in grand *belle epoque* style. South are the striking green domes of **Suez Canal House**, built in time

The central district of Port Said around the canal is full of fascinating architecture.

for the inauguration of the canal in 1869, but, unfortunately, off limits to visitors. There's also a **National Museum** (☎ *237 419, Sharia Palestine; admission E£12; open 9am-4pm Sat-Thur, 9am-11am & 1pm-4pm Fri*) and a small **Military Museum** (☎ *224 657, Sharia 23rd of July; admission E£6; open 9am-3pm Sat-Thur*).

If you decide to stay overnight (or miss the last bus back to Cairo, see Getting There & Away), try the *Akri Palace Hotel* (☎ *221 013, 24 Sharia al-Gomhuriyya*), a Greek-owned place which has reasonably clean singles/doubles with balconies for E£20/25, or doubles with bath for E£37. Alternatively, try *Hotel de la Poste* (☎ *224 048, 42 Sharia al-Gomhuriyya*), which has singles/doubles for US$8/12, or US$10/14 with bath and balcony, and a fading elegance.

Getting There & Away

If you don't want to risk a service taxi or spend the night in town, then beware – the last train and buses for Cairo all depart Port Said by 6.05pm.

Superjet buses to Cairo (E£15, three hours) leave 11 times a day from a terminal in front of the train station. West Delta Bus Co services for Cairo depart hourly from the Ferial Gardens between 6am and 6pm daily and fares range from E£13 to E£15.

There are five trains departing daily to Cairo. These take four hours. There are no 1st-class services. Fares are E£14 for 2nd-class air-con, E£5.50 for 2nd-class ordinary and E£3 for 3rd class.

Service taxis depart from a garage about 2km west of the centre. You'll need to take a taxi to get out there: ask for '*al-mahattat servees*'. The fare to Cairo is E£10.

QANATER (NILE BARRAGES)
☎ 02

The Nile Barrages and the city of Qanater (which simply means 'Barrages') lie 16km north of Cairo where the Nile splits into the eastern Damietta branch and the western Rosetta branch. On Fridays and public holidays this is *the* favourite spot for picnicking Cairenes who flock up here by boat. The barrages, begun in the early 19th century, were

successfully completed several decades later. The series of basins and locks, on both main branches of the Nile and two side canals, ensured the vital, large-scale regulation of the Nile into the Delta region, and led to a great increase in cotton production.

The **Damietta Barrage** consists of 71 sluices stretching 521m across the river; the **Rosetta Barrage** is 438m long with 61 sluices. Between the two is a 1km-wide area filled with beautiful gardens and cafes. It's a decent place to rent a bicycle (E£2 per hour) or a felucca and take a relaxing tour.

The town of Qanater, at the fork of the river, is officially the start of the Delta region.

Getting There & Away

To get to the barrages from Cairo you can take a river bus for E£2 from Maspero in front of the Radio & Television building, just north of the Ramses Hilton in central Cairo. The trip takes about 1½ hours. A faster, but less relaxing, way to get there is by taking bus No 930 from Midan Ataba bus station or bus No 950 from Ahmed Helmy bus station behind Ramses train station.

WADI NATRUN

About 100km north-west of Cairo, Wadi Natrun is a long, narrow depression in the desert just west of the Delta region sheltering several ancient Coptic monasteries. A visit to these places should explain the endurance of the ancient Coptic Christian sect. It is the desert, in a sense, that has been the protector of the faith, for it was there that thousands of Christians retreated to escape Roman persecution in the 4th century AD. They lived in caves, or built monasteries, and developed the monastic tradition that was later adopted by European Christians. At one time there were 60 monasteries scattered across the valley, but today just four remain.

All four holy retreats are surrounded by high, mud-brick walls and appear similar to desert fortresses, which, in effect, they also were, because they had to provide protection from attack for the monks within.

At **Deir Anba Bishoi**, the Monastery of St Bishoi, it is possible to explore the massive

EXCURSIONS

fortified keep just inside the walls, entered by a drawbridge. The figure for whom the monastery is named is St Bishoi, a 5th-century hermit to whom Jesus Christ is said to have twice appeared. The church at the heart of the monastery is said to contain the saint's body, fresh as the day he died, enclosed within a sealed tube that lies on a shrine to the left of the main altar.

Bishoi is also commemorated at the neighbouring **Deir as-Suriani**, the Monastery of the Syrians, so named because it was for centuries occupied by Syrian monks. Its main church, dedicated to St Mary, is built over the saint's supposed cave, which can still be visited. Of even greater interest are the Coptic wall paintings and icons, some of which date back to the 8th century.

Of the other two monasteries, **Deir al-Baramus**, a little to the north, has five churches, a keep, and an unusual refectory, while **Deir Abu Makar**, 20km south-east, is the most secluded of the monasteries,

and permission to visit must be organised in advance.

The religious life, which the monasteries have protected for centuries, is currently thriving. The Coptic pope is still chosen from among the Wadi Natrun monks, and monasticism is experiencing a revival, with younger Copts again donning robes and embroidered hoods to live within these ancient walls in the desert.

Getting There & Away

You can get a West Delta Bus Co bus to the village of Bir Hooker for E£3 from Cairo's Turgoman garage. Departures are every hour from 6.30am. From the village you have to negotiate for a taxi to make the rounds of the monasteries, along roads that are more potholes than surface. Expect to pay around E£20. If you go on a Friday or Sunday, when the monasteries are crowded with pious Copts, you shouldn't have any trouble picking up a lift.

Language

Arabic is the official language of Egypt. However, the Arabic spoken on the streets differs greatly from the standard Arabic written in newspapers, spoken on the radio or recited in prayers at the mosque.

Egyptian Colloquial Arabic (ECA) is fun, but difficult to learn. It is basically a dialect of the standard language but so different in many respects as to be virtually another language. As with most dialects, it is the everyday language that differs the most from that of Egypt's other Arabic-speaking neighbours. More specialised or educated language tends to be pretty much the same across the Arab world, although pronunciation may vary considerably.

There is no official written form of the Egyptian Arabic dialect, although there is no practical reason for this – Nobel Prize-winning author Naguib Mahfouz has no trouble writing out whole passages using predominantly Egyptian (or Cairene) slang.

If you take the time to learn even a few words and phrases, you'll discover and experience much more while travelling in Cairo. For a more comprehensive guide to the language, get hold of Lonely Planet's *Egyptian Arabic phrasebook*.

Pronunciation

Pronunciation of Arabic can be somewhat tongue-tying for someone unfamiliar with the intonation and combination of sounds. Pronounce the transliterated words and phrases slowly and clearly.

The following guide should help, but it isn't complete because the myriad rules governing pronunciation and vowel use are too extensive to be covered here.

Short Vowels

a   as in 'had' (sometimes very short)
e   as in 'bet' (sometimes very short)
i   as in 'hit'
o   as in 'hot'
u   as the 'oo' in 'book'

Long Vowels

Long vowels are indicated by a macron (stroke above the letter).

ā   as the 'a' in 'father'
ē   as the 'e' in 'ten', but lengthened
ī   as the 'e' in 'ear', only softer
ō   as the 'o' in 'four'
ū   as the 'oo' in 'food'

You may also see long vowels transliterated as double vowels, eg, 'aa' (ā), 'ee' (ī) and 'oo' (ū).

Diphthongs

aw   as the 'ow' in 'how'
ay   as the 'y' in 'by'
ei   as the 'a' in 'cake'

These last two are tricky, as one can slide into the other in certain words, depending on who is pronouncing them. Remember these rules are an outline and are far from exhaustive.

Consonants

Pronunciation for all Arabic consonants is covered in the alphabet table on the following page. Note that when double consonants occur in transliterations, each consonant is pronounced. For example, *el-hammam*, (bathhouse), is pronounced 'el-ham-mam'.

Other Sounds

Arabic has two sounds that are very tricky for non-Arabs to produce, the 'ayn and the glottal stop. The letter 'ayn represents a sound with no English equivalent – it is similar to the glottal stop (which is not actually represented in the alphabet) but the muscles at the back of the throat are gagged more forcefully and air is allowed to escape, creating a sound that has been described as reminiscent of someone being strangled! In many transliteration systems 'ayn is represented by an opening quotation mark, and the glottal stop by a closing quotation mark. In order to simplify the transliterations in this

LANGUAGE

The Arabic Alphabet

Final	Medial	Initial	Alone	Transliteration	Pronunciation
ا			ا	ā	as the 'a' in 'father'
ب	ب	ب	ب	b	as in 'bet'
ت	ت	ت	ت	t	as in 'ten'
ث	ث	ث	ث	th	as in 'thin'
ج	ج	ج	ج	g	as in 'go'
ح	ح	ح	ح	H	a strongly whispered 'h', almost like a sigh of relief
خ	خ	خ	خ	kh	as the 'ch' in Scottish *loch*
د			د	d	as in 'dim'
ذ			ذ	dh	as the 'th' in 'this'
ر			ر	r	a rolled 'r', as in the Spanish word *caro*
ز			ز	z	as in 'zip'
س	س	س	س	s	as in 'so', never as in 'wisdom'
ش	ش	ش	ش	sh	as in 'ship'
ص	ص	ص	ص	ş	emphatic 's'
ض	ض	ض	ض	ḍ	emphatic 'd'
ط	ط	ط	ط	ţ	emphatic 't'
ظ	ظ	ظ	ظ	ẓ	emphatic 'z'
ع	ع	ع	ع	'	the Arabic letter 'ayn; pronounce as a glottal stop – like the closing of the throat before saying 'Oh oh!' (see Other Sounds on p.223)
غ	غ	غ	غ	gh	a guttural sound like Parisian 'r'
ف	ف	ف	ف	f	as in 'far'
ق	ق	ق	ق	q	a strongly guttural 'k' sound; in Egyptian Arabic often pronounced as a glottal stop
ك	ك	ك	ك	k	as in 'king'
ل	ل	ل	ل	l	as in 'lamb'
م	م	م	م	m	as in 'me'
ن	ن	ن	ن	n	as in 'name'
ه	ه	ه	ه	h	as in 'ham'
و			و	w	as in 'wet'; or
				ū	long, as the 'oo' in 'food'; or
				aw	as the 'ow' in 'how'
ي	ي	ي	ي	y	as in 'yes'; or
				ī	as the 'e' in 'ear', only softer; or
				ay	as the 'y' in 'by' or as the 'ay' in 'way'

Vowels Not all Arabic vowel sounds are represented in the alphabet. See Pronunciation on p.223 for a list of all Arabic vowel sounds.
Emphatic Consonants To simplify the transliteration system used in this book, the emphatic consonants have not been included.

language guide, we have not distinguished between the 'ayn and the glottal stop, using the closing quotation mark to represent both sounds – people will still understand you.

Transliteration

Converting what for most outsiders is just a bunch of squiggles into meaningful words (ie, those written using the Roman alphabet) is a tricky business – in fact no really satisfactory system of transliteration has been established, and probably never will be. For this edition, an attempt has been made to standardise some spellings of place names and the like. There is only one article in Arabic: *al* (the). It is also sometimes written as 'il' or 'el' and sometimes modifies to reflect the first consonant of the following noun. For example, in Saladin's name, Salah ad-Din (meaning 'righteousness of the faith'), the 'al' has been modified to 'ad' before the 'd' of 'Din'. The use of *el* is seen only in a few circumstances such as well-known places (Sharm el-Sheikh) or where locals have used it in restaurant and hotel names.

French and English have had a big influence which has led to all sorts of interesting ideas on transliteration, so don't be taken aback if you start noticing half a dozen different spellings for the same thing. For some reason, the letters 'q' and 'k' have caused enormous problems, and have been interchanged willy-nilly in transliteration. Some examples of an Arabic 'q' receiving such treatment are *souq* (market), often

The Transliteration Dilemma

TE Lawrence, when asked by his publishers to clarify 'inconsistencies in the spelling of proper names' in *Seven Pillars of Wisdom* – his account of the Arab Revolt in WWI – wrote back:

Arabic names won't go into English. There are some "scientific systems" of transliteration, helpful to people who know Arabic not to need helping, but a washout for the world. I spell my names anyhow, to show what rot the systems are.

written 'souk'; *qasr* (castle), sometimes written 'kasr'; and the Cairo suburb of Doqqi, often written 'Dokki'.

Greetings & Civilities

Arabic is more formal than English, especially with greetings; thus even the simplest greetings, such as 'hello', vary according to when and how they are used. In addition, each greeting requires a certain response that varies according to whether it is being said to a male, female or group of people.

Hello.
  salām 'alēkum
  (lit: peace upon you)
(response)
  wa 'alēkum es salām
  (lit: and peace upon you)
Hello/Welcome.
  ahlan wa sahlan
(response)
  ahlan bīk (to male)
  ahlan bīkī (to female)
  ahlan bīkum (to group)
Pleased to meet you. (when first meeting)
  tasharrafna (polite)
  fursa sa'īda (informal)
Good morning.
  sabāH al-khēr
(response)
  sabāH an-nūr
Good evening.
  misa' al-khēr
(response)
  misa' an-nūr
Good night.
  tisbaH 'ala khēr (to m)
  tisbaHī 'ala khēr (to f)
  tisbaHu 'ala khēr (to group)
(response; also used as 'Good afternoon' in the late afternoon)
  wenta bikhēr (to m)
  wentī bikhēr (to f)
  wentū bikhēr (to group)
Goodbye.
  ma'as salāma (lit: go in safety)

Basics

There are three ways to say 'please' in Egyptian Arabic, each of which is used somewhat differently:

min fadlak/fadlik/fadlukum (to m/f/group), when asking for something in a shop; *law samaHt/samaHtī/samaHtu* (to m/f/group), similar, but more formal; *tfaddal/tfaddalī/ tfaddalū* (to m/f/group), when offering something, for example, a chair or bus seat, or when inviting someone into your home or to join in a meal. The same words preceded by 'i' (eg, *itfaddal*) can be used to mean much the same thing or 'Please, go ahead' (and do something).

Excuse me.
  'an iznak, esmaHlī (to m)
  'an iznik, esmaHīlī (to f)
  'an iznukum, esmaHūlī (to group)
Thank you (very much).
  shukran (gazīlan)
You're welcome.
  'afwan, al-'affu
Yes.
  aywa or *na'am* (more formal)
No.
  la'
Sorry.
  'assif

A useful word to know is *imshī*, which means 'Go away'. Use this at tourist sites when you are being besieged by children. Do not use it on adults; instead, just say, *la' shukran* ('No thank you').

Small Talk

How are you?
  izzayyak? (to m)
  izzayyik? (to f)
  izzayyukum? (to group)
I'm fine.
  kwayyis ilHamdu lillah
  (to m, lit: fine, thanks be to God)
  kwaysa ilHamdu lillah (to f)
  kwaysīn ilHamdu lillah (to group)

(On their own, *kwayyis*, *kwaysa* and *kwaysīn* literally mean 'good' or 'fine', but are rarely heard alone in response to 'How are you?')

What's your name? *ismak ēh?* (to m)
                  ismīk ēh? (to f)
My name is ...   *ismī ...*

Language Difficulties

Do you speak English?	*enta bititkallim inglīzī?* (to m)
	entī bititkallimī inglīzī? (to f)
I understand.	*ana fāhem/fahma* (m/f)
I don't understand.	*ana mish fāhem/ fahma* (m/f)

Getting Around

bicycle	*'agala/bīcīklēt*
car	*sayyāra/'arabiyya*
ferry	*ma'atiya*

Where is the ...?	*fein ...?*
airport	*matār*
bus station	*maHattat al-otobīs*
bus stop	*maw'if al-otobīs*
railway station	*maHattat al-'atr*
street	*ash-shāri'*
ticket office	*maktab at-tazāker*

When does the ... leave/arrive?	*emta qiyam/wusuul...?*
bus	*al-otobīs*
train	*al-'atr*
boat	*al-markib*

How far is ...?	*kam kilo li ...?*
I want to go to ...	*ana 'ayiz arūH ...*
Does this bus go to ...?	*al-otobīs da yerūH ...?*
How many buses per day go to ...?	*kam otobīs fil yōm yerūH...?*
Please tell me when we arrive in ...	*min fadlak, ullī emta Hanūsel ...*

Signs	
Entry	مدخل
Exit	خروج
Toilets (Men)	حمام للرجال
Toilets (Women)	حمام للنساء
Hospital	مستشفى
Police	الشرطة
Prohibited	ممنوع

What is the fare to ...?	*bikam at-tazkara li ...?*
May I/we sit here?	*mumkin eglis/neglis hena?*
Stop here, please.	*wa'if/hassib hena, min fadlak*
Please wait for me.	*mumkin tantazarnī*
Where can I rent a bicycle?	*fein e'aggar 'agala?*

Directions

Where is the hotel ...?	*fein al-funduq ...?*
Can you show me the way to the hotel ...?	*mumkin tewarrīnī at-tarīqlil-funduq ...?*
Where?	*fein?*
here	*hena*
there	*henek*
this address	*al-'anwān da*
north	*shimāl*
south	*ganūb*
east	*shark*
west	*gharb*

Around Town

Where is the ...?	*fein ...?*
bank	*al-bank*
barber	*al-Hallē'*
beach	*al-plā/ash-shaata*
citadel	*al-'ala*
embassy	*as-sifāra*
female toilet	*twalēt al-Harīmī*
market	*as-sūq*
male toilet	*twalēt ar-ragel*
monastery	*dēr*
mosque	*al-gāme'*
museum	*al-matHaf*
old city	*al-medīna/al-'adīma*
palace	*al-'asr*
police station	*al-bolīs*
post office	*al-bōsta/ maktab al-barīd*
restaurant	*al-mat'am*
zoo	*Hadīqat al-Haywān*

Accommodation

I'd like to see the rooms.	*awiz ashūf al-owad*
May I see other rooms?	*mumkin ashūf owad tānī?*

Numbers

Arabic numerals are simple to learn and, unlike the written language, run from left to right. Pay attention to the order of the words in numbers from 21 to 99.

0	٠	*sifr*
1	١	*wāHid*
2	٢	*itnein*
3	٣	*talāta*
4	٤	*arba'a*
5	٥	*khamsa*
6	٦	*sitta*
7	٧	*sab'a*
8	٨	*tmanya*
9	٩	*tis'a*
10	١٠	*'ashara*
11	١١	*Hidāshar*
12	١٢	*itnāshar*
13	١٣	*talattāshar*
14	١٤	*arba'tāshar*
15	١٥	*khamastāshar*
16	١٦	*sittāshar*
17	١٧	*saba'tāshar*
18	١٨	*tamantāshar*
19	١٩	*tisa'tāshar*
20	٢٠	*'ishrīn*
21	٢١	*wāHid wi 'ishrīn*
22	٢٢	*itnein wi 'ishrīn*
30	٣٠	*talatīn*
40	٤٠	*arba'īn*
50	٥٠	*khamsīn*
60	٦٠	*sittīn*
70	٧٠	*sab'īn*
80	٨٠	*tamanīn*
90	٩٠	*tis'īn*
100	١٠٠	*myya*
101	١٠١	*myya wi wāHid*
200	٢٠٠	*mītein*
300	٣٠٠	*talāt mia*
1000	١٠٠٠	*'alf*
2000	٢٠٠٠	*'alfein*
3000	٣٠٠٠	*talāttalāf*

Ordinal Numbers

first	*'awwal*
second	*tānī*
third	*tālit*
fourth	*rābi'*
fifth	*khāmis*

How much is the room per night?	*kam ugrat al-odda bil-laila?*
Do you have any cheaper rooms?	*fī owad arkhas?*
It's too expensive.	*da ghālī 'awī*
This is fine.	*da kwayyis*
air-conditioning	*takyīf hawa*

Shopping

Where can I buy ...?	*fein mumkin ashtirī ...?*
How much is this/that ...?	*bikam da ...?*
It costs too much.	*da ghālī 'awī*
Do you have ...?	*fī 'andak ...?*

Money

The Egyptians have names for their own money, used in most everyday transactions.

pound	*guinay*
½ pound (50 pt)	*nuss guinay*
¼ pound (25 pt)	*ruba' guinay*
20 pt	*riyal*
10 pt	*barisa*
5 pt	*shilling*

I want to change ...	*ana 'ayiz usarraf ...*
money	*fulūs*
travellers cheques	*shīkāt siyaHiyya*

Time & Dates

What time is it?	*sā'ah kam?*
When?	*emta?*
day	*yom*
month	*shaher*
today	*el nharda*
tomorrow	*bokra*
week	*esbuwa*
year	*sana*
yesterday	*mberrah*
early	*badrī*
late	*mut'akhar*
daily	*kull yōm*

Sunday	*(yōm) al-aHadd*
Monday	*(yōm) al-itnīn*
Tuesday	*(yōm) at-talāt*
Wednesday	*(yōm) al-arba'a*
Thursday	*(yōm) al-khamīs*
Friday	*(yōm) al-gum'a*
Saturday	*(yōm) as-sabt*

Emergencies

Help!	*el-Ha'nī!*
Call a doctor!	*itassal-ī bi-doktōr!*
Call an ambulance!	*ittasal-ī bil-is'āf!*
Call the police!	*itassal bil-bolīs!*
I've been robbed.	*ana itsara't*
Thief!	*Harāmi!*
I'm lost.	*ana tāyih/tāyha*
Go away!	*imshī!*
Where are the toilets?	*fein al-twalēt?*

January	*yanāyir*
February	*fibrāyir*
March	*māris*
April	*abrīl*
May	*māyu*
June	*yunyu*
July	*yulyu*
August	*aghustus*
September	*sibtimbir*
October	*'uktūbir*
November	*nufimbir*
December	*disimbir*

Health

Where is the hospital?	*fein al mustashfa?*
My friend is ill.	*sadīqi 'ayan*
I'm allergic ...	*'andī Hasasiyya ...*
to antibiotics	*min mudād Hayawi*
to penicillin	*min binisilīn*
I'm ...	*'indī ...*
asthmatic	*azmit rabū*
diabetic	*is sukkar*
epileptic	*sara'*
antiseptic	*mutahhir*
aspirin	*asbirin*
condoms	*kabābīt*
diarrhoea	*is-hāl*
fever	*sukhūna*
headache	*sudā'*
pharmacy	*agzakhana*
sanitary napkins	
stomachache	*waga' fil batn*
tampons	*hifāz al-'āda al-shahriyya*

Glossary

Abbasids – Islamic dynasty that ruled from Baghdad (AD 750–1258)
abeyya – women's gown
ablaq – banding of different coloured stone, typical of Mamluk building
abu – father, saint
ahwa – coffee, also coffeehouse
AUC – American University in Cairo
Ayyubids – Egyptian-based Islamic dynasty (AD 1169–1250) founded by Salah ad-Din

bab – gate or door
baksheesh – tip
beit – house
bey – term of respect
burg – tower

caliph – Islamic ruler
Canopic jars – pottery jars that held the embalmed internal organs and viscera (liver, stomach, lungs, intestines) of the mummified pharaoh
caravanserai – merchants' inn enclosing a courtyard, providing accommodation and a marketplace
cartouche – oval-shaped figure enclosing the *hieroglyphs* of royal or divine names in ancient Egypt

darb – track, street
deir – monastery, convent

eid – feast
emir – Islamic ruler, military commander or governor

fellaheen – the peasant farmers or agricultural workers who make up the majority of Egypt's population; 'fellaheen' literally means ploughman or tiller of the soil
finial – top part of a *minaret*

galabeyya – full-length robe worn by men
gezira – island
haj – pilgrimage to Mecca
hammam – bathhouse
higab – woman's headscarf

Hejira – Islamic calendar; also refers to Mohammed's flight from Mecca to Medina in AD 622
hieroglyphs – ancient Egyptian form of writing which used pictures and symbols to represent objects, words or sounds

ibn – son of
imam – a man schooled in Islam and who often doubles as the *muezzin*
iwan – vaulted hall opening into a central court in the *madrassa* of a mosque

al-jeel – a type of music characterised by a hand-clapping rhythm overlaid with a catchy vocal; translates as 'the generation'

khan – another name for a *caravanserai*
khanqah – *Sufi* monastery
khedive – Egyptian viceroy under Ottoman suzerainty
kuttab – Quranic school

madrassa – school where Islamic law is taught
mahatta – station
mashrabiyya – ornate carved wooden panel or screen; a feature of Islamic architecture
Masr – Egypt (also means Cairo)
mastaba – Arabic word for 'bench'; mudbrick structure in the shape of a bench above tombs that was the basis for later pyramids
midan – town or city square
mihrab – niche in the wall of a mosque that indicates the direction of Mecca
minaret – mosque tower
minbar – pulpit in a mosque
moulid – festival celebrating the birthday of a local saint or holy person
muezzin – mosque official who calls the faithful to prayer five times a day from the *minaret*
muqarnas – stalactite-type stone carving used to decorate doorways and window recesses

oud – a type of lute

papyrus – plant identified with Lower Egypt; writing material made from the pith of this plant; a document written on such paper

qa'a – reception room
qasr – palace

Ramadan – ninth month of the lunar Islamic calendar during which Muslims fast from sunrise to sunset

sabil – public drinking fountain
sabil-kuttab – combination of a *sabil* with a Quranic school
sarcophagus – huge stone or marble coffin used to encase other wooden coffins and the mummy of the pharaoh or queen
serdab – hidden cellar in a tomb, or a stone room in front of some pyramids, containing a coffin with a lifesize, lifelike, painted statue of the dead pharaoh

servees – service taxi
shaabi – working class or 'popular' music which has satirical or politically provocative lyrics and is cruder than *al-jeel*
sharia – Arabic for road or street
sheesha – water pipe
souq – market
Sufi – follower of any of the Islamic mystical orders that emphasise dancing, chanting and trances in order to attain unity with God

tarboosh – the hat known elsewhere as a fez

umm – mother of
Umayyads – a Damascus-based Islamic dynasty who ruled from AD 658–750

wikala – another name for a *caravanserai*

zawiya – small school dedicated to the teachings of a particular sheikh

Thanks

Many thanks to the travellers who used the last edition and wrote to us with helpful hints, useful advice and interesting anecdotes:

Sumanth Addagaria, Jane Akshar, Francesca Albertini, Amanda S Anderson, Peter Arvantely, GE Ashworth, Cathy Atkinson, MJ Bache, Billy-Jo Basinger, Wolfram Beck, John Bedford, Melanie Bell, Maria & Tony Benfield, Laurent Bianchi, Annacarin & Nils Billing, JL Bishop, Steve Blair, Joanna Blunt, Julien Bodart, Peter Boodell, Mary Boyd, Carlo Brand, Lance Brendish, Gunner Brunke, Dennis Bullard, Sandi Burford-Poole, Mike Burns, Sally Burrows, Maret Busch, Andrew Cameron, Mariana Carneiro, Jon & Sonja Carter, Colleen Chan, Viviana Cocurullo, George Coulouris, Linton Cull, Rob Curry, Paul Deering, Karlheinz Dienelt, Kate Douglas, Lorrie Drumm, Tilman Duerbeck, Hussein Elazm, Kerrieann Enright, Tim Eyre, Lyndon Ferguson, Lisa Flynn, Franca Franceschini, Scott Furness, Marzia Gandini, Stefan Gasser, Sandra Geisler, Yutan Getzler, Paul W Gioffi, Katherine A Giuffre, James Grass, Zach Greig, Daniel Groeber, Ed Gruhl, Sandra Guenther, Matteo Guidotti, Dr Arun Gupta, Linda Haddrell, Chris Heal, Roos Hermans, Lee & Mei Hook, Sue Hopenwasser, Ian Horrocks, Frances B Hunt, John Hunt, Sylwia Hyzopska, Kirby Inwood, Graham James, Derek Jay, Farouk Jehan, Mona Johansen, Don Jones, Mark Jones, Peter Jones, Oscar Kafati, Mike Katz, Tim Kealy, Alison Keefe, Wendy Keeney, Lee Kessler, Heidi Korhonen, G Krishnan, Dale & Debbie Krumreich, Peter Kurze, Gilles Lamere, Mary-Justine Lanyon, Paul Lelievre, Marcus Lim, Terry Maguire, Barbara Mansvelt, Susan Mares-Pilling, Will Maynez, Kathleen McCann, Malcolm Mckay, John McKie, Wendy Meskes, Markella Mikkelsen, Lee Gerard Molloy, Anita Montvazski, Guy Moorhouse, Marcel Mourad, Brennan Mulligan, Gyle H Nashed, Lorenzo Nastasi, Emma O'Connell, Anna Olsson, Lars Oltrogge, Shawn Owen, Ben Owens, Eric Owens, Anita Paltrinieri, Emily Peckham, Katja & Henry Petzold, Sean Plamondon, Shelley Potter, Seth Powell, Jo Price, Peter & Erika Pucsok, Justin Reed, Caroline Reynolds, Albert Rogers, Darren Ross, Errol Salvador, R Bart Sangal, Monique Schoone, Adam Schreck, Christine Shalaby, Fiona Shaw, Peter Shaw, Saeed Sheshehgar, Eric Sieberath, Stephan Siemer, Helen Silverberg, Jass Sio, Bob Skinner, John Skuthorpe, Sarah Smyth, Helena Soderlind, Ralph Somma, Zoe Sowden, Ilia Starr, Peter Stein, J Swinden, Rick Thomas, Mary Tilton-Jakab, Julie Toth, Toni Tremp, Heli Vainio, Thomas Vaughan, Tamara Veenendaal, Lisette Verzijl, Edwin Visser, Kerry & John Wallace, Dawid & Kathy Welgemoed, Jeroen Wiersma, Debra Winters, Gareth Woodham, Christine Yip, Haseena Zachariah

LONELY PLANET

You already know that Lonely Planet produces more than this one guidebook, but you might not be aware of the other products we have on this region. Here is a selection of titles that you may want to check out as well:

Middle East
ISBN 0 86442 701 8
US$24.95 • UK£14.99

Egypt
ISBN 1 86450 298 3
US$19.99 • UK£12.99

Egyptian Arabic phrasebook
ISBN 1 86450 183 9
US$7.99 • UK£4.50

Jerusalem
ISBN 0 86442 784 0
US$14.95 • UK£8.99

Libya
ISBN 0 86442 699 2
US$16.99 • UK£11.99

Israel & the Palestinian Territories
ISBN 0 86442 691 7
US$17.95 • UK£11.99

Istanbul to Cairo on a shoestring
ISBN 0 86442 749 2
US$16.95 • UK£10.99

Africa on a shoestring
ISBN 0 86442 663 1
US$29.99 • UK£17.99

Read This First: Africa
ISBN 1 86450 066 2
US$14.95 • UK£8.99

Diving & Snorkeling Red Sea
ISBN 1 86450 205 3
US$19.99 • UK£12.99

Cairo City Map
ISBN 1 86450 257 6
US$5.99 • UK£3.99

Healthy Travel Africa
ISBN 1 86450 050 6
US$5.95 • UK£3.99

Available wherever books are sold

Index

Text

Bold indicates maps.

233

Bold indicates maps.

Places to Stay

Places to Eat

Boxed Text

MAP 1 – GREATER CAIRO

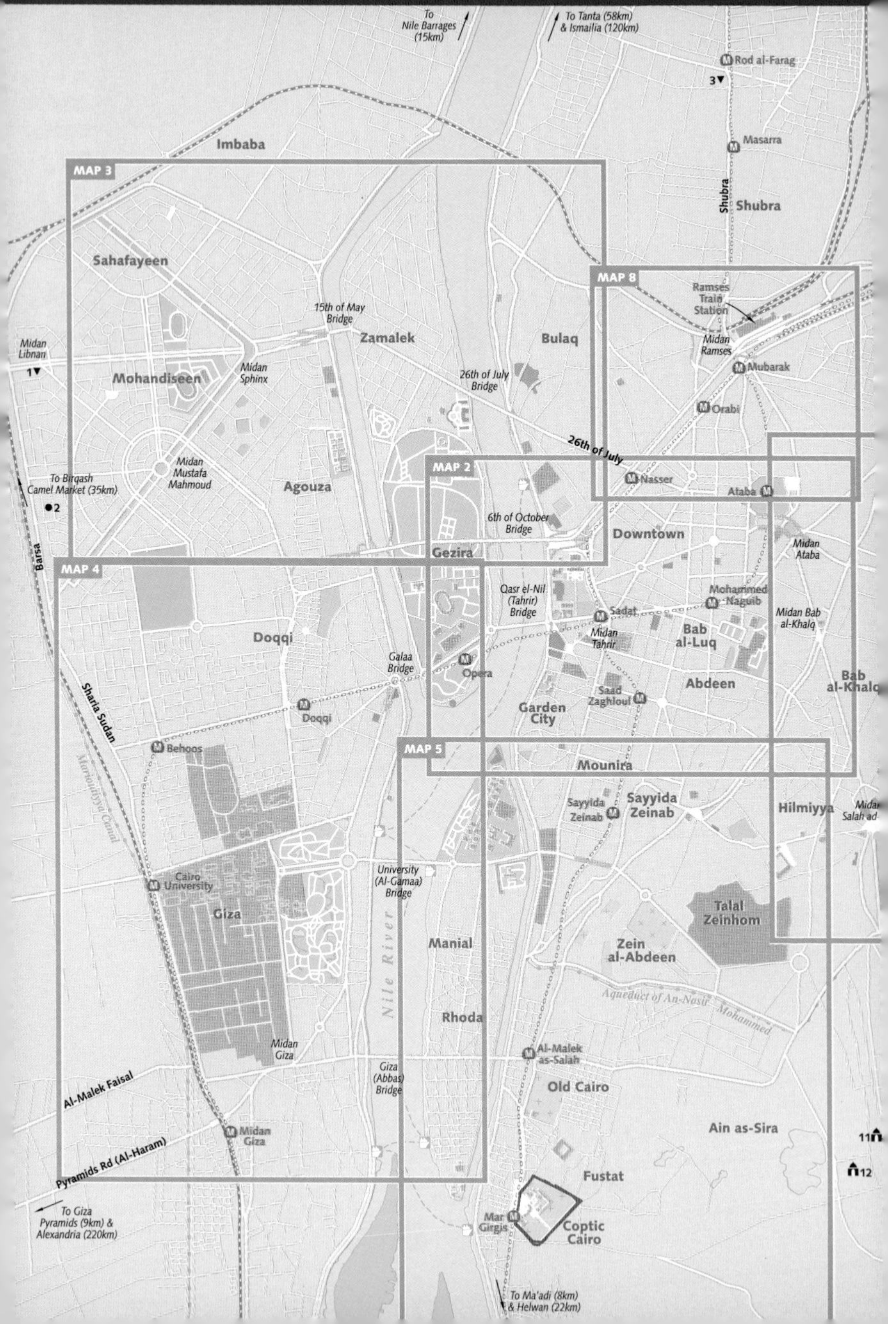

To Nile Barrages (15km)

To Tanta (58km) & Ismailia (120km)

M Rod al-Farag

3▼

M Masarra

Imbaba

Shubra

MAP 3

Shubra

Sahafayeen

15th of May Bridge

Zamalek

Bulaq

MAP 8

Ramses Train Station

Midan Ramses

Midan Libnani

1▼

Mohandiseen

Midan Sphinx

26th of July Bridge

M Mubarak

M Orabi

26th of July

To Birqash Camel Market (35km)

●2

Midan Mustafa Mahmoud

Agouza

MAP 2

6th of October Bridge

Gezira

M Nasser

Ataba M

Downtown

Midan Ataba

Barsa

Sharia Sudan

MAP 4

Doqqi

Galaa Bridge

Qasr el-Nil (Tahrir) Bridge

Sadat

Midan Tahrir

Mohammed Naguib

Bab al-Luq

Midan Bab al-Khalq

Bab al-Khalq

M Doqqi

M Opera

Garden City

Saad Zaghloul

Abdeen

M Behoos

MAP 5

Mounira

Hilmiyya

Midan Salah ad

Sayyida Zeinab

Sayyida Zeinab

M Cairo University

University (Al-Gamaa) Bridge

Giza

Manial

Zein al-Abdeen

Talal Zeinhom

Aqueduct of An-Nasir Mohammed

Nile River

Rhoda

Mahmudiyya Canal

Midan Giza

Giza (Abbas) Bridge

Al-Malek as-Salah M

Old Cairo

11🏛

Ain as-Sira

Al-Malek Faisal

M Midan Giza

🏛12

Pyramids Rd (Al-Haram)

Fustat

To Giza Pyramids (9km) & Alexandria (220km)

Mar Girgis M

Coptic Cairo

To Ma'adi (8km) & Helwan (22km)

MAP 1 – GREATER CAIRO

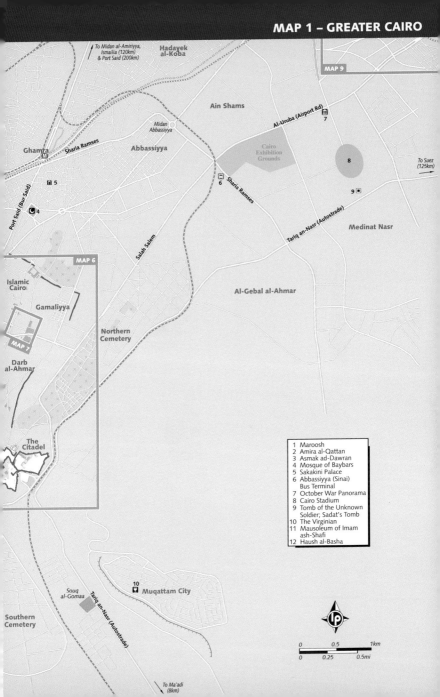

To Midan al-Amiriyya,
Ismailia (120km)
& Port Said (200km)

Hadayek
al-Koba

Ain Shams

Al-Uruba (Airport Rd)
7

MAP 9

Midan
Abbassiyya

Cairo
Exhibition
Grounds

8

To Suez
(125km)

Ghamra

Sharia Ramses

Abbassiyya

6

Sharia Ramses

9

Port Said (Bur Said)

5

4

Salah Salem

Tariq an-Nasr (Autostrade)

Medinat Nasr

MAP 6

Al-Gebal al-Ahmar

Islamic
Cairo

Gamaliyya

MAP 7

Northern
Cemetery

Darb
al-Ahmar

The
Citadel

1 Maroosh
2 Amira al-Qattan
3 Asmak ad-Dawran
4 Mosque of Baybars
5 Sakakini Palace
6 Abbassiyya (Sinai)
   Bus Terminal
7 October War Panorama
8 Cairo Stadium
9 Tomb of the Unknown
   Soldier; Sadat's Tomb
10 The Virginian
11 Mausoleum of Imam
   ash-Shafi
12 Haush al-Basha

Souq
al-Gomaa

10 Muqattam City

Tariq an-Nasr (Autostrade)

Southern
Cemetery

0   0.5   1km
0   0.25   0.5mi

To Ma'adi
(8km)

MAP 2 - DOWNTOWN

To Zamalek
▼ 1
To Bulaq
Al-Sultan Abu
Galal Abu Talib
Sharkis al-Wustany

Maspero River Bus Terminal
TV & Radio Building

6th October Flyover (Galaa)

🏛 4
Ramses

Qanater Boats
Comiche el-Nil

MAP 8

Dr. Abdel Hamid S

Marouf

42 ▼

Champollion

2 ❖

3

🏛 43

Midan Abdel Moniem Riad

🚇 60

Downtown

🏛

6th of October
6th of October Bridge
Comiche el-Nil

MAP 3

Mahmoud Bassiouni

🚇 61

55 🏛
★ 56

To Doqqi

Saray al-Gezira
Saray al-Gezira
Pedestrian Corniche

Egyptian Museum

62 🏛

🔆 58 ▼
59 ● 81
Midan
Talaat Harb

Gezira
Club

Andalusian Gardens ❖

Town Hall

67 ●
68 ●
Qasr el-Nil

80
79 ▼
78 ▼ 77
75

Gezira
63

▼ 64

65

Al-Bustan

72
73

🔆 66

🔆 69

70
●

71

Ahly
Stadium

Arab League Building

Midan Tahrir
🚇 Sadat

Tahrir
▼ 102

● 103
104

MAP 4

Tahrir

Midan Saad Zaghloul

Qasr el-Nil (Tahrir) Bridge

Tahrir

▼ 116 ▼ 117
118

🏛 109
108

● 107

105
●

114
🔆 Mogamma

▼ 115

American University in Cairo (AUC)

110
111

Gezira Exhibition Grounds

🚇 Opera

106

112 ▼
Felucca Landing ⚓

113

Midan Simon Bolivar
🚇 123

Nile River

Nady al-Qahira Garden ❖

124

Cairo Centre Building

People's Assembly

125

Latin America

Lazoughli

Maglis ash-Shaab

131

Ahmed Ragheb

Rustum Basha

Ibrahimy

● 126

127

Hussein Higazy

Saad Zaghloul

0   200   400m
0   200   400yd

Garden City

Kamelash-Shennawi
Ahmed Basha
Ibrahim Basha Naguib
Al-Harass

Dareh Saad

Ismail Abaza

Al-Kubra

Al-Falaki

Gamal ad-Din Abu al-Mahasin
Al-Bitash

● 129

Qasr al-Ainy

Saad Zaghloul
🚇

Dok Dok Felucca Landing ⚓

MAP 5

Safiyya Zaghloul

🏛 128

Mansour

130

To Old Cairo

MAP 2 – DOWNTOWN

PLACES TO STAY

3 Ramses Hilton;
  Windows on the World
7 Ambassador
8 Carlton Hotel
10 Sultan Hotel I-III; Safary
  Hotel; Hotel Venice
17 Windsor Hotel; Windsor Bar
25 Hotel Minerva
27 Richmond Hotel
30 Pension Roma
41 Odeon Palace Hotel
56 Dahab Hotel;
  Onyx Internet Cafe
65 Nile Hilton; Taverne du
  Champs de Mars;
  American Express;
  EgyptAir; Jackie's
70 New Sun Hotel;
  New Zealand Embassy
72 Magic Hotel
78 Lotus Hotel
86 Cosmopolitan Hotel
89 Berlin Hotel
100 Amin Hotel
104 Ismailia House Hotel
105 Garden City House Hotel
106 Semiramis Inter-Continental;
  The Grill
113 Helnan Shepheard's
130 Le Méridien Cairo;
  Hard Rock Cafe; Nubian Village
131 Gezira Sheraton

PLACES TO EAT

1 Morocco
14 Akher Sa'a
15 Alfy Bey; Sheherazade
16 Peking Restaurant
22 El-Abd
42 Abu Tarek
46 At-Tahrir
50 Simonds
58 El-Abd; ILLI
64 Da Mario; Abu Ali
67 Arabesque
75 Felfela Takeaway
76 Felfela Restaurant
79 Estoril
82 Cafe Riche
96 Le Bistro
99 Gomhuriyya Restaurant
102 Fatatri at-Tahrir
112 MS Scarabee
116 KFC; Pizza Hut
117 McDonald's
119 Lux

OTHER

2 Ramses Hilton Annexe;
  Ramses Hilton I & II
  Cinemas
4 Entomological Society
  Museum
5 Isaaf Pharmacy
6 Al-Agaty
9 Ash-Shams
11 Leyaleena; Nicolakis
12 Cafeteria Port Tawfiq
13 New Arizona
18 Sednaoui Department Store
19 Ezbekiyya Book Market
20 National Theatre
21 Al-Andalus
23 Cinema Miami
24 Metro; Excelsior Restaurant
26 Lehnert & Landrock
28 Palmyra
29 Shar Hashamaim
  Synagogue
31 Main Tourist Office;
  Tourist Police
32 Postal Museum
33 Main Post Office
34 Poste Restante
35 EMS Office
36 Senouhi
37 Groppi's Garden
38 Anglo-Egyptian Bookshop
39 Buonanno Internet Cafe
40 Kodak Shop
43 Late Night Coffeehouses
44 Odeon Cinema
45 Talaat Harb Shopping
  Centre
47 Anglo-Eastern Pharmacy
48 Cap d'Or
49 Gallerie Hathout
51 French Consulate
53 Cinema Radio
54 Townhouse Gallery
55 Atelier du Caire Gallery
57 4U Internet Cafe
59 Thomas Cook
60 Airport Bus; Local Bus
  Services; Pyramid
  Minibuses
61 Pyramids Bus
62 Mashrabia Gallery
63 Cairo Tower
66 Nile Hilton
  Shopping Mall;
  Nile Hilton Cybercafe
68 Goethe Institut
69 Telephone Centrale
71 Masr Travel
73 EgyptAir
74 Al-Bustan Centre;
  St@rnet Cyber Cafe
77 Stella Bar
80 American Express
81 L'Orientaliste
83 Zahret al-Bustan
84 Espace Karim-Francis
  Gallery
85 Photo Centre
87 Western Union
88 Egypt Free Shop
90 Salon Vert
91 Livres d'France
92 Osiris Auction House
93 St Joseph's Church
94 Egypt Free Shop
95 Exit
97 Antar Photostores
98 Cafeteria Horreyya
101 Cairo-Berlin Gallery
103 Ali Baba Cafeteria
107 Casino el-Nil
108 Arts Palace
109 National Museum of
  Egyptian Modern Art
110 Hanagar Art Centre
111 Cairo Opera House
114 Omar Makram Mosque
115 AUC Bookstore
118 Wallace Theatre
120 Telephone Centrale
121 Museum of
  Islamic Art
122 Abdeen Palace Museum
123 InternetEgypt
124 US Embassy; American
  Cultural Center
125 British Embassy
126 Sudanese Embassy &
  Consulate
127 Canadian Embassy
128 Mausoleum of Saad
  Zaghloul
129 DHL

MAP 3 – MOHANDISEEN, AGOUZA & ZAMALEK

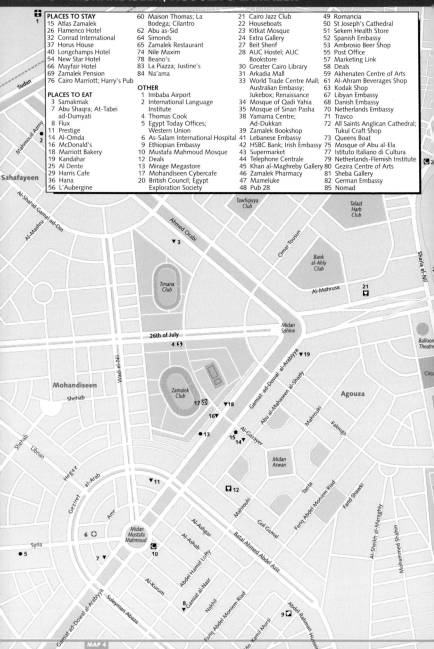

PLACES TO STAY
15 Atlas Zamalek
26 Flamenco Hotel
32 Conrad International
37 Horus House
40 Longchamps Hotel
54 New Star Hotel
66 Mayfair Hotel
69 Zamalek Pension
76 Cairo Marriott; Harry's Pub

PLACES TO EAT
3 Samakmak
7 Abu Shaqra; At-Tabei ad-Dumyati
8 Flux
11 Prestige
14 Al-Omda
16 McDonald's
18 Marriott Bakery
19 Kandahar
25 Al Dente
29 Harris Cafe
36 Hana
56 L'Aubergine

60 Maison Thomas; La Bodega; Cilantro
62 Abu as-Sid
64 Simonds
65 Zamalek Restaurant
74 Nile Maxim
78 Beano's
83 La Piazza; Justine's
84 Na'ama

OTHER
1 Imbaba Airport
2 International Language Institute
4 Thomas Cook
5 Egypt Today Offices; Western Union
6 As-Salam International Hospital
9 Ethiopian Embassy
10 Mustafa Mahmoud Mosque
12 Deals
13 Mirage Megastore
17 Mohandiseen Cybercafe
20 British Council; Egypt Exploration Society

21 Cairo Jazz Club
22 Houseboats
23 Kitkat Mosque
24 Extra Gallery
27 Beit Sherif
28 AUC Hostel; AUC Bookstore
30 Greater Cairo Library
31 Arkadia Mall
33 World Trade Centre Mall; Australian Embassy; Jukebox; Renaissance
34 Mosque of Qadi Yahia
35 Mosque of Sinan Pasha
38 Yamama Centre; Ad-Dukkan
39 Zamalek Bookshop
41 Lebanese Embassy
42 HSBC Bank; Irish Embassy
43 Supermarket
44 Telephone Centrale
45 Khan al-Maghreby Gallery
46 Zamalek Pharmacy
47 Mameluke
48 Pub 28

49 Romancia
50 St Joseph's Cathedral
51 Sekem Health Store
52 Spanish Embassy
53 Ambrosio Beer Shop
55 Post Office
57 Marketing Link
58 Deals
59 Akhenaten Centre of Arts
61 Al-Ahram Beverages Shop
63 Kodak Shop
67 Libyan Embassy
68 Danish Embassy
70 Netherlands Embassy
71 Travco
72 All Saints Anglican Cathedral; Tukul Craft Shop
73 Queens Boat
75 Mosque of Abu al-Ela
77 Istituto Italiano di Cultura
79 Netherlands-Flemish Institute
80 Gezira Centre of Arts
81 Sheba Gallery
82 German Embassy
85 Nomad

MAP 3 – MOHANDISEEN, AGOUZA & ZAMALEK

MAP 4 – DOQQI & GIZA

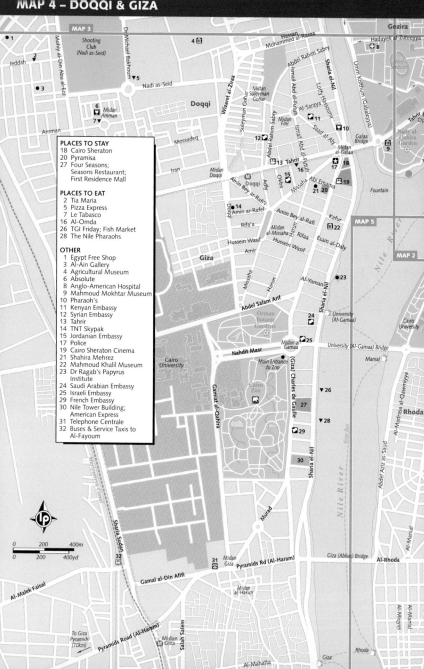

MAP 3

Gezira

Shooting Club (Nadi as-Seid)

Hadayek al-Zohreyya

4 ▼5

Nadi as-Seid

Doqqi

Midan Amman

Amman

Mossadeq

Iran

Midan Doqqi

Giza

Rifa'a

Amir

Abdel Salam Arif

Orman Botanic Gardens

Cairo University

Nahdit Masr

Midan al-Gamaa

University (Al-Gamaa)

University (Al-Gamaa) Bridge

Cairo University

Manial

Main Entrance to Zoo

Cairo Zoo

Rhoda

Midan Giza

Pyramids Rd (Al-Haram)

Gamal al-Din Afifi

Midan al-Hakim

To Giza Pyramids (10km)

Pyramids Road (Al-Haram)

Midan Giza

Al-Malek Faisal

Al-Mahatta

Giza

Rhoda

Nile River

River Bus

MAP 5

MAP 2

Fountain

Kafur

Esam al-Daly

Al-Yaman

Giza (Abbas) Bridge

Al-Rhoda

PLACES TO STAY
18 Cairo Sheraton
20 Pyramisa
27 Four Seasons;
   Seasons Restaurant;
   First Residence Mall

PLACES TO EAT
2 Tia Maria
5 Pizza Express
7 Le Tabasco
16 Al-Omda
26 TGI Friday; Fish Market
28 The Nile Pharaohs

OTHER
1 Egypt Free Shop
3 Al-Ain Gallery
4 Agricultural Museum
6 Absolute
8 Anglo-American Hospital
9 Mahmoud Mokhtar Museum
10 Pharaoh's
11 Kenyan Embassy
12 Syrian Embassy
13 Tahrir
14 TNT Skypak
15 Jordanian Embassy
17 Police
19 Cairo Sheraton Cinema
21 Shahira Mehrez
22 Mahmoud Khalil Museum
23 Dr Ragab's Papyrus Institute
24 Saudi Arabian Embassy
25 Israeli Embassy
29 French Embassy
30 Nile Tower Building; American Express
31 Telephone Centrale
32 Buses & Service Taxis to Al-Fayoum

0   200   400m
0   200   400yd

LP

LEE FOSTER

The Nile is the lifeblood of Cairo, serving as a transport artery for river buses, barges and feluccas.

PHIL WEYMOUTH

For distances that are too far to walk, taxis are the most convenient way to get around Cairo.

RUSSELL MOUNTFORD

The Mosque of Ibn Tulun is perhaps the most impressive medieval monument in Cairo.

CHRISTINE OSBORNE

The river bus may not be the fastest form of transport but it's a relaxing way of getting around.

MAP 5 – SAYYIDA ZEINAB, RHODA & OLD CAIRO

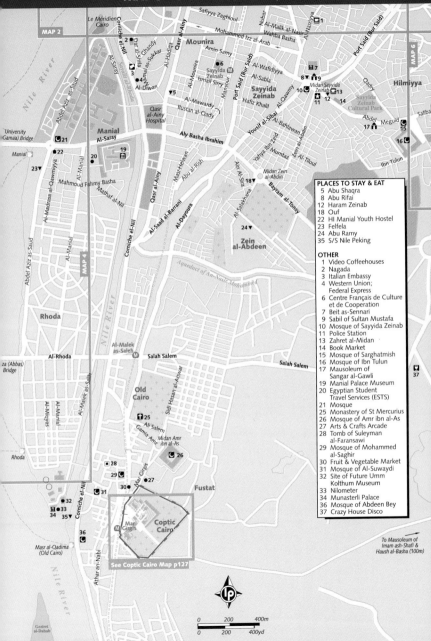

PLACES TO STAY & EAT
5 Abu Shaqra
8 Abu Rifai
12 Haram Zeinab
18 Ouf
22 HI Manial Youth Hostel
23 Felfela
24 Abu Ramy
35 S/S Nile Peking

OTHER
1 Video Coffeehouses
2 Nagada
3 Italian Embassy
4 Western Union;
   Federal Express
6 Centre Français de Culture
   et de Cooperation
7 Beit as-Sennari
9 Sabil of Sultan Mustafa
10 Mosque of Sayyida Zeinab
11 Police Station
13 Zahret al-Midan
14 Book Market
15 Mosque of Sarghatmish
16 Mosque of Ibn Tulun
17 Mausoleum of
   Sangar al-Gawli
19 Manial Palace Museum
20 Egyptian Student
   Travel Services (ESTS)
21 Mosque
25 Monastery of St Mercurius
26 Mosque of Amr ibn al-As
27 Arts & Crafts Arcade
28 Tomb of Suleyman
   al-Faransawi
29 Mosque of Mohammed
   al-Saghir
30 Fruit & Vegetable Market
31 Mosque of Al-Suwaydi
32 Site of Future Umm
   Kolthum Museum
33 Nilometer
34 Munasterli Palace
36 Mosque of Abdeen Bey
37 Crazy House Disco

See Coptic Cairo Map p127

To Mausoleum of
Imam ash-Shafi &
Haush al-Basha (100m)

0   200   400m
0   200   400yd

MAP 6 – ISLAMIC CAIRO

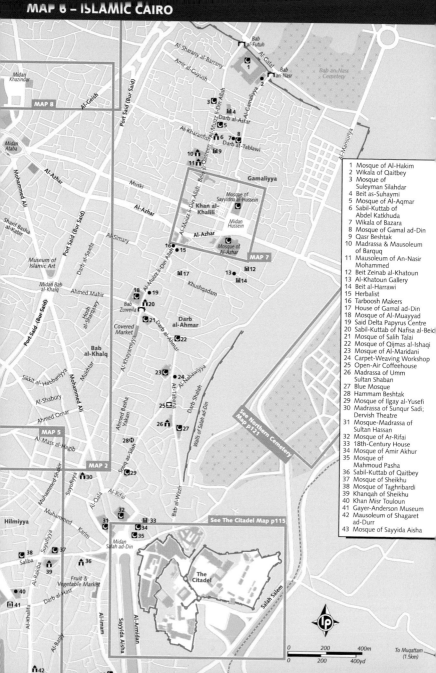

1 Mosque of Al-Hakim
2 Wikala of Qaitbey
3 Mosque of Suleyman Silahdar
4 Beit as-Suhaymi
5 Mosque of Al-Aqmar
6 Sabil-Kuttab of Abdel Katkhuda
7 Wikala of Bazara
8 Mosque of Gamal ad-Din
9 Qasr Beshtak
10 Madrassa & Mausoleum of Barquq
11 Mausoleum of An-Nasir Mohammed
12 Beit Zeinab al-Khatoun
13 Al-Khatoun Gallery
14 Beit al-Harrawi
15 Herbalist
16 Tarboosh Makers
17 House of Gamal ad-Din
18 Mosque of Al-Muayyad
19 Said Delta Papyrus Centre
20 Sabil-Kuttab of Nafisa al-Beid
21 Mosque of Salih Talai
22 Mosque of Qijmas al-Ishaqi
23 Mosque of Al-Maridani
24 Carpet-Weaving Workshop
25 Open-Air Coffeehouse
26 Madrassa of Umm Sultan Shaban
27 Blue Mosque
28 Hammam Beshtak
29 Mosque of Ilgay al-Yusefi
30 Madrassa of Sunqur Sadi; Dervish Theatre
31 Mosque-Madrassa of Sultan Hassan
32 Mosque of Ar-Rifai
33 18th-Century House
34 Mosque of Amir Akhur
35 Mosque of Mahmoud Pasha
36 Sabil-Kuttab of Qaitbey
37 Mosque of Sheikhu
38 Mosque of Taghribardi
39 Khanqah of Sheikhu
40 Khan Misr Touloun
41 Gayer-Anderson Museum
42 Mausoleum of Shagaret ad-Durr
43 Mosque of Sayyida Aisha

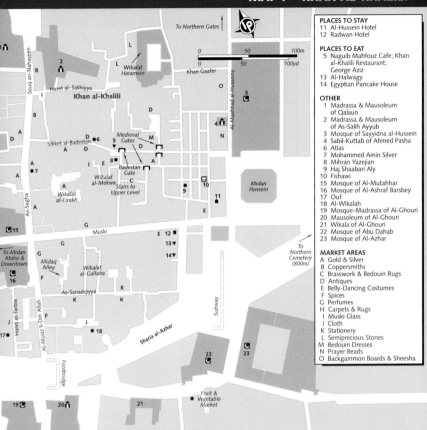

MAP 7 – KHAN AL-KHALILI

PLACES TO STAY
11 Al-Hussein Hotel
12 Radwan Hotel

PLACES TO EAT
5 Naguib Mahfouz Cafe; Khan al-Khalili Restaurant; George Aziz
13 Al-Halwagy
14 Egyptian Pancake House

OTHER
1 Madrassa & Mausoleum of Qalaun
2 Madrassa & Mausoleum of As-Salih Ayyub
3 Mosque of Sayyidna al-Hussein
4 Sabil-Kuttab of Ahmed Pasha
6 Atlas
7 Mohammed Amin Silver
8 Mihran Yazejian
9 Haj Shaaban Aly
10 Fishawi
15 Mosque of Al-Mutahhar
16 Mosque of Al-Ashraf Barsbey
17 Ouf
18 Al-Wikalah
19 Mosque-Madrassa of Al-Ghouri
20 Mausoleum of Al-Ghouri
21 Wikala of Al-Ghouri
22 Mosque of Abu Dahab
23 Mosque of Al-Azhar

MARKET AREAS
A Gold & Silver
B Coppersmiths
C Brasswork & Bedouin Rugs
D Antiques
E Belly-Dancing Costumes
F Spices
G Perfumes
H Carpets & Rugs
I Muski Glass
J Cloth
K Stationery
L Semiprecious Stones
M Bedouin Dresses
N Prayer Beads
O Backgammon Boards & Sheesha

Glittering rows of brass and copper items are shown off to advantage at night in the Khan al-Khalili bazaar.

LEE FOSTER

MAP 8 – AROUND MIDAN RAMSES

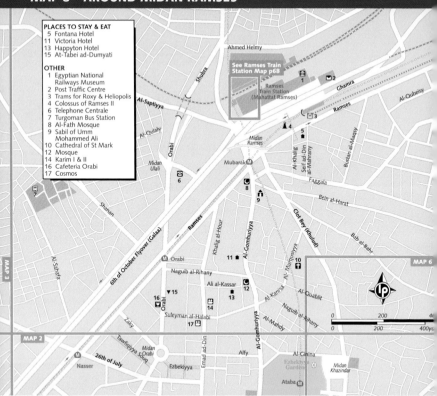

PLACES TO STAY & EAT
5 Fontana Hotel
11 Victoria Hotel
13 Happyton Hotel
15 At-Tabei ad-Dumyati

OTHER
1 Egyptian National
   Railways Museum
2 Post Traffic Centre
3 Trams for Roxy & Heliopolis
4 Colossus of Ramses II
6 Telephone Centrale
7 Turgoman Bus Station
8 Al-Fath Mosque
9 Sabil of Umm
   Mohammed Ali
10 Cathedral of St Mark
12 Mosque
14 Karim I & II
16 Cafeteria Orabi
17 Cosmos

Midan Ramses, the northern gateway onto central Cairo, is a jumble of flyovers and arterial roads.

MAP 9 – HELIOPOLIS

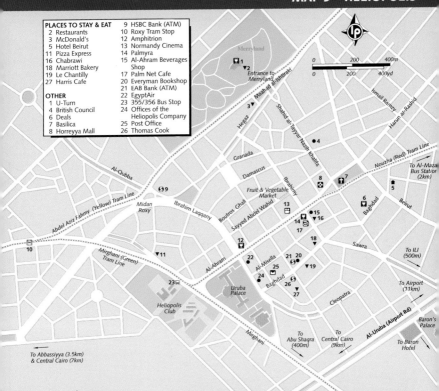

PLACES TO STAY & EAT
2 Restaurants
3 McDonald's
5 Hotel Beirut
11 Pizza Express
16 Chabrawi
18 Marriott Bakery
19 Le Chantilly
27 Harris Cafe

OTHER
1 U-Turn
4 British Council
6 Deals
7 Basilica
8 Horreyya Mall

9 HSBC Bank (ATM)
10 Roxy Tram Stop
12 Amphitrion
13 Normandy Cinema
14 Palmyra
15 Al-Ahram Beverages Shop
17 Palm Net Cafe
20 Everyman Bookshop
21 EAB Bank (ATM)
22 EgyptAir
23 355/356 Bus Stop
24 Offices of the Heliopolis Company
25 Post Office
26 Thomas Cook

The exterior of the Baron's Palace is adorned with sandstone Buddhas, geishas, elephants and serpents.

MAP LEGEND

CITY ROUTES

Freeway .... Freeway		.... Unsealed Road
Highway .... Primary Road		.... One Way Street
Road .... Secondary Road		.... Pedestrian Street
Street .... Street		.... Stepped Street
Lane .... Lane		.... Tunnel
.... On/Off Ramp		.... Footbridge

REGIONAL ROUTES

.... Tollway, Freeway
.... Primary Road
.... Secondary Road
.... Minor Road

BOUNDARIES

.... International
.... State
.... Disputed
.... Fortified Wall

HYDROGRAPHY

.... River, Creek
.... Canal
.... Lake
.... Dry Lake; Salt Lake
.... Spring; Rapids
.... Waterfalls

TRANSPORT ROUTES & STATIONS

.... Train
.... Underground Train
.... Metro
.... Tramway
.... Cable Car, Chairlift
.... Ferry or River Bus
.... Walking Trail
.... Walking Tour
.... Path
.... Pier or Jetty

AREA FEATURES

.... Building
.... Park, Gardens
.... Mall
.... Market
.... Hotel
.... Cemetery
.... Campus
.... Sports Ground

POPULATION SYMBOLS

| ✪ CAPITAL .... National Capital | ● CITY .... City | ● Village .... Village |
| ◉ CAPITAL .... State Capital | ● Town .... Town | .... Urban Area |

MAP SYMBOLS

| ■ .... Place to Stay | ▼ .... Place to Eat | ● .... Point of Interest |

.... Airfield	.... Cinema	.... Mosque	.... Shopping Centre
.... Airport	.... Embassy	.... Museum or Art Gallery	.... Synagogue
.... Anchorage	.... Hammam	.... Pyramid	.... Telephone
.... Bank	.... Historic Building	.... Petrol or Gas Station	.... Toilet
.... Bus Terminal	.... Hospital	.... Police Station	.... Tomb
.... Coffeehouse	.... Internet Cafe	.... Post Office	.... Tourist Information
.... Cave	.... Islamic Monument	.... Pub or Bar	.... Transport
.... Church	.... Monument	.... Ruins	.... Zoo

Note: not all symbols displayed above appear in this book

LONELY PLANET OFFICES

Australia
Locked Bag 1, Footscray, Victoria 3011
☎ 03 8379 8000 fax 03 8379 8111
email: talk2us@lonelyplanet.com.au

USA
150 Linden St, Oakland, CA 94607
☎ 510 893 8555 TOLL FREE: 800 275 8555
fax 510 893 8572
email: info@lonelyplanet.com

UK
10a Spring Place, London NW5 3BH
☎ 020 7428 4800 fax 020 7428 4828
email: go@lonelyplanet.co.uk

France
1 rue du Dahomey, 75011 Paris
☎ 01 55 25 33 00 fax 01 55 25 33 01
email: bip@lonelyplanet.fr
www.lonelyplanet.fr

World Wide Web: www.lonelyplanet.com *or* AOL keyword: lp
Lonely Planet Images: lpi@lonelyplanet.com.au